Debt, Trust, and Reputation

Starting in the late nineteenth century, colonial rule in India took an active interest in regulating financial markets beyond the bridgeheads of European capital in intercontinental trade. Regulatory efforts were part of a modernizing project seeking to produce alignments between British and Indian business procedures, and to create the financial basis for the incipient industrialization in India. For vast sections of Indian society, however, they pushed credit–debt relations into the realm of extra-legality, while the new, regulated agents of finance remained incapable of serving – and equally unwilling to serve – their needs.

Combining historical and ethnographic approaches, the book questions underlying assumptions of modernization in finance that continue to prevail in postcolonial India. It delineates the socioeconomic responses produced, and studies the reputational economies of debt that characterize the extra-legal markets that have emerged in consequence. Deeply embedded into communication flows on trust and reputation, these extra-legal markets turned out to be significantly more exploitative than their colonial predecessors.

Sebastian Schwecke writes on South Asian history, economy, and society, combining a broad spectrum of disciplines. His recent works include the co-edited *Rethinking Markets in Modern India: Embedded Exchange and Contested Jurisdiction* (Cambridge University Press, 2020). He is the founding director of the Max Weber Forum for South Asian Studies, Delhi.

METAMORPHOSES OF THE POLITICAL: MULTIDISCIPLINARY APPROACHES

The Series is a publishing collaboration of Cambridge University Press with The M. S. Merian–R. Tagore International Centre of Advanced Studies 'Metamorphoses of the Political' (ICAS:MP). It seeks to publish new books that both expand and de-centre current perspectives on politics and the 'political' in the contemporary world. It examines, from a wide array of disciplinary and methodological approaches, how the 'political' has been conceptualized, articulated and transformed in specific arenas of contestation during the 'long twentieth century'. Though primarily located in India and the Global South, the Series seeks to interrogate and contribute to wider debates about global processes and politics. It is in this sense that the Series is imagined as one that is regionally focused but globally engaged, providing a context for interrogations of universalized theories of self, society and politics.

Series Editors:

- Niraja Gopal Jayal, formerly at Jawaharlal Nehru University, New Delhi
- Shail Mayaram, formerly at Centre for the Study of Developing Societies, Delhi
- Samita Sen, University of Cambridge, Cambridge
- Awadhendra Sharan, Centre for the Study of Developing Societies, Delhi
- Sanjay Srivastava, University College London, UK
- Ravi Vasudevan, Centre for the Study of Developing Societies, Delhi
- Sebastian Vollmer, University of Gottingen, Germany

ICAS:MP is an Indo-German research collaboration of six Indian and German institutions. It combines the benefits of an open, interdisciplinary forum for intellectual exchange with the advantages of a cutting-edge research centre. Located in New Delhi, ICAS:MP critically intervenes in global debates in the social sciences and humanities.

Other Titles in the Series

- *The Secret Life of AnOther Indian Nationalism: Transitions from the Pax Britannica to the Pax Americana* • Shail Mayaram
- *Properties of Rent: Community, Capital and Politics in Globalising Delhi* • Sushmita Pati
- *Saffron Republic: Hindu Nationalism and State Power in India* • Edited by Thomas Blom Hansen and Srirupa Roy
- *Women, Gender and Religious Nationalism* • Edited by Amrita Basu and Tanika Sarkar

Debt, Trust, and Reputation

Extra-legal Finance in Northern India

Sebastian Schwecke

Metamorphoses of the Political
Merian Tagore International Centre of Advanced Studies

CAMBRIDGE
UNIVERSITY PRESS

CAMBRIDGE
UNIVERSITY PRESS

University Printing House, Cambridge CB2 8BS, United Kingdom

One Liberty Plaza, 20th Floor, New York, NY 10006, USA

477 Williamstown Road, Port Melbourne, vic 3207, Australia

314 to 321, 3rd Floor, Plot No.3, Splendor Forum, Jasola District Centre, New Delhi 110025, India

103 Penang Road, #05–06/07, Visioncrest Commercial, Singapore 238467

Cambridge University Press is part of the University of Cambridge.

It furthers the University's mission by disseminating knowledge in the pursuit of education, learning and research at the highest international levels of excellence.

www.cambridge.org
Information on this title: www.cambridge.org/9781316517260

© Sebastian Schwecke 2022

First published 2022

Printed in India by Thomson Press India Ltd.

A catalogue record for this publication is available from the British Library

ISBN 978-1-316-51726-0 Hardback

For Michaela

Contents

Tables and Figures

Tables

Figures

Acknowledgements

When I first started thinking about this research project, I decided that the only place I could do it in was in Banaras – not only for its history, or the importance of extra-legal practices of exchange in its economy, but primarily because of the people I knew there. Little did I know how much help, assistance, and friendship I would receive throughout the time I spent in the city since 1999. This book would not have been possible otherwise. First and foremost, my thanks need to be expressed to all these people in Banaras who went far out of their way to help me. In particular, I wish to express my gratitude for their efforts, company, and friendship to the following people: Rakesh Kumar Singh, Anoop Sharma, Ajay Pandey, Chandra Kishore Singh, Navneet Raman, Sudhakar Yadav, Neelam Atri, Shashank Singh, Ram Lakhan, and Dipak and Miriya Malik. This list should be longer, but it would get far too long if I included anyone who I am grateful to. As an honorary Banarsi, however, I should include Andy Rotman, whose advice and discussions on trust and reputation were particularly important for shaping the book's argument as it developed.

This book is derived from my habilitation thesis at the Philosophical Faculty of Göttingen University. My research benefited greatly from the highly conducive atmosphere at the Centre for Modern Indian Studies (CeMIS) at Göttingen, the International Institute of Asian Studies at Leiden, and the Indian Institute of Management Calcutta. I wish to express my heartfelt thanks to all the scholars at these institutions who helped to make my stay there such an enjoyable experience. Parts of my research was funded by mobility grants from CeMIS, while a major part of my research into the banking families of Banaras was funded by a mobility grant from the Erasmus Mundus Experts4Asia programme for which I had been affiliated to the economics department of Pune University. I am particularly grateful to the anonymous reviewers of this book who helped me considerably in addressing at least some of its flaws. Ravi Ahuja was instrumental in shaping the original research idea. I am highly thankful for all his support, help, and friendship. I am also grateful to Srirupa Roy, Hartmut Elsenhans, Indivar Kamtekar, Samita Sen, Lakshmi Subramanian, Ritu Birla, Tirthankar Roy, Jon Keune, Saikat Maitra, Patrick Desplat, Parikshit Ghosh, Dhanmanjiri Sathe, Dwaipayan Bhattacharya, and Debjani Mazumder for their help and encouragement as well as for offering – at various points of time – ideas that I could build upon. In particular, I want to thank Ajay Gandhi, Douglas E. Haynes, and Barbara Harriss-White for all their help over these years. My last thank you is reserved for Michaela Dimmers, who not only introduced me to Banaras more than two decades ago but whose presence in my life was always the greatest help I could have hoped for.

Abbreviations

BHU	Banaras Hindu University
CCUP	*Report of the Co-operative Committee of the United Provinces of Agra and Oudh*
BoB	Bank of Benares
ICS	Indian Civil Service
RBI	Reserve Bank of India
ROSCA	rotating savings and credit association
SBB	State Bank of Banaras
SHG	self-help group
UPBEC	United Provinces Banking Enquiry Committee
UPBECR	*United Provinces Banking Enquiry Committee Report*

Part I A Tangled Jungle of Disorderly Transactions

Introduction

'Can you imagine that I am handing out interest-free loans right now?' I was asked in December 2016 by a moneylender in Banaras (Varanasi)[1] who normally charged a rate of 30 per cent per month. A few weeks earlier the Indian government overnight had withdrawn banknotes of 500- and 1,000-rupee denominations, the vast majority of all cash in circulation – certainly one of the biggest policy misadventures in recent history. Since the 'demonetization' misadventure had not included any apparent planning for a re-monetization, trade in the city's 'bazaar' had collapsed, by some local estimates upwards of 80 per cent. While many extra-legal lenders were simultaneously engaged in commerce, and therefore affected by the policy, it also constituted a business opportunity. Old denominations could be exchanged for new ones only with significant difficulties, in an endless-seeming array of fresh regulations restricted to very low amounts. For richer Indians, exchanging old banknotes that had become practically worthless depended considerably on finding poorer people who would exchange them in their stead. The market value of the 'old' banknotes in Banaras, as elsewhere, dropped drastically. They became available to buyers within days of the policy announcement for 75 per cent of their nominal value. By early December this value had dropped to 60 per cent, and to 40 per cent around mid-December. One way of getting the devalued banknotes into the banking system hinged on loans by moneylenders. The depositors – frequently depicted obnoxiously as 'money mules' or *chotu*s (lit. little ones) in the parlance of India's upper-middle classes – made deposits consisting of (frequently interest-free) loans given to them by moneylenders. Consisting of devalued banknotes, these loans thus entered the banking system, and could be withdrawn in legal tender a few months later to repay the moneylenders. For the depositors, this practice brought about a significant respite from economic distress.

When I asked the lender why he did not charge interest, he proceeded to outline an argument that I had already become familiar with in my fieldwork. The agreed-upon interest rates for a transaction mostly served as a guideline. Eventually, given their exceedingly exploitative character, almost all debtors would default. For the lenders, anticipated returns on investment were rarely fixed by the contractual agreement. Instead, repayment remained flexible as long as the lender ultimately considered the returns to be sufficient or – more precisely according to the treatment of credit in economic anthropology – they were commensurate with the lender's expectations. Having obtained profits of 40–60 per cent, there was no reason to insist on interest payments, and not charging them made people eager to enter into transactions, thus maximizing overall profits. And, as the lender confided over cups of tea afterwards, it felt good to enter a transaction without acrimony, one that helped both sides.

Petty money lending of this sort constitutes a criminal offence in the state of Uttar Pradesh, which includes Banaras. Other forms of extra-legal finance relating to either credit or speculation are not technically illegal but typically comprise practices that are semi-legal at best. This book depicts the evolution of financial markets operating without recourse to legal practices, predominantly in an urban north Indian setting, centring on the city of Banaras. The study straddles the divide between social and economic history, and economic anthropology, and is based on archival and ethnographic research conducted between 2011 and 2019. It is informed by an understanding of socio-economic relations and their cultural embeddedness that emphasizes the engagement of market participants in various overlapping economic segments following different functional logics than Indian capitalism, and intersecting with it.[2] This book weaves together histories of market framing and market responses that led to the coalescence of a comprehensively extra-legal economic segment. It explores the anchoring of diverse financial practices – from petty money lending and extra-legal 'trade credit' flows to forms of financial speculation – in a reputational economy that allows these financial markets to flourish in the absence of state-centred enforcement mechanisms for contractual obligations in spite of their (increasingly) exploitative character.

The book is based on two intertwined approaches – the historical analysis of market-framing processes and market responses leading to the emergence of a comprehensively extra-legal segment of the Indian economy, and an anthropological analysis of these developments combining historical anthropology with ethnographic research. The starting point of the analysis is a discussion of the ambiguities of the credit–debt relationship, especially the reputational underpinnings of the extra-legal credit contract in colonial India.

Taking issue primarily with the argument of disrupted moral economies of debt, the analysis commences with a study of the ambiguities of the credit contract in the nineteenth-century Indian economy. Drawing on the history of usury, the history and anthropology of the bazaar, and the anthropology of credit–debt, it demonstrates how European and Indian conceptions of the credit contract differed in their handling of pervasive uncertainty anchored in the enhanced future orientation of the credit contract as opposed to other contractual forms (Peebles 2010). It is argued that the conception of a 'moral economy' disrupted by 'capitalism' rests on a faulty application of European historical experiences of credit. In the early modern European credit contract, the conception of shared uncertainty between creditor and debtor prevalent in the medieval conception of credit was overcome by fixing the creditor's risks at the time of contractual agreement. Instead, the management of enhanced future uncertainty in the Indian case rested primarily on permitting the renegotiation of obligations within the limits set by communicating reputational fallouts of default.[3] The increased penetration of liberal contractual law disrupted the reputational mechanisms for renegotiating obligations, rooted in patterns of ethical emulation and loose forms of status-related arbitration, rather than a moral economy based on conceptions of generalized equity. Essentially, the concept of the credit contract in India since the mid-nineteenth century was brought in accordance with its European equivalent, in which the risks of the creditor were contained through the legal form while the uncertainties faced by the debtor were unaddressed, extending the common intelligibility of 'capitalist' credit to Indian financial markets.

Faced with growing perceptions of a crisis of indebtedness primarily in rural India, and growing nationalist sentiments that contributed to the emergence of a narrative on the disruption of moral economies, the colonial state incipiently started to address the fallout of the abolition of the usury laws in the last decades of the nineteenth century, but without showing any willingness to undermine the common intelligibility of 'capitalist' credit. By the mid-1890s, and based on the historical experience of legislation and the cooperative movement in Germany and Austria,[4] a broad consensus had emerged among the colonial administration that 'indigenous' credit practices needed to be contained. Based on continental European models and recent legal innovations in British law, the predominant argument sought the withdrawal of liberal contractual law (and the state's role in enforcing transactional obligations) from credit markets targeting poorer strata and the petty bourgeoisie in the Indian hinterland. The direction of market-framing policies shifted from the utilitarian assumption that laissez-faire approaches would facilitate credit flows and reduce borrowing costs to an admission of failure that necessitated the removal of state assistance in accumulation through its regulatory apparatus. Market-framing policies shifted towards state regulation at the same time as state assistance was expanded in the 'modern' segment of financial markets. While the numerous critics of this policy shift pointed out that this would lead to increased exploitation by lenders forced to operate in an extra-legal manner – although having the advantage of obscuring state complicity in exploitation – its proponents highlighted the anticipated successes of alleviating measures such as cooperation, and the final aim of forcing debtors to shift to the 'modern' banking sector through the deterioration of 'indigenous' credit conditions. Policy debates centred on the need to provide British Indian courts with comprehensive discretionary powers to remove contractually stipulated obligations from all credit contracts outside the small spectrum of 'organized' banks, a policy eventually enacted in the Usurious Loans Act, 1918.

Colonial legislation obstructed the gradual shift of credit relations in India towards the common intelligibility of the 'capitalist' credit contract, and reinforced tendencies of lenders to shift towards extra-legal modes of operation. Combined with broader economic developments, however, the separation of financial markets into a state-supported banking system and the mass of extra-legal financial transactions gradually undermined the higher spectrum of 'traditional' Indian finance. As the practices that marked 'indigenous' banking and the social ties between these financiers and lower-level lenders provided key elements for the governance of enforcement mechanisms, the gradual demise of the apex of 'traditional' financial markets had significant impacts on the ability of creditors to enforce contractual obligations in extra-legal ways. By the 1920s, colonial sources studying the 'bazaar economy' of India commonly identified a process of 'amateurization' (see Yang 1998), a widespread decline of sophisticated business forms and their replacement by practices of a more limited transactional scale. Credit relationships within the extra-legal economy of debt relying on reputational means for stabilizing the market were strongly affected, gradually shifting from modes of operation relying on 'bazaar' models of enforcing obligations through mercantile ethics and social ties to models reminiscent of the operation of trust and association depicted by Keith Hart for west African slum economies (Hart 1973, 1988). Similar to the guiding question posed by Hart – of what replaced contractual law in the governance of market relations – extra-legal credit markets in India bereft of both enforcement mechanisms created new but significantly limited transactional grammars depending crucially on long-term interpersonal relations of trust, and their extension at need through communication flows centring on an impoverished form of reputation. The latter became depicted locally as *vishvaas*, a Hindi term contextually denoting both trust and reputation, as opposed to the elaborate system of mercantile ethics depicted by C. A. Bayly (1983) as a conception of merchant's 'credit' (*sakh*). The reputational economy of debt in Banaras gradually shifted to an 'impoverished' (or rather, adjusted) system of information flows on reliability primarily through neighbourhood and 'bazaar' gossip.

Once the initial optimism over the anticipated success of legislative measures in the colonial administration (and subsequently in independent India) started to dissipate, the Indian state reacted to the continued crisis of indebtedness by a flurry of interventions that by and large failed to alleviate credit conditions for the mass of the Indian population. The various measures remained stringently tied to the common intelligibility of 'capitalist' credit relations, and thus tended to reinforce the separation of the extra-legal economy from a state-supported 'capitalist' credit market with functioning enforcement mechanisms that permitted the facilitation of credit flows for prosperous social segments and large-scale businesses, and where regulation allowed for the lowering of borrowing costs. The dissection of the two market segments in Banaras – sporadic interaction notwithstanding – became fully established by the late 1960s, roughly corresponding in time with the nationalization of India's banks, which marked the final stage in the decline of 'indigenous' banking in the city. By the late 1930s, the Reserve Bank of India openly argued that the aim of facilitating credit flows to lower the costs of borrowing for the poorer social segments needed to be substituted for a policy that restricted the access of these strata to credit to contain indebtedness. Late colonial as well as postcolonial Indian policies – despite being couched in idioms of 'financial inclusion' – have tended to follow the latter's prescriptions, imposing restrictions on debtors that impeded a shift from reputational to the juridical-procedural parameters of 'capitalist' finance, and insulated the 'modern' banking sector from the need to address the riskier credit demands of a major part of the population.

The extra-legal financial markets that emerged in Banaras in the process remained 'amateurish', based on interpersonal relations of trust and association that, in turn, created a reputational system communicated primarily through gossip, and allowed its participants to establish wider market relations. This system stabilized an economic segment following an operational logic that was fundamentally detached from the dominant capitalist segment of the economy, and which became significantly more exploitative than colonial credit markets, despite the continued ability of the debtors to renegotiate transactional obligations through reputational means. At the same time, the inherent limitations of market relations based on trust resulted in mechanisms by which lenders and debtors sought to create enclaves of 'sophistication' in order to stabilize riskier transactional patterns. While the regulatory processes for the 'capitalist' financial market segment tended to reinforce its juridical-procedural underpinnings, processes of 'sophistication' within the extra-legal market segment conversely buttressed its reputational dimensions, thus strengthening the divide between the operational logics of the two markets. For the petty bourgeoisie that dominated much of the 'bazaar' in Banaras – whether as lenders or borrowers – this divide imposed a need to navigate two contradictory logics of credit, although skilled market participants managed to use this profitably. For the mass of the poorer population – primarily, though not exclusively, as debtors – it restricted credit access to the most exploitative segment of Indian finance.

Outline of the book

This book is divided into two parts. Part I emphasizes the role of the Indian state in shaping credit markets, and creating the division between a juridically-procedurally defined 'capitalist' and a reputationally defined extra-legal financial market. Part II highlights the reactions by market participants to the disappearance of both the legal and the 'traditional' enforcement mechanisms for contractual obligations, and the resulting emergence of a reputational economy dependent almost comprehensively on trust.

Chapter 2 (Contract) serves a threefold purpose: (*a*) It outlines the argument on the credit contract, and the divergence between juridical-procedural and reputational mechanisms of enforcing obligations inherent in the credit relationship; (*b*) it engages with the historical literature on the emergence of capitalism in India, the bazaar economy, and finance (including money lending), thus outlining the historical background of the market-framing processes that commenced in the 1890s; (*c*) it introduces the historical background of the case study on Banaras, particularly its considerable importance for the financing of the inland trade in India in the eighteenth and nineteenth centuries, and the characteristics of its bazaar economy. Accordingly, the chapter intertwines a historical anthropology of credit, the bazaar, and contractual law with a historical outline of major developments in India, including the abolition of the usury laws in 1855 and the Deccan Riots in 1875.

Chapter 3 (Discretion) focuses on advancing the historical narrative, primarily studying the debates that led to the withdrawal of contractual law from extra-legal financial markets. The narrative starts by setting out the complex (and often conflicting) stances taken by British Indian courts on issues concerning credit obligations, detailing the extent to which the abolition of the usury laws remained contested legally in the 1870s and 1880s. Its main part, in turn, focuses on policy discourses in India and Britain between 1895 and 1918. The chapter provides a detailed reading of the various arguments for state interference in 'indigenous' finance, and the criticism thereof, eventually coalescing into the predominance of the legal doctrine of unconscionable bargains that lay at the heart of legislation against money lending in both Britain and India, and facilitated the removal of contractual law from much of Indian finance.

Chapter 4 (Containment), first, depicts the flurry of legislative efforts, especially in the United Provinces (present-day Uttar Pradesh), after the realization that the effects of the Usurious Loans Act had not had a significant impact on the extent of indebtedness. Second, it establishes that while the exploitative character of money lending was not changing considerably, its reliance on reputational means of governance significantly increased, outlining incipient changes in the governance structure of this reputational economy that coalesced into the demise of 'indigenous' banking. It provides a detailed reading of the main socio-economic characteristics of this market and its increasing 'amateurization', the complex intertwining of extra-legal practices in lending, and state attempts to legislate against money lending as well as to provide alleviative measures. Demonstrating the failure of these attempts, the chapter, third, emphasizes how policy debates gradually shifted – from an optimistic assessment of state capacities to provide relief towards the realization that the state's efforts could only succeed in containing debt by restricting access to credit.

Chapter 5 (Trust) advances the historical narrative into the 1960s, but its main emphasis is on historical anthropology. Historically, it demonstrates the increasingly exploitative character of extra-legal finance, on the one hand, and engages with the gradual formalization of 'organized' banking, on the other. It outlines the collapse of reputational mechanisms on 'modern' financial markets in the 1950s and 1960s, and the growing reliance on an 'impoverished' reputational mechanism for stabilizing debt relationships in extra-legal finance. Anthropologically, the main purpose of the chapter lies in demonstrating the operation of trust in financial markets, and its links to a reputational economy operating in parallel to the monetary economy.

In Chapter 6 (Obligation), the historical anthropology focus of the previous chapter is taken up again and brought to its conclusion. The main purpose of this chapter is to depict the collapse of the reputational mechanisms of enforcing obligations through strong social ties, especially in Banaras. For this purpose, the primary focus of the chapter remains on the demise of 'indigenous' banking that is used to depict the workings of Bayly's concept of mercantile ethics, and the importance of reputational standing even in times of monetary decline. The chapter proceeds to outline the rapid collapse of an entire market segment, and the corresponding undermining of structures of obligation that depended primarily on emulation and on the existence of an elevated segment within the credit economy capable of arbitration. Conversely, it also demonstrates the partial resilience of reputational systems of enforcing obligations through strong social ties in parts of rural India.

Chapter 7 (Disappearance) brings the narrative into the present. The chapter complements the historical narrative of money lending, supplementing the arguments in Chapters 5 and 6, which emphasized 'organized' and 'indigenous' banking. Persistent efforts by the Indian state to enforce the juridical-procedural elements of the credit contract reinforced responses by extra-legal entrepreneurs to find viable modes of operation based on trust and reputation. In the process, credit and exploitation through debt became increasingly invisible to the Indian state and media discourses, notwithstanding intermittent periods of attention to specific aspects of a more or less ubiquitous, everyday experience for vast sections of the Indian population.

Finally, Chapter 8 (Reputation) supplements the historical narrative and the historical anthropology approach of the preceding chapters by adding an ethnographic study of extra-legal finance in Banaras. The ethnographic approach highlights the complexity of the market and its reputational underpinnings. Observing the characteristics of extra-legal finance, the chapter establishes the considerable increase in exploitation that accompanied the withdrawal of contractual law. The main emphasis, however, is on depicting the functioning of the emergent reputational economy in the absence of mechanisms for enforcing obligations. The chapter highlights the operational modes of an 'amateurish' reputational economy, and their anchoring in communication flows centring on gossip. It demonstrates the importance of reputational information centring on trust in facilitating the renegotiation of obligations without viable enforcement mechanisms, and studies the differences across segments of extra-legal finance. The chapter also analyses the emergence of enclaves of sophistication within a largely 'amateurized' market, and the ways in which an 'impoverished' concept of reputation has been employed in highly sophisticated ways for determining trust and stabilizing credit relations.

A brief note on transliterations and translations

For the sake of simplicity, I have used a highly simplified system of transliterating terms in Indian languages other than English that omits diacritical signs. Long vowels instead are marked by a doubling of the Latin character, except where these terms are generally used in the literature without indications of vowel length. All translations from Hindi in this book are by me, unless marked otherwise.

Notes

1. The north Indian city of Banaras has had several names throughout its long history and is presently named 'Varanasi' in official discourse. In colonial times, it was known officially as 'Benares', an anglicized spelling of its name during its heyday as a commercial and financial centre of India. In its religious role, it is often depicted as Kashi, although from a strictly religious point of view the area known as Kashi covers only a part of the present city. While the name Varanasi is commonly used nowadays, a major part of the local population continues to refer to it as Banaras, according to the Hindi transcription of its earlier name. Among many scholars, it has become an unspoken convention to refer to the city in the latter way, too, as a way of highlighting its heritage without directly using the name used by the colonial rulers of India.
2. See Polanyi (2001 [1944]) and Granovetter (2011a).
3. It is noteworthy here to revisit Arjun Appadurai's depiction of the contract – not merely the credit contract but stated in the context of futures trade that combines elements of the credit and the commodity contracts – as a promise about an uncertain future, signifying the need to engage more deeply with the language involved in contract-making (Appadurai 2016). On the language of credit contracts in India, see Rawal (2015).
4. See, for instance, Suter (2017).

2

Contract

This raises the question of what takes the place of law as the major source of sanctions in economic relations.[1]

Trust, shame, and the reputational credit contract

When I started to observe participants in the elaborate arena of social and economic practices that constitutes the reputational economy of debt in the north Indian city of Banaras, two correlated features became visible almost immediately. The first was the accessibility of many of the people involved, in spite of the extra-legal and at times even straightforwardly illegal character of the financial practices they partook in. The second was the apparent lack of details in the information I learned from speaking to debtors compared to what I managed to learn from creditors. Let me begin by discussing the first of these features. Markets depend on information flows. They are, in fact, embedded in information flows. Narges Erami and Arang Keshavarzian (2015) have highlighted the difference between a criminal market and a bazaar in their study on the latter's involvement in smuggling activities in post-revolutionary Iran. The criminal market, in this example, needed to rely on information flows that were clandestine, thus compromising the availability of robust knowledge on who was involved in dealings, to what extent, and in which role. Not knowing or, better from an anthropological perspective, not having sufficient information to trust one's assessment of the reliability and robustness of information (Corsín Jiménez 2011) introduced high levels of suspicion into a market that was characterized by *knowability*, the ability to add to the information readily available and identify its robustness at need.

Conservative norms and ethics – a recurring feature of 'traditional' mercantile groups visible in the Iranian bazaar as much as in a plethora of contexts across temporal, spatial, and cultural boundaries – nurtured by shared religious practice, shared social space and cultural practice, and strong commonalities in socio-economic organization rooted in class, community, and kinship structures created a sense of being able to know. The sense informed a sense of being able to trust, and the latter in turn facilitated recourse to collective action to punish transgressions once the loosely organized collective of merchants reached the conclusion that such a transgression had occurred. Diego Gambetta argued that trust begins with 'acting *as if* one trusted' until further information permitted the establishment of more stable beliefs (Gambetta 2004, 234, original emphasis). On extra-legal financial markets in Banaras, these more stable beliefs – as will be argued in much greater detail later – were rarely possible. In the Iranian bazaar studied by Erami and Keshavarzian, the more stable beliefs rested on the *social and cultural* embeddedness of the bazaar upheld by weak and diffuse ties that not only permitted the enforcement of obligations through collective action at need but, crucially, also allowed merchants to enter and express 'credible and prolonged commitments to one another' (Erami and Keshavarzian 2015, 126). Clandestine transactions, in turn, undermined this ability, disrupting the social entity of the bazaar.

Notably, Gambetta's definition cited here excludes the operation of more stable beliefs from trust. Defined as 'acting *as if* one trusted', the act of trusting precedes the availability of sufficient information, and instead consists of the pretence of future informational sufficiency. To maintain this pretence, markets that cannot rely on sufficiently robust information to allow for credible commitments need to be steeped in information flows, in a constant chatter of *insufficiently* robust information. Smuggling in post-revolutionary Iran, being clandestine, fostered strong hierarchical ties among its participants, according to Erami and Keshavarzian – at least implicitly of ties that could be enforced, and likely were at least occasionally enforced by violence. Extra-legal financial markets in Banaras, instead, depend on the constant background noise of reputational communication. The market participants need to be accessible, partially to provide sufficiently robust information at need, but partially also to provide the possibility for everyone involved to pretend that this information was just around the corner, that continuing to listen to it would eventually provide the additional amount of information necessary to make the transition from acting as if one trusted to making credible commitments. The heightened uncertainty of an extra-legal market frequently reduces trust to what for all practical purposes constitutes the first stage of a trust-based relationship that creates the basis on which the experiential character of trust can play out and stabilize it – the pretence of trust to allow oneself to enter a relationship where there cannot be any certainty.

Studying the credit practices of Kashmiri merchants in the contemporary period, Aditi Saraf (2021) has characterized the operation of trust on these markets as 'reflective improvidence', a notion that in her analysis was rooted in local practice rather than meant as a contribution to the theorization of trust in general. Reflective improvidence was an outcome of the quasi-perpetual deferment of payment in credit relations among the traders in which both custom and habit, but also the realization that pervasive uncertainty on these markets could lead to the reversal of the creditor–debtor relationship at short notice, made creditors advance money despite the heightened awareness that dues were unlikely to be paid. Nevertheless, the term remains particularly apt to describe not only the first stage of an ideal-type trust relationship in which the pretence of acting as if one trusted formed the first stage of trust before experiential parameters or additional information increased the robustness of available information. It can very well be extended to the operation of trust in the practical realm – including the feedback loop of prior experience with and communication of trust – as long as the arena in which trust operates is marked by heightened uncertainty. Depicting the fluidity of political and economic contexts faced by Kashmiri merchants, but which could easily be mistaken for a discussion of Banarsi moneylenders and their clients, Saraf argued that 'people continually recast trust *in ways that indexed the impossibility of its fulfillment … without abandoning the notion altogether*' (Saraf 2021, 388, emphasis added).

Heightened uncertainty in the markets faced by both these groups accentuated the importance of Gambetta's act of pretence to the extent where the likelihood of trust ever being fulfilled fully became remote, but where the need to deal in trust nevertheless remained paramount. The accessibility of the market's participants needed to be marked. When the weak and diffuse yet, comparatively speaking, still much stronger ties of social and cultural embeddedness remained insufficient to enforce obligations, the market's embeddedness in informational flows necessitated the constant involvement in communication. Accessibility and participation in gossip constituted the lifeblood of credit, producing knowability wherever it was possible and, just as importantly, facilitating the pretence that knowability would be produced in the near future wherever it was not.

To some extent the markets created thus, whether for trade credit in Kashmir or for extra-legal financial transactions in Banaras, resembled the West African slum economy described by Keith Hart for Nima in Ghana (Hart 1973, 1988, 190). At the same time, credit was not extended to strangers. The invocation of friendship and the 'pretension of familiarity [constituted] the normal rhetoric of economic life' (Hart 1988, 190), especially by the borrower. Credit flows in contemporary Banaras, though, are regularly extended on very low levels of social proximity.

It is difficult to ascertain the precise difference here as the languages of friendship and familiarity in Ghana and India may differ substantially, and may thus hide commonalities. The pretensions of familiarity cited by Hart and the accessibility of Banarsi creditors and debtors rooted in the imperative to act as if one trusted in order to trust show a clear resemblance in the way they highlight the importance of pretension and pretence, the attempt to deceive others as well as oneself, at least in some cases, for the operation of relatively stable economic relations with strangers. Yet Hart's description shows the manifold uses of familiarity (or friendship, howsoever defined) once the credit relation has been established, with a track record of commodity exchange reinforced by the fairly strong ties established by gift-giving having created the necessary groundwork in establishing social proximity. Similarly, Saraf's Kashmiri merchants very clearly operated in a context of pre-existing social ties and social proximity, using the tool of reflective improvidence to maintain credit ties despite the awareness of the enhanced likelihood of default or constant deferring of payments. The high likelihood of default constituted an additional source of friction in the operation of credit markets not depicted by Hart for Nima, where credit formed a learning process, and people 'found out by trial and error what worked for them', with a high failure rate (Hart 1988, 190–91), indicating that failures frequently terminated credit relations – as opposed to the example of Kashmiri merchants – and thus constricted credit flows to personal networks of friendship and association.

The failure rate in stabilizing credit relations and the default/deferment rate – as will be shown profusely below – were extremely high. The main difference in the case of extra-legal finance in Banaras – when foregrounding the act of pretence inherent in making the market work – was in the manner in which acting as if one trusted was employed to start new credit relationships, in addition to working under conditions of very high default rates. And in this respect, the main contrast was the addressee of communicating the act of pretending which, in turn, increased the need for accessibility. The act of pretence was addressed to a larger public instead of a known or knowable person. The operation of trust on extra-legal financial markets in contemporary Banaras certainly involved very strong interpersonal features, yet the pretension of trust as a prerequisite to enter and maintain trust relationships in the face of a high likelihood of future breaches of trust needed to be communicated beyond the immediate network of social proximity precisely to allow business conduct beyond its narrow confines. The addressee of the act of pretence was an amorphous collective of participants in the communication structure of the market, primarily driven by gossip, in which more robust information could be established at need, though without ever reaching substantial levels of knowability, and only with significant difficulty. In this way, I as a person without any social standing relevant to the market still served as a conduit of information flows, and communicating with me still served to magnify the reputational information underlying the constant chatter of never-established informational robustness.

Those engaged in the business of giving or taking extra-legal loans were still frequently shy of meeting me, especially at the outset of my research, yet they were very rarely inaccessible, with the exception of legally operating lenders, which will be discussed in Chapter 8. Once accepting to talk to me, almost anyone I met opened up substantially, confiding 'secrets' as much as cherished hopes, or ruthlessly depicting the 'realities' of extra-legal finance. What I became involved in was the process of reputational gossip-making that addressed the collective of market participants far beyond any individual's social networks, yet still within the limits of what could at least be pretended to be identifiable people whose qualities could be learned from listening to the gossip. The information I learned eventually coalesced into an understanding of the market, but it took a long while before I understood that the people I observed actually were answering questions on how the market operated rather than telling me about people who took part in the market. I was fed a steady stream of information that at the surface appeared to centre on personal networks but that really was all about the kind of reputational information that needed to be advanced by different participants in order to make it easier for other participants to take the initial step of convincing oneself to act as if one trusted, or of disregarding the experience of (minor) breaches of trust that may have been communicated by gossip earlier. I was not so much studying a market; I was learning it. A particularly frustrating pattern in this regard was the behaviour of many of the debtors in this market that I spoke to, the second feature that became visible almost immediately – the apparent lack of robust and reliable information on details of financial transactions provided by debtors rather than creditors.

Information that was detailed yet at the same time sufficiently robust was not always readily forthcoming when talking to creditors. For instance, it occasionally was inconsistent with other information passed on by the same person, or contradictory to information passed on by another source that was used for corroboration, or hinting at generalized patterns in the market that were absent from first-hand or second-hand experiences recounted. More frequently, it simply gave the appearance of telling me what I presumably wanted to hear rather than what the interlocutor thought. But with creditors, the chances of finding a person willing to provide detailed *and* robust information were approximately even. With debtors, these chances went down drastically. I had started field research without being fully convinced about the likelihood of being able to access extra-legal lenders, and therefore had deliberately set my priority on seeking out debtors, but had soon discovered that the information I received from speaking with them seemed to be insufficient for my purposes. I initially put it down to debtors' shame over being indebted. In contrast to the almost proverbial willingness to discuss pecuniary matters publicly that is often times attributed to Indians, I thought of debt as a state of economic affairs related to one's own failure, thereby facilitating recourse to means of not only justification but also of concealment. Eventually, I came to understand the responses by debtors differently, still linked to shame, but in a much more nuanced way.

One particularly striking instance was related to an encounter I had with a debtor who actually was a master artisan, though I did not know this when I first met him. I had received a call from a friend asking me to come over to his place immediately. He had a person he occasionally employed over at his place, my friend told me on the phone, but he could not keep him there for long. However, this man was practically always in debt to extra-legal moneylenders, and he could tell me all I needed to know about them, if I hurried. What followed was a long discussion in which I first met the initially somewhat sullen artisan, then gradually managed to coax him into relating his experiences with indebtedness to extra-legal moneylenders. As it turned out, the artisan – a carpenter known for his skill – had progressively fallen on very hard times. Originally from a family of master artisans, he had inherited several houses, a substantial amount of real estate, even though the houses were of relatively small size. Carpentry, however, was a difficult business, especially at the higher end of demand. Highly skilled carpentry was expensive. Most families who could afford to employ a carpenter were simply looking for someone who would do the work cheaply. They would then complain about the shoddy work the carpenter did and look down even on highly skilled carpenters like him. If the carpenter asked for the wages that he considered his due, he was compared to run-of-the-mill carpenters and declined. Rich people who valued skilled carpentry, however, increasingly tended to buy new ready-made items, further compressing the market.

Over the years, the artisan's life had taken a number of drastic turns for the worse, partially related to moneylenders. His wife had died while his children were still relatively young. Wages for his work were still fairly high, he admitted, but he received less and less offers. At times, he could not work for long stretches of time as his children fell sick frequently, and he needed to take care of them. After bouts of his children's sickness, he needed money, and the only way he could get this money was by turning to moneylenders. The lenders charged him very high rates which he could not repay. He had owned several houses in the city, and he had to pledge one after the other as collateral. Within a period of four years, he had lost all but one of the houses he owned, and now was truly desperate as he could not use this one as collateral, so that the next time his children fell ill he would be left with no chance to obtain credit. The friend who had called me over was the last person who would still pay him the wages his work deserved, and therefore he was always glad to come here where he was treated fairly. However, there could never be enough work for him in this household, so even the small hope of continuing to work here was turning sour.

There was another side to the artisan's narrative. As soon as he left, my friend took me aside and started relating the 'true' story. In this, the artisan was not only highly skilled, he was also among the very best carpenters available in Banaras, which was why he was being employed at my friend's place – highly plausible as he appreciated artisanship and was willing to pay a high price for it. He was employed there on a monthly basis, whether there was work for him or not, and earned a sum of 25,000 rupees, approximately four to five times what a shopworker in this area of town could hope to earn in a month at the time. There would always have been additional work for him, but other employers did not pay as much, and the artisan considered employment elsewhere disdainful since these employers did not know artisanship well enough to appreciate his skill and treated him accordingly. He could afford to pass on extra work as the wages he got were normally sufficient to live a fairly decent life, and in earlier years, they had been sufficient for him to buy real estate. When he had first complained about his debts, my friend had tried to arrange additional work for him, but he had not completed the jobs he took on, and now it was getting difficult to find anyone who would employ him. In addition, he was an epsilon alcoholic. It was true that his children fell sick frequently, but that was mostly after he had been away from home on periodic drinking binges that at times went on for as long as a week, leaving his young children uncared for at home. Since he spent all his savings during these excesses, he did not have any money left afterwards and needed to take on loans. As he did not take on any other employment even when he needed additional income, he eventually forfeited the houses he had used as collateral.

I sought out one of the moneylenders the artisan had mentioned. The lender professed that he had originally given the artisan good rates, significantly below the usual rate for small loans, but he had had great difficulties in recovering interest payments. At one time, the artisan had simply disappeared and the lender had not been able to find him for several weeks. Instead, he had taken on loans from a different moneylender, but had defaulted there as well. When he reappeared, he had pleaded for a new loan and had offered the collateral himself as he knew that he would not receive credit otherwise, being of a dubious moral character. The lender not only was aware of his alcoholism, and had been aware of it when he first entered business with him, but was also aware of his skill and income. He agreed that he exploited the artisan's addiction, but depicted the situation as a moral hazard. He had known the artisan's family, including his wife and children, though not closely. Everyone knew that the children were left to their own devices in the artisan's absence, and originally people had given small sums of money for free out of pity. Yet they had never received what the lender considered due recognition of this kind of help, and eventually all that was left to the artisan was to approach extra-legal lenders like him for money. In the end, it was not the lender's fault if the artisan continued to fall into debt traps, and it was difficult not to extend a loan if one knew that the children needed help.

I am not recounting this case to blame or exculpate either of the people involved. After having spent a significant time talking to a variety of people who knew the case, or had heard of it somewhere, I am convinced that the inherent tragedy is pronounced, but that none of the stories I heard is entirely correct. Whatever their content, at the same time, the patterns that emerge from it were fairly visible in other cases I came across. Alcoholism, or addiction in general, was frequently pointed out as the reason for indebtedness, and certainly exacerbated debt traps. There were also reasons for it, and it was not always clear whether the extent to which it was depicted was correct. Disdain for employment that was considered demeaning was a widespread motive, and sometimes the same people who would point out this disdain as a fault, or as responsible for indebtedness, would speak highly of it in other cases where it was considered a sign of dignity, especially when it was not related to (known) debts. The opprobrium of not taking care of one's children was marked, and shared by everyone I talked to in this case, typically as a sign of addiction, but on second thought some people I spoke to also expressed doubts on the accuracy of the common depiction, indicating that it may have been exaggerated in the way that gossip tends to work in a place like Banaras. That a debtor would first seek out friends or people considered relatively close before going to a moneylender happened often, especially if debt was not a recurring experience. That people who had given money, whether as gifts or as loans with substantially better conditions, were offended by a debtor's behaviour afterwards was common, whether or not there was a direct cause given by the debtor. Merely the fact that the artisan was rumoured to have continued neglecting his children had in some cases been cited as justification for feeling disrespected. Finally, that moneylenders would take the opportunity to obtain valuable collateral if it could be expected to be the outcome of locking up capital for a fairly short period of time was hardly surprising.

There were also inconsistencies within the narrative. While the children's sickness would incur expenses, especially if the artisan was forced to eschew work for a sustained period of time, medical bills – unless involving hospitalization which appeared implausible as no one I spoke to recounted it – would never be sufficient to demand significant levels of debt. Foregoing work would not have had much of an impact on the artisan's income if he did not seek out additional work and was paid monthly regardless of the time he spent working, and I had no reason to doubt the sincerity of his employer. The level of wages he received, in turn, would be sufficient for most types of maladies the artisan's children might have caught. Moneylenders who were lending to a locally known figure with an income approaching lower-middle-class status (and real estate property) were not usually charging very high rates, and these would tend to decline if the loans were secured. Obviously, repeated default would over time lead to worse outcomes as well-reputed lenders would shy away from the artisan. Yet most lenders in Banaras who could extend loans at the scale of the collateral of a house in the city, even a small one, would be reputable lenders as their clients had sufficient means. In any case, a loan at the scale where it would make use of a house as collateral would never be taken on for paying medical bills. These bills were unlikely to have simply accumulated to this extent either, as no medical shop would ever consider advancing drugs on credit to such an extent, since doing so would likely bankrupt the shop's owners.

The inconsistencies in the narrative, in turn, are linked to the manner in which reputation, shame, blame, exculpation, and gossip frequently interact in depictions of indebtedness in Banaras. Asking moneylenders how they operated did not elicit similar responses as the need for accessibility and the pretence of knowability counteracted it. It constituted a very typical feature when discussing cases of debt, though, and in turn, the crucial underlying reason for this frequency rested on the specific operation of extra-legal credit agreements in the city that emphasized their renegotiation stage. Debtors' shame as well as the need to blame someone or something that was beyond the debtor's control outweighed the creditors' shame. This statement may appear commonsensical given the widespread prevalence of understanding debt as failure, as mentioned earlier. But in the context of present-day Banaras – where any form of extra-legal finance elicits public reproach and the figure of the moneylender to the poor is particularly loathed publicly, while indebtedness among the poor is widely considered a routine matter – this outcome is striking. Moreover, debtors I observed were rarely ashamed of acknowledging their debts. Instead, their responses fell into a pattern in which the inability to comply with repayment obligations emerged as the key element eliciting shame, making it necessary to conceal individual responsibility for default rather than for debt in general.

There are two patterns visible here that need to be distinguished analytically, though both are handled simultaneously by debtors and both, in fact, are highly correlated to the emphasis in extra-legal debt relations on the renegotiation stage of the credit contract: the first relates to the actual practice of renegotiating obligations after default and will be discussed at significantly greater detail in subsequent chapters, especially Chapter 8. Briefly summarized here, extra-legal financial markets have responded to the high levels of uncertainty they are dealing with by producing an operational grammar that centres on the handling of default. Debtors use a range of practices to renegotiate obligations with the aim to cope with the excessive exploitation that goes hand in hand with extra-legal debt. Creditors use a similar range of practices to maintain exceedingly high rates of profit in spite of very high rates of default in the absence of viable enforcement strategies for the recovery of dues. In present-day Banaras, these practices by market participants create a reputational economy of debt in which a central concern for all transactional parties is to minimize the reputational fallout of default and its handling. Integral to this exercise of reputational aspects in the credit relationship is the public visibility and assessment of one's own behaviour, so that a debtor's presentation of his or her narrative to me necessarily forms part of a reputational performance addressing the general public of market participants. Crucially, for the indebted transactional party likely to default in the near future, this understanding of reputational information flows corresponds to the need to showcase that the instances leading to the act of default were beyond one's own control. In fact, they needed to be beyond one's own control at all times, even pre-emptively, as the reputational dynamics hinged on the debtor not having defaulted on his or her own 'volition' – with the latter obviously being a fairly vague and highly contested category, considering the socioeconomic status and abilities of many debtors.

Beyond the performative aspect of renegotiating obligations, the heightened shame inherent in default (as opposed to debt) needs to be seen separate analytically, even though it too is related in present-day Banaras to the reputational underpinnings of extra-legal financial markets. Extra-legal credit in contemporary Banaras hardly ever encompassed a significant negotiation stage. Instead, the creditors' terms were almost always accepted straightforwardly by the debtors, and the renegotiation stage of the credit contract was emphasized in creditor–debtor relations. Renegotiating obligations provided means of redress and coping mechanisms to the debtors, with the reputational dynamics of the market forcing creditors to act leniently after a while. At the same time, however, renegotiations crippled the debtors' ability to avoid paying the maximum amounts that could be extracted from them without the creditors losing reputation. This maximum was almost invariably lower than the amount contractually stipulated in the negotiation stage of the contract, but as the stipulated interest rates tended to operate as instruments allowing the creditors to extract the maximum as rapidly as possible, this deviation did not lessen the extent of exploitation – it made a high rate of exploitation possible.

Shame took on a crucial role in this context. The trade-off that made it possible to escape the stipulated interest rates came with the price of a much deeper (and often times much less reflected) shame for the debtor. It perennially threatened to compromise the one value the debtor was capable of seeking to uphold even in contexts of high poverty, and the one value the debtor needed to uphold for future creditworthiness – his or her reputation. Conversely, the creditor gained reputation by being lenient, even under highly exploitative conditions. Material losses corresponded to reputational gains that would in turn help to stabilize future material gains that offset temporary losses due to lenience. The act of lenience also allowed the lender to minimize the fallout of public reproach, saving face and thus making it possible to discuss business in accordance with the imperative of feeding the reputational information flows through gossip. For the debtors, what was left under these conditions was to appeal to circumstances beyond one's own control – accidents, systemic injustices, bad luck, acts of god. The master artisan emphasized the frequent sickness of his children as a way out of an impossible situation, not necessarily as a device to absolve himself from blame. Admitting blame would have threatened the only viable way to cope with the operational logic of the reputational economy of debt. Asking him about his own responsibility, I realized much too late, was inconsiderate not because I was asking him to explain a failure associated with being in debt. I was asking him to project a face-saving narrative that he knew would be called out by people around him in ways that damaged his reputation.

The tendency of debtors to appeal to circumstances beyond one's own control when discussing default instead of debt even where it appeared to be futile as the last recourse of a person in danger of irrevocably losing reputation went beyond class boundaries. One of the people I had spent a significant amount of time with discussing the master artisan's debts and the reasons for his persistent defaulting came from a family that had owned significant amounts of land and real estate. We had discussed his family's current and past debts frequently, and while being indebted was clearly a routine experience despite the family's prosperity, it was discussed straightforwardly down to minute details, without any apparent evocation of shame. Discussions of debt, in fact, to some extent resembled discussing the cash flows of an enterprise. There were expenses associated with the need for taking on loans, but they could be handled as long as new earnings ensured liquidity. They were part of a perennial give-and-take that made it possible to have available the right amount of liquid capital at all times.

We had also frequently discussed the locally well-known fact that the family had been more prosperous in the past and had at one time owned significant property nearby which had been used as collateral. Though the family clearly did not own the land and real estate anymore, it took the same person a very long time to admit that the family had gradually *lost* its immovable property as collateral. Knowing that the property had been lost was fine as long as it had not been discussed. The discussion, however, would have made it unavoidable to consider the real problem – that the cash flow had broken down sufficiently often, that the family had needed to fall back on defaulting, that therefore its reputation had (at some time) been tarnished with the shame of default. When we finally started to discuss the family's defaults, the reaction fell into patterns closely resembling the master artisan's responses: the family had intermittently fallen on hard times as was not uncommon for elite families in mid-twentieth-century Banaras. The reasons for this intermittent decline had been beyond the control of the family, or else the family might have had the chance to escape decline but only by sacrificing its reputation and taking on morally dubious business opportunities. The moneylender, in turn, had not been constrained by moral considerations. He could not be depicted entirely immorally since he was an ancestor of a common friend, and was therefore praised as a 'great devotee'. Yet, despite his piety, he had been 'heartless'. Heartlessness, obviously, constituted a moral category that indirectly emphasized the question of default. It formed the debtor's way out of admitting the failure to adhere to contractual obligations. It highlighted the renegotiation of obligations that formed part of extra-legal credit, and alluded to the act of default as the *creditor's* failure to prolong the renegotiation stage of the credit contract.

Default as the ultimate problem for communicating reputational information on an extra-legal credit market could only be admitted as the insinuation that someone else had been responsible too. The pattern of maintaining face by pointing out that even if the debtor may have been at fault to some extent, it must have been the lender's fault as well, since the lender *should have* allowed the renegotiation of contractual obligations to continue just a little bit longer, presented a persistent problem for me in recording debtors' narratives. Almost invariably, the increase in formality brought about by the act of recording went hand in hand with a considerably heightened tendency of the interlocutor to engage in an elaborate exercise of blaming rather than discussing experiences. At times, the same interlocutor would portray the topics of our discussion very differently as soon as I switched of the tape recorder.

Talking to debtors and understanding the need to maintain reputation even under the adverse conditions of default helped me significantly to comprehend the differences between my original understanding of the credit contract and the operation of credit relations that rely more strongly on reputational modes of governing – as extra-legal credit contracts do. There is, however, no fundamental difference between the legally enforceable contracts I had been thinking of and their extra-legal counterparts. Instead, the scale of embeddedness of these transactions in reputational information flows emphasizes a differentiation according to the relative importance accruing to various stages of credit contracts, with extra-legal credit placing emphasis on what should be defined as the 'future' stage of a credit contract as against the heightened importance of its 'present' stage in the modern notion of credit.

Credit contracts follow a temporal sequence that resemble the past, present, and future stages or, respectively, can be defined as the sequential stages of negotiation, agreement, and renegotiation, complemented by a highly complex feedback loop between the latter and the next negotiation stage. The 'modern' notion of credit contracts that underlies what in the Indian discourse became classified as 'organized' banking seeks to impoverish this temporality of credit contracts. Thus, the feedback loop is (in theory) restricted to the operation of a quantifiable track record, while the negotiation stage relies on the prospective debtors informing themselves on the credit schemes offered by various competing financial institutions. The renegotiation stage, in turn, is largely kept hidden from the operation of 'credit' – and only thought of as a last resort to escape over-indebtedness – and consists of tightly regulated procedures applying to specific contexts in which debtors are allowed to default through debt rescheduling, insolvency, and bankruptcy proceedings.

On extra-legal financial markets such as the reputational economy of debt I observed in Banaras, the relative importance attributed to the various stages of the credit contract changed considerably from this blueprint. The negotiation stage, in fact, hardly existed. It was very rare for any prospective debtor even to try and engage a lender in a negotiation of transactional obligations including interest rates. When I had started field research in Banaras, I had been baffled by the seeming contradiction in debtors' assertions that they were keenly aware of the 'rules of the game' and used them to their own advantage, while simultaneously making certain I understood that the interest rates hardly ever changed. As will be shown in much greater detail in Chapter 8, the prevalent interest rates were widely known and hardly ever deviated from. At the same time, there were strong differences between interest and profit rates, and in many ways the exceedingly high interest rates were intended to speed up the process until the ubiquity of default ushered in the renegotiation stage. It was here, in the renegotiation stage, that the actual costs of borrowing were agreed upon through a series of interactions between lender and borrower. It was in the renegotiation stage that the reputational economy of debt and the materiality of transactions overlapped to such an extent that it allowed the conversion – with difficulty, and in specific contexts – of reputation into credit. It was the centrality of the renegotiation stage for extra-legal finance combined with the complexity of the feedback loop that made it possible for the credit contract to become embedded in information flows on reputation to such an extent as to make the material and the reputational economies of debt almost inseparable. In order to understand the emergence of this market, it is necessary to engage with anthropological theory on contracts, exchange, and credit, but it is also necessary to study the history of the framing of credit markets in India since the mid-nineteenth century.

The contract takes a central place in economic anthropology, partially as it is characterized as an antipode to the gift as an area of inquiry in early economic anthropology (Raheja 1988; Malinowski 2014 [1922]; Hann and Hart 2011). With the Maussian intervention in the debate in 1925, demonstrating balanced reciprocity (Mauss 1970), the discourse shifted to a more nuanced observation of the differences between contract and gift, less pre-occupied with the intention of giving in the gift and more focused on receiving return values. With the concept gaining traction, the contrast between gift and contract could not anymore be comprehensively located in the negation of gainful activity in the gift but shifted to a differentiation between the commensurability of the return value in gift exchange and the stipulated return value in contractual exchange. This more nuanced distinction resulted in increased attention to the actual practice of contractual exchange.

According to David Graeber (Graeber 2001; see also Graeber 2011), the stipulations of the contract are enunciated and visible, though following Émile Durkheim's emphasis on the 'non-contractual element in the contract' (Durkheim 2013; Hart 1988, 180) the extent of enunciation and visibility of contractual stipulations remain open to interpretation, further narrowing the gap to the gift under balanced reciprocity. Keith Hart, contrasting contractual relations to kinship-based ones defined as 'an extrapolation of statuses typical of traditional ideology and practice' (Hart 1988, 178), stressed yet another element in the contract – its enforceability as a legally sanctioned agreement. Here, the contract emerged as synonymous with a particular type of contract defined as operating in legally codified manners, notwithstanding contractual agreements that operate without recourse to the law. The emphasis on enforceability obviously does not resolve the distinction between gift and contract but adds yet another layer of complexity: the return value in exchange relations may be enforced in multiple ways – whether by the spirit *hau* in the Polynesian examples that gave rise to this discourse, by extrapolations of statuses perceived as 'tradition', or by extrapolations of statuses denominated as the law. The difference is located in the manners of enforcing obligations to return a more or less clearly defined value to the other transactional party. The enunciated and visible element in the contract, accordingly, lends itself to structures of obligation underlying exchange that emphasize an enforcement through arbitration, while, conversely, Graeber's silent and invisible elements in the contract facilitate an enforcement of obligations through reputational means. Enforceability through reputational means facilitates deeper social ties between transactional parties, while enforceability through arbitration facilitates stronger ties of the transactional parties to the arbitrator, with contractual law – backed by the modern state's monopoly on violence – emerging as one of the strongest (and most political rather than social) forms of these ties. When asking what replaced the law in 'informal' economic relations among Ghanaian migrants,

Hart referred to the contract under contractual law. A major part of my argument addresses the same question, outlining the emergence of new forms of extra-legal finance in northern India. In this chapter, however, the focus of the argument is on the related question of how contractual law replaced other viable forms of enforcing the obligation to return value in mid-nineteenth-century India.

As I have argued elsewhere (Schwecke 2020), the future orientation of credit further diminishes the distinction between credit contracts and gift-giving under balanced reciprocity when observed from the perspective of the return value. In medieval Britain, the archbishops of Canterbury circumvented the prohibition of usury by transferring the principal of their loans as a gift, expecting a return gift in instalments that 'incidentally' corresponded to the 6 per cent per annum interest permissible in law for non-Christian lenders (Bellot 1906). As Hart has noted (Hart 2018), in money lending transactions entrepreneurial success depends less on the rate of interest but the rate of default. The heightened uncertainty imposed by its enhanced future orientation on the credit contract in contrast to the commodity contract serves as an impediment to be bridged by any structure of enforcing obligation. In markets depending on relatively 'weak' ties, the obstacles for enforcement are tantamount to a decrease in expected returns on investment, regardless of their fixed nature in the enunciated and visible element of the contract. Essentially, returns on investment in many forms of money lending are closer to being 'commensurate' with expected returns than to the returns stipulated in the contractual agreement. Citing Hart, Gustav Peebles (2010, 230) noted that barter served as an index of the instability of sociopolitical regimes, while credit conversely indicated stability and lasting ties, a phenomenon also addressed in the tendency of 'immediate-return' societies to avoid credit relations (Day, Papataxiarches, and Stewart 1999). Barter differs from gift exchange under balanced reciprocity in that the former's C–C relationship (in its Marxian denomination)[2] is transformed into a commensurate value, at most an unknowable gain expected to be commensurate, and should be depicted accordingly as $C-C^?$. While certainly being gainful, the *extent* of the gain in an $M-M'$ credit transaction without strong enforcement is diminished in its knowability, narrowing the gap to gift exchange – $M-M'^?$.

While the unknowability of the return value is heightened in contexts of low levels of enforcement, the principle remains the same even in credit contracts operating under conditions of strong enforcement of contractual law that constitute the majority of credit transactions that are commonly associated with the credit contract nowadays, even in contexts such as India, where credit transactions beyond the reach of the state's enforcement apparatus remain widespread. Marcel Mauss' discussion of the gift had been highlighting the stabilizing effect that sequential gift exchange based on balanced reciprocity had over time since information flows on both transactional sides' expectations decreased the level of unknowability involved (Mauss 1970). Sequential exchange in credit relations operates according to the same logic – at all times, though the 'modern' credit contract seeks to minimize the extent of uncertainty by incorporating strong enforcement mechanisms for obligations. In their (relative) absence, the experiential nature of trust and the increases in knowledge that underlie the operation of balanced reciprocity for both gift exchange and credit – all of which tend to stabilize transactional relations over time, though there are significant differences in the operation of trust and balanced reciprocity – gain in importance. Extra-legal credit markets do not necessarily lack strong enforcement mechanisms for obligations, though broadly speaking the guarantee of contractual validity through the law in contemporary nation-states constitutes one of the strongest known historical forms of doing so. Historically, many market participants on extra-legal credit markets have instead relied on relatively strong social ties for the provision of enforcement mechanisms, visible even in contemporary India.

In cases with high extents of extra-legality, as Isabelle Guérin has noted for rural southern India, the inherent impediment to the enforcement of transactional obligations facilitates a stronger recourse to non-legal social ties, augmenting social relations through debt and providing new avenues for livelihood strategies to debtors. Credit and debt, she notes, express 'the size of one's social network', and needed to be interpreted as 'a kind of wealth', despite 'the possible consequences of dependency and exploitation inherent in debt' (Guérin 2014, 45).[3] Conversely, in order to overcome the need to develop social networks that are sufficiently strong to allow for credit contracts, the level of enforcing obligations through the law in contexts defined by a strong contractual law-based enforcement strategy needs to be significantly higher for credit than for commodity contracts. The commodity form in a transaction lowers the uncertainty associated with the future orientation of the exchange relationship, and thereby facilitates the ease with which enforcement structures based on arbitration enter credit markets as regulatory authority. Where credit involves commodity elements – such as in the use of desirable collaterals, especially land – the shift towards the use of arbitration in the governance of credit is marked, as will be pointed out repeatedly with regard to the Indian historical experience later.

Given these difficulties, it is unsurprising that a vast majority of credit transactions in India remained beyond the purview of the law well into the twentieth century. British Indian courts certainly adjudicated debt cases beforehand, yet there is a broad consensus that marks the abolition of the usury laws in 1855 as a decisive threshold in bringing credit markets under the purview of contractual law, in the process arguably even bringing about a fully capitalist system of finance in India. The latter point was forcefully made by David Hardiman (1996b, 1996a) and will be discussed subsequently in greater detail. Yet the general argument was widely shared at the time across a wide spectrum of British and Indian public opinion. Indian nationalist and British opinion differed on the question of responsibility for its outcomes, not on the importance of the event in itself. In Hardiman's interpretation, the abolition of the usury laws replaced the prevalent 'moral' economies of debt embedded into village structures with contractual relations enforced by the British Indian state (Hardiman 1996b, 125–26). It disrupted more or less harmonic 'extrapolations of statuses typical of traditional ideology and practice' that are depicted in this argument as 'moral', replacing these with the legal enforcement of contractual obligations that constituted a hallmark of capitalist modernity. Keith Hart's depiction of the shift in economic practices from 'kinship' to 'trust' in the transition from a rural to a slum economy after migration – part of his much larger work on informality – was part of an endeavour to establish a critique of the emergence of corporate personality in law, particularly in business law, taking on the qualities of real personalities in the abstraction that is the law.[4] Hardiman's depiction resembles this process to some extent. The 'moral' economies of debt he describes were rooted in the very real social structures of a different corporate nature that governed Indian rural society, and are depicted as less exploitative than their capitalist counterparts that at heart rely on processes of abstraction. Yet the predominant way of governing credit relations in India in the absence of strong commodity elements, and frequently enough even in their presence, still relied on a reputational basis that both limited and facilitated highly exploitative forms of credit. As will be shown profusely in the following chapters, the act of lenience in a reputational economy of debt (instead of a merely 'moral' one) can frequently be part of the exercise of renegotiating obligations that governs many credit relations and can be just as exploitative as its 'capitalist' counterparts.

Abolishing usury

In the history of ideas on usury, the case for the abolition of usury laws is inextricably tied to the exchange between Jeremy Bentham and Adam Smith in the final decades of the eighteenth century, though earlier debates had controversially discussed usury in early modern British history (Codr 2016). Bentham's letter to his mentor, making the case for non-intervention by the state and asking the latter to rethink his defence of usury laws, became the foundation for legislative efforts to 'rationalize' credit markets in the spirit of free-market ideology. The economist Joseph Persky portrayed the exchange of ideas in ways that are reminiscent of the debate over the conceptualization of the Deccan Riots as a 'non-event' (see later) by Neil Charlesworth (1972) – as a 'modest dispute' with major ramifications:

> [T]he entire affair amounts to nothing more than a modest dispute between a failing master ... and an over-eager disciple.... Yet the argument struck a fundamental chord ... Chesterton ... identified Bentham's essay on usury as the very beginning of the 'modern world.' I tend to agree with him. (Persky 2007, 228)

Persky's self-avowedly 'ambitious' claim on the relationship between the abolition of usury and 'modernity' is based on an argument that perceives the extension of the free-market principle even to credit contracts as a breakthrough towards the shaping of social relations through self-interest (Persky 2007, 235).[5] Bentham's aims in proposing the abolition of usury laws are depicted in ways that combine the pessimistic understanding of the limits for state intervention on markets – widely shared among nineteenth-century colonial administrators – with a celebration of risk-taking entrepreneurship that would have seemed out of place in this period and were much more commonly expressed in the run-up to the financial crisis of 2008. Persky's argument rests strongly on Bentham's validation of the premium due to the 'projectors' that convinced Adam Smith of the need for legislation against usury – risk-taking entrepreneurs prone to engage in speculative business practices. In the financially more conservative atmosphere of nineteenth-century India, the interpretation of Bentham's ideas emphasized the state's inability to prevent the evasion of its laws, the claimed logical inconsistency in the applicability of different legislations for credit and commodity markets, and the efficacy of non-intervention by the state as a supply-side measure for lowering the costs of borrowing. Bentham's pessimistic conception of the ability of the state to safeguard 'prodigals' and 'simpletons' (Bentham 1787/1818) in the face of opportunities for misguided consumption remained broadly accepted in mid-nineteenth-century British India. It faded in importance, though, at least until it was challenged in the last quarter of the nineteenth century by the legal doctrine of 'expectant heirs' underlying the emergence of 'unconscionability' as the key test for state intervention.

The abolition of the usury laws in India in 1855 followed their abolition in Britain in the preceding year. While the Usury Laws (Repeal) Act (Act XXVIII of 1855) in British India did not include a statement of aims, the debates in the House of Commons for the British act provide ample evidence for the weight attributed to Bentham's arguments among British legislators.[6] Act XXVIII of 1855 repealed Section XXX of the 'Act for Establishing Certain Regulations for the Better Management of the Affairs of the East India Company as well in India as in Europe'[7] which addressed credit transactions with Indians by Company employees. More importantly for Indian debtors, it also repealed several sections and clauses in the Bengal, Madras, and Bombay codes that primarily governed the Presidency towns. Its most important stipulation for the vast majority of credit transactions, especially in the *mufassil*, related to paragraph II of the act that provided legal protection to mutually agreed interest rates in credit contracts:

> In any suit in which interest is recoverable, the amount shall be adjudged or decreed by the Court at the rate (if any) agreed upon by the parties; and if no rate shall have been agreed upon, at such rate as the Court shall deem reasonable.[8]

The British and Indian acts overturned a long-term development in European thought that had held 'moderate usury' as morally and legally permissible in contrast to excessive usury (Bernstein 1965, 848). Carl F. Taeusch related the development of permissible forms of usury – in late-eighteenth-century Britain defined in law as 5 per cent per annum – to a conflation of interest and rent (Taeusch 1942, 304). The 'modern' interpretation of usury became restated in the late nineteenth century, but was temporarily undermined with the enactment of Bentham's ideas (see Mews and Abraham 2007). Jean Francois Bissonnette has depicted the lasting effect of Bentham's ideas as a 'de-politicization' of credit relations and conversely demonstrated the continued political nature of credit (Bissonnette 2019, 455–57), though his discussion centres on questions of political control rather than the construction of interest. It is noteworthy, however, that credit needs to be understood as an inherently political construction, especially in its 'modern' form. It is the political construction of 'modern' credit that allows the enforcement of credit obligations through (typically state-led) arbitration which, in turn, impoverishes the temporality of the credit contract by seeking to minimize all its temporal stages other than negotiation and, even more importantly, agreement. In the Indian context, it was the political intervention of the high-colonial era state that in turn provided barriers to the exercise of the renegotiation stage, except under significantly constricted circumstances and following stringently specified procedural rules. Procedural stipulations, an intensely political category, facilitated the turn towards what should be classified as the actuarial pretence (see Zelizer 1978) – that predictions of the future are not rooted in personal judgement or divination, to employ Laura Bear's term for it (Bear 2015), and therefore one's trust in one's own ability to judge correctly, but in methodologies of achieving calculability, thus turning 'trust' into 'risk', and informing creditors and debtors alike to the extent that increasingly high levels of debt were perceived as viable.

The practical consequences for Indian debtors were far-reaching, even though it is unclear whether the act directly influenced prevalent interest rates that typically had been significantly higher than legally permitted by the so-called 'old' usury laws. As discussed in greater detail later, administrators in the Northwestern Provinces or United Provinces in the late nineteenth and early twentieth centuries observed long-term trends in interest rates that were depicted as either stable or declining. While there is sufficient evidence from official sources to identify exceptions to these trends, the complexity of credit practices governing the costs of borrowing impedes the identification of validated long-term trends of this sweeping nature. Obviously, though, in protecting interest rates agreed upon at the time of the contractual agreement regardless of their conscionability, the act placed creditors at an advantage over debtors – an argument that many proponents of Bentham's ideas readily accepted, arguing that increases in credit supply would sufficiently reduce borrowing costs to offset this advantage.

The 1855 act, however, fundamentally changed the structure of enforcement of contractual obligations, at least in theory, disincentivizing creditors to allow renegotiations of contractual terms according to changed circumstances: one element of the future orientation of the credit contract – the costs of borrowing – was legally fixed at the time of agreement, while another element – the means for repayment – remained pervasively uncertain. Benthamite ideas on usury rested crucially on the conflation of credit and commodity contracts, negating the differences caused by the credit contract's increased future orientation and undermining one of the crucial ways in which societies relying on extra-legal credit markets have responded to its heightened uncertainty. The repeal of the usury laws was primarily based on substituting often vaguely defined moral ideas (Mews and Abraham 2007) with a process of rationalization, and intended as a supply-side measure for the facilitation of credit. Yet its outcome in the nature of the credit contract's practice in India was a legislative effort to fix M–M'? as M–M'.

With this disincentive for renegotiation, legislation added another key element, shifting the 'permissible' credit contract to a procedurally pre-defined form. In theory, legislative efforts brought about considerable changes in the procedural form for credit contracts. Read in combination with the Indian Evidence Act, 1872, which codified the form of evidence permissible in legal suits, the 1855 act provided legally stipulated form to credit transactions that emphasized their written codification unless falling under 'undue influence' as defined by the Indian Contracts Act, 1872.[9] In its interaction with the subsequent legislations that according to Ritu Birla constituted a process of defining the 'proper swindle' (Birla 2009), the abolition of the usury laws had lasting indirect effects that – in contrast to its intentions – were not subsequently countermanded through the Usurious Loans Act of 1918.

The credit contract, contractual law, and capitalist finance in modern India

While the introduction of liberal contractual law in the Indian economy has a much longer history, it was its increased penetration of business practices since the second half of the nineteenth century that brought about its centrality for the development of capitalism in India.[10] Birla's account of the definition of the 'proper swindle' provides considerable insights into this development. The link between the development of contractual law and the development of capitalism in India is easily traceable from a Weberian standpoint, but the argument developed here seeks to make a broader point: that the dissection of the Indian economy into state-supported and state-neglected segments was based on the employment of procedural logics in service of the changing needs of the Indian state and that these procedural changes brought about a divergence in the operational modes of markets, forcing a major share of the Indian population to interact simultaneously with economic segments (of 'formal' and 'informal', or 'organized' and 'unorganized' sectors) following very different and frequently conflicting regimes of accumulation that can be defined as procedurally capitalist and reputational economies. Liberal contractual law emerged as a key element in this process precisely because it was fundamental to the procedurally capitalist economy but withheld or removed from the reputational one. The case of financial markets provides an excellent study area to demonstrate how these processes developed since financial markets have minimal exposure – relative to others – to the factors of labour and commodities, magnifying the visibility of procedural dimensions.

As an entry point to the discussion of the relationship between capitalism and its procedural basis, I want to explore the ambiguity of finance for capitalist accumulation, especially the ambiguity of interest. As discussed by Taeusch, the distinction between usury and interest in modern European thought rested on the definition of the former as 'excessive' charges for borrowing. This interpretation – barring its temporary undermining through Bentham's ideas – gradually developed in a secular process out of the Christian tradition of perceiving usury/interest as sin. According to Taeusch (1942, 304–05), both Catholic and Protestant traditions started to reinterpret usury/interest as rent, that is, as a charge on the use of an asset, and therefore permissible as long as it remained reasonable. This reinterpretation replaced a concept of usury which permitted lending only through the institution of partnership that, in turn, corresponded to the obligation of the lender to share both the borrower's gains *and* losses, a practice still visible in Islamic banking (Mews and Abraham 2007). This conception sought to reconcile the vagaries arising from the heightened future orientation of the credit contract relative to the commodity contract: the lender's gains would correspond to the future development of the borrower's fortunes. Bentham's idea on the permissibility of all usury fixed the lender's gains at the time of contractual agreement without alleviating the borrower's future uncertainty over the ability to repay principal plus interest. The reinterpretation of Christian thought on usury followed the same reasoning except for the *laissez-faire* conception of allowing the market to fix prices free of its embeddedness in moral discourses other than utility maximization.

The lender was re-imagined as a landlord or landlady, conflating money and land as goods that could be used for a charge. The conception of interest in the contemporary period remains little changed from its early modern foundations, which comprise very strong non-capitalist components. The argument on the ambiguity of interest could easily be extended in various directions, by employing it in connection with studies emphasizing differentiations within capital, for instance, Giovanni Arrighi's argument on financialization as the final stage of each capitalist conjuncture (Arrighi 1996) and its incipient statement by Fernand Braudel (1982, 246), or Hartmut Elsenhans's argument that speculative finance capital needs to be seen as a non-capitalist element within capitalism as it leads to the entrenchment of rentier structures (Elsenhans 2007, 2015). Added to the ambiguities of finance in terms of its relationship with capitalism through the differences between the credit and the commodity contract, and the relationship of interest and rent is the Marxian conception of M–M' markets in cutting out both labour and the commodity form that informed Marx's treatment of exchange as circulation (Marx 1967). Jairus Banaji has dealt extensively with this ambiguity of finance as capitalist in his studies of mercantile capitalism in the Indian Ocean region (Banaji 2016) and of money lending in western India (Banaji 1977). The chief virtue of Banaji's fascinating studies lies in the way in which he is able to make a persuasive case for the realignment of mercantile accumulation and control over production as the basis for a mercantile capitalism distinct from, though interacting with, its industrial equivalent.

Banaji clearly distinguishes between mercantile accumulation and mercantile capitalist accumulation, with the latter located within mercantile efforts to exert control over the production process. His work traces the development of mercantile control over production, especially in the putting-out systems and produce trade primarily dominated by European capital. While his work deals predominantly with capital flows and the organization of production through these, and therefore neglects the form of enforcing obligation, his argument implicitly locates the latter in commodity and labour contracts rather than in credit. Defining mercantile capitalism through the attempt to seek control over production obviously has the drawback of relegating the majority of mercantile practices in India during this period to the non-capitalist realm. Banaji clearly accepts this, though many scholars working on capitalism in India would disagree. This drawback has repercussions on the history of finance in India, including the history of banking, as a significant share of financial and banking operations in India were focusing on financing trade – without seeking control over production.

A reading of Banaji's work on money lending reinforces these conclusions. Banaji's area of choice to study petty finance is rooted in the advance system, a less sophisticated relation of the putting-out system. While the putting-out system depended on complex flows of capital as advances through agents and middlemen into artisanal production, its sophistication allowed for direct control by (mercantile) capitalists over the production process in terms of specifying the output, though not in other dimensions (see Perlin 1983). The advance system, in contrast, centred on an exploitation of indebtedness of the agricultural and artisanal household, related to seasonal fluctuations in demand.[11] The predominant pattern was one of dependency, allowing merchants to control the artisan's or farmer's output in its price dimension but not in the specification of the product. As the advance system constituted one of the main modes of organizing artisanal labour, and will therefore be discussed subsequently, the main points to draw from Banaji's work for understanding the evolution of contracts and their relationship with the development of capitalism will be highlighted here, instead.

Banaji's work on money lending – observing the functioning of the credit contract – adds another layer to its complexity. While the credit contract comprises elements that bring it closer to the gift under balanced reciprocity, it also can operate in ways that at least partially enable labour control, thus bringing it closer to the work contract. It is noteworthy here that Mauss' study of Polynesian societies was undertaking an inquiry not only into the gift but equally into prestations, collective social services typically rendered to elites (Mauss 1970). The advance system in India operated on an extra-legal obligation of the producer to sell the finished product to the creditor, a system that did not need to be fixed in contractual terms and in this way approximates the 'non-contractual element in the contract'. Systems of ensuring obligations were met may have been compromised in times of low labour supply due to the operation of a political logic in making the credit market work: obligations could not be enforced or even stipulated when the negotiating power of artisanal labour was high. Historically, however, the penetration of liberal contractual law into Indian credit markets occurred at a time when labour (especially artisanal labour) possessed very low negotiating power, being squeezed by both the aftermath of India's deindustrialization and its incipient shift to industrialization, especially in the textile sector where these processes combined to force artisanal production into market niches (see Roy 1999; Haynes 2012).[12]

The credit contract thus emerges as an ambiguous and complex instrument that contextually takes on elements resembling reciprocal gift exchange, rent, and the work contract. What the combined reading of Banaji's work on mercantile capitalism and money lending demonstrates is that only the last of these resemblances can be used as a key element in defining capitalism in a Marxist approach. What is more, its links with the commodity contract are tenuous at best, as long as credit is predominantly perceived as transferring resources over time. Munn's argument that credit facilitates movement through space–time (Munn 1986) can be interpreted in its contractual dimension when foregoing the 'modern' distinction between credit instruments and bills of exchange. It is noteworthy here that the Middle Eastern and South Asian early modern economies placed a less categorical distinction on the difference between transfers over time or space, with the *hundi* and *hawala* denominating instruments that worked as both (Martin 2009).

As mentioned earlier, the central drawback in understanding the relationship between credit, liberal contractual law, and capitalism in India in Banaji's approach is that it leaves out a vast realm of commercial activity in which credit was used to finance trade without exerting control over the production process, or to finance consumption and subsistence. These areas delineate a market for credit practices that necessitates a study beyond the strictly defined Marxist paradigm to identify their relationship with capitalism. The debate on these credit practices is inextricably linked with debates on mercantile practice in general, including Sanjay Subrahmanyam's concept of portfolio capitalists and C. A. Bayly's study of north Indian burgher towns which also provides considerable information on the case of Banaras and will be highlighted here for this reason. These approaches, in turn, are associated with questions on the 'bazaar economy' that will be discussed subsequently.

Bayly's intricate study of the burgher towns of the north Indian plains in the eighteenth and early nineteenth centuries – and the network of markets and business practices linking them – depicts the embeddedness of economic practice into sociocultural life in the advent of colonialism, detailing the sophistication of mercantile practices and ethics, especially regarding the inland trade, located at the junction of two prominent poles: the market town and the merchant family firm (Bayly 1983). Subrahmanyam's concept of 'portfolio capitalists' strongly intersected with Bayly's work (Subrahmanyam and Bayly 1988). Focusing originally on southern India, the concept was designed to correct the tendency of earlier literature to highlight aspects of community-centric associational life in mercantile organization rather than emphasizing the individual entrepreneur or firm in ways that enabled their depiction as capitalist enterprises of an 'Indian' historical lineage. It implicitly delineated a schism between capitalist traditions that marked the production of colonial 'modernity'.

Bayly's work focuses on the commercial networks linking cities and their hinterland that considerably expanded in the eighteenth century at the same time as the political stability brought about by the Mughal empire collapsed. Businesses in this time of political instability needed to find stabilizing practices beyond the reach of the imperial successor states and its local manifestations. The eighteenth century thus saw an increased reliance on business practices centring on what economic anthropology would describe as extra-legality, with Bayly stressing the importance of the family firm and of mercantile ethics. As will be discussed in greater detail in Chapters 5 and 6, other authors have emphasized caste and community structures to demonstrate the high extent of social embeddedness of markets, while Bayly consciously depicted these as more important for trading diasporas than for the inland trade.

Focusing among other areas on the city of Banaras in the central Gangetic plains – at the time one of the most important entrepôts for the inland trade and one of the biggest financial hubs of India – Bayly describes the family firm as not only a central organizational unit of Indian commerce but one that served key business functions. It operated as a skilling and networking unit, allowed for strategic expansions of business undertakings through marriage alliances and branch offices in distant cities, and minimized the need for politico-legal exposure, while keeping capital under unified control. While Birla demonstrated that the colonial state in the late nineteenth century (strategically) depicted the family firm as a family first (Birla 2009, 49), Bayly shows how the institutions of the family and the firm were merged inextricably.

The role of the family firm as an informational unit, in facilitating opacity and in communicating standing, needs to be understood in its relationship with the importance of mercantile ethics, signifying the reputational underpinnings of mercantile practice. Bayly's analysis of north Indian mercantile ethics in the eighteenth and early nineteenth centuries draws heavily on sources depicting the worlds of Banarsi bankers. Located at the intersection of the main east–west 'artery of trade' (Das Gupta 2001) in northern India – the Ganges river and the Grand Trunk Road – with the main southward trade route that linked the north Indian cities to economic centres such as Pune and Hyderabad, the city had emerged as one of the most important financial centres in India in the eighteenth century. Its religious role as a centre of an expanding pilgrimage system across the subcontinent helped in stabilizing bullion supplies – a key concern in a credit market centring on the *hundi* – while its 'discovery' as an ancient site of Hindu learning principally by the Maratha aristocracy (and the absence of strong political control by Awadh) (Mishra 1975) magnified the opportunities to tap into networks of political patronage. In addition, the city had emerged as a major site for artisanal production, and was benefiting from the proximity of similar artisanal centres such as the region around Azamgarh (Pandey 1981). In the mid-eighteenth century, tensions between the Bhumihar dynasty effectively ruling most of the countryside around the city and the Nawabdom of Awadh heightened effective control by mercantile houses over the city's affairs, including its bazaar. Linked to larger political and military developments, Banaras soon passed under indirect British rule, while the city itself was taken over by the British after a short-lived revolt by one of its nominal rulers,

Chet Singh, in 1781. (The Princely State of Banaras did not extend to the city itself, and centred on the small town of Ramnagar.) British rule soon led to upheavals not only within the city (Freitag 1989, 1995) but also in the nearby countryside when the area's land tenure system became permanently settled, providing investment opportunities to the city's mercantile elite (Cohn 1960; Mishra 1975). In terms of trade and finance, British rule initially benefited the merchants and bankers of Banaras – who had played an important role in financing the East India Company's conquest of India[13] – in providing political and legal stability, and in tying the city to the rising fortunes of the new capital, Calcutta. The link to Calcutta cemented the role of Banaras for colonial-era Orientalist scholarship as a reservoir of supposedly authentic Hinduism which, in turn, aided the reimagination of the city's religious practices, a central aspect of what Vasudha Dalmia (1997) termed the 'nationalization of Hindu tradition'. With its economy turning relatively stagnant around the mid-nineteenth century, the religious reimagination of Banaras combined with its artisanal industries served to sustain the city, even though it declined significantly since the late nineteenth century and even more sharply with the relative decline of Calcutta in the mid-twentieth century.

In its commercial heyday, however, its strong entrenchment as a religious centre bolstered the mercantile ethics followed by its commercial and financial elite. Bayly describes mercantile ethics as revolving around the notion of *sakh* (literally: credit), a holistic concept of ethical behaviour for mercantile groups that foregrounded reliability, thrift, and piety, and in turn was inextricably linked to a reputational standing that was reflected in the financial system dominated by the *hundi*. Its lynchpin was in the family firm that allowed the communication of reputation as a *family's* reputation rather than an individual one, and ascribed codes for publicly visible behaviour, while keeping from public knowledge information that was deemed to be reputationally damaging. Bayly highlights the tendency of successful merchants and bankers to be seen taking care of the cowsheds attached to their homes (Bayly 2011, 172), thus highlighting one dimension of piety and its links with the reputational underpinnings of the *hundi*. Not being seen to engage in pious activity damaged the merchant's reputation and lowered the value of his or her *hundi*s in the bazaar. While the facades of bankers' residences in Chowk were already opulent,[14] mercantile residential quarters became increasingly lavish the further away they were from public view (see Desai 2017). Piety and thrift were related in one other way: while it was important to showcase thriftiness, it was equally important to communicate the extent to which thrift was a matter of choice rather than need. Since displays of conspicuous consumption were contrary to thrift, religious patronage provided an opportunity to demonstrate wealth without attracting public displeasure for sumptuous spending. The importance of religious patronage will be discussed in greater detail in Chapter 6 in the context of its decline in the mid-twentieth century and its ramifications for the system of enforcing obligations.

While piety and thrift shaped mercantile ethics through the reputational underpinnings of the *hundi*, demonstrations of reliability interacted most directly with the notion of *sakh* in its monetary dimensions. In one of the old banking families of Banaras, a narrative handed down through generations related to a late-nineteenth-century occurrence when the family head was visited by a new British collector. On being asked at this first meeting for a substantial loan, the head of the family called for the head *munim* (accountant) who – aware that the family's reputation was tested – proceeded to ask whether he wanted the loan in coins of a particular year of coinage.[15] The value of a family's *hundi*s depended strongly on the assurance of the drawer's ability to encash them at short notice, so that a lack of liquidity had direct repercussions on the family's reputational standing, and therefore the family's ability to raise credit. The importance of the city's constant bullion supply needs to be seen in this perspective. Similarly, the family firm provided much-needed opacity in an economy depending on reputational communication flows: it allowed the firm to hide the state of its finances during business downturns, as long as the appearance of reliability could be maintained.

In many ways, the enforcement of obligations in this economy remained strongly reputational. To turn to a court of law for arbitration remained fraught with dangers as the courts relied on certain forms of evidence, particularly account books, and at least partially publicized this evidence. The difficulties faced by 'indigenous' bankers in making use of the British Indian legal system were particularly pronounced in credit markets where the difference between communicated reputation and the actuality of business affairs was not only greater than in commodity exchange, but where public awareness of this difference was disastrous. The *hundi* simply did not correspond to the stipulations of liberal contractual law, a fact that partially explains the difficulties of the British in bringing it under the sway of commercial law. The Negotiable Instruments Act of 1881 defined *hundi*s as outside its purview unless they specifically stated that they were adhering to the act's stipulations (Birla 2009; Martin 2009) – which negated significant parts of the *hundi*'s utility. The penetration of the Indian economy by liberal contractual law had more significant effects in disrupting the credit market than meets the eye. It affected the ways in which businesses were run in fundamental ways. The financial segment defined in British Indian sources as either 'indigenous' or 'native' banking remained mostly outside Banaji's definition of mercantile capitalism, though it formed the apex of the commercial system dominating the inland trade. Subrahmanyam's definition of the concept of 'portfolio capitalists' indicates that these bankers needed to be perceived as at least partially capitalist, though. What definitions such as Subrahmanyam's lack in stringency from a strictly Marxist perspective, they compensate by their ability to be linked to non-Marxist conceptions of capitalism, and by being able to capture nuances in Indian economic history beyond the bridgeheads of European capital that dominated intercontinental trade but failed to penetrate the inland trade to a similar extent.

Bayly's work on the organization of Indian finance in the inland trade through mercantile ethics and the family firm strongly emphasized its apex, the system of 'indigenous' banking, despite its focus on rural–urban links and the development of market towns, where his work concentrates on commodity exchange to a much greater extent than credit networks. For obvious reasons, credit and commodity exchange cannot be separated completely, yet the differences between the credit and the commodity contract outlined earlier necessitate close attention to their distinctiveness. One of the reasons for Bayly's neglect of lower-order credit markets – apart from the paucity of sources – is linked to visible tendencies of emulation. In some ways, the lower-order markets mirrored organizational principles that were more pronounced at higher levels of lending. Partially, this is related to top-down credit flows that tied lower-order credit markets to these higher levels through several stages of intermediation, necessitating a common framework of intelligibility (see Perlin 1993, 2020). At the same time, Indian credit markets comprised traces of segmentation: the function of the *hundi* for long-distance and large-scale markets was provided at lower-order markets by an assortment of credit instruments frequently depicted as *chitti*s or *chit*s. Understudied as these instruments are, it remains clear that they followed less elaborate and possibly less sophisticated operational logics than the *hundi*, yet were based on similar principles, either derived from or constitutive of the reputational grammar of Indian finance that was expressed in the *hundi* trade, and shared a common intelligibility. The topmost layer of Indian finance may have eschewed trading in *chitti*s and being involved in the local bazaar beyond several stages of intermediation, but even among 'indigenous' bankers there is ample evidence for combining these trades. In some ways reminiscent of debates in the

1980s and early 1990s on medieval and early modern statehood in India (Stein 1985; Kulke 1997), higher-order markets provided a blueprint for the organization of market behaviour at lower levels to be followed in ways adjusted to the different contextual parameters, or vice versa. The penetration of Indian credit markets by liberal contractual law struck at these operational modes and their common intelligibility at various levels in the nineteenth century but was restricted at the lower end through processes described in Chapters 3 and 4, while facilitating the collapse of the topmost layer of this credit market as discussed in Chapter 6, disrupting the market's governing apex.

Before concluding the discussion of the relationship between the credit contract, contractual law, and capitalism, and moving on to the Deccan Riots and their aftermath, it is necessary to portray the links between credit markets and the larger economic system, a discussion that is inextricably related to debates on the 'bazaar' and the 'bazaar economy'. In Indian historiography, the 'bazaar economy' has been most comprehensively (and influentially) depicted by Rajat Kanta Ray (1995). Taking issue primarily with the work of J. C. van Leur (1955) – and also with Clifford Geertz's early work on the bazaar in Indonesia (Geertz 1963) – Ray's engagement with the bazaar is driven partially by the desire to portray it as a sophisticated commercial arena. Van Leur, working in the service of the Dutch colonial state (Wertheim 1954), portrayed the difference between Asian commerce rooted in the 'bazaar' and European firms active in the Asian trade predominantly as one of scale. Economies of scale allowed European firms to dominate the bulk trade, while their small-scale Indonesian counterparts in this argument exploited the niches left beyond European commercial predominance, effectively remaining pedlars. The gist of his argument certainly resembles the more sophisticated conceptualization of mercantile capitalism in the Indian Ocean by Banaji outlined previously. In contrast to Banaji's work, it fails to accept the large scale in its own right of the 'bazaar economy', a fact also pointed out by Sushil Chaudhury (2019). Geertz's work on the Indonesian 'bazaar' emphasized its low profit margins – an aspect also found in his subsequent engagement with the 'bazaar' in Morocco (Geertz 1979) that, however, introduced a framework that relied on information flows and social ties. Low profit margins do not necessarily lead to low-scale business operations. In fact, bulk trade constitutes one of the possibilities for ensuring the viability of trade on low margins, though its pursuance by traders with low profit expectations and high labour inputs constitutes an equally viable route. The latter interpretation, in turn, allows for the conflation of low profit margins and 'pedlars', visible in some of Geertz's work. Ray's frustration with this interpretation is as pronounced as it is, in turn, based on a derogatory characterization of peddling, very much in line with many major works on economic history. With a few exceptions – prominently Fernand Braudel's celebration of peddling in early modern Europe as 'a way of getting around the sacrosanct market, ... of cocking a snook at established authority' (Braudel 1982, 80) – disregard for the pettiness of transactions has tended to go hand in hand with condescension for the people involved in this form of exchange.

Highlighting large-scale business operations, Ray set up a different characterization of the 'bazaar economy', combining elements from world systems theory with an emphasis on institutional arrangements that demonstrated its difference from European models of business organization. Ray's interpretative framework remains the most detailed conception of the bazaar economy in India. At the same time, it implicitly sets important restrictions on further inquiry by its cogency – temporally, geographically, and organizationally. Temporally, it provides a historical narrative of the rise and demise of the 'bazaar' that coincides loosely with the end of colonial rule, by which time the bazaar economy is portrayed as subordinated to 'global' capitalism. Geographically, it severs the linkages between lower-order markets and the 'bazaar' and locates the latter's most sophisticated form predominantly in the overseas trade. Organizationally, it emphasizes various institutions – predominantly the *hundi* and the *arhat* (a managing agency) – and in this way impedes a broader engagement between anthropological and historiographical scholarship on the 'bazaar' in the context of modern South Asia. The *arhat* system of managing agencies intersected with both the credit practices centring on the *hundi* and the organizational foundation of Indian commerce in the family firm. Its lower-order aspects, represented by the role of *arhatiya*s in credit flows, constituted a major element linking rural and urban economies in the late colonial period. Ray's subsequent work on the changes in the 'bazaar economy' during this period placed greater emphasis on the inland trade and included a wider range of 'bazaar' institutions, chiefly the system of storage (*goladari*) and its links with middlemen structures in Indian commerce that established extra-legal forms of future trading. However, for the purposes of this chapter, the discussion will focus on the *hundi*.

Ray traces the *hundi* as a financial instrument over several centuries, locating its roots in the difficulties in transferring military funds to armies away from the imperial centres (Ray 1995), before it emerged in the full-fledged form as a mercantile instrument in the eighteenth century. Broadly speaking, he identifies the *hundi* as a range of instruments allowing the transfer of money over space, noting how its various forms provided a more diverse range of practices than the European-origin bill of exchange (Ray 1995). The definition of the *hundi* broadly follows established convention in the history of Indian banking (Jain 1929). The versatility of the *hundi* in allowing nuanced financial transactions has been highlighted by a range of scholars, including David Rudner (1989) and Marina Martin (2009), providing complex ways in which the functions of European-origin financial instruments could be combined or separated and added to social ties and reputational standing. Most *hundi*s fell into two analytical categories of *muddati* and *darshani* *hundi*s, or time and sight bills. Rudner's work is exemplary in demonstrating the various terminologies, uses, and utilities of different *hundi*s as used by Nattukottai Chettiar bankers (Rudner 1989). To broadly define *hundi*s as time and sight bills does not give justice to the complexity of their actual use, but it helps in understanding the main differences.

A time bill allowed the drawer to issue a credit document in which the full amount of the stated principal would be paid at a specified due date. A sight bill did not specify a due date and instead stipulated that the full principal would be paid to the document's bearer. The main difference to European practices was in the discountability of the *hundi* in its actual practice. Both time and sight bills were discountable, though discountability was more pronounced in the case of sight bills since these remained in circulation longer. The discountability of the *hundi* rested on the assurance by the drawer that the stated principal would be paid on sight of the document in its head office and branches. In the meantime, however, the *hundi* would pass through the hands of various third parties who would buy the *hundi* at discounted rates based on the expected likelihood of this assurance being honoured or of finding another buyer who would be willing to pay a price commensurate with expected returns on the initial investment. In the case of time bills, the price of a *hundi* therefore was partially correlated to the due date. For both time and sight bills, other considerations involved the distance to the drawer's nearest office deemed capable of encashing the *hundi*, the drawer's reputation, and – in case the drawer's reputation was difficult to establish – the reputation of the local market(s) in which the drawer was located. Essentially, the *hundi* allowed a merchant family to transform its reputation into a form of extra-legal credit.

The *hundi* provided a wide range of reputational registers to be employed: personal or family reputations in cases where communication flows were strong, that is, in cases where transactions were frequent enough to establish significant knowledge of the other party involved; and a more diffuse reputational register based on assumptions that the structures of the local 'bazaar' in which the drawer was located would be sufficiently strong to allow an enforcement of obligations in case the drawer attempted to default. The latter is reminiscent of the system of denominating belonging (*nisba*) in the Moroccan bazaar studied by Geertz, even if the Moroccan practice was more elaborate (Geertz 1979, 142–43), though caste belonging added another layer to it in India (Rudner 1994). Ray's work remains preoccupied with large mercantile enterprises that benefited from both these reputational registers. Similarly, Bayly's work on the *hundi* draws heavily on the context of north Indian towns which had developed robust mechanisms of enforcing obligations, through community structures but also through mercantile ethics and related associational structures such as the Naupatti Sabha – a loose association of the heads of the city's main banking families – depicted by Bayly for Banaras (Bayly 1983, 180–81). Rudner, in turn, highlights the role of community and community-specific religious practice among the Nattukottai Chettiars, though the favourable terms on which intra-community *hundi*s could be drawn in this case (Rudner 1989) already points to the difficulties faced by other merchants.

The common practice of cutting the *hundi* into two halves and paying the stated principal only when the two documents were matched by payee and drawer or drawee in cases where it was considered essential to ensure enhanced trustworthiness demonstrates that the reputational underpinnings of the *hundi* were not always sufficient to maintain strong ties between the transactional parties. Ray's argument on the scale of the 'bazaar economy' led him to locate the 'bazaar' at the apex of this economy, strongly intersecting with its involvement in the Indian Ocean trade, and to differentiate the 'bazaar' from lower-order markets (Ray 1995) where these difficulties were more pronounced. Bayly's depiction of the strong links between these lower-order markets and the apex of the system, reinforced by other scholarship on the 'bazaar' (Sen 1998; Yang 1998), establishes that such an interpretation needs to be treated with caution, especially considering the broad continuities in the use of *hundi*s (and *chitti*s) between markets at various scales of operations.

Anand Yang's depiction of the 'bazaar' in nineteenth- and early-twentieth-century northern India uses an expression that is widely found in colonial sources from the last decades of colonial rule, 'amateurization' (Yang 1998, 245–46; see also Schwecke 2018). Yang's treatment of the 'bazaar' – pre-occupied as it is with exploring the India of the bazaar rather than the bazaar in India – is strongly at odds with Ray's identification of the 'bazaar economy' with its apex. The 'bazaar' here emerges as a broad socio-cultural spectrum linking local markets to market towns and beyond to the bridgeheads of European capital. Credit practices remain central in Yang's treatment of the 'bazaar', but their lower-order expressions remain interconnected with the *hundi* trade, instead emphasizing the bottom-up links between rural lenders, intermediating creditors, and the large banking families (Yang 1998, 83, 272). The characterization of much of the inland trade as the mainstay of commerce in India as 'amateurish' reflects a misunderstanding among colonial-era observers – that commercial and financial practices on lower-order markets should be judged from the perspective of the functioning of higher-order markets, either European-dominated ones or those controlled by 'native' bankers. This characterization, correspondingly, neglects the relationship between 'sophistication' and contextual suitability. After all, European or European-style lenders were largely incapable of extending their operations into the Indian hinterland, and 'indigenous' bankers depended crucially on the intermediation of supposedly 'amateurish' lenders. While I will continue to use the terms 'sophisticated' and 'amateurish' in the following, their use will be restricted either to the description of colonial discourses or to identify one of the main underlying reasons for the perception of 'amateurization' in colonial sources: the growing detachment between economic segments especially on credit markets or, to use a phrase coined by Amiya Kumar Bagchi (1985) in the context of the Bengali banking crisis of the 1830s, between 'controlled' and 'uncontrolled' credit.

The 'amateurish' nature of much of the 'bazaar' in Yang's depiction, in turn, resembles the 'bazaar' as depicted in economic anthropology, especially by Geertz. Notwithstanding the difficulties in describing the 'bazaar' through the use of terms like 'pedlars' or petty margins of profit, Ray's argument that the lower-order markets should not be interpreted as part of the 'bazaar economy' based on their linguistic denomination in India as *haath*s or *shandie*s does not reflect the deep links between higher- and lower-order markets not only in terms of capital flows but also in the common intelligibility of their practices. Geertz's later engagement with the 'bazaar' in the Moroccan town of Sefrou highlights the importance of petty margins (and includes a pedlar component), but fundamentally it locates the 'bazaar' in an economy defined by deeply embedded enforcement mechanisms for transactional obligations, and an informational regime seeking to manage pervasive uncertainty. Community structures of Jewish, Arab, and Berber origin as well as distinctions between town-born and 'outsider' groups facilitated social cohesion (Geertz 1979, 142–50), while the aforementioned *nisba* system allowed for flexible uses of identification, important for the flow of reputational information (Geertz 1979, 198–201). Religious institutions like the *habus* (a particular form of trusts) provided competitive advantages to the regular participants of the 'bazaar' (*suwaqqa*) and kept capital within the locality (Geertz 1979, 151–54). Membership in religious brotherhoods (*zawia*) created complex overlaps between religious and occupational status groups (*henta*), reinforcing communication as well as trust (Geertz 1979, 154–62). Trust, in turn, was further facilitated through clientelization and mercantile ethics expressed in a particular culture of bargaining and protected by an institution of extra-legal arbitration and 'honest broker-ship' centring on the office of the *amin* (Geertz 1979, 192–97). The Bihari bazaar depicted by Yang differed in the precise intersection of market and society, with Indian social structures taking on similar functional roles, but it does not differ in ways that would have impeded the establishment of common intelligibility between a Bihari and a Berber merchant. The one exception to this is the office of the *amin* for which no clear equivalent can be found in the Indian 'bazaar', though various *panchayat*s and associations were involved in arbitration (see Rudner 1989).

The credit contract – through its reputational underpinnings – served as a crucial link between the 'amateurish' and 'sophisticated' segments of the market, a link that does not correspond to either Marxist or Weberian assumptions on the development of capitalism. It also did not share the degree of common intelligibility in the 'bazaar economy' with the conception of credit and the credit contract that had developed in Europe after the dissolution of the conception of credit relations as partnership. While the relationship between capitalism and finance needs to be seen as ambiguous in any case, the increased penetration of Indian financial markets by liberal contractual law created a shift in economic practices that established a framework of common intelligibility that allowed a deeper involvement of Indian and European big finance capital. Liberal contractual law imposed 'propriety' – in the sense used by Birla – on Indian financial practices, an imposition that affected Indian extra-legal credit markets much more than the 'mercantile capitalist' practices depicted by Banaji which had significantly greater impacts on the organization of labour.

The reputational credit contract and liberal contractual law

The reputational credit contract that was the mainstay of Indian commerce rested on an assumption that future obligations were subject to change but that this change affected the reputational standing of the drawer, lowering the value of the drawer's *hundi*s. As both Bayly and Rudner show clearly, the negative impact of losing reputation would go significantly beyond the borrower's creditworthiness, but the credit system remained central to it. As will be shown in the following chapters, this principle of a reputational credit contract was very much operational in money lending transactions as well, where the credit contract was based on more exploitative terms and, hence, the likelihood of default was anticipated to a degree that credit obligations remained renegotiable. Conditions for future obligations were fixed at the time of transactional agreement, but the conception that they needed to adhere to this fixed state regardless of changed circumstances was diminished, except in the sense that they needed to follow a reputational rationale – they needed to be communicated and legitimized in order to minimize their reputational fallout.

David Hardiman's depiction of the rural credit economy in western India before the abolition of the usury laws as a moral economy following E. P. Thompson (1971), to which I will return later, does not capture the reputational underpinnings of the credit contract. Notwithstanding the embeddedness of credit markets in moral discourses in general, Thompson's concept of the moral economy rested on assertions of an entitlement to a 'fair' price that constituted a key element in western discourses on usury (Bernstein 1965; Rockoff 2003; Mews and Ibrahim Abraham 2007). In contrast, Jonathan Parry noted that '[c]ertainly nothing suggests the severity with which medieval [European] thought judged usury (as equivalent to sodomy in its opposition to natural increase)' (Parry 1989, 79). In the Indian case practices of usury depended much less on conceptions of fairness but on the reputational management of the problems arising from the future orientation of credit.

Several conceptions of a 'fair' price for the costs of borrowing existed in India, though their impact on lending practices from the eighteenth century to the present was negligible at least in the area comprising the Northwestern or United Provinces, and probably much beyond. Many depictions of the history of interest rates in India start with or highlight the conception of 'permissible' interest rates in the *Manusmrti* which gave a framework for interest depending on caste status (*varna*): 2 per cent for Brahmins, 4 per cent for Kshatriyas, 6 per cent for Vaishyas, and 8 per cent for Shudras. Fixing 'permissible' interest rates depending on caste status – apart from its discriminatory content – can be interpreted in ways that also comprise reputational dimensions of lending and risk assessments by the lender (Bayly 1983, 407). Higher ranked status groups can be perceived to lend reputation to its members, thus providing an informational grid for decision-making apart from appeasing notions of hierarchical superiority. For a text that sought to codify norms of behaviour along hierarchical lines between status groups, the intent to ignore other transactional contexts appears plausible, and more nuanced (and less hierarchical) ways of linking belonging and creditworthiness persisted well into the twentieth century. Conversely, from the lender's perspective the risk perception of default may well have been linked to questions of belonging to status groups as the likelihood of continued liquidity as well as of an ability of the borrower to seek assistance from a more prosperous member of a higher status group in times of imminent default may well have been judged to be higher. It is noteworthy that the *Arthashastra*, roughly originating in the same period, directly related interest rates to risk assessment: it proposed interest rates that were rising in accordance with the type of lending, differentiating between financing trade and agriculture, and with geographical distance between the merchant and the targeted market. In practice, interest rates in India deviated strongly from either system especially in the period studied here,[16] and these rates did not relate to a legal and moral enforcement mechanism as the usury laws of Europe had.

A different tradition of fixing a 'fair' price for credit existed through the conception of *damdupat* (and its variations), which did not fix interest rates but instead fixed limits for the accumulation of interest. *Damdupat* will be discussed in greater detail in the following chapter in the context of attempts to introduce legal measures against exploitation through credit after the Deccan Riots. Gyan Pandey (Pandey 1981, 32) argued that negative perceptions of money lending had been of recent origin in the mid-nineteenth century, and that the image of the moneylender in *bhakti* traditions had been positive, an assessment that might corroborate Hardiman's interpretation of rural debt markets as 'moral economies' in the Thompsonian meaning of the term.

> This [hatred of the moneylender] appears, contrary to one's expectations, to have been quite a novel phenomenon.… [T]he bhakti saints had extolled the services of the moneylender, and even likened the relationship between peasant and moneylender to that between a *bhakt* (devotee) and *bhagwan* (object of worship, god). By the latter half of the eighteenth century … the popular perception of this relationship changed radically. Thus the term *mahajan* (substantial trader, moneylender) had come to be used in UP in the later nineteenth century as the Kahar's slang for human excrement. (Pandey 1981, 32)

The reference to the *bhakti* saints and their extolling of the virtues of the moneylenders before the abolition of the usury laws may appear surprising, despite the diversity of religious practices and thought in *bhakti*. Given the wide spectrum of devotional practices and discourses in *bhakti*, it is difficult to ascertain how common these praises were. Considering my limited knowledge of *bhakti* traditions, I asked the *bhakti* scholar Jon Keune to post a query for me on the Regional Bhakti Scholars Network (RBSN) on references to moneylenders in *bhakti* discourses – laudatory or otherwise.[17]

Winand M. Callewaert drew my attention to the *Bhakti Dictionary* published by him which indicated references to the term *sahukar* in the Dadu *sakhi*s, the *Namadeva*, and the *parcai* of Pipa by Anantadasa (Callewaert 2009, 2049). Tyler Williams in his response also referred to the positive depictions of moneylenders in the discourses of Dadu and the less laudatory references in the *parcai* of Pipa by Anantadasa, in addition to references in other discourses where the mentioning of terms indicating money lending is less straightforward and it was difficult to ascertain whether they were 'laudatory, derogative, or simply descriptive',[18] a point also referred to by R. Jeremy Saul.[19] Williams' work on merchants in Rajasthani *bhakti* traditions depicts the differences between various traditions regarding the treatment of material wealth, and emotional attachment to material wealth. Drawing parallels to the roughly isochrone movement of merchants into political and administrative positions of power, and the rationale of merchants allying themselves to *bhakti* sects offering military protection to trade, his work also depicts merchant devotees as financing religious congregations and celebrations (T. Williams 2019, 196–99). Neelima Shukla-Bhatt related an aspect of the sacred biography of Narasinha Mehta that will be depicted subsequently, also referenced briefly by Gandhi in his Gujarati autobiography (Shukla-Bhatt 2014). Depicting the tendency of devotees to carry promissory notes on pilgrimage, Shukla-Bhatt described a narrative in which pilgrims were sent to the penniless Narasinha Mehta by fellow Nagar Brahmins to ask for promissory notes to be encashed in Dwarka. Aware of a prank played on him to avenge the inclusion of lower-caste members in his devotional practice, Narasinha drew a promissory note to Sheth Shamalsha of Dwarka – an appellation of Krishna – before spending the money on fellow devotees. On arriving in Dwarka, the pilgrims were told that no moneylender of this name existed, only for Krishna to appear as Sheth Shamalsha to the pilgrims.

> [Krishna] profusely apologized for being late; and gave them [an] additional amount of money as compensation for the trouble they went through. He also asked the pilgrims to convey the message to Narasinha that there were abundant funds in his account at Shamalsha's firm, so he (Narasinha) should feel free to write promissory notes whenever he wished.[20]

The positive depiction of lending practices in the example provided by Shukla-Bhatt is noteworthy in the way it reinforces the conception of mercantile ethics provided by C. A. Bayly, even though lending here takes place in the immediate context of pilgrimage. Another case of a positive reference to credit practices was provided by Jaroslav Strnad, citing an example from Kabir depicted in Callewaert and Swapna Sharma (2000). Noting that the translation of some terms was 'problematic', Strnad depicted verses 2 and 3 of Kabir's *pad* no. 115 as saying:

> If you do not honour the promissory note …, you will break away from the Lord …. Having given the capital, he will put you in jail; on whose intercession will you be released?[21]

The aforementioned examples provide an indication of *bhakti* discourses on credit practices and money lending that refers to these either through the devotees in their capacity as merchants and creditors, including their role in financing devotional practice, or with reference to the interplay of religious tradition and mercantile ethics. Honouring promissory notes, however, clearly refers to mercantile debt, instead of the petty debts incurred by, for instance, farmers, and none of the responses to my query indicates significant concern over the services of moneylenders to less prosperous debtors – who were unlikely to document debts through *hundi*s or similar promissory documents – though Pandey's reference to praises for moneylenders is given in this context. While it is certainly conceivable that the moral imperative to honour debt obligations would have extended to the poor, it is notable that this honouring does not indicate a conception of equity in the costs of borrowing but rather an understanding that freely agreed-upon contractual obligations must be met.

Actual interest rates in India in the second half of the nineteenth century followed very different logics and were contextually adjusted in more complex ways. The digest of cases on debt litigation in British India collected by H. H. L. Bellot (see Chapter 3) depicts a great variety of interest rates and widely differing ideas on whether these were morally justified. Even restricting the sample to the early cases (from 1867 to 1887) in the digest referred to courts in the Northwestern Provinces, there are wide variations between prevalent rates, between the courts' perceptions of a 'fair' price for the costs of borrowing, and between what defendants considered inequitable. It needs to be kept in mind that contrary to expectations based on the contents of the Usury Laws (Repeal) Act 1855, there was very little juridical consensus on the treatment of credit contracts under the 'sanctity' of liberal contractual law. The Allahabad High Court as the apex court for the Northwestern Provinces in particular refused to give up conceptions of equity in debt cases in many instances. In addition, while interest rates were at times held permissible at the contractually stipulated rate, litigation centred strongly on the question of permissible penalties for default. In the following, I will give a very brief outline of these cases under the assumption that the decision to file suit meant that they were considered to be inequitable.

In 1867, the court in *Sheoburts* v. *Dharee Thakoor* accepted the principle of *damdupat* as a limitation of accumulated interest, the only case in which it was invoked and held valid within the period under study here.[22] In *Kuar Lachman* v. *Pirbhu Lal* (1874), the court held that a penalty imposed upon default amounting to 6.25 per cent was inequitable and reduced the rate after default to the stipulated rate of interest at 1.75 per cent per month, which had not been questioned by the defendant. The court held that rates for penalties needed to comply with considerations of equity in order to be permissible.[23] In a case in 1880 where the debtor had accepted a principal of 50 rupees on the stipulation that it be returned within four days, otherwise attracting an interest rate of 2 per cent per day as interest, the Allahabad High Court disallowed and reduced the rate with the argument that the contractually stated rate was not an interest rate but a penalty, thus allowing the court to interfere under the Indian Contracts Act. Implicitly, the court acknowledged here that the rate of 2 per cent per day would have been allowed as a contractually agreed interest rate if not for its nature as a penalty.[24] In *Kurram Singh* v. *Bhawani*, 1881, the court disallowed a rate of 37.5 per cent per annum in a mortgage case on the grounds of this being a penalty and reduced it to the originally stipulated interest rate of 7.5 per cent per annum.[25]

In *Kharag Singh* v. *Bhola Nath*, in the same year, the High Court reduced a penalty rate of 2 per cent per month to 1.5 per cent per month instead of the stipulated interest rate of 1.25 per cent per month,[26] while in *Bhola Nath* v. *Fateh Singh*, two years later, the same court allowed an interest rate of 6.25 per cent per month to be compounded as penalty upon default. The debtor had opposed the contractual stipulation that on default the outstanding interest payments should be added to the outstanding principal, and interest paid on the compounded amount, as well as the unfairness of the original interest rate. The court of first instance had perceived the interest rate as 'extremely high, usurious, and exorbitant' and proceeded to allow an interest rate of 1 per cent per month, a decision which was overturned in this judgment.[27]

In the same year, the High Court held that an interest rate of 2 per cent per month was 'not exorbitant' as an interest rate (not a penalty) upon default for an otherwise interest-free loan.[28] In the following year, in turn, the court provided an opening to undermine its earlier strict distinction between interest and penalties: it decreed that an enhanced interest upon default of 1.5 per cent per month for a loan of 5,000 rupees with a stipulated interest rate of 1.0625 per cent per month was not in the nature of a penalty but comprised an arrangement for deferred payment as was common in commodity contracts.[29] Finally, the Allahabad High Court in *Dip Narain Rai* v. *Dipan Rai*, 1886, held that a penalty constituted an insurance for the creditor against the risk of default, and therefore could be in the nature of either an increased simple interest rate or a compound interest rate of the stipulated simple interest before default, but not both. In this case, the contractual stipulations had consisted of a principal paid in two rates of 1,475 rupees and 725 rupees, respectively, with a simple interest rate of 9 per cent per annum and a compound interest rate of 15 per cent per annum upon default for the first rate, and a compound interest rate of 24 per cent per annum upon default for the second rate.[30]

The brief survey of ideas on equity in costs of borrowing shows a remarkable complexity, apart from the fact that interest rates were not in any clear way linked to an understanding of 'permissible' rates beyond contextual factors. It needs to be kept in mind that there would have been a much wider deviation of rates, too, if the sample included rates of transactions that did not go into litigation or even if it included litigation in the small causes courts. If the moral element of the 'moral economy' of debt was related to an understanding of 'fair' prices as in the assertions on the price of bread by the English 'crowd' depicted by Thompson, it should have found an expression that closely resembled European usury laws – permitting interest at a specific level – or a variation of its Indian counterparts which permitted variations of interest according to contextual circumstances like status group belonging, or risk assessment, or in the more fluid Indian conception of permitting interest accumulation up to a specific point.

Hardiman's argument, however, emphasizes the centrality of the imposition of liberal contractual law through the abolition of the usury laws. The latter, he argues, supplanted a 'moral economy' between moneylenders and debtors by strong state backing for lenders in a 'policy of laissez-faire in the market – supported if necessary by the deployment of soldiers and police to prevent popular disturbance' (Hardiman 1996b, 126) and replaced '[t]he existing system of customary enforcement of debt-agreements ... with a system of contract, enforced by law' (Hardiman 1996b, 125).

The 'system of customary enforcement of debt agreements' rested either on status and its respective relationship with risk or – as shown earlier – on an underlying reputational character of credit markets. As discussed in the beginning of this chapter, the former component changed from Hart's 'extrapolations of statuses perceived as tradition' to those extrapolations of statuses denominated as law – a significant shift in many ways but not one that should have been expected to have had a highly negative impact on the majority of debtors in rural India, unless village society in pre-1855 India is imagined as a surprisingly harmonic entity. Understanding the village economy as a system that combined elements of solidarity embedded in social practice with strongly hierarchical patterns of exploitation, the main change brought about by the deeper penetration of the market by liberal contractual law was the opportunity for the creditor provided by the law to legitimize withholding 'solidarity'. Hardiman's argument strongly emphasizes this point (Hardiman 1996a), and it is plausible that this impact would have been important for indebted peasants. Yet this opportunity to legitimize withholding solidarity was not an assertion of claims for a 'fair' price as in Thompson's conception of the moral economy. Rather, it formed the debtor's perspective on the benefits of a reputational understanding of the credit contract in allowing the renegotiation of contractual obligations according to changed circumstances as long as these could be communicated in terms not affecting the defaulting debtor's reputation.

Towards the withdrawal of liberal contractual law from petty finance

Hardiman's argument strongly rested on his analysis of the so-called Deccan Riots, which been extensively documented (Catanach 1970; Charlesworth 1972; Hardiman 1996a). Charlesworth had depicted the riots as a 'non-event', primarily based on the idea that in comparison with other disturbances throughout British India in the nineteenth century, the Deccan Riots did not seem to be important enough to warrant the political attention they received, a perception that is closely reminiscent of Bayly's notion of 'information panics' impacting colonial policy (Bayly 1999). Hardiman countered this by pointing out not only the scope of the riots – which in some ways buttresses Charlesworth's argument – but also the relatively new forms of protest associated with it, and the manner of subaltern self-organization (Hardiman 1996a). With reference to William Sewell's conception of the event and its interaction with structure in the study of history (Sewell 2005), the riots certainly were 'eventful' in that they constituted an important threshold in the history of framing credit markets in India, thus having considerable long-term implications.

Hardiman's perception of the outcome of the riots in terms of changing government policy is deeply pessimistic (Hardiman 1996a). A major reason for this assessment lies in his neglect of later developments, that is, the market-framing exercises that were only taking shape from the mid-1890s onwards. It can also be linked to an understanding of government intervention as a policy that would have created significant improvements on the exploitation of subaltern strata by moneylenders. In this respect, the Deccan Riots formed one of the events shaping government policy in the following decades, leading to the enactment of the Usurious Loans Bill and reinforcing government intervention in other redress mechanisms, including the cooperative movement, agricultural banking, and the criminalization of unregistered money lending. The Deccan Riots certainly had an impact on attitudes among government officials. Their most significant effect, however, was in shaping a perception of urgency for government intervention. The particular shape this government intervention eventually coalesced into reinforced processes that resulted in the establishment of new forms of extra-legal finance that turned out to be at least as exploitative for poorer debtors than the rural credit markets of the 1870s. Seen from this perspective, Hardiman's pessimistic assessment of the aftermath of the riots in terms of policy is well justified, though hardly in terms of this aftermath's non-eventfulness.

The riots broke out in 1875, though the report of the Deccan Riots Commission traces 'premonitory' disturbances to late 1874.[31] It eventually covered several dozen villages in the Poona and Ahmednagar districts of the Bombay Presidency. The riots predominantly targeted moneylenders rather than the colonial state. At the same time, the colonial government reacted by suppressing the riots militarily. Hardiman's depiction of the riots is by far the most detailed (Hardiman 1996a) apart from its 'official' interpretation in the *Deccan Riots Committee Report*, and there is no need to replicate it here as its significance for the argument rests on its aftermath, not the riots themselves.

Two aspects related to the riots, especially in their depiction by Hardiman, however, need to be briefly mentioned here: First, Hardiman's narrative on the riots stresses distinctions made by the protesters between 'locals' and 'outsiders' (Hardiman 1996a). His account mentions instances where 'local' moneylenders were spared by the protesters who, instead, primarily targeted those lenders who had only recently settled in the region and frequently lived apart from the villagers, including in nearby small towns. Many of these were Marwari lenders. Hardiman emphasizes this point partially to provide evidence for the disruption of the 'moral economy' of lending in rural India that was being disrupted by the imposition of liberal contractual law, highlighting it as an example of claims to solidarity within the village community. I will engage with this argument in greater detail in Chapter 5, discussing it from the perspective of strains on the mechanisms for enforcing obligations that facilitated shifts within the reputational economy of debt from market mechanisms relying on obligation towards mechanisms relying on trust. Second, Hardiman emphasizes instances where the target of protests was less the moneylender, but instead the moneylenders' account books, which frequently were destroyed by the protesters (Hardiman 1996b, 144–45). It is on this point that the argument developed here has the greatest extent of convergence with Hardiman's.

Hardiman describes the destruction of account books as one of the main aims of those protesting. This, he argues, showed the awareness of subaltern debtors of the larger changes in the economy of debt brought about by the abolition of the usury laws under which debt contracts became governed by contractual law. Debtors, accordingly, were aware of the prerequisites of the British Indian legal system that defined admissible evidence and gave preference to the enunciated and visible element in the contract rather than its silent and invisible counterpart which accepted the possibility of changed circumstances that needed to be managed in a debt relationship. Hardiman also highlights the strategic component in targeting the account books rather than the lenders, citing instances where protesting crowds were demanding that the lenders give up the account books in order to escape violence against them or their property – which strongly reinforces the argument outlined earlier.

Hardiman combines the two arguments outlined here on the protesters' awareness of the requirements of the legal system and their acceptance of 'locals' rather than outsiders as moneylenders in order to show the villagers' acceptance of 'traditional' lending practices and their embeddedness in the 'moral economy' of debt, and their opposition to the forms of lending embedded in the legal structure of an expanding capitalist credit market (Hardiman 1996b, 115–19). The argument I am developing here, in contrast, rests on an interpretation of these protest strategies as related to the reputational dimension of credit contracts: the penetration of credit markets by liberal contractual law undermined the possibility of managing future uncertainty in debt relations through reputational means by fixing one element of this future orientation – repayment obligations – at the time of contractual agreement, and thus in favour of the creditor. This fixing of future uncertainty in the present, being enunciated and visible, was favoured under the British Indian legal structure, while at the same time not being accepted in socio-economic relations of debt that hitherto had included a reputational mechanism for redress that worked at least partially in favour of the debtor. The insider–outsider dynamic addresses this shift merely in the likelihood of seeking the state's help in enforcing obligations. In fact, the protesters' willingness to refrain from targeting lenders who turned over their account books reinforces the interpretation that what the villagers demanded was continued validity for this reputational redress mechanism. 'Local' lenders were, after all, also targeted, if to a lesser extent. The protesters' aims were thus less informed by a clear understanding of equity in the costs of borrowing, which is anyway unlikely given the wide spread of interest rates in India at the time and the character of prevalent interest rates in rural society that is difficult to portray as non-exploitative whether by 'locals' or 'outsiders'. They were informed by the more fluid possibility of managing uncertainty through reputational means. In other words, what the protesters attacked was not the morality defined by the level of exploitation, but the transformation of the credit contract from its reputational to its juridical-procedural character which defined its intelligibility as 'capitalist'.[32] It is noteworthy here that the Deccan Riots took place in the context of famine, and therefore would have been perceived as an instance of future uncertainty that fully justified renegotiations of past obligations without negative reputational fallout, while other parts of British India that were not as affected by famine conditions did not experience significant disturbances. Interpreting the causes for the violence, the *Deccan Riots Committee Report* noted:

> We come now to consider the causes … of hostility on the part of the ryot towards the sowcar. A condition of indebtedness would not of itself produce such a feeling. The needy man might be expected to regard the person who supplies his needs rather with gratitude than dislike. It is only when indebtedness is attended with circumstances which produce in the mind of the debtor a sense of hardship, of unfair treatment, of being oppressed and having no redress, that a feeling of hostility is aroused....[33]

Leaving aside the patronizing tone of the statement, and its striking inability to understand the complex moralities underlying debt relationships from the debtor's perspective, the link drawn between the idea of inequity and the absence of redress mechanisms is informative. As will be discussed in the following chapters, legislative efforts after the Deccan Riots were very much seeking to provide opportunities for redress. Yet they did so in ways that were constricted by the imperative of preserving the common intelligibility of the juridical-procedural underpinnings of 'capitalist' finance, refusing to engage with the established reputational mechanisms of renegotiating obligations. Fixing repayment obligations at the time of contractual agreement remained paramount. It constituted an unbreachable boundary that informed an understanding of credit in which this attempt to tie future developments to the transactional context in the present needed to be made 'conscionable' through a variety of procedural means. The imbalance between creditor and debtor created in this way was implicitly acknowledged in the report by linking the question of usury to the creditor's risk, that is, to the uncertainty faced by the creditor because of the enhanced future orientation of the credit contract, but not to the uncertainty of the debtor, which the latter, in this argument, ought to be able to calculate in advance. The report affirmed that usury could only be established if interest rates deviated from the protection against uncertainty needed by the creditor, thus detaching the debt relationship from the idea of partnership or of reputationally governed redress. Eventually proceeding to state that high rates were justified by these high risks, it noted:

> The rate of interest chargeable upon a loan … is determined by the risk as to repayment. The risk in each case depends upon the assets and character of the debtor. Usury means the taking of higher interest than is required to cover the risk.[34]

Hardiman's depiction of the Deccan Riots Committee is deeply pessimistic, essentially pointing out that no relevant action was initiated that could have alleviated the situation of indebted peasants (Hardiman 1996a). There is absolutely no doubt that using this yardstick, the report's recommendations were pointless, though its long-term implications were significant, even if these also did not lead to an alleviation of credit market conditions. The recommendations can be summarized as a refusal to re-enact usury laws, and to pass some protective measures for debtors such as the abolition of imprisonment for debt[35] and legislation against the confiscation of assets falling under a vague definition of means for subsistence.[36] (Imprisonment for debt was not abolished. Instead, it was significantly restricted several decades later in that courts were constrained in using it by the Criminal Procedure Code [Amendment] Act, XXI of 1936.[37]) Additionally, the report recommended measures to make the courts more accessible for indebted peasants in line with its general direction towards establishing juridical-procedural mechanisms for redress in contrast to the existing reputational ones. It also recommended the enactment of an insolvency law that would have provided debtors the opportunity to make use of the legal structure to escape its contractual obligations, thereby further undermining the reputational economy of debt on which their access to credit had been based, and shifting credit markets even more in the direction of 'capitalist' finance.[38] Insolvency proceedings tended to have little impact on alleviating indebtedness precisely because insolvency – as a juridical-procedural form of default – did not correspond to the reputational mechanisms for communicating default, and thereby threatened to undermine a debtor's reputational standing to the extent that gaining new credit was practically impossible. In contrast to subsequent debates, the committee expressed its view that these measures would serve to restrict access to credit for poor households rather than facilitating it, an interpretation that was taken up again only several decades later by the Reserve Bank of India. The committee, however, perceived this anticipated outcome as beneficial. It argued that creating hurdles for the recovery of loans would increase the costs of borrowing to a level where poor households were unable to afford them, thus creating a condition where the 'worst class of borrowers' was prevented 'from obtaining loans altogether'. In turn, this would force 'the money lender [sic] ... to restrict his dealings to the more solvent and respectable borrowers [to avoid being] burdened with the risks of the bad debtors'.[39] Its recommended policies, correspondingly, did not seek to facilitate access to credit but were foreshadowing the subsequent warnings of the Reserve Bank against the 'dangers of facile credit' (see Chapter 4) and to contain the perceived crisis of indebtedness by making it more difficult for India's poorer strata to access credit.

In the short term, the government of India passed the Dekkhan Agriculturists' Relief Act (Act XVII of 1879) to provide some alleviating measures without significant success, though the act needs to be seen as one of the first instances of direct government intervention. Latika Chaudhury and Anand Swamy (Swamy and Chaudhury 2014) have provided a more optimistic assessment of the act in its objectives to provide relief to debtors.

The responses to the Deccan Riots by both the colonial government and the incipient nationalist movement remained complex, if not confused. In later sources, both sides started to agree on some need to alleviate rural distress caused by indebtedness, with Indian nationalists either placing blame on the government and absolving moneylenders, or blaming both moneylenders and the British Indian government. British officials, in turn, increasingly attempted to pass the blame for agrarian indebtedness to the moneylenders, and pointed out legislative efforts as signs of British goodwill towards poor farmers. The Deccan Riots, however, placed questions of rural indebtedness, and the related question of the transfer of land to non-agriculturists on the political agenda, though without reaching clear conclusions. David Washbrook, relying strongly on Charlesworth's study of the riots, described the British reaction as 'paranoia' (Washbrook 1981, 685) related to the experience of revolt in the mid-1850s.

> It is also unclear, given the social character of the early nationalist movement, what kind of connection it could have made with a marginal peasantry being driven off the land.... [M]ost of nationalism's popular following seems to have come from urban commercial and mercantile groups who frequently were expressing frustrations at the limitations posed to their exploitation of the countryside by the raj ... But the evidence that the threat was real is not strong. It was the shadow of the Mutiny rather than a cold examination of the facts, which turned the petty Deccan Riots into the justification for a far-reaching policy of peasant protection, and every act of bazaar violence into the augury of mass revolt. (Washbrook 1981, 686)

K. C. Suri, in turn, studied the contradictions in the agrarian policy of the early Congress, though without specifically mentioning the Deccan Riots, highlighting the 11th session of the Congress at Poona which passed a resolution against enacting restrictions on the transfer of land as collateral as a remedial measure for agricultural indebtedness that depicted such an approach as a 'retrograde measure' (Suri 1987, 26).[40] By the late 1920s, an interpretation of the changes on rural credit markets had consolidated among both Indian and British observers that is highly reminiscent of Hardiman's argument on the disruption of a 'moral economy' by 'capitalist' finance, supported by contractual law. Premchand's novel *Godaan*, first published in 1936, provides ample evidence to this.[41] Relatively critical British Indian officials followed the same argumentation as for instance in the argument by Malcolm Lyall Darling, cited in the *United Provinces Banking Enquiry Committee Report*, that social harmony between debtors and moneylenders had been prevalent in rural India until the 1860s, when it was disrupted by British legislation.[42]

The Deccan Riots constituted a major threshold for market-framing policy, reinforcing tendencies to extend the common intelligibility of 'capitalist' finance. They cannot, though, be seen to have caused these changes. Bagchi's argument on 'controlled' and 'uncontrolled' credit in the transformation from Indian to British Indian capital is particularly instructive in this context, depicting the perceived imperative for colonial policy in extending 'capitalist' finance in the Bengali banking crisis of the 1830s (Bagchi 1985). Similarly, Birla's study of the Indian Contracts Act of 1872 (Birla 2009, 35–36), including the insertion of the legal doctrine of undue influence, points to a growing understanding that the 'sanctity' of the liberal contract needed to be constricted in juridical-procedural ways that did not affect the expansion of the legal grammar of capitalism. Instead, it reinforced it by filling gaps neglected in the adoption of a comprehensively *laissez-faire* attitude, similarly to the implicit intention of insolvency legislation to shift the possibility of redress in the face of future uncertainty from reputational to juridical-procedural means.

The abolition of the usury laws in the mid-nineteenth century had encompassed a broad spectrum of countries. In the last decades of the nineteenth century, however, many continental European countries started to shift to new policies regarding legislation on petty loans, while the United States never fully implemented it (Rockoff 2003). In Germany and Austria, and slightly later in France, different mechanisms for regulatory support by the state to cooperative banks had emerged in the last quarter of the nineteenth century that allowed more stringent legislation against money lending (see Farr 2001; Guinnane 2001). Britain shifted relatively late towards an emulation of these policies, but their characteristics were well known among British Indian officials who understood these models as an opportunity to tackle the question of agrarian indebtedness – whether out of a sense of paranoia as argued by Washbrook or to alleviate poverty and thus stabilize British rule as frequently argued by those engaging in these debates. If colonial policy on the credit contract had been dominated for most of the nineteenth century by efforts to bring it under the comprehensive sway of a common capitalist intelligibility, from the 1890s onwards the legislative impact on framing credit markets shifted towards the removal of liberal contractual law from the operations of petty credit markets, and its expansion in large-scale credit.

Conclusion

Keith Hart, writing about the slum economy in Nima, had raised 'the question of what takes the place of law as the major source of sanctions in economic relations' (Hart 1988, 185). Market-framing policies in British India since the 1890s shifted towards providing the basis for an inquiry into this question, but in order to arrive at a conclusion it first needed to be explored what the law had actually replaced as a source of sanctions on Indian credit markets. Staying briefly with Hart's depiction of the operations of kinship, trust, and contract in 'informal' entrepreneurship, it can very well be argued that the market-framing policies of the colonial state – seeking to create the conditions for a deeper penetration of credit markets in India by contractual law – provided an equivalent to the effects of migration on entrepreneurship in this Ghanaian slum economy that Hart depicted as having destroyed kinship-based models of economic activity based on 'extrapolations of statuses typical of traditional ideology and practice' (Hart 1988, 178). In the Indian case, what had been disrupted was a reputational understanding of the credit contract that allowed the management of future uncertainty through a limited permissibility of renegotiating obligations. These mechanisms for renegotiating obligations (or delaying the enforcement) were embedded in social ties, either in relatively loose forms of association between individuals – of the kind that Hart depicted as 'trust' – or in significantly stronger social ties based on religion and mercantile ethics, on kinship, and on caste and community.

Within the creditor–debtor relationship, the redefinition of the credit contract through the deeper penetration of the market by liberal contractual law reinforced shifts in its balance. The authority of the state and its potential to use violence for enforcement tilted the balance of the credit contract in favour of the creditor, not at the time of contractual agreement – where this imbalance was in any case present – but at the equally crucial time of renegotiations necessary to make the likelihood of default 'manageable'. Liberal contractual law provided protection to the creditor against the vagaries of the future orientation of the credit contract. It is important to avoid an interpretation of this development that is one-sided: credit is much too complex and nuanced a topic to be fruitfully studied in this way and even less from ideological positions that have pre-allotted blame.

The liberal argument for fixing the future uncertainty faced by the creditor in debt transactions rested strongly on the assumption that favouring the creditor would facilitate lending, that is, it would make capital available for lending that otherwise would be idle, or that would not be lent to 'unbankable' people. In short, it would make capital available for lending to the poor as well, and thus allow poorer segments of society to share in the benefits accruing from credit, through supply-side measures also bringing down the costs of borrowing. Cooperative credit in continental Europe in the late nineteenth century strongly followed this logic and serves as an example that the liberal argument should not be dismissed. In colonial India, the likelihood that such a process would have been successful is certainly low. Yet it needs to be emphasized that the reputational mechanisms for redress – apart from being strongly unequal themselves, and rooted in 'traditional' hierarchies – may have balanced the creditor–debtor relationship at the time of renegotiation of obligations but certainly did not lower the costs of borrowing which were exorbitant by European standards at the time. The test for the liberal argument is in its ability to expand credit to less secure debtors without increasing their costs of borrowing, while the test for the system of lending based on reputational redress mechanisms was in making credit available without leading to highly exploitative costs of borrowing. As the subsequent chapters will demonstrate, the combination of market framing policies and market responses that coalesced in India since the late nineteenth century, at least from the perspective of poorer debtors, tended to bring out the negative dimensions of both these models.

Notes

1. Hart (1988, 185).
2. Marx classified markets according to the involvement of commodities (C) and money (M), with the dash following either depicting a realized increase over its original amount. Thus, barter was depicted as C–C, the ideal-type peasant involved in selling produce at a market to buy other goods as C–M–C. The capitalist exchange of goods, in turn, was depicted as M–C–M', while credit markets were denominated as M–M'.
3. See also Guérin, D'Espalier, and Venkatasubramanian (2013).
4. I am highly grateful to Keith Hart for making this point forcefully in private correspondence. See Hart and Ortiz (2014).
5. For a more general treatment of the idea of the permissibility of usury from liberal perspectives, see, for instance, Labat and Block (2012). For a contrasting perspective on the merits of more accommodative enforcement policies by banks, see Zazzaro (2005).
6. Available online at https://api.parliament.uk/historic-hansard/commons/1854/aug/04/usury-laws-repeal-bill (last accessed 27 January 2020).
7. Cap. 63 of 13 Geo. III.
8. 'Act XXVIII of 1855. Passed by the Legislative Council of India. An Act for the Repeal of the Usury Laws', in Index to the Acts Passed by the Legislative Council of India in the Year 1855, available online at http://legislative.gov.in/sites/default/files/legislative_references/1855.pdf (last accessed 27 January 2020).
9. For a discussion of both the Indian Evidence Act, 1872, and the Indian Contracts Act, 1872, including the insertion of the legal doctrine of undue influence relating to the legal history of Indian markets, see Birla (2009).
10. In contrast, credit practices among British officials in Calcutta in the early nineteenth century strongly followed extra-legal operational modes, emphasizing its reputational underpinnings as for instance shown by Peter Robb (2013).

11. Beyond Banaji's work, see, among others, Roy (1999), Kumar (1988), Swarnalatha (2005), Sahai (2006), Haynes (2012), and Venkatesan (2009).

12. For a broad discussion of the discrepancies in developmental trajectories between India and Europe, see Parthasarathi (2011).

13. On the collaboration between Indian bankers and the British, see Subramanian (1987).

14. For a description from the early twentieth century, see Anonymous (1918, 146–48).

15. Interview with Navneet Raman, Banaras. Records of all interviews cited here in possession of the author.

16. On the complexity of credit practices in medieval and early modern India, see, for instance, the various contributions in Bagchi (2002) or Irfan Habib's depiction of the development of medieval credit markets (Habib 1964).

17. I want to use this opportunity to express my gratitude to not only Jon but also the various respondents who went to great lengths to provide significant detail, only a selection of which can be discussed here.

18. Email by Tyler Williams to Jon Keune, posted on the RBSN, 21 March 2020. All RBSN emails in possession of the author.

19. Email by R. Jeremy Saul to Jon Keune, posted on the RBSN, 27 March 2020.

20. Email by Neelima Shukla-Bhatt to Jon Keune, posted on the RBSN, 27 March 2020.

21. Email by Jaroslav Strnad to Jon Keune, posted on the RBSN, 21 March 2020.

22. *Sheoburts* v. *Dharee Thakoor* (3 Agra Rep. 194), 1867, digest provided in Bellot (1906, 395).

23. *Kuar Lachman* v. *Pirbhu Lal* (6 N.W.P.H.C. 358), 1874, digest provided in Bellot (1906, 395).

24. *Bansidhar* v. *Bu Ali Khan* (3 All. 260), 1880, digest provided in Bellot (1906, 396).

25. *Khurram Singh* v. *Bhawani* (3 All. 440), 1881, digest provided in Bellot (1906, 396–97).

26. *Kharag Singh* v. *Bhola Nath* (4 All. 8), 1881, digest provided in Bellot (1906, 397).

27. *Bhola Nath* v. *Fateh Singh* (6 All. 63), 1883, digest provided in Bellot (1906, 401).

28. *Kunjbehari Lal* v. *Ilahi Baksh* (6 All. 64), 1883, digest provided in Bellot (1906, 401).

29. *Narain Das* v. *Chait Ram* (6 All. 179), 1884, digest provided in Bellot (1906, 402–03).

30. *Dip Narain Rai* v. *Dipan Rai* (8 All. 185), 1886, digest provided in Bellot (1906, 403).

31. Government of the United Kingdom, Report of the Commission Appointed in India to Inquire into the Causes of the Riots which Took Place in the Year 1875, in the Poona and Ahmednagar Districts of the Bombay Presidency. Presented to Both Houses of Parliament by Command of Her Majesty, London, 1878, 1 (in the following referred to as Deccan Riots Committee Report). On the larger pattern of rural disturbances in the mid-nineteenth century that Hardiman and Pandey perceived the Deccan Riots to be part of, see Stokes (1969).

32. The juridical system in India well into the second half of the twentieth century, in turn, needs to be divided into system relying on and originating from the idea of the nation-state, and systems of localized authority as depicted by Bernard S. Cohn (1965). There have been some attempts by the Indian state – both colonial and postcolonial – to employ the latter on credit arbitration for its localized knowledge, but in this study the focus will remain on the higher levels of juridical arbitration.

33. Deccan Riots Committee Report, 1878, 32–33.

34. Deccan Riots Committee Report, 1878, 33.

35. For a discussion of imprisonment for debt in Europe, and the moral discourses over it, see Peebles (2013).

36. Deccan Riots Committee Report, 1878, 57–58.

37. See Perianna Goundan v. Sellappa Goundan and Ors. (2MLJ 1068, 1938).

38. Deccan Riots Committee Report, 1878, 58–59.

39. Deccan Riots Committee Report, 1878, 59.

40. See also P. V. Rao (2009; 2003).

41. See Upadhyay (2011). Upadhyay depicts Premchand's narrative on usury as a 'total breakdown of [a] moral economy' (Upadhyay 2011, 1247) as a consequence of a loss of mutuality.

42. *United Provinces Banking Enquiry Committee Report*, Vol. I, 1929, 190 [the four volumes of this report are in the following referred to as *UPBECR* I–IV.]

3

Discretion

> *The fact is lost sight of that besides minors, females, idiots and others legally incapable of making contracts, except under certain safeguards, there are millions of illiterate persons in this country who are quite as incapable mentally and morally, and ought to be equally incapacitated by law.*[1]

The decision to repeal the usury laws in British India did not remain uncontested, not only by protesting farmers, but also in the legislatures and courts. While one of its effects certainly was to enhance the importance attributed to the written form of contracts, the actual practice of debt relations in Indian society remained to some extent unaffected by it. The vast majority of debt contracts did not lead to litigation. Instead, moneylenders frequently relied on written contracts and court litigation either as a last resort in cases of default or to 'fleece' debtors once the accumulation of interest payments had led to default. The Deccan Riots formed a major threshold in the development of British Indian policy, especially in the development of law and legal interpretation. Yet the comprehensive sway of the Benthamite doctrine on the futility of usury laws had been challenged even before, especially in tenancy laws. Thus, for instance, the Bengal Landlord and Tenant Procedure Act of 1869 (Act VIII B. C. of 1869),[2] concerning the procedure of suits between landlords and tenants, in Section 21 provided an interest rate of 12 per cent per annum for arrears in rent, unless otherwise provided for by written contract. Read together with Section 67 of the same act, stipulating the signing of a *kabuliyat* for outstanding arrears in rent for transfers of landed property between tenant and (new) landlord, the act in practice imposed an effective maximum interest rate for a significant number of debt relations.

The effects of legal measures on the actual practice of debt relations should not be overstated as even where suits were instigated, especially the subordinate courts were unlikely to employ this legal reasoning to set aside the evidence of a written contract. The case of the aforementioned act, however, emerged as one of the early cornerstones in the development of legal doctrine regarding debt cases. In 1899, the Calcutta High Court in *Kali Nath Sen* v. *Trilokhya Nath Roy* held that '[a] stipulation for the payment of interest at an unusual and exorbitant rate cannot be supposed to be an incident of a tenancy which would attach to it even after a sale for arrears in rent'.[3] In their judgment, Justices Banerjee and Rampini interpreted the specific wording 'unless otherwise provided by written agreement' as stipulating an ordinary rate of interest, thus ingeniously conflating the ordinariness of written agreements in these cases with a thumb rule for what constituted an acceptable interest rate in contravention of the actually stipulated rates in the ordinary written agreements. Opining that the sale of property with attached sub-tenancies as well as the incidence of payments of arrears constituted ordinary incidences of tenancy in India, while by definition the payment of an 'unusual and exorbitant rate' of interest did not, the judges held that the sale of property invalidated the continued attachment of the written debt contract to the tenancy.[4] Arguing that tenants needed to be included among the social groups requiring special protection in line with the Privy Council judgment in 1885 in *Kamini Sundari Chaodhrani* v. *Kali Prosunno Ghose*,[5] the judgment also laid an important legal base for the preferential treatment of farmers in subsequent Indian debt and debt relief legislation: the Privy Council ruling had extended British legal practice of the late nineteenth century to India, which distinguished debtors on the basis of their assumed mental and moral capacity of understanding debt contracts, with minors, women, persons of assumed low intelligence, and 'expectant heirs' exempted from the legal assumption of having entered into debt contracts out of their own free will. In combination, the two reasonings led the justices to award interest to the plaintiff at the 'ordinary' interest rate of 12 per cent per annum on the arrears in rent, thus establishing an effective maximum rate of interest in contravention of the Usury Laws (Repeal) Act of 1855, though one that remained contested among legal practitioners afterwards. The notion that 12 per cent per annum constituted the threshold for a morally defensible interest rate was widely held among the administration at the time and continued to inform opinions on legislative measures regarding credit markets well into the twentieth century, though most legislation from the 1920s onwards shifted towards the maximum rate of 24 per cent per annum.

It should be noted that court judgments after the Deccan Riots did not lead to the constitution of a coherent legal practice. Rather, legislation differed widely across the provinces of British India, and in many cases continued to differentiate between the Presidency towns and the *mufassil*, while different High Courts followed conflicting lines of argumentation. In turn, the subordinate courts frequently failed to follow the guidelines established by the High Courts, preferring to leave contentious matters to the courts of appeal and thereby significantly affecting the success of litigation against moneylenders. Suits on debt contracts that did not comprise mortgages of land as collateral were typically handled by small causes courts. By informing elite public opinion on the 'evils of usury', the legal debate among High Court justices, based on documentary evidence restricted largely to high-value land mortgages, reinforced an emerging discourse that presented indebtedness primarily as an agricultural problem and at times appeared to locate the problems of indebtedness in British India at the level of landlords falling prey to the machinations of unscrupulous *mahajan*s. It also contributed to the notion that debt relief and credit market regulations were needed to prevent the expulsion of farmers from their lands and their migration to the cities. Both reinforced a conservative strand of argumentation within debt legislation in India that lent itself to the protection of prevalent social hierarchies in rural society, while the latter argument stood in opposition to simultaneously emerging policies of industrialization and its prerequisite in expanding 'organized' finance.

The immediate effect of the erratic nature of the extension of protective measures against usury through legal re-interpretation rather than a project of comprehensive legislation rested in an increasingly pervasive understanding that the solution to the (apparent) crisis of indebtedness lay with the courts. The root causes for the crisis of indebtedness thus became implicitly a question that needed to be addressed by reforming legal procedure rather than by economic interventions. In turn, the moral argument on the necessity of debt legislation – while never comprehensively becoming detached from its intentions to help the poor – developed a significant second strand, partially as a counterargument to utilitarian ideas, reflecting on the need to save the courts from visible complicity in oppression.

A major issue of contention emerged in the late nineteenth century, with conflicting views of different High Courts on the issue of penalties exacted for delays in instalments as part of written contractual obligations. Penalties in the form of increased interest rates constituted an important element in debt contracts, and their legal enforcement through court judgments formed one of the most important areas of legal debate. The issue was particularly contentious as it struck directly at the growing awareness that the courts' 'complicity in oppression' was morally indefensible and needed to be rectified.

In 1869, the Bombay High Court had held in *Motoji* v. *Shekh Hosain* that a stipulation for interest payment of 75 per cent per annum after default on monthly instalments in an otherwise interest-free loan amounted to a penalty and was therefore not covered by the Usury Laws (Repeal) Act. A similar ruling was passed by the Bombay High Court in 1873 in *Pava* v. *Govind*. In both cases, the High Court judged that penalties did not need to be strictly enforced according to the stipulations of the written contract. In contrast to the relatively clear line adopted by the Bombay High Court, the Calcutta High Court continued to pass several contradictory judgments, upholding the precedence of its counterpart in the Bombay Presidency in several instances, but also passing opposing judgments. Thus, in *Mackintosh* v. *Hunt*, the High Court held that interest rates of 10 per cent per month in case of default did not constitute a penalty, though it also held that the stipulated rate of interest was exorbitant and therefore could not be enforced. In *Mackintosh* v. *Craw*, the High Court reinforced its interpretation that increased interest after default did not constitute a penalty, and proceeded to allow the strict enforcement of interest payments. This line of legal interpretation was consolidated in *Arjan Bibi* v. *Asgar Ali Chawdhuri* (with an increased interest rate of 2 *anna*s to the rupee per month, or 12.5 per cent per month) and *Baijnath Singh* v. *Shah Ali Husain* (48 per cent per annum).[6]

The legal debate on the nature of penalties and their relation to the Usury Laws (Repeal) Act gained considerable traction after a series of judgments by the Allahabad High Court between 1880 and 1885. In 1880, the High Court disallowed the strict enforcement of a daily interest rate after default amounting to 730 per cent per annum, holding that the interest after default was in the nature of a penalty *because* it was 'extortionate', reinforced by another judgment in the same year (*Chuhar Lal* v. *Mir*). In *Kunjbehari Lal* v. *Hahi Bulesh* (1883), however, the High Court held that an interest rate of 24 per cent per annum after default did not form a penalty and did not warrant court interference. The Allahabad High Court, accordingly, shifted the debate on penalties from the deliberations of the original judgments by the Bombay High Court on the admissibility of *increased* rates of interest in cases of default towards the question whether the specific interest rates were appropriate. The High Court's intervention was interpreted widely as a call to entrust the courts of British India with discretionary powers to set aside interest rates as 'extortionate' or, in legal parlance, as 'unconscionable bargains'.[7]

Damdupat and the emergence of the doctrine of unconscionable bargains

The shift towards granting discretionary powers to the courts adjudicating debt contracts is of central importance for the subsequent development of extra-legal credit markets in India. The essential component of this shift was the enactment of the Usurious Loans Bill in 1918. In turn, its codification in Indian law followed earlier examples of legislation, first in continental Europe (in particular in Germany in 1880), then subsequently in the United Kingdom with the Money-lenders Act of 1900, although all these pieces of legislation differ in their details. In the immediate circumstances of the 1890s in India, however, this shift in legal doctrine was only gradually coalescing into the defining feature of debt legislation. It vied not only with the slowly diminishing prevalence of utilitarian ideas on the futility of usury legislation and the preference for 'unfettered' markets. Market regulation, it continued to be argued, would only lead to regulatory evasion that would turn to the detriment of the debtor as lenders extracted additional charges either as compensation for their need to transgress legal stipulations or by contracting markets and, accordingly, increasing the monopoly position of 'unsavoury' lenders. The shift towards vesting the courts with discretionary powers also competed with ideas to re-enact the core elements of usury legislation, especially by imposing maximum rates of interest, or by the peculiarly Indian tradition of usury regulation that linked the extraction of interest to the amount of the principal (*damdupat*).[8] While these two elements of 'old' usury laws constituted the main competitors in British Indian legal thought for the imposition of the doctrine of unconscionable bargains – and the enactment of maximum interest rates eventually re-emerged as a central component of debt legislation – even the third core element, especially of European traditions of usury legislation – 'lending to the Other, not thy brother' – occasionally resurfaced on the margins of deliberations on legislative measures.

The proponents of discretionary powers tended to view elements that could be linked to the 'old' usury laws with caution, at times even with disdain – a recurring feature of the debates on the Bill to Regulate the Award of Interest in Suits for Simple Money-Debts and Mortgage-Debts in 1895 and, to a lesser extent, the Usurious Loans Bill in 1917, as discussed later. The combination of Benthamite disdain for the 'old' usury laws and the advocacy of discretionary powers can be represented in the deliberations of F. A. Nicholson, one of the most important proponents of agricultural banks and cooperative banking in India and, correspondingly, an influential figure in the rejection of the 1895 bill that proposed to extend the operation of *damdupat* to all of British India, and – eventually – the shift towards the doctrine of unconscionable bargains in debt legislation. Nicholson's recommendations in the wake of the debate on *damdupat* constituted one of the most sophisticated responses to the proposed bill and merit a detailed discussion in the way they demonstrate the entanglement of utilitarian thought with the newly emerging discourse on procedurally defined modernity.

Nicholson's deliberations began with setting out principled reasons for his rejection of *damdupat* that strictly followed Bentham's dictum:

> The proposal is a reversion to the old law of '*damdupat*' ... It is a usury law, pure and simple, which limits the contractual power of parties; it is a usury law which though not regulating the rate of interest by an arbitrary standard, restricts the amount of interest by an equally arbitrary limitation. While I do not desire to condemn a law merely because it is a member of a legal family rejected by the English commercial and legislative instinct, I cannot but remember that no usury law ... has ever yet succeeded, ... while such law has always been found to interfere with business, to increase interest, and to promote fraud and falsehood.[9]

Nicholson proceeded to enlist the typical utilitarian arguments on the futility of usury laws in the face of their likely evasion, enriched by commenting upon the (assumed) intention of the proposed bill to restrict the operations of morally indefensible moneylenders exploiting the needy out of greed, rather than intending to find universally applicable solutions to regulate credit practices. This intention was depicted as a self-defeating objective as the morally indefensible stratum of moneylenders would be encouraged to evade regulations, while 'honest' lenders would be forced out of business. Detailing avenues for evasion, including the general difficulty of enacting *damdupat* in a system relying on documentation in current accounts by moneylenders, Nicholson's arguments still appear to be almost a rehearsal of Benthamite thoughts. Yet Nicholson's deliberations swiftly moved from stating the inevitability of evasions to the (supposed) solution:

> But the law will chiefly be ineffective because it will not touch the mass of rural usury. It is but comparatively seldom that interest is even allowed to rise at any one time to the amount of the principal; the transactions are largely continuous, with an annual settlement of accounts and perhaps fresh bonds.... Nor is the usual rate of interest such as to make interest equal to the principal in two or even in three years.... In above 3,000 small cause suits ... I have noticed no such case. In the class of rural cases so often quoted where a man borrows 100 rupees, pays various amounts for a series of years, and yet finds himself ... with a debt of perhaps 300 rupees, the whole bond has long before been replaced by a fresh bond.... The proposed law cannot per se deal with such cases, but only a law which ... enables a court to go behind the bond actually sued upon.[10]

The proposal to extend the operation of the principle of *damdupat* was, instead, undermining the sanctity not only of contractual law but of the procedural underpinnings of modernity itself:

> As shown above ... there will be a marked and increasing tendency to fraud. Documents will falsely recite consideration, and will be duly sworn to; ... debtors will falsely plead and bring false witnesses; ... parties will begin to treat false recitals as venial and false swearing as praiseworthy; written contracts will be looked on with suspicion.[11]

Concluding, Nicholson continued to reiterate what in his opinion presented the only possible solution to the problem of usury, the granting of discretionary powers to the courts:

> If a usury law is desirable at all ... it should give the Courts power ... to decide in each particular case ... whether there has been usury or not. That seems already to be the tendency of the Bombay and Allahabad High Courts, to 'examine into the character of agreements ... and, to decline to enforce such agreements unless they are shown to be fair and reasonable'.[12]

Nicholson's recommendations carried weight among proponents of discretionary powers and were eventually cited by the Chief Secretary to the government at Fort St. George as the most forcible statement of arguments against the bill.[13] As Collector of Anantapur in the Madras Presidency, he had been commissioned to conduct a study into agricultural and cooperative banks that also dealt with their viability in southern India.[14] Though most of his study dealt with the experience in continental Europe, he also engaged with the idea of constituting cooperative banking in the Madras Presidency based on an appropriation of the *nidhi* system. H. W. Wolff, an established authority on cooperation in Britain who subsequently became a key figure in the emergence of the cooperative movement in India, described Nicholson's report as a key inspiration.[15] Incidentally, a relatively minor aspect of Nicholson's argumentation regarding the inefficacy of the bill proposing the extension of *damdupat* to all provinces of British India re-emerged in the 1898 *Report of the Select Committee on Money-lending* in the House of Commons as one of the key arguments that persuaded the committee to forgo the option of maximum rates of interest in favour of granting discretion to the courts: without giving evidence, but probably related to his report to the Madras government where the 'old' usury laws of several US states are mentioned in passing, Nicholson had argued that for US states that had passed usury laws limiting interest to 6 per cent per annum, census data had shown that the actual average of interest rates was higher at 7 to 8 per cent per annum The committee, without going into the matter in greater detail, cited Nicholson's argument as proof – a rare instance, and buttressed by a reflection that the majority of Indian judges asked for recommendations on the 1895 *damdupat* bill was also in favour of granting discretionary powers[16] – and proceeded to recommend this solution.[17]

The legal doctrine of 'unconscionable bargains' developed in parallel in India and the United Kingdom. One of the leading proponents of this doctrine in Britain was H. H. L. Bellot, a barrister who – together with R. J. Willis – published the highly influential *The Law Relating to Unconscionable Bargains with Money-lenders* in 1897.[18] Bellot's work, though just recently published, was cited in the *Report of the Select Committee on Money-lending* as a 'most excellent work'. Bellot's own assessment of his influence on the shape of subsequent money lending legislation in Britain was self-congratulatory but probably correct in pointing out the contribution towards incorporating the doctrine of 'unconscionable bargains' into British law as well as the close relationship of this doctrine with utilitarian thought (Bellot 1906, 7–8).

Bellot's intervention in the debates was both timely and fortunate, as the committee began to take evidence in 1897 without taking notice of his publication, but decided to discontinue its work without recommending remedies, instead asking for a re-constitution of the committee in 1898.[19] The term 'unconscionable bargains' only entered the committee's debate in 1898. In the event, the re-constituted committee recommended the adoption of the doctrine of 'unconscionable bargains' and the granting of full discretionary powers to the courts to adjudicate suits on moneylenders' transactions. The committee's recommendations were finally enacted in the (United Kingdom) Money-lenders Act of 1900 which, in turn, formed the blueprint for subsequent Indian legislation in the form of the Usurious Loans Act of 1918. The two laws differ principally on the question of requiring moneylenders to register their businesses. The requirement for registration was taken up in India in subsequent legislation as the effects of the Usurious Loans Act on checking usury remained significantly below expectations. After the mid-1930s, most Indian provinces (and in independent India, states) shifted to the adoption of maximum rates of interest without, however, restricting the discretionary powers of the courts.

The history of the shift in elite public opinion in the course of the 1890s – both in Britain and in British India – towards granting discretion to the courts to settle disputes on credit transactions thus unfolded in relative complex ways. It was to a significant extent related to the experience of continental

European blueprints. It was based on ideas that stood in direct opposition to the prevalence of the Benthamite doctrine, yet it fundamentally developed from within this doctrine. The opposition to maximum rates of interest among the proponents of discretionary powers acted as a symbolic representation of utilitarian concerns, even while it was proposing to vest the judiciary with the authority of interfering in markets. Finally, while the proponents of discretionary powers 'won' the arguments on two occasions in India and one occasion in Britain, their arguments were hardly uncontested. Nevertheless, to its proponents the doctrine of 'unconscionable bargains' marked an important step in the advent of modernity, visible in the frequent juxtaposition of the 'old' usury laws and the 'new' doctrine. Bellot, in particular, celebrated the new legislation as evidence for a civilizational process, inexorably following a progression of stages (Bellot 1906, 28–29).

The deliberations of the committee are of interest for the Indian history of money lending legislation in one other aspect: they show the remarkable extent to which decisions on money lending legislation were based on a concern for 'young men' who were induced by moneylenders to gamble recklessly, in the process pledging their 'character' and 'position' before finally being forced to pledge 'the benevolence and friendship of those to whom [they] belong',[20] putting stress on families and communities who otherwise appear to be remarkably affluent. It would be incorrect to state that the committee did not take into consideration the concerns of poorer debtors: it certainly evicted a strong interest in cooperative finance, for instance. Yet the recommendations remained strongly informed by concerns for the affluent, but reckless or ignorant, and the effects of their indebtedness on wealthy families. In line with the origins of the doctrine of 'unconscionable bargains' in the exercise of discretionary powers to lessen hardships for 'expectant heirs' (typically depicted as male affluent adolescents) who – apart from 'women' and 'idiots', as depicted in a particularly ghastly way in the quotation at the outset of this chapter – could not be considered fully trustworthy as to the exercise of their contractual obligations freely entered into, the proponents of discretionary powers remained strongly concerned with the foolishness of the children of otherwise respectable families. These concerns, in turn, closely resemble the apprehensions of the British Indian administration on landlords forced to transfer land to moneylenders that remained remarkably persistent well into the twentieth century. These apprehensions formed a recurring feature in the deliberations on both the 1895 bill on *damdupat* and the Usurious Loans Bill in 1917.

The direction taken by legislation in Britain affected the development of opinions on legislation against money lending in India to a significant extent without, however, comprehensively overcoming resistance from followers of the utilitarian dogma and the proponents of the 'old' usury laws. The recommendations collected by the Indian government on the proposal to enact a bill on *damdupat* in 1895 and on the Usurious Loans Bill in 1917 provide two of the most comprehensive sets of sources available on the history of extra-legal credit markets in India at the time. The Bill to Regulate the Award of Interest in Suits for Simple Money-Debts and Mortgage-Debts of 1895 formed one of the few serious attempts to engage in money lending legislation at the all-India level between the Deccan Riots and the first attempt to acquire recommendations on the Usurious Loans Bill in 1913.

The bill was drawn up for the Legislative Council by Mohiny Mohun Roy and was deliberately phrased in concise ways, seeking to remedy a growing crisis of indebtedness through a general and simple method that would not allow for the institution of exceptions of whatever kind. It proposed that '[n]o Civil Court shall in any suit for a simple money-debt or a mortgage-debt instituted after the commencement of this Act, decree or award interest exceeding in amount the original principal, or, where there has been payment in reduction of the principal, exceeding in amount the reduced principal'.[21] The statement of objects drawn up by Roy remained far from elaborate. It cited a single case of litigation in which a compound interest rate of 33 per cent that had amounted to an average simple interest rate of 175 per cent per annum over the course of ten years had been allowed by the Calcutta High Court, and argued that the bill sought to rectify an anomaly in jurisdiction. Hidden behind the argument on correcting an anomaly was a brief statement that went beyond this intention, but was toned down to a considerable extent, concluding with the statement that '[t]he object of this Bill is to remove the existing anomaly of practice and to place a limit upon the award of interest'.[22]

In effect, the bill proposed to extend the principle of *damdupat*, which was followed by British Indian courts in the Presidency towns and the entire Bombay Presidency (where it had been extended to the *mufassil* after the Deccan Riots) in cases where at least one of the opposing parties in a suit was a Hindu to the rest of the country and to all communities. The fact that at least some British Indian courts were already making use of the principle may have been one of the considerations in seeking to make this the centrepiece of debt legislation in India. In addition, it was considered by many British administrators and judges to hold scriptural sanctity – even though it was not widely known outside the Bombay Presidency and there was a noticeable lack of enthusiasm among many Indian respondents to the bill.

The principle of *damdupat*, in essence restricting the *extraction* of interest to the amount of the principal, has evoked a significant amount of attention – despite the fact that it has arguably been rather ineffective in regulating usurious practices. As recently as 2010, Mandar Oak and Anand Swamy published a case for *damdupat* as a neat principle for regulating credit transactions (Oak and Swamy 2010). It is important to note here that the rule of *damdupat* makes considerably more sense under a reputational system of credit based on renegotiating obligations after the contractual agreement – as an indication of the commensurability of the expected return value – than under the juridical-procedural parameters of the 'modern' credit contract that is presupposed by Oak and Swamy. The historical inefficacy of the principle in checking exploitative credit practices is linked to a combination of factors: (*a*) it does not prohibit high interest rates, only the accumulation of interest beyond a specific limit; (*b*) many debtors prefer to settle outstanding debts as fast as possible, especially if interest rates are high, and many creditors prefer debtors to settle outstanding dues fast; (*c*) it provides a disincentive for lenders to provide long-term credit and an incentive for lenders to make it mandatory for debtors to settle outstanding debts before reaching the threshold of accumulation; (*d*) it could easily be evaded by declaring interest as penalties, as long as penalties were accepted by Indian courts; and (*e*) it can easily be evaded by a variety of other means, chiefly by pressurizing the debtor to sign a fresh contract once the limitation is reached, by overstating the amount of the principal or deducting interest in advance, or by not documenting interest payments. In addition, the recommendations on the 1895 bill make it clear that in late-nineteenth-century India the principle of *damdupat* was not necessarily followed by all courts, even where it was operational, with especially subordinate and small causes courts prone to disregard the rule in favour of the written contract. As with many other issues regarding indebtedness in India, the British Indian administration's sources of information were biased in favour of more affluent debtors.

While the rule of *damdupat* has frequently been interpreted as a limit on the accumulation of interest in total – an interpretation typically followed by the courts – this interpretation was, in fact, contentious. Thus, Basil Lang, Advocate General in the Bombay Presidency, depicted the rule as 'limit[ing] the amount recoverable at one time by way of interest to the amount of the principal'.[23] That an advocate general could interpret the rule sufficiently different makes it doubtful whether jurisdiction even in the Bombay

Presidency was in any way uniform. That the interpretation of the rule was still contentious was affirmed by other respondents. S. Srinivasan Raghavaiyangar, Inspector General of Registration in the Madras Presidency, called upon the government to fix its legal interpretation to refer to total accumulation.[24] W. H. Crowe, District Judge of Poona, went to the extent of including a quotation from an edition of the *Manusmrti* that supported the opposite view.[25] The District Judge of Satara, S. Tagore, in turn, called attention to the omission of grain loans in the bill and suggested that it be remedied by invoking the less well-known Hindu civil law tradition of *kantipat* – in his experience operational in grain deals in the Bombay Presidency – which would have limited the accumulation of interest to twice the principal.[26]

Given the large defects of the bill, it is not surprising that it failed to receive sanction. Rather, the government started deliberations on alternative remedies. The alternatives were laid out as vesting courts with larger discretionary powers regarding undue influence, to empower courts to reduce penalties or additional interest in cases of default, or to require moneylenders to comply with specific accounting practices, including the regular issuance of statements on accounts to the debtors.[27] These options were falling behind considerably in contrast with a major part of the recommendations. In the event, the government did not even follow up on these options, and the matter was set to rest for almost two decades, before the first circulation of the Usurious Loans Bill. What is remarkable about the recommendations collected is not their outcome but the fact that a majority of respondents chose to provide detailed commentaries on possible remedies that had neither been asked for nor were related to remedies proposed.

To understand the government's inactivity – in the face of a strong perception of a crisis of indebtedness in the recommendations – the conclusion drawn by the Select Committee on Money-lending in Britain on the clear-cut preference for vesting the courts with discretionary powers needs to be questioned. The contention that there was a clear majority of recommendations for this view, in fact, was an over-simplification.

> [B]ut substantially they are all on the same line, you say. - Yes. I might just give the numbers. Taking the judges, I should say that of 30 who have given an opinion on the matter, 17 are in favour of giving discretion to the courts; others say, without giving their reasons, that they approve of the Bill, ... and the remainder say that they think the Bill will neither do harm nor good.[28]

This testimony – the only estimation given in the minutes of evidence – leading to the conclusion of a clear majority opinion is misleading in many ways.

First, it considered only the judges, disregarding responses sent by administrative officers as well as some concerned associations. The corpus of responses comprises approximately 90 communiqués. A significant number of these responses, in turn, summarized opinions, sometimes going to great lengths to include the opinions of lower-rank officers and subordinate judges, many of whom had greater experience in these matters, or were added to provide a 'native' view. Counting the judges mentioned by name, the number of 30 certainly does not represent all the judges who commented on the matter. More importantly, though, the number of specific opinions does not really signify the level of support – many respondents mentioned other remedies as well or differed on details. Rather than counting votes, it seems more promising to provide a classification of remedies proposed.

The third option eventually proposed by the government, enforcing specific accounting practices for moneylenders, is rather surprising, as this remedy had hardly been mentioned in the recommendations and, if at all, only in passing. Similarly, the related question of moneylenders' registration was hardly discussed. Among the less ubiquitous remedies proposed were also recommendations on a reform of the bankruptcy laws in favour of defaulting debtors – a solution that was frequently suggested by proponents of utilitarian positions to avoid any significant interference with 'free' markets. One respondent proposed a remedy based on the policies adopted with regard to 'encumbered estates' which is remarkable in that it outlined a form of legislation that was otherwise completely ignored: by granting the courts authority to appoint a 'receiver' who would take over the management of the immobile property pledged as collateral (rather than letting the lender acquire the collateral as compensation), the proceeds from the management of the collateral held in trust were to be used to liquidate the defaulting borrower's debt.

But the main body of responses fell into five categories, occasionally advanced simultaneously. Apart from a significant number of stridently utilitarian positions with minor variations that opposed any clear interference in credit markets – as distinct from positions that remained informed by Benthamite doctrine but accepted the necessity of intervention – there were several proposals to fix the problem by an amendment of the Evidence Act, suggesting a reversal of the burden of proof on the plaintiff where the latter was a moneylender. Another proposal, the frequency of which was probably linked to an understanding that *damdupat* acted as a form of limitation, was to impose short limitations for suits in debt cases, thus shortening the time in which a suit could be filed, though the recommended time spans varied from several months to above ten years. It needs to be pointed out here that the courts had not accepted any limitations in debt cases until recently, and frequently adjudicated several decades-old cases. An imposition on short limitation rules would have reduced outstanding dues that needed to be awarded to a successfully pleading lender, and the number of cases brought before the courts. In the terminology used by its proponents, it was supposed to positively affect the morals of debtors and creditors alike, inducing the former to take contractual obligations more seriously, and preventing the latter from letting unpaid interest accumulate for long periods of time.

The most ubiquitous remedy proposed, apart from variants of discretionary powers, was to fix maximum interest rates, the very policy direction opposed most strongly by utilitarianists and proponents of discretion alike. Maximum interest rates proposed started from 6 per cent per annum – one of the maximum rates imposed in early modern Britain by the 'old' usury laws. By far the largest number of proposals on these lines considered a rate of 12 per cent per annum to be equitable, though a significant body of recommendations suggested interest rates of 24 (or 25) per cent per annum as more suitable, based on assessments on prevailing market rates. In addition, there were a number of proposals to fix maximum interest rates for several categories of loans defined by the amount of the principal. A significant number of proposals did not recommend fixing maximum rates in terms of percentages of the principal, but through different means. These included the respondents who favoured the imposition of *damdupat*. Despite the repudiation of the bill's principles by a large majority, this group still consisted of a significant number of respondents. In contrast, a relatively large group of respondents were simply recommending the prohibition of compound interest, but leaving simple interest rates to be fixed by the market.

While the proponents of discretionary powers were the largest group of respondents, this group, too, needs to be subdivided. The majority of respondents proposing discretionary powers favoured granting full discretionary powers to the courts, though opinions were divided whether these should be reserved for the High Courts, or be granted to subordinate courts. At the same time, there were many respondents who favoured restricted discretionary powers. One of the typical restrictions proposed was for cases dealing with groups considered to need special protection by the law, here typically 'the ignorant' rather than women, people recklessly accumulating debts, and 'expectant heirs'. These proposals differed from the aforementioned amendments to the Evidence Act in being more broadly concerned with unconscionable bargains rather than undue influence, apart from granting much more significant discretionary powers in cases needing special protection. In contrast, a significant proportion of recommendations suggested the restriction of discretionary powers to enquiries into undue influence, but recommended full discretionary powers for ordering inquiries instead of merely reversing the burden of proof. Another group of responses favoured full discretion in declaring rates of interest to be in the nature of penalties, sometimes in combination with a threshold of 12 per cent per annum above which all interest was to be declared voidable – one of the few instances where the combination of the doctrine of unconscionable bargains and maximum rates of interest went together. Lastly, a relatively small group of responses favoured to vest the courts with powers – at their discretion – to either ask for the submission of bona fides in order to prove the claimants' reliability and respectability, or requiring bona fides to be submitted by moneylenders as plaintiffs. Compared to the larger group of proponents of full discretion, the other sub-groups were, therefore, proposing severely diluted discretionary powers.

The categorization of perceived remedies to the debt crisis demonstrates the extent to which the direction of policy, despite a growing consensus that something needed to be done, was still unclear. The government reacted with caution, gradually moving in the direction of granting discretionary powers to the courts, but stopping half-way, and finally letting the matter rest for almost two decades. The deliberations in 1895 showed that the option of fixing maximum interest rates was off the table. It had been attacked both on principle as well as on its anticipated futility by utilitarianists and proponents of discretionary powers alike, that is, by the previously established consensus as well as by the incipiently predominant new doctrine. If Mohiny Mohun Roy had hoped to introduce a maximum rate of interest through the backdoor, the proposal needs to be seen as an abject failure in the way it contributed to the consolidation of a new idea of market framing.

The growing distance in time to the shock of the Deccan Riots and their impact on the emerging nationalist movement certainly contributed to the relative inaction, as did the relatively conservative political atmosphere at the turn of the century. The perceived need to reform the Indian economy through procedural modernization – the definition of the 'proper swindle' – receded from the priorities of the colonial government in the face of growing domestic adversity. Similarly, the perception of a need for legal reform on credit markets within the United Kingdom decreased considerably after the enactment of the Money-lenders Act in 1900, providing a rupture in the short period of co-evolution of legal doctrines in both countries. As the issue of money lending increasingly failed to attract attention in the metropolis, the problems faced in the colony may have seemed to be less pressing. By the time the issue was taken up again for consideration, the metropolis had once again taken on a role of leadership to be emulated by the colony, not only with respect to money lending legislation, but also in the development of 'organized' banking and the newly emerging cooperative movement.

The Usurious Loans Act

It may be tempting to link the re-emergence of money lending as a matter requiring the urgent attention of British Indian policy-makers to the growing economic crisis in the wake of the First World War. However, the Usurious Loans Bill was first drafted in 1913, and circulated for deliberations at a much larger scale than the *damdupat* bill in 1895. While the government apparently perceived this to be a matter of concern, the administration's response indicated its continued apathy: not a single response was forthcoming until the government re-circulated the bill along with a reminder in 1917 and, even then, several responses indicated frustration with the government's efforts at a time of war, exemplified by the minute of dissent by Sita Nath Roy as part of the concluding report of the Select Committee appointed to study the responses.[29] By the end of 1917, in contrast, a considerable body of responses had been returned, the largest contribution of which originated from the United Provinces which had hardly figured in the deliberations in 1895. In contrast to the recommendations sent on the 1895 bill that had been dominated by responses from the Bombay Presidency and Bengal, the volume of responses from the Bombay Presidency had decreased, and the response from Bengal consisted of a short statement by the judges of the Calcutta High Court, stating their approval primarily based on the resemblance to the Money-lenders Act in Britain.[30]

The original version of the Usurious Loans Bill had been a straightforward proposal to grant full discretionary powers to the courts to reopen and settle *any* debt-related case, including the reapportioning of interest rates and interest payments, in which interest rates were supposed to be excessive, or where the signing of the contract had been influenced by conditions that were considered unfair. It is significant to note that the original draft bill was understood by all respondents to apply to suits by lenders and borrowers alike, while the subsequent Usurious Loans Act of 1918 restricted its operation to suits filed for the recovery of loans by creditors. (In 1926, it was amended to include redemptions of collaterals.) The discussion here will focus on the draft bill, though the effects of this restriction will be discussed subsequently.

The circulated bill was accompanied by a range of questions, asking for deliberations on specific aspects, concerning its area of application and legal definitions of terminology, and on whether a range of other features should be included. In particular, the government's queries related to the question of (a) including British Baluchistan in the bill's area of application,[31] (b) whether loans in kind or pawn-broking should be covered under the term 'loan', (c) whether there should be a minimum rate of interest stipulated in the bill below which interest was not to be considered 'excessive', (d) whether discretionary powers should be extended to subordinate courts, (e) whether courts should have the powers to reopen cases settled before the commencement of the act, (f) whether courts were empowered to re-apportion paid interest in cases that had been settled before the commencement of the act, and (g) whether the bill should include a maximum rate of interest, or include *damdupat*. In many ways, these queries resembled the sample of recommendations sent to the government on the 1895 bill, though the weight given to granting full discretionary powers had changed significantly in its favour.

The responses, especially from the United Provinces, mirrored this significant consolidation in favour of discretionary powers. As the following discussion will be primarily based on the responses from the United Provinces, a brief summary of opinions from other provinces will be provided here: the Chief Commissioners of Coorg, Delhi, Ajmer-Merwara, Baluchistan, and the Northwestern Frontier Provinces broadly agreed with the provisions of the bill without offering extensive deliberations on any of the provisions, as did the judges of the Calcutta High Court and the government of Bihar and Orissa. The Chief Commissioner of Assam related that he and the majority of persons contacted by him agreed with the provisions of the bill and opined that his agreement was based precisely on the likely effect of the bill to make it more *difficult* for farmers to borrow money, supposedly in line with government policy – a significant undercurrent within legislative intentions that foreshadowed the specific variant of 'containment' policies discussed in the following chapter.[32] The Bombay government opposed any provision of re-opening cases with regard to non-agricultural debtors but agreed otherwise. At the same time, it forwarded opinions by the judges of the Bombay High Court and the Bombay Indian Merchants' Chamber and Bureau which comprehensively agreed with the provisions. The Madras government forwarded a sample of opinions from its administrative officers and judges which differed considerably: the Southern Indian Chamber of Merchants expressed its satisfaction with the provisions 'notwithstanding their drastic character'.[33] Both the Board of Revenue, and the Registrar of Co-operative Societies supported the bill, but the government also forwarded two opposing views, one of a district judge in Trichinopoly who voiced considerable misgivings on the level of uncertainty in debtor–creditor relations that would be introduced by the bill, and one by the Inspector General of Registration, arguing that the bill would affect the availability of credit and increase the costs of recovering loans. The Lieutenant Governor of the Punjab agreed with the bill, but stated that despite general agreement in the administration and judiciary, the bill would be opposed by the money lending communities, and forwarded a small sample of opinions representing these. The sample included a statement by the Manager of the Alliance Bank of Shimla agreeing with the legislation, but cautioning the government to ensure judiciousness in the exercise of discretionary powers, and two straightforward oppositions to the bill by Pundit Sheo Narain, and by the Punjab Hindu Sabha. The former pointed out that the courts already possessed discretionary powers (with regard to undue influence, fraud, and so on), and protested against any court interference with securities held by a creditor, 'and still more emphatically against the disgorgement by the creditor of any benefits already derived'.[34] In turn, the Hindu Sabha vented its strong opposition to the bill based on the contention that 'existing law already greatly favour[ed] debtors especially agricultural debtors, that the proposed measure [would] be a direct incentive to debtors to evade payment and that the uncertainty of law resulting from the wide discretion vested in Courts [would] greatly interfere with money-lending and thus hamper trade and economic progress'.[35] The main opposition to the bill, however, came from the Central Provinces. The Chief Commissioner summed up the responses from the judiciary and administrative as highly critical of the bill, foresaw major difficulties in its implementation, and, instead, proposed a solution based on *damdupat*.

Within the United Provinces, the majority of responses was in favour of the bill, or preferred a wider application of discretionary powers. However, as in the case of the 1895 bill, the consolidation of opinions in favour of discretion hid continuing underlying disagreements and misapprehensions on the course of state policy regarding credit markets. A significant share of these disagreements originated from Indian respondents who remained more strongly evocative of utilitarian principles than British respondents, though this divergence was clearly related to the relative proximity of many Indian respondents to the commercial aspects of everyday lives in northern India, and occasionally to money lending and indigenous banking businesses, rather than showing a division on 'ethnic' lines. Similarly, Indian respondents were more likely to favour the imposition of maximum rates of interest than their British counterparts.

The continued utilitarian opposition to government efforts to intervene on credit markets was voiced most strongly by Pandit Sita Ram of the Municipal Board of Meerut:

> The Bill ... removes a certain fetter from the discretion of courts ... and I fear that the suggested remedy will become worse than the malady itself. History informs us that laws that have gone far deep into the ordinary relations of mankind in their every-day life, ... have proved nothing but a failure.... Bentham's dictum that all attempts made directly to suppress usury have only increased the evil is well known.[36]

He proceeded to argue that an anomaly was developing in Indian law in which the general direction of the law was the reinforcement of statutory law, while the law on money lending was reintroducing an emphasis on case law through discretionary powers. If at all there was a need for legislation, the government should 'also take into consideration the creditor's point of view' and needed to consider imposing a maximum rate of interest, followed by a reduction in the limitation period for bringing suits in credit cases, and an imposition of the requirement for moneylenders to register their businesses. In an interesting reversal of a widely used catchphrase, he stated that courts should not be allowed to become instruments of 'active relief to the debtor', as it was sufficient if they were prevented from being used as 'instruments of oppression'.[37] If the bill was to be enacted, he preferred the inclusion of a minimum simple interest of 12 per cent per annum as a rule of limitation, which was after a short initial period to be enlarged to 12 per cent per annum compound interest with yearly rests.

Pandit Sita Ram's deliberations depict an interesting evolution of utilitarian principles regarding credit transactions that demonstrate their development in increasing opposition not anymore to the idea of fixing interest rates by law but to the doctrine of unconscionable bargains. Compared to the ideas expressed on the 1895 bill on the imposition of *damdupat*, the difference is striking, exemplified by Nicholson's deliberations that developed the proposal of discretionary powers from an originally utilitarian proposition. In contrast, Sita Ram's contention can be read as a preference for a *laissez-faire* approach to credit markets, followed in this sequence by a proposal to fix maximum interest rates, or to impose a minimum interest rate for the operation of discretionary powers, in both cases fixing rates below which markets were to operate freely. The common concern was for 'the creditor's point of view', and the avoidance of 'harassing and prolonged litigation',[38] with the apprehension being that this would eventually turn to the detriment of the debtor as well, in line with Bentham's dictum.

> [T]he natural outcome of the Bill is likely to be the invention of new devices to override the law. I fear that the debtor, compelled by necessity, would, under it, either have to consent to the terms of his sowcar [sahukar] or go without a loan....[39]

Sita Ram's arguments are particularly noteworthy in that they were forwarded to the government of the United Provinces by the Commissioner of Meerut Division, H. M. R. Hopkins, in a way that illustrates the government's growing hostility to these arguments:

> I ... forward the enclosed copies of the replies received ... together with the instructive criticism of Pandit Sita Ram of Meerut which is interesting as indicating the line of opposition likely to be taken by money-lenders.... It is not to be expected that the Bill will stop usury and ... will not be evaded, but it is an honest attempt to ... control the evil....[40]

The continued sway of utilitarian positions was also manifested in the response of Kanhaiya Lal as Additional Judicial Commissioner of Awadh, a much more senior officer than Sita Ram, who shared the concern over the introduction of uncertainty into money lending transactions and proposed an amendment of the Contracts Act, demonstrating an even more fundamental opposition to the bill despite the less confrontational wording:

> The sanctity of contracts entered into with all the solemnity and formalities required by law will thus ... be seriously imperiled to the prejudice of the creditor and the demoralization of the debtor.... [All] that in my opinion seems to be needed to protect the necessitous debtor is to amend ... the Indian Contract Act so as to lay the burden on the creditor to prove that the bargain was not obtained by undue influence ... where it was on the face of it hard and unconscionable.[41]

In turn, Sita Ram's contention that if legislation was necessary at all, it should follow the model of the 'old' usury laws was seconded by probably the most influential Indian respondent from the United Provinces, Babu Brij Nandan Prasad, a former member of the United Provinces Legislative Council.

> The object of the Bill is 'to save the foolish from the extortions of the money-lenders.' So before a person can avail of its provisions he should satisfactorily prove that he was a fool. But the very fact that he can prove ... such a difficult

point should go to show that he could not be what he tries to prove that he was, ordinarily a person who enters into a contract voluntarily is to be held bound by its terms. Is there any reason why money-lending contracts should be viewed in a different light? … Is there any reason to think that persons who can look after their ordinary business in life, who can purchase and sell property and do other work somehow lose their understanding when they enter into a loan transaction? … I don't think legislation should encourage men to break their contracts and to put themselves forward as idiots and imbeciles.[42]

Babu Brij Nandan Prasad continued to relay his thoughts on the supposed urgency of legislation which he related to a spike in litigation in 1909 and 1910 when the Privy Council, having earlier changed the limitation rule for bringing suits from sixty to twelve years, decided to extend the operation of the previous rule by two years, inducing creditors and debtors alike to sue before the commencement of the new rules. The temptation to settle old debt relations within this short period of time, in his view, had affected political perceptions of the crisis as lenders and borrowers alike had brought suits – 'some probably fraudulently arrived at'[43] – while the opportunity presented to settle old debt relations had tended to inflate the amounts of claimed outstanding interest, in this way 'excit[ing] a sense of prejudice against the money-lenders'.[44]

In contrast to many Indian respondents, British respondents who remained critical of the direction of market-framing policies referred to utilitarian positions to a much lesser extent, likely related to the shift in legal doctrine in Britain. One of the predominant criticisms, instead, was related to fears of overburdening the judiciary, expected to be overwhelmed with litigation cases and the disentangling of intricate past debt relations in ways hampered by an anticipated lacuna in 'proper' documentation – and the generally lamented lack of morality among debtors and creditors alike. These fears were widespread among proponents of discretionary powers as well, especially among respondents from eastern United Provinces. They were utilized in arguments designed to make a case against legislation, reminiscent of Benthamite disdain for usury legislation without open references to it.

H. W. Pike, Commissioner of Faizabad Division, stated his agreement with Babu Brij Nandan Prasad's position, though his reasons differed to some extent. In his argument, British money lending legislation had worked well since British people would think twice before approaching a court while Indians would rush to file suits on the slightest chance of success, making the legislation a 'temptation to try their luck … irresistible to debtors', since '[d]ebtors [were] quite ready enough in this country to repudiate their responsibilities without being helped'.[45]

A partially related argument with a different conclusion was put forward by A. W. Pim, District Officer at Banaras. Calling the bill an attempt to deal with a 'genuine evil', his contention was that while it might 'fulfil a useful purpose by marking the disapproval of usurious contracts by the Legislature',[46] he doubted whether it would improve conditions for 'honest debtors'. Owing to the numbers and intricacy of suits, the bill would lead to conflicting judgments in the absence of standards for application, introducing uncertainty into credit transactions. This, in turn, would be to the detriment of honest creditors, while dishonest lenders would evade its provisions. What had previously been thought of as good debts, were likely to be invalidated. At the same time, it would increase the temptations for dishonest debtors to avoid their contractual obligations. Eventually, the availability of credit would be reduced, and interest rates would rise. Pim differed from the respondents discussed earlier, however, in that he believed discretionary powers – if granted at all – should be comprehensive rather than subject to limitations.

The responses discussed here demonstrate considerable unease over the direction of credit market policies, despite the consolidation of views in favour of discretionary powers. An underlying current in the criticisms of the bill was related to unfavourable perceptions of the Money-lenders Act in Britain. Pike's argument in this respect is instructive: it contended that the act had worked as people in Britain were not likely to make use of it. If correct, this may have had two reasons, either related to a withdrawal of moneylenders from demanding excessive interest rates or related to a withdrawal of debtors from making use of the legal system and the establishment of extra-legal credit markets.

Whatever the direct effects of legislation on money lending operations in Britain following the enactment of the act in 1900, its (relative) success was linked to the establishment of alternatives in the form of new credit agencies and the gradual growth of prosperity for lower classes in Britain (compared to India). Conditions in India for the success of money lending legislation were significantly different, and the 'success' of the Usurious Loans Act was directly linked to the withdrawal of creditors and debtors alike from the legal system of arbitration rather than the disappearance of usury. The legal developments – the very idea of framing credit markets through the doctrine of unconscionable bargains – need to be understood in the way their effects were anticipated at their inception, including the possibility of a withdrawal of credit markets to extra-legal fashions of operation.

Pandit Sita Ram, in his response, had alluded to doubts on the efficacy of the British act, though not with reference to the extent of litigation. Rather, citing a speech by Madan Mohan Malviya, he referred to court judgments in Britain that allowed interest rates of up to 60 per cent per annum. Babu Brij Nandan Prasad in his criticism of the British act went to the extent of citing an 'eminent' British judge in *Samuel* v. *Cayley*:

> There had been only one Judge who could have ... understood this Statute: that was King Solomon. If there ever was another it was, he thought, Sancho Panza.[47]

Rather than focusing on the opponents of the bill, it is instructive to observe the perceptions of the British Money-lenders Act by its proponents. Among several responses that lauded the draft bill for being on the lines of the British act, there were several more nuanced positions. The District Magistrate of Mirzapur, F. S. P. Swann, while agreeing with the general direction of the bill, perceived it to be too complicated, as it applied to a wider variety of loans than the British act which he described as 'not entirely successful'.[48] He also contested the idea of a minimum rate of interest at 12 per cent per annum, stating that cooperative societies were unable to lend below 18 per cent. Justice C. Walsh (Allahabad High Court) described the draft of the Usurious Loans Bill as excellent precisely because it was simpler than the British act and avoided registration clauses which (in Britain) had 'led to so much litigation',[49] proceeding to argue that the bill should be redrafted to remove opportunities for a second appeal in order to prevent lenders from entangling debtors in prolonged litigation, and reduce the burden on the judiciary.

The question of the efficacy of the British act, in turn, was inextricably tied to the anticipated effects on the scope of future litigation, with widely differing estimates. Thus, the District Judge of Kanpur, E. H. Ashworth, cited his agreement with the unanimity among his subordinate judges that the bill would not protract hearings or overburden the judiciary, but still recommended a limitation of its applicability to the 'class technically known as money-lenders' (a phrase from the British act) to remove not only banks and cooperative societies from its operation but also pawn-brokers. Expressing his strong approval of the bill, he added:

> My approval of this principle is not based on any great optimism as to relief that will be actually afforded ... to borrowers, but it is based on the consideration that no courts should be compelled to give judgments ... which ... are oppressive.[50]

Ashworth's assessment was contested by W. R. G. Moir, District Judge of Gorakhpur, who feared that 'Courts might be overwhelmed with the history of transactions' and that '[h]alf the usurers in the country who applied to the courts for recovery of debts might be forced to disgorge their ill-gotten gains and driven to the bankruptcy courts'.[51] While voicing apprehensions on the intricacy of cases to be settled, he concluded by re-affirming his agreement with the bill precisely because it would reduce the amount of litigation by forcing lenders to seek extra-legal means of operation:

> This Act will make cases for recovery of money lent much more complicated than ... at present; but it will probably have the effect of reducing the number of such cases brought into courts, as creditors will prefer to settle these matters out of court....[52]

Read together, Ashworth's and Moir's statements are particularly informative on one of the underlying rationales for the doctrine of discretionary powers: while it could not be assumed that the bill would afford significant relief to debtors – as it forced moneylenders to avoid the legal system and develop extra-legal ways of enforcing obligations – any reduction in the numbers of suits filed was positive, lowering the burden on the judiciary, at the same time also removing the moral burden of being seen to pass oppressive judgments. If the crisis of indebtedness could not seriously be expected to be mitigated by legislation, at the least it would not reflect any longer on the image of the state. It needs to be pointed out that this line of argumentation was far from representative for the responses to the draft bill from the United Provinces, the majority of which remained solidly optimistic as to its alleviating effects. The importance of these specific responses, rather, is in the accuracy of the prediction on likely outcomes of the doctrine of unconscionable bargains in India.

The discussion on the draft Usurious Loans Bill temporarily resolved the debate in favour of granting discretionary powers to the courts rather than enacting maximum rates. Compared to the debate in 1895 the number of proponents of maximum rates in any form dropped significantly, and where interest limitations were still considered advisable, it was typically in the form of *damdupat*. In the United Provinces, the government clearly stated its opposition to any form of maximum rates, in agreement with a circular by the Lieutenant Governor from December 1914 that proposed legislation on discretionary powers.[53] In addition, the few proponents of maximum rates of interest widely diverged in the intent of their recommendations.

While some preferred maximum rates as the least objectionable form of (altogether) unwanted legislation, others contested the efficacy of discretionary powers or the judiciary's capability of dealing with the expected fallout. In turn, a number of respondents accepted the desirability of discretionary powers but sought the enactment of maximum rates as an additional step to solve the problem of money lending, exemplified by Justice P. C. Banerji, who stated that the 'Bill d[id] not seem to go far enough' and that it 'would have been well had a maximum rate of interest been prescribed'.[54] A particular strident approach was taken by Sitla Prasad Bajpai, who favoured granting discretionary powers within a limitation of minimum rates of interest in addition to maximum rates of interest and the imposition of an accumulation limit through the use of *damdupat* on otherwise non-usurious loans, though he was rather lenient on the threshold of usury, recommending a maximum rate of 24 per cent per annum compound interest at half-yearly rests.[55] Similarly, F. B. Sherring, also of the Lucknow District Court, proposed maximum rates in addition to discretionary powers, in his case at a lower rate of 36 per cent per annum and 24 per cent per annum simple interest for unsecured and secured loans, respectively.[56] The wide divergence of interest rates thought to be acceptable, reflecting differences in locally prevailing rates and personal sentiments on what constituted usury, is noticeable in the recommendations of judges from other courts, for instance, R. P. Dewhurst from Gonda, who recommended 15 per cent per annum and 8 per cent per annum simple interest, respectively, for unsecured and secured loans.[57] At the other end of the spectrum was Babu Brij Nandan Prasad, who, as pointed out earlier, did not favour legislation of any kind, preferring legislation that would have facilitated the recovery of outstanding dues by moneylenders as a supply-side remedy. Being pessimistic as to the likelihood of the government's acceptance, Prasad noted his opposition to discretionary powers by pointing out that it would be preferable to impose *damdupat*, though if at all necessary it would be better to simply fix a maximum rate at 1 per cent per month simple interest above which the burden of proof on whether the contract was conscionable should be reversed, in the process highlighting one particular fault in the operation of discretionary powers: if these were granted, in time, High Court rulings would come to fix rates in any case, so the government could also simply go ahead and impose maximum rates directly.[58]

While the discussion of the draft Usurious Loans Bill set the stage for a legislative approach relying exclusively on discretionary powers, setting aside – if only for a few years – the possibility of fixing interest rates, the debate is instructive not only in the weight of arguments favouring discretion but just as importantly in the way it incipiently foreclosed a variety of other options. Full discretionary powers emerged as the only viable option of legislation, closing the options of granting lesser forms of discretion to the courts, mediated by various limitation rules or restrictions to cases of undue influence. Compared to the 1890s, the question of whether subordinate courts were considered trustworthy of handling full discretion disappeared almost entirely, as did the applicability of the doctrine in appeals. Anticipations of a chaotic jumble of conflicting jurisdictions eventually turned out to be unfounded, but it is questionable whether this resulted from a well-designed legislation or the failure of the Usurious Loans Act to facilitate the actual adjudication of debt cases with the incipient shift of money lending to increasingly extra-legal modes of operation.

Another option which was foreclosed – for several years – was the registration of money lending businesses and the imposition of specified accounting procedures. As pointed out in Walsh's argumentation, the Indian government selected a simplified approach compared to British legislation in avoiding registration clauses. These clauses may have been considered a burden on the administrative infrastructure in India, but the debate simply omitted the question. The avoidance of registration clauses and specifications of accounting procedures, especially in the light of concerns over judicial and administrative overburdening, showcase a recurring feature in the intention of legislative approaches of the Indian state to questions of indebtedness: to solve the problem of debt crises with a minimum of effort and costs, relying instead as far as possible on means related to what Arjun Appadurai depicted as the 'legal and magical proceduralism' of capitalism (Appadurai 2015).

A major shift in the debate on money lending legislation that can be captured in a comparison of the legislative proposals in 1895 and 1917 is the significant decrease in concerns over evasions of the legal framework. This is most noticeable in the recommendations sent by respondents like Walsh and Ashworth that implied that reductions in litigation on debt cases were positive, even if it meant that matters were settled out of court. But the lack of concern over debt contracts that did not lead to litigation was much more widespread, even though it is only visible in the absence of concerns over evasions: in 1895, the remnants of utilitarian doctrine on debt legislation used these concerns as an argument on the futility of usury legislation, and a widely held assumption was that moneylenders would anyway find means to defeat the purposes of state intervention. In 1917, the ground facts on the ability of the Indian state to check evasions had not changed, but the issue had lost its potency as an argumentative tool with the decline of the utilitarian position and the ascent of the doctrine of unconscionable bargains. In consequence, it did not even figure in the majority of responses or else became construed as an unavoidable feature of Indian society that nevertheless should not distract the state from the overriding concern of ridding itself from the moral dilemma of passing oppressive judgments, the 'moral minimum' of not being *overtly* associated with exploitation. Evasion of the law became a concern only of the few remaining proponents of utilitarianism like Babu Brij Nandan Prasad or an argumentative trope used by people representing the interests of lenders. While the debates of 1895 and 1917 show a significant discrepancy on the question of evasion, a clear commonality between both debates is the shared lack of interest in selecting a remedy that relied on affirmative economic policy rather than legal codifications. Partially, this can be linked to the character of the debates as responses to particular legislative measures, though the large-scale absence of responses pointing out the need for economic policy interventions remains glaring.

The rare instances in which the idea of improving economic conditions in India as a way of remedying the crisis of indebtedness were at all referred to fell into two categories: (*a*) references to the way in which legislation would tend to restrict the capital available for lending that invoked arguments on supply and demand to argue that interest rates would rise as an outcome and (*b*) typically vague arguments that an improvement in the economic conditions or 'civilizational advances'[59] in India would tend to lower interest rates. In 1917, the issue of improving economic conditions, rather than mere references to supply and demand, was exclusively voiced by opponents of legislation. Pandit Sita Ram deplored the hampering of business through the restriction of capital available for lending and proceeded to quote Raja Rampal Singh, a member of the Viceroy's Council, that the bill would 'affect injuriously the credit system of the country'.[60] Sita Ram proceeded to state his belief that money lending in India would prevail as long as the country did not develop a full-fledged system of 'organized' and cooperative banking. The more interesting criticism on these lines came from the responses of Babu Brij Nandan Prasad and the District Officer of Benares, A. W. Pim. While stating his anticipation on the draft bill's negative effects on credit supply, and his belief that interest rates would fall when the country became more prosperous, Prasad clearly saw the improvement of economic conditions as the best way of solving the debt crisis, though his later statements demonstrate that he did not have relief measures for poor indebted farmers in mind. Instead, his argument dwelled on the way in which legislation should aim to improve the conditions of enforcing obligations in debt contracts which, in turn, would provide an incentive for lenders to commit higher amounts of capital to lending, thereby lowering interest rates. The argument was further elaborated by Pim, who emphasized his opposition to the bill on the grounds that the very direction of policy on money lending was wrong and that it should instead proceed in the direction of tightening insolvency stipulations.

> Under Indian conditions ... these legal complications would tend to raise the general rate of interest and ... restrict the capital available for loans whereas a lowering of the rate of interest is what is mainly required.... Legislation cannot do much towards increasing the ... capital available, but it may ... make the use of that capital more effective and ... the most hopeful directions in which legislative action is possible are not those contemplated in this Bill. Rates of interest must be high when honest creditors find it almost impossible to realize their money and the decrees of civil courts are practically useless to them. Insolvency proceedings in particular are widely availed of simply for the purpose of swindling honest creditors.... [61]

The arguments by Prasad and Pim are interesting not only in that they propagate an approach to legislation that would roll back debtor protection and favour creditors – a reasonable approach from the perspective of classical liberalism, though in direct contravention of the stated aims of government policy. Rather, they need to be seen in the context of the specific social groups implicitly targeted. While the discourse on money lending heavily made use of moral arguments on the need to alleviate the sufferings of the poor, British legislation had been heavily influenced by concerns over the plight of affluent but reckless or naïve male adolescents, apart from 'expectant heirs'. In India, these groups were substituted by others. Much of the literature on the cooperative movement clearly remained concerned with poor farmers, though it needs to be noted that the definition of the poor employed in this discourse frequently veered towards the landed peasantry. In the context of the debate on the draft Usurious Loans Bill, one of the main underlying target groups evoking concern, rather, were landlords in distress. Colonial concerns over the figure of 'distressed landlords' are well documented (in the specific context of Banaras, see Cohn 1960, Mishra 1975). Both Prasad and Pim were based in areas of the United Provinces that were associated with the relative decline of landed aristocracies, Awadh and the Benares Division respectively. The proposed facilitation of debt enforcement through law along the lines of classical liberalism certainly would have been to the disadvantage of some landlords indebted to *mahajan*s and *sarraf*s. Yet even indebted landlords remained in the habit of lending to the landed peasantry and especially their tenants, so that the 'improvement and simplification' of insolvency proceedings would primarily have resulted in facilitating the accumulation of capital through lending at the top of the social hierarchies, even if it may also have led to a trickle-down effect that would have left social status untouched. While the government eventually decided to extend the provisions of the Usurious Loans Bill to all loans in kind, this matter – affecting primarily poorer sections of society – was still thought to be sufficiently contentious to necessitate deliberate discussion. And though the debate demonstrated near unanimity with respect to grain loans, the only respondent from the United Provinces deliberately emphasizing the need to include other forms of loans in kind that predominantly affected the poor in urban and semi-urban areas was F. S. P. Swann, District Magistrate of Mirzapur, who depicted lending practices in small-scale industries rather than agricultural loans as 'the worst kind of Shylockism'.[62]

The concern for 'landlords in distress' was widely shared among respondents in the United Provinces, though rarely stated directly. J. Campbell, Deputy Commissioner of Kheri, for instance, supported the inclusion of grain loans, though in a half-hearted manner, stating that the principals in these cases tended to be 'small amounts', and while rates in Kheri were typically of the relatively high *derha* kind (see Chapter 4), they would 'probably come before the courts on very few occasions'.[63] His main concern, however, was with the question whether the stipulations of the bill should be applicable to transferees of land pledged as collateral, an issue that exclusively affected litigation involving large-scale land-owners. His response demonstrates a deep concern for asymmetric levels of knowledge in debt cases in this particular context that appears particularly evocative when contrasted to his off-hand comments on grain loans.

> [T]he creditor is the man with the money, with brains, with … connections. The debtor will … be unable even to state his own case properly. If the rights of transferees … are to be recognized, the insertion of a qualifying 'bona fide' will not … serve … in preventing the evil it sets out to combat. I do not see why the transferee should not be placed in precisely the same position as the creditor…. [I]f this position stands, the money-lender may … be trusted to render the Act a dead letter.[64]

In a similar way, S. R. Daniels, District Judge of Allahabad, stated that the legislative approach was particularly advisable and superior as it specifically empowered the courts to deal with cases where moneylenders had deliberately led interest accumulate so that they could 'swallow up the entire estate' of an 'improvident zamindar'.[65] In turn, Dr. Tej Bahadur Sapru, advocate at the Allahabad High Court, asked whether banks should be included in the stipulations of the Usurious Loans Bill, specifically on the grounds that some of the most important landlords in the United Provinces were heavily indebted to banks charging interest that was considered usurious in the case of moneylenders and would have been reduced if discretionary powers applied.

The concern over the applicability of the bill to banks and cooperative banks was stated forcefully by a number of respondents, with varying intentions, either to protect these businesses from adherence to the strictures imposed on moneylenders or to save debtors from obligations that were not considered exploitative as long as they were employed by 'modern' lending agencies. These concerns were voiced despite the fact that the government had not specifically asked for recommendations on this issue in the context of a draft bill that remained silent on the applicability to banks and cooperatives. Following its enactment, the Home Department deliberated whether arbitrators under the Co-operative Societies Act of 1912 needed specific exemption from the Usurious Loans Act, and eventually decided that the act did not apply to cooperatives.[66] Subsequent regulations on banking and cooperative banking excluded these businesses from the operation of the Usurious Loans Act, while the various money lending pieces of legislation after 1918 consistently used a definition of the term 'moneylender' that excluded both banks and cooperatives. Both types of businesses, however, frequently stipulated interest rates that would have been depicted as usurious by all but the most permissive respondents from the United Provinces in the debate.

In the examples used by Sapru, banks had been charging interest to *zamindars* of 24 per cent per annum compounded at half-yearly rests for principals in the range of several lakh[67] rupees, which corresponds to the (compound) *sawai* rate of interest charged for small (and unsecured) agricultural loans. Other banks, according to Sapru, were frequently charging interest between 10 and 18 per cent per annum compounded at half-yearly rests which was still significantly more expensive than the widely held assumption that 12 per cent per annum simple interest constituted a 'conscionable' rate. Kanhaiya Lal opposed the bill on the grounds that it would 'introduce an element of uncertainty in *all* money dealings'.[68] His subsequent elaboration, however, shows that he was concerned whether the bill applied to banks, which he depicted as lending *generally* at rates of 6–12 per cent per annum compound interest with half-yearly rests, with bonds or promissory notes being renewed at regular intervals in the fashion of moneylenders. Aware that these rates were significantly more expensive than typical agricultural loans that would be settled much earlier, he opposed the bill among other reasons as he (wrongly) interpreted it as giving the opportunity for debtors to re-open bank transactions through litigation.[69]

The widespread concerns over 'landlords in distress' in combination with the decreasing consideration given to questions of evasion (mostly relevant for poorer borrowers) and the predominance of the 'moral minimum' of not being overtly associated with exploitation show the narrow target clientele supposed to benefit from legislation. Concerns over usury in itself were hardly the most important driving factors behind the legislative efforts as shown by the lack of concern over bank lending rates that would have been considered usurious in the case of moneylenders. The legal doctrine of unconscionable bargains did not affect levels of indebtedness in India in a significant way or contribute to a lowering of interest rates for the poorer sections of Indian society – on the contrary, at least in the long run it contributed to massive hikes in interest rates in money lending. Vesting the courts with comprehensive discretionary powers proved to be a dead-end, though it still forms one of the cornerstones of money lending legislation in India. The act needed supplementary legislation within a few years, bringing back some of the remedies dropped since the 1890s, notably maximum interest rates and prescriptions for registration and accountancy that – in turn – also failed to improve the situation on the ground. As such, the Usurious Loans Act has often been disregarded as an ineffectual law.

The restriction of the act to suits brought by creditors mentioned at the outset of this discussion was cited by Justice Walsh as one of the most debilitating measures for the efficacy of the act, though it is doubtful whether an omission would have led to a different outcome.[70] The restriction, obviously, reduced its efficacy for debtors against moneylenders, but it also had the converse effect of heightening the improbability of lenders to seek redress through the legal system that, through this measure, appears to have been actively shaped with the intention of leaving lenders the opportunity to continue their practices extra-legally. Read in this way, the act served as an incentive for usurious creditors to seek extra-legal means. The Usurious Loans Act constituted the single-most important legislative step in reversing the process of bringing money lending under the sway of liberal contractual law.

As will be shown later, this suited at least parts of the Indian state and its planners, as it partially removed the burden of devising means to cater to the interests of the poorer and petty bourgeois sections of Indian society through 'organized' banking. The definition of the 'proper swindle' in finance may have been overtly pre-occupied with questions of proceduralism, yet it included an underlying class angle. Although Holmwood's call for extending discretionary powers of the courts – as cited at the outset of this chapter – was meant differently, the direction of legislation facilitated the removal of the law from credit markets catering to the needs of millions of Indians. The stridency of the Usurious Loans Act as well as later money lending legislation was accompanied by the withdrawal of the state from concerns over the effects of money lending on the poor and the withdrawal towards the 'formal' credit sector. It offered improvement merely to the richest sections of Indian society. Referring to the discussion in Chapter 2, the Indian state attempted (and failed) to fix the redress mechanism in the handling of the enhanced uncertainty in credit contracts by juridical-procedural means in order to enhance and preserve the common intelligibility underlying 'capitalist' finance.

Notes

1. Letter No. 479, dated Gaya, 2 July 1895, by H. Holmwood, Esq., District Judge Gaya, to the Officiating Under-Secretary to the Government of Bengal, Judicial Department, cited in United Kingdom, *Report of the Select Committee on Money Lending, 1898, Minutes of Evidence*, 190 (in the following referred to as *Select Committee Report*).
2. Cited in Jogindra Chandra Maulik, The Rent Law of Bengal, L. P. (Act VIII, 1869, B. C.) with All Important Rulings of the High Court in Rent Suits up to the Present Date and with Elucidatory Notes and an Appendix Containing Abstracts of the Stamp and Registration Acts (Calcutta: Thacker, Spink and Co, 1875).
3. Kali Nath Sen v. Trilokhya Nath Roy, cited in The Lawyer's Companion Office, Trichinopoly and Madras (ed.), The Indian Decisions (New Series). Being a Re-print of All the Decisions of the Privy Council on Appeals from India and of the Various High Courts and Other Superior Courts in India Reported in Both the Official and Non-official Reports from 1875. Calcutta, Vol. XIII (1898–1899) (Trichinopoly and Madras: The Law Printing House and The Lawyer's Companion Office, 1914), 805.
4. Ibid., 806–08.
5. Kamini Sundari Chaodhrani v. Kali Prosunno Ghose, cited in George Wheeler, Privy Council Law. A Synopsis of All the Appeals Decided by the Judicial Committee (Including Indian Appeals) from 1876 to 1891 Inclusive; Together with a Précis of All the Important Cases from the Supreme Court of Canada in Which Special Leave to Appeal Has Been

Granted or Refused, or in Which Appeals Have Been Heard (London: Stevens and Sons, 1893). Please note that the spelling of the title of this judgment varies significantly across sources.

6. A short discussion of the conflicting judgments is provided in the *Select Committee Report*, 190–91.

7. See for instance Letter No. 850, dated Berhampore 17 July 1895, from F. B. Taylor, B.A., District Judge of Murshidabad to the Chief Secretary to the Government of Bengal, *Select Committee Report*, 195.

8. The early history of the regulatory attempts regarding *damdupat* is recounted among others in Vicajee (1900).

9. Letter from F. A. Nicholson, Esq., I.C.S., to the Chief Secretary to Government, dated Yercaud, 10 August 1895, *Select Committee Report*, 213 (original emphasis).

10. Ibid., 214.

11. Ibid.

12. Ibid.

13. Letter from the Chief Secretary to the Government of Fort St. George, to the Secretary to the Government of India, Legislative Department, *Select Committee Report*, 209.

14. F. A. Nicholson, Report Regarding the Possibility of Introducing Land and Agricultural Banks into the Madras Presidency (Madras: Government Press, 1897).

15. *Select Committee Report*, 51.

16. The recommendations were attached to the report as true excerpts. The minutes of evidence show that the recommendations on the 1895 *damdupat* bill were discussed by the committee, with F. J. Willis, private secretary to the parliamentary secretary, providing a synopsis of the recommendations that highlighted the issue of discretion. See *Select Committee Report*, 87–88.

17. For Nicholson's statement, see: Letter from F. A. Nicholson, Esq., I.C.S., to the Chief Secretary to Government, dated Yercaud, 10 August 1895, *Select Committee Report*, 213; for the committee's citation of it, see: *Select Committee Report*, XVII. Nicholson's report to the Madras government mentions the usury laws in the United States only once, including the restrictions on interest above 6 per cent per annum, but without mentioning the census data on higher interest rates (Nicholson, *Report*, 247).

18. In the following, citations from Bellot's work are from the subsequent edition of this work, published in 1906 by Bellot alone under a different title, *The Legal Principles and Practices of Bargains with Money-Lenders in the United Kingdom of Great Britain and Ireland, British India, and the Colonies*.

19. On the importance of Bellot's intervention in the debate on the act, see Baty (1906).

20. *Select Committee Report*, IV.
21. The Bill to Regulate the Award of Interest in Suits for Simple Money-Debts and Mortgage-Debts, 1895, cited in *Select Committee Report*, 176.
22. Ibid., emphasis added.
23. Letter no. 33, dated 23 April 1895 from Mr. Basil Lang, Advocate General to the Under Secretary to Government, Judicial Department, *Select Committee Report*, 176.
24. Letter no. 2425-G from the Inspector-General of Registration to the Chief Secretary to Government, dated Madras, 10 August 1895, *Select Committee Report*, 215.
25. Letter from Mr. W. H. Crowe, I.C.S., District Judge, Poona, to the Secretary to Government, Judicial Department, *Select Committee Report*, 177.
26. Letter no. 1587 from S. Tagore, I.C.S., District Judge of Satara, to the Secretary to Government, Bombay, dated 29 June 1895, *Select Committee Report*, 180.
27. Letter from the Chief Secretary to the Government of Fort St. George, to the Secretary to the Government of India, Legislative Department, *Select Committee Report*, 209.
28. *Select Committee Report*, 88.
29. National Archives of India, New Delhi, Home Department files, Judl. – Mar. – 342–45 – Part B, The Usurious Loans Bill, *Select Committee Report*, dated 11 March 1918 (In the following referred to as Report on the Usurious Loans Bill).
30. Report on the Usurious Loans Bill, Office Memo from the Legislative Department, no. 314, dated the 31st January 1918.
31. This question was related to the fact that the Usury Laws (Repeal) Act of 1855 was not in force in British Baluchistan, and the province still maintained maximum rates of interest fixed by law.
32. Report on the Usurious Loans Bill, Office Memo from the Legislative Department, no. 314, dated the 31st January 1918.
33. Report on the Usurious Loans Bill.
34. Report on the Usurious Loans Bill, Office Memo from the Legislative Department, no. 314, dated the 31st January 1918.
35. Ibid.
36. Letter from Pandit Sita Ram, Hon. Magistrate and Junior Vice-Chairman, Municipal Board Meerut, dated Meerut 19-11-17, in United Provinces (file no. 12), Report on the Usurious Loans Bill.
37. Ibid.
38. Ibid.
39. Ibid.

40. Letter from H. M. R. Hopkins, Commissioner Meerut Division, no. 556/ XIX-1/17-18, dated Meerut, 8 December 1917, in United Provinces (file no. 12), Report on the Usurious Loans Bill.

41. Letter from Kanhaiya Lal, Esq., 2nd Additional Judicial Commissioner Oudh, 3 December 1917, in United Provinces (file no. 12), Report on the Usurious Loans Bill.

42. Letter from Babu Brij Nandan Prasad, Vakil, High Court, Ex-Member UP Legislative Council, dated Moradabad 3 December 1917, in United Provinces (file no. 12), Report on the Usurious Loans Bill.

43. Ibid.

44. Ibid.

45. Letter from H. W. Pike, Esq., Commissioner Fyzabad Division, no. 833/ XIX-66-7, dated Fyzabad the 22nd/26th December 1917, in United Provinces (file no. 12), Report on the Usurious Loans Bill.

46. Letter from A.W. Pim, Esq., Dist Officer Benares, to Commissioner Benares Division, in United Provinces (file no. 12), Report on the Usurious Loans Bill.

47. Letter from Babu Brij Nandan Prasad, Vakil, High Court, Ex-Member UP Legislative Council, dated Moradabad 3 December 1917, in United Provinces (file no. 12), Report on the Usurious Loans Bill.

48. Letter from F. S. P. Swann, Esq., C.I.E., Dist Magistrate Mirzapur to Commissioner Benares Division, No. 162, dated Mirzapur 21 November 1917, in United Provinces (file no. 12), Report on the Usurious Loans Bill.

49. Précis of opinions of Chief Justice and judges of the High Court, in letter No. 3750/47, dated Allahabad, the 13th December 1917, from B.H. Bourdillon, Esq. Registrar, High Court of Judicature at Allahabad to Sec to Govt, UP, in United Provinces (file no. 12), Report on the Usurious Loans Bill.

50. Letter from E. H. Ashworth, Esq., Dist Judge Cawnpore, Cawnpore 20 November 1917, in United Provinces (file no. 12), Report on the Usurious Loans Bill.

51. Letter from W. R. G. Moir, Esq., Dist Judge Gorakhpur, no. 763/XIV, 21 November 1917, in United Provinces (file no. 12), Report on the Usurious Loans Bill.

52. Ibid.

53. Letter by M. Keane, I.C.S., Secretary to the Government of U.P., to the Secretary to the Government of India, Legislative Department, no. 27-C, dated 6 February 1918, in United Provinces (file no. 12), Report on the Usurious Loans Bill.

54. Letter by Justice P. C. Banerji, dated 3 December 1917, in United Provinces (file no. 12), Report on the Usurious Loans Bill.

55. Letter by Sitla Prasad Bajpai, Second Additional District Judge, Lucknow, no. 944/XIV, dated 26 November 1917, in United Provinces (file no. 12), Report on the Usurious Loans Bill.

56. Letter by F. B. Sherring, Esq., District Judge Lucknow, no. 943/XIV, dated 29 November 1917, in United Provinces (file no. 12), Report on the Usurious Loans Bill.

57. Letter by R. P. Dewhurst, Esq., M.A., F.R.G.S., District Judge Gonda, no. 798/XV, dated Gonda, 30 November 1917, in United Provinces (file no. 12), Report on the Usurious Loans Bill.

58. Letter from Babu Brij Nandan Prasad, Vakil, High Court, Ex-Member UP Legislative Council, dated Moradabad 3 December 1917, in United Provinces (file no. 12), Report on the Usurious Loans Bill.

59. Letter by Kunj Behari Sen, Esq., First Additional District Judge Aligarh, no. 452/XV, dated 27 November 1917, in United Provinces (file no. 12), Report on the Usurious Loans Bill.

60. Letter from Pandit Sita Ram, Hon. Magistrate and Junior Vice-Chairman, Municipal Board Meerut, dated Meerut 19-11-17, in United Provinces (file no. 12), Report on the Usurious Loans Bill.

61. Letter from A.W. Pim, Esq., Dist Officer Benares, to Commissioner Benares Division, in United Provinces (file no. 12), Report on the Usurious Loans Bill.

62. Letter from F. S. P. Swann, Esq., C.I.E., Dist Magistrate Mirzapur To Commissioner Benares Division, No. 162, dated Mirzapur 21 November 1917, in United Provinces (file no. 12), Report on the Usurious Loans Bill.

63. Letter from J. Campbell, Esq., Deputy Commissioner Kheri, no. 416, dated Kheri, 17 November 1917, in United Provinces (file no. 12), Report on the Usurious Loans Bill.

64. Ibid.

65. Notes A, May 1918: Notes in the Home Department (in Proceedings, May, 1918, Nos. 39–56), in United Provinces (file no. 12), Report on the Usurious Loans Bill.

66. Question of exempting awards under the Co-operative Societies Act, 1912 (II of 1912), from the provisions of the Usurious Loans Act, 1918 (X of 1918), National Archives, Delhi, Home Dept. (Judicial) 1918 – Judl. – May – 147 – Part B.

67. 'Lakh' and 'crore' are units of the numbering system prevalent in South Asia; 1 lakh is equal to 100,000 and 100 lakhs is equal to 1 crore.

68. Letter from Kanhaiya Lal, Esq., 2nd Additional Judicial Commissioner Oudh, 3 December 1917, in United Provinces (file no. 12), Report on the Usurious Loans Bill (emphasis added).

69. Ibid.

70. C. Walsh, preface to his edition of the Usurious Loans Act, cited in Jafri (1931, 343).

4

Containment

A British bank is run with precision A British home requires nothing less! Tradition, discipline, and rules must be the tools Without them – disorder! Chaos! Moral disintegration! In short, you have a ghastly mess![1]

The shift in policy towards granting the courts discretionary powers led to a significant drop in litigation cases reaching the higher-level courts, visible almost as soon as the Usurious Loans Bill was enacted in 1918. There are indications that matters of usury continued to be dealt with for a time by small causes courts, though. *In principle*, the shift in legal doctrine on credit markets marked a significant rupture. It rescinded the operation of contractual law for transactions that were defined to be usurious, just as much as the repeal of the usury laws in 1855 – *in principle* – had imposed contractual law on the earlier economies of debt. The policy shift towards the doctrine of unconscionable bargains clearly relates to the endeavour to define propriety in economic relations, though the definition of the 'proper swindle' (Birla 2009) with regard to credit markets took on an ambiguity that needs to be emphasized here. While marking a broad array of credit transactions as improper, and dissecting these from the proper debt relations that continued to fall under the purview of contractual law, the shift towards discretionary powers did not envision state supervision of propriety through regulation. It did not constitute a move towards enhanced formality. On the contrary, it (vaguely) delineated an economic enclave in which state regulation would remain incoherent and arbitrary, and implicitly envisioned creditors in this segment to seek redress in extra-legal manners.[2] While 'proper' debt transactions became increasingly subjected to regulatory regimes, their 'improper' equivalent was implicitly intended to remain fuzzy.

While it is difficult to ascertain the precise effects of the new policy with respect to the lower courts, the influence of the shift in legal doctrine on the actual operations of credit markets can only be seen in long-term developments. Credit markets in northern India were extremely complex and could not be expected to become neatly detached into two segments within a short period of time. The United Provinces Banking Enquiry Committee described the credit markets they encountered in 1929–30 in derogative fashion as 'a tangled jungle of disorderly transactions',[3] marking their disapproval of the messy character of Indian business relations, despite the fact that colonial interventions through the use of discretionary powers increased rather than decreased the complexity of markets.

The Usurious Loans Act has frequently been interpreted in Indian economic history as a 'non-event' – to employ Charlesworth's term for the Deccan Riots. This interpretation is mostly related to the characterization of the act by the Royal Commission on Agriculture, which remarked that it was 'practically a dead letter in every province in India',[4] although this assessment was disputed.[5] It also rests on an assumption that the Usurious Loans Act should have had the effect of diminishing usury, and that its failure in this therefore reflects a general failure of money lending legislation, neglecting the possibility that the act had other significant results, especially in dissecting 'formal' and 'informal' segments in Indian finance. Financial entrepreneurs were reacting to the new policy by gradually withdrawing from the legal system. In the short term, this affected business practices only in minor ways: the majority of credit transactions even before the enactment, after all, never went into litigation. Rather than removing the majority of credit transactions from the legal system, the Usurious Loans Act served to arrest the gradually increasing reliance of creditors on juridical-procedural parameters characterizing the common intelligibility of 'capitalist' finance. In the long run, however, this withdrawal of contractual guarantees through the state significantly changed the coordinates of lending practices for extra-legal credit.

The misunderstandings on the changes brought about by the Usurious Loans Act even within the British Indian administration can be illustrated by the striking case of Sir Cecil Walsh. Signed in his capacity as a recently retired puisne judge at Allahabad, Walsh had published a searing critique of the Usurious Loans Act in the *Morning Post* in 1929. Specifically, he emphasized the act's original intention to apply to all suits, that is, even to suits brought by debtors. Arguing that the original bill would have been an 'admirable act', he proceeded to state that it had been 'amended to death' by the Select Committee.[6] Opening a conversation with officials in the Colonial Office, he proceeded to clarify that 'after deep research [he] found hardly any reported cases since the Act' had been implemented 'in a country which is rampant with litigation, and swamped by reports', finally stating that this amounted to 'one of the biggest blunders [he] ever saw'.[7] The Select Committee, he argued, had acted 'in the interest of the capitalist and money-lending class' in watering down the bill, in itself not an entirely implausible though unconfirmed suggestion. The Colonial Office reacted furiously, mostly on the grounds that Walsh had published his article before contacting them. It pointed out that while there were 'other statements in his letter [that were] not accurate', the Usurious Loans Act had been amended three years earlier, precisely to remove the limitation on suits brought by debtors.[8] However, the amendment had not led to noteworthy increases in litigation.

It is hardly possible to comprehensively map changes that occurred over the period in the emerging segment of 'informal' finance between 1918 and the last years of colonial rule even in a restricted area such as the United Provinces, not necessarily because of the lack available sources – this period is extensively documented – but because of the complexity of the market: the United Provinces Banking Enquiry Committee Report, running into four volumes with a total of over 2,000 pages, attempted to set out both an analytical framework and an overview but primarily managed to demonstrate the opacity of this intricate web of market relations. The expression 'a tangled jungle of disorderly transactions' does not only mark a derogative approach towards the state of Indian finance but also the committee's perplexity in the face of its task to unravel these relationships. In view of this, the intention of this chapter is less to portray the precise changes on credit markets in northern India but to set out an argument on broad lines of development. Apart from successive legislation and institution-building processes reinforcing the separation of credit practices, dimensions of financial markets in India that are particularly demonstrative of the changes (and lack of change) include the development of interest rates and other costs of borrowing, the business practices of extra-legal lenders, the social composition of lenders in the extra-legal segment, the social embeddedness of lending practices, especially in family or community structures, the growth of organized banking and cooperative finance, and the scale of extra-legal lending after 1918. Lastly, the intention of this chapter is to set out an argument that the last decades of colonial rule were significant for the development of credit markets in India in that they marked an increasing dominance of the strand of thought incipiently visible in the debates on the Usurious Loans Bill that rather than facilitating credit conditions for the poor and the petty bourgeoisie, it should be the aim of the state to contain debt by limiting the access to credit for non-productive uses or for uses the productiveness of which could not be documented within 'proper' banking formats, that is, the vast majority of loans needed by the mass of the population.

Improper transactions

One of the pervasively visible driving forces of legislation was the desire by the state to bring 'good' credit practices under the purview of regulation, implicitly leaving credit markets that carried high risks either to the cooperative movement (the hoped-for outcome) or to the emerging 'informal' segment of finance that was supposed to disappear over time. The Indian state's policy was designed to provide incentives for relatively prosperous borrowers to benefit from state regulation and, at the same time, to prevent 'dishonest', non-modern, and exploitative lenders from making use of these incentives. The definitions of who was considered dishonest, anachronistic, or even exploitative changed according to contexts, especially with regard to the spectrum of 'indigenous' banking, but there was a stable consensus that its embodiment was the moneylender. While it was well understood that money lending practices were diverse, the figurative triad of the *sahukar*, Bania, and Kabuli formed a background for debates that implicitly defined what was perceived as undesirable. Other lenders, accordingly, were judged according to their perceived equation with these figures, at times actively seeking to showcase their distinctiveness and at other times conflated with them to demonstrate their undesirability. The opacity of the term 'moneylender' needs to be kept in mind not only when discussing the social composition of types of lenders and their target clienteles but also in a depiction of prevailing interest rates.

The *UPBECR* treated the legal framing of credit markets in India as unfinished, suggesting both broader and stricter regulation of the formal segment of Indian finance, while maintaining ambiguity in its assessment of the Usurious Loans Act. Concerning the Usurious Loans Act, the committee's members vacillated between outright condemnation and an interpretation that it might have been partially successful. Eventually, the committee settled on an assessment that the act would in the future become more widely used and therefore effective. This assessment was based almost exclusively on the statements of two witnesses, the written statement by Shah Muhammad Sulaiman, judge at the Allahabad High Court of Judicature,[9] and the written statement and oral evidence of Jitendra Nath Roy, judge at the small causes court in Lucknow.[10] Sulaiman had pointed out that he was aware of the usage of the act in the lower courts and that one reason for its relatively rare use in the higher courts was that the limitation for registered mortgage deeds executed before 1918 had not yet expired. In turn, Roy clearly stated that he himself was using the act 'almost every day' and that it was widely used in the small causes courts of Lucknow.[11] The committee's report also proceeded to note that other witnesses had presented complaints that the act was being used to the detriment of creditors, a claim which the committee rejected with an argument that demonstrates the tendency of the Indian state's policy to distinguish between lenders serving 'good' debts whose businesses needed to be facilitated, while leaving a swath of riskier forms of lending to the 'undesirable' creditors, disregarding the consequences for less prosperous borrowers.

> There can be no doubt that ... the scales are weighted against the moneylender. We cannot, however, conceal from ourselves that to some extent he is himself to blame if his legal position is weak. Induced by the hope of a high return ... he is apt to take risks which no prudent man would take, and if ... he loses thereby, he is entitled to blame only himself and not the law.[12]

The committee also marked its disapproval of the lack of guidelines for the courts to define excessive rates of interest, complained that lower court officials tended to be dishonest and help debtors against creditors, and showed a considerable interest in condemning the allegedly prevalent practice of courts in the United Provinces to reduce interest allowed on contracts under litigation after the date of filing suits to 6 per cent per annum regardless of whether the contractual rates of interest were considered usurious.[13] These observations provide a good starting point to a discussion of interest rates in northern India in the last decades of colonial rule.

The committee did not suggest the imposition of maximum rates of interest for money lending, but went along – despite some misgivings – with the line of legislation seeking to address interest rates through the courts' discretionary powers. Contrary to some anticipations in the debate on the Usurious Loans Bill, the definition of excessive rates had not yet coalesced into unified practice by 1930, being hampered by the heterogeneity of credit conditions and a lack of consensus. While many commentators on credit policies tried to demonstrate the need to distinguish between acceptable rates in a variety of contexts, others referred to moral arguments on the impermissibility of rates above specific thresholds, frequently 12, 15, or 24 per cent per annum. As the evidence given by Roy was accorded special weight, and is relatively detailed as to the practice of a small causes court, it provides an important entry point into this discussion.

While stating explicitly that the Usurious Loans Act was '[c]ertainly not [a dead letter] in the small cause courts of Lucknow',[14] Roy proceeded to outline the practices of his court.

[W]e do not require to use [the act] generally, because as soon as the interest comes to, say, 75 per cent. we at once reduce it to half. The *Agha* and *Kabuli* moneylenders charge two annas per rupee, i.e. 150 per cent. These people know that the court will not allow more than six pies per rupee, i.e. 37 ½ per cent. So if they go to court they take care to see that the interest is put down at six pies per rupee. If any stray cases come where the interest is usurious it is at once reduced.... [H]aving regard to the risk that the creditor has to run, we allow six pies and it has almost become a custom.[15]

Roy went on to state that courts in general were still left at discretion to define usury, with some courts being more lenient than others, and proceeded to suggest the insertion of a definition of usury in the Usurious Loans Act, arguing that there was a deviation of small causes courts from the preferences of higher courts which typically held monthly rates of 1 per cent to be 'reasonable'.[16] Roy's deposition was followed by the evidence provided by Pandit Raj Rajeshwar Sahai, Subordinate Judge at Muzaffarnagar, who depicted prevalent interest rates between 1 and 2 per cent per month, arguing that these were 'not exorbitant' in 'the circumstances under which [moneylenders] take the risk of advancing the loan',[17] and Pandit Vishnu Ram Mehta, Officiating Additional Sessions Judge at Benares. The latter depicted common interest rates in his area as 2 per cent per month or (rarely) above for cash loans, 25 per cent per annum for loans in kind, or 37.5 per cent per annum for small loans.[18]

The sample of depositions already shows several features of interest rates that need to be highlighted. The rates mentioned here broadly correspond to interest rate patterns that are relatively typical for colonial India, much more so than the rate of 6 per cent per annum to which courts in the United Provinces reduced interest between the filing suits and the recovery of loans. The latter rate has no clear relation to interest rate patterns in modern Indian history, and its frequent recurrence in colonial debates is more likely to be linked to British historical experience, thus informing the moral argument of colonial officials. While the rates considered to be below the threshold of usury vary from 1 per cent to roughly 3 per cent per month, the prevalent rates charged by moneylenders especially were likely to differ significantly, with 12.5 per cent per month forming the current rate in Lucknow for borrowers who needed to approach Kabulis. Even the officially stated rates that were accepted by Roy allow for some variation. As pointed out by S. N. A. Jafri, loans were often repaid in instalments but the interest rates tended to be calculated for the whole principal for the entire duration of the loan, thus raising the actual interest rates significantly, in his example from 36 to 75 per cent per annum (Jafri 1931, 326). The figures accessed by the courts tended to obscure additional costs such as up-front payments as 'cuts' deducted from the principal. Moreover, the depiction of annual rates obscured compounding and the frequency of rests, which frequently constituted integral parts of loans. While the courts were typically taking these matters into account, the explanatory depiction of contractual obligations as annual simple interest rates for the benefit of colonial officials tended to hide the complexity of prevalent rates.[19]

The *UPBECR* shows a wide variation of interest rates in the United Provinces, even for smaller sums, so that the depiction of patterns within the costs of borrowing is hardly possible. Lenders changed their business strategies according to circumstances, rather than following a 'local rate'. The depiction of locally prevailing rates in the report typically followed the pattern set out earlier in the statements by Roy, Sahai, and Mehta, stating one rate but allowing significant space for deviation. As the committee had specifically asked for a representation of *the* locally prevailing rates, it is probable that witnesses would have given rough estimations, based on assessments of plausibility rather than accuracy. This would also explain the relatively vague depictions of prevalent rates by some witnesses. It is more promising to dissect interest rates according to the purpose of borrowing and providing room for adjustments relating to reputation, seasonal fluctuations, and need.

For Allahabad district, encompassing much of the rural areas around Banaras, the evidence provided by Thakur Ram Singh, Assistant Commissioner of Income Tax at Banaras, depicts the costs of borrowing as outlined here.[20]

- Large loans advanced on mortgages typically included interest rates between 6 and 12 per cent per annum, according to the quality of the land. This range of rates varied according to the borrower's reputation, falling to 4–8 per cent per annum for reputable borrowers but at times going up to 24 per cent per annum.
- Similar rates were current for large loans advanced against promissory notes, though these did not fall as low as 4 per cent on good reputation. These loans were typically facilitated by brokers charging a one-time commission of approximately 3 per cent (6 *pie*s in the rupee).
- Large loans by the big 'indigenous' bankers to aristocratic families typically on personal security tended to fall below this range, including a commission fee (*nazrana*) between 2 and 5 per cent.
- Advances against *hundi*s fell into the range of 6–12 per cent for *muddati hundi*s, and between one and two *anna*s per rupee (6.25–12.5 per cent

per annum) for *darshani hundi*s. Loans against *sarkhat*s – informally drawn-up promissory notes in the bazaar – were issued for rates between 9 and 12 per cent per annum, or between 10.5 and 12 per cent per annum for less well-known traders, but falling to 6 per cent in slack season.[21]

- Pawn-brokers advanced loans against ornaments for one *paisa* per rupee per month (approximately 1.56 per cent, though erroneously depicted as 1.9 per cent), going up to 2 per cent per month for less reputable borrowers. For higher-value ornaments, rates were lower at 9–12 per cent per annum.
- Private limited companies engaged in lending were charging rates of 18–24 per cent per annum, higher than most 'indigenous' bankers, partially due to high commissions by the Imperial Bank (up to 25 per cent) for collection of cheques.

For the poorer segments of the population, the rates quoted by Singh were significantly higher:

- Loans in kind for farmers typically followed the *sawai* rate, though in some places the *derha* rate was prevalent (both discussed later).
- Loans based on the *qist* system (also discussed later) typically included interest rates of 44 per cent per annum, though Singh mentions *qist*s with lower rates, for instance repayments of an 11 rupees advance in twelve monthly instalments of 1 rupee.
- Very poor borrowers needed to fall back on 'Punjabi' or Kabuli moneylenders typically charging two *anna*s per rupee per month (12.5 per cent), but also advancing loans in kind on either the *sawai* or *derha* systems.

Singh's outline demonstrates the deviation of interest rates by purpose of borrowing from statements depicting 'locally prevalent' interest rates. Compared to the patterns of interest rates in Benares district before 1918, there are some significant changes, though without a clear direction. The district gazetteer for Benares of 1909 depicted interest rates as having been stable for over a century, 'much the same to-day as they were in the time of Jonathan Duncan' in the late eighteenth century, typically following the *derha* or *sawai* rates for loans in kind to farmers (the latter increasingly prominent), with the *ugahi* system (see later) operating for *qist*s, while it was possible to contract (supposedly even petty) loans on good personal reputation for 18 per cent per annum, or for 12–15 per cent per annum against the security of 'articles' pledged.[22] While any comparison between the rates of 1909 and 1930 needs to be conducted with caution due to the complexity of interest rates, there appears to have been a slight fall in the rates for *qist*s (from about 48 to

44 per cent per annum), a continuation of the shift from *derha* to *sawai* rates for loans in rural areas, and a rise of rates against the security of ornaments from 12–15 per cent to approximately 18–24 per cent per annum The rate depicted in the gazetteer for loans against personal security (that is, good reputation) of 18 per cent per annum does not correspond clearly to rates provided by Singh, and appears low for petty loans. It likely relates to unsecured loans between petty traders and shopkeepers rather than mid-level traders dealing in loans against *sarkhat*s. The change in the *ugahi* rate is likely to be related to variations in the system rather than declining rates. With the continued existence of *derha* rates – though less pervasive than *sawai* rates – the only clearly visible change for an assessment of fluctuations between 1909 and 1930 is the rise of rates in pawn-brokering, which, though significant, might relate to differences in the personal assessments by the gazetteer and Singh of what constituted low-value ornaments. All in all, the picture is one of continuity rather than change.

Interest rates in late colonial money lending were rarely quoted in percentages but used forms of quotation that provided indications of the amount of payment over time. In these ways, they tended to facilitate information flows on the costs of borrowing to the parts of the population that frequently lacked arithmetic skills needed to calculate percentage-based rates. These quotation systems comprised their own fallacies which could be exploited by lenders who wanted to obscure the costs of borrowing. However, in many cases these systems of quotation simply followed established patterns of indicating costs that neither lenders nor borrowers sought to deviate from, as they constituted common frameworks of reference. From the perspective of colonial officials, these quotations were interpreted as 'traditional' credit systems, enshrined in custom. The rates most commonly referred to in colonial sources with respect to the United Provinces – *derha, sawai, ugahi*, and *rozahi* – are described later.

The former two systems of quotation were linked to the main harvest seasons – notwithstanding sub-regional patterns of seasonal deviation. Being strongly but not exclusively related to essential features of the rural economy, they tended to comprise elements that embodied the characteristics of rural credit markets, most visibly in the case of compound interest. The *UPBECR* strongly deplored the 'flimsiness'[23] of securities that Indian farmers could offer, leaving only undesirable collaterals – the pawning of household goods, cattle stock (more likely to be sold than pledged), and *jajmani* rights or other transferable privileges apart from land. In the context of the 1920s and 1930s, the notion of creditors forcing farmers off their land, or else leaving tenants under the control of absentee landlords lacking knowledge about agriculture, was fairly widespread, in part out of concern with indebted peasants, but just as importantly linked to anxieties on the indebtedness of landlords. Bagchi's argument on British responsibility for the emergence of land as the principal rural credit security (Bagchi 1981, 32) was already foreshadowed in the committee's report.

> There remains the farmer's principal asset, his land. Ever since rights on land have been settled and land has required a selling value, the most common form of long-term credit throughout India has been based on land mortgage.[24]

As collateral, land (and fruit trees) could be pledged either as mortgages or as usufruct mortgages. These could be pledged by agriculturists with legal land titles either as landlords or, in permanent settlement areas, by permanent or fixed-rate tenancy holders (and in Benares district additionally by occupancy tenants in the *pargana* of Kaswar Raja).[25] While there is sufficient evidence that especially urban-based moneylenders were not keen to acquire large tracts of land, preferring cash over obtaining the collateral, the high value of the security enabled lending at (relatively) low rates, but also facilitated the inclusion of compound rates of interest in contractual obligations. Both *derha* and *sawai* rates, correspondingly, frequently constituted compound rates of interest. The two rates differed principally on the respective sum of interest payment, either half or a quarter of the principal at the end of the harvest season. Typically, this would relate to a six-monthly interval, and colonial officials almost invariably assumed that debts would be contracted for agricultural purposes at the start of the season, so that both rates were calculated as roughly 8 or 4 per cent per month compound interest at half-yearly rests. Most colonial sources do not explicitly state the general assumption of compound interest.

The compounding of interest at half-yearly rests did not affect the interest rate significantly if repayments were carried out in time. Arrears, however, would quickly lead to an escalation of interest payments, and one of the moral arguments by colonial officials against moneylenders was the assumed tendency of creditors to let arrears accumulate with the intention to acquire the collateral, in the process making the courts 'complicit in exploitation' – a strategy that would not make sense in case of 'flimsy' securities, or simple interest rates. The *UPBECR* commented that 'the creditor by compounding the interest ... and by refusing to accept repayment in instalments makes redemption [of the mortgage] difficult even if the debtor desires to redeem; and most landlords are bad payers'.[26] While it is apparent that the Usurious Loans Act was to a considerable extent intended precisely to check the tendency of creditors to rely on the law enforcement agencies to administer the transfer of the security, the period between 1918 and the early 1930s does not demonstrate any significant effect of the law, as compound rates evident in the *derha* and *sawai* forms of quoting the costs of borrowing remained largely unchanged, with the tendency to apply the lower *sawai* rate already well established beforehand. Reasons for this failure necessarily include an extent of conjecture: courts may have accepted at least the *sawai* rate as 'locally prevalent' or 'customary', and therefore not usurious; or the courts may simply have been evaded in the transfer of land, for instance through the use of *benami* transfers or, especially in usufruct mortgages, through extra-legal practices of claiming harvest shares. In turn, the limitation rule to suits on mortgages contracted before 1918 reduced the number of unsuccessful suits by creditors, while the act's original limitation to suits brought by creditors might have dissuaded lenders to enter litigation without, however, affecting their propensity to quote the *sawai* or *derha* rates. It needs to be pointed out that legal practice after 1918 tended to reduce interest considerably in litigation, at least after the process of compounding started. In this way, legislation may have slowed the processes of land acquisition by lenders without necessarily halting them. The committee looked into these matters before the crash in agricultural prices during the Great Recession became apparent (see Rothermund 1992), so that land was still desirable for creditors. With regard to extra-legal forms of land transfers, the *UPBECR* noted the unclear extent to which agriculturists were engaging in practices of subleasing, especially concerning usufruct mortgages that were illegal under the tenancy laws of the United Provinces.

> The mortgagee, in the role of the subtenant, takes over the land, pays the landlord's rent, and either cultivates [the land] or re-lets it to somebody else, very often to the mortgagor himself, at a competitive rent.... Such a transfer is entirely illegal, rendering both parties liable to ejectment by the landlord; to the debtor it is also highly unprofitable. Since the usufruct is set against the interest only, the debt at the end of the sublease stands where it did at the beginning.[27]

These forms of subleases were not considered sufficiently problematic in sources on earlier periods. While not constituting conclusive evidence for a new phenomenon, the considerable extent to which the committee expressed concern over these extra-legal subleases, in the face of an apparent lack of concern over increases in overall mortgages in the United Provinces,[28] may indicate an incipient shift of agricultural credit systems towards extra-legality, though one that was not sufficiently pronounced to affect the registration of mortgages in general.

Usufruct mortgages involved a high level of complexity in terms of calculating borrowing costs, as they were based on uncertain future yields instead of the *sawai* or *derha* rates. The Inspector of Co-operative Societies in the United Provinces, Satya Prakash, depicted an example of a carpenter in Sripalpur, Basti district, who had borrowed 32 rupees. against the usufruct of his jack trees. Calculating the yield in market prices for the last two years, Prakash depicted the rate as 78 per cent per annum simple interest.[29] As usufruct mortgages were unlikely to be redeemed by farmers – in the assumed absence of additional income – they were highly profitable for the lenders.

While there is a link between the availability of desirable high-value collateral and the incidence of compound interest, the *sawai* and *derha* rates were also used as systems of quotation for non-agricultural loans. Colonial officials frequently asserted a prevalence of the rates for grain loans but quoted equivalent rates for other loans in kind or for cash loans. Partially, this can be explained by the predominant forms of debtor–creditor relationships, especially in the countryside: grain dealers and other merchants constituted the lenders of choice for many rural Indians but supplied not only seeds and food items; rather, they supplied cash loans for a variety of purposes as well as providing a range of manufactured goods on credit.[30] The village studies conducted for the *UPBECR* provide ample evidence for the centrality of debt in rural life beyond the harvest cycles. In the case of Benares district, for instance, the report on Dhangaria village lists the reasons for cash loans as (*a*) payment of old debts, (*b*) marriage and funeral ceremonies, (*c*) payment of rent and interest on loans, (*d*) purchase of bullocks, (*e*) purchase of milch cattle, (*f*) repairing and building of houses, (*g*) trade in corn and sugar, (*h*) family expenses, (*i*) litigation, and (*j*) investment in land mortgage.[31] This list, in turn, does not even include miscellaneous purchases in cash by poorer villagers. With the prevalence of systems of quoting borrowing costs based on the *sawai* and *derha* rates, many lenders simply fell back on these for other loans. In these cases, compound interest at the same rates and rests frequently applied to loans unrelated to the harvests and the desirability of the collateral, especially if loans were recorded as part of a current account by the lender, reinforcing the escalation of debts over time. In other instances, contracts for non-agricultural credit followed a simple interest variety of the *sawai* and *derha* rates. The widespread omission by observers at the time to explicitly mark deviations from the compound interest assumption prevents any estimation of the frequency of simple interest rates within the *sawai* and *derha* rates, though some sources allude to these as mostly or frequently comprising compound interest.

Sawai and *derha* rates formed an informational grid for borrowing costs in rural United Provinces. These rates were not applied uniformly, though. Local deviations continued to exist, both in the terminology and in lending practices. For instance, in the district of Basti grain loans to ploughmen (rather than landed farmers) were occasionally depicted as following a *harwaha* rate, equal to *sawai*, but set apart in terminology. At the same time, *sawai* rates in some of the district's villages differed in including yearly instead of seasonal rests. More importantly, though rarely reported in the *UPBECR*, the assumption of six-monthly repayment periods was faulty, as loans continued to be contracted in the middle of the harvest seasons but would still follow the *sawai* or *derha* systems of calculating interest.[32] Total interest would be calculated for a six-month period, even though repayment was due already after three or four months. In contrast, kinship or social proximity tended to decrease interest rates actually charged, though not necessarily the ways of quotation. Prakash depicted interest rates for these cases in Basti to be as low as one-eighth of the principal, while also stating that some lenders would charge rates mid-way between the *sawai* and *derha* rates, that is, three-eighths of the principal. In turn, while contracts would still specify compound rates of interest at yearly rests, lenders in Basti district were shown by him to charge only simple interest rates to landlords.[33]

In contrast, the *ugahi* and *rozahi* rates formed an informational grid underlying the *qist*[34] system and therefore unrelated to collaterals. Constituting unsecured loans, *qist*s formed one of the prevalent system of lending in urban areas but extended widely into the countryside for loans unrelated to agricultural production. In turn, *qist*s need to be distinguished from loans secured on 'personal security', that is, the borrower's reputation, in that they were contracted in contexts of low social intimacy, making it necessary for the lender to visit debtors at frequent intervals to ensure repayments. While many *qistwallah*s were itinerant, or operated across wide tracts of land, *qist* rates were significantly lower than the rates of operationally similar loans provided by Kabulis as the former lent to a clientele of relatively 'respectable' lower-class persons.

While the *rozahi* (lit.: daily) rates were higher and less widely used at the time of the Banking Enquiry Committee than *ugahi* (lit.: collection) rates, both included a set of transactions based on the intervals of repayment and the amounts of the principals. As depicted by Jitendra Nath Roy, *rozahi* formed the more effort-intensive of the two systems for the lender but included an internal variation according to repayment intervals: a loan of 10 rupees was repaid in 2 months and 22 days through daily instalments of

10 *paise*,[35] leading to a total repayment of approximately 12 rupees and 13 *anna*s. Alternatively, repayment would be lower in daily instalments of 5 *paise* for 5 months and 15 days. In turn, the *ugahi* rate was made up by a repayment of a 10 rupees loan in 12 monthly instalments of 1 rupee, with arrears in payment frequently being charged with an interest rate of 6 *pie*s to the rupee per month.[36] Accordingly, while interest rates (calculated over the entire period of the loan) would fluctuate widely according to the duration of the loans in the three different systems, the borrowing costs at the end of the loan period were roughly similar, indicating that the moneylenders were not calculating according to their effort, or even the return on investment per day or month as capital outlay in the first-mentioned system of *rozahi* would yield significantly higher annual profits than the other two. Rather, the consideration was that a loan of 10 rupees should bring a return between 2 and 3 rupees for short-duration periods, regardless of whether these were approximately three or six months, or one year. While the significantly lower interest rates in case of the *ugahi* rate may be explained by the relative lack of input costs by the lender, necessitating only monthly visits, the most effort-intensive variety (the second *rozahi* rate) has lower interest rates than its shorter equivalent. As the *ugahi* rate allowed lenders to cover wider areas of operation, and therefore focus on relatively 'respectable' borrowers who could be trusted to repay large instalments of 1 rupee, the lower interest rates in this case are plausible. With the same reasoning, however, the significant increase of the effective daily interest rates for the 82 larger daily instalments of 10 *paise* in contrast with the 165 instalments at 5 *paise* remains puzzling.

*Qist*s were changing according to circumstances. The *UPBECR* reported recent varieties of *qist*s from Banaras:

> Four new types of loan are reported from Benares: in two cases the principal is repayable in monthly instalments of one rupee, in the other two it is repayable in daily instalments of one anna. The amounts are respectively Rs. 16 repayable in 20 monthly or 330 daily instalments; and Rs. 20 repayable in 25 monthly or 395 daily instalments.[37]

The profits in these loans would have been 4 or 5 rupees, respectively, again regardless of their duration, but roughly equivalent to the expectations of overall returns from *ugahi* and *rozahi* rates. In the cases reported from Banaras the lower interest rates for monthly over daily instalments are broadly consistent with a reduction in the lender's effort. Being unrelated to collaterals, these rates were invariably charged as simple interest, and in this way *qist*s were significantly better suited to loans for consumption purposes. Roy's example of 5 *paise* instalments might simply be a misrepresentation, an interpretation that is partly corroborated by the absence of similar figures in the *UPBECR*. The monthly interest rates in this example are significantly lower even than the *rozahi* rates given for the 'new types of loans' in Banaras. Having stated this, as judge in a small causes court, Roy was likely more knowledgeable in dealing with litigation on *qist*s than many of his superiors.

Setting aside the example of 5 *paise* instalments, the rates quoted for *ugahi* and *rozahi* systems of *qist*s still demonstrate a significant discrepancy. While *ugahi* rates were surprisingly low considering the lack of security other than reputation, falling into a range from 20 to 25 per cent interest per annum, the rates following the *rozahi* system show significantly wider variation, from less than 3 per cent per month to above 10 per cent per month. The difference is attributable in part to the higher principals of the 'new' rates in Banaras – though the daily repayment rate in the 10 *paise* example depicted by Jitendra Nath Roy is higher than the daily instalments of one *anna* in Banaras. The difference might also show a degree of regional fluctuation[38] or, more likely, prevalent rates at different times of the year related to fluctuations in money markets. Tirthankar Roy (2016) shows the wide range of fluctuations in *bazaar* rates, though these differed significantly from *qist*s. Signifying lower principals, *qist* rates were not likely to be fluctuating considerably with money supply. Rather, the wide range of interest rates needs to be understood as showing the range of prevalent systems of *qist*s of the *rozahi* type, indicating room for adjustment to the borrower's reputation and socio-economic status in which the *rozahi* rates could be settled somewhere between the prevalent *ugahi* and Kabuli rates, each marking the opposite end of the spectrum of rates at which lower-class borrowers could obtain loans.

While the two systems of *qist*s indicate the spectrum of rates for unsecured loans to poorer clienteles, and the *sawai* and *derha* rates the prevalent rates on loans secured by land mortgages, the highest rates, targeting the least 'reputable' borrowers, were offered by lenders who were frequently identified by their ethnic origin as Kabulis or Pathans. In practice, the difference between a Kabuli rate and the high-end spectrum of interest rates for loans offered by *qistwallah*s was not necessarily significant. While the *qist* system as well as *sawai* and *derha* rates were depicted in colonial sources as 'traditional' rates – lending the legitimacy of custom to a range of interest rates the higher end of which would have been considered unconscionable by Indian courts, and was often associated with enforcement practices that differed from Kabuli practice in gradations rather than principle – Kabuli lending was not included under the rubric of tradition. The allusion to foreign and communally charged social origins, in contrast, implied an Otherness that set them apart from the mainstream of money lending, and reinforced both apprehension and condemnation. Rather than perceiving Kabulis as another group of lenders engaged in lending at the higher range of interest rates associated with the *qist* system, official discourse strove to set it apart from the latter, highlighting an ethnic origin that was neglected elsewhere and focusing on enforcement practices rather than interest rates. Official discourse tended to be strongly engaged in a dissection of moneylenders on the basis of their 'desirability' and status, conflating class, caste, and community prejudices. The Upper India Chamber of Commerce summed up their disdain for lenders targeting the poorer sections of society in the following terms, demonstrating gradations from approval to condemnation, after having depicted petty moneylenders in general as full of 'envy, hatred and malice and all uncharitableness':

The sarraf is regarded with respect. The sahukar is relied on and regarded with confidence. The arhatia is also relied on as a rule, and looked to by the beopari for guidance. The village Mahajan is regarded with somewhat mixed feelings… The qistwallah though resorted to perforce, is detested because of his usury and grasping attitude. The Kabuli is not only hated as an usurer but is detested because of his method of entrapping his victims and is feared because of his aggressiveness and readiness to resort to personal violence.[39]

Jitendra Nath Roy had depicted Kabuli (and 'Agha', another term depicting Muslim community) lenders to charge interest rates at 150 per cent per annum, though he asserted that contracts would be drawn on the 'permissible' rate of 6 *pie*s per rupee.[40] The difference between the legally stated and the actually enforced rates of interest demonstrates one of the ways in which lenders were digressing from their earlier practices after the Usurious Loans Act. The written contract became an additional security for the lender, guaranteeing legal enforcement of the principal and a share of the accumulated interest, while the larger share of interest was legally unsecured. While Roy's deposition made it clear that the common practice in Lucknow small causes courts was to reduce interest, his statement demonstrates his awareness and concern about the way the 'sanctity of the contract' had become merely a fall-back option for moneylenders:

The moneylender says that he will charge two annas per rupee per month. The borrower agrees to pay that, knowing that if he refuses … he will not get the loan. The creditor advances money on this explicit understanding. Now, when he comes to the court for the recovery of the debt his interest is substantially reduced. That is a sort of injustice to the creditor.[41]

What appears to be a throwback to the doctrine of undue influence, needs to be seen in the immediate context of the statement, deploring the differences in the exercise of discretion by the courts which threatened the clarity of legal principles. While most witnesses to the committee perceived the typical Kabuli rate to be 12.5 per cent per month, there are some significant discrepancies shown by others, partially linked to the stereotypical representation of Kabulis as lending to the poorest, and to industrial workers. In the United Provinces, a province without dense industrial clusters beyond Kanpur (see C. Joshi 2003), Kabuli lenders were engaging in lending to much more varied social strata, including peasants, artisans, and low-value service and clerical professions. Even for Cawnpore district, the Assistant Commissioner of Income Tax stated that Kabuli moneylenders 'did not count for much' and were mainly engaged in lending to the 'poorer classes of Anglo-Indians' and menial servants as much as to mill-hands.[42]

When lending to different strata than industrial workers, Kabulis followed the prevalent systems for lending to these target clienteles at the higher end of these ranges. Thus, when lending to peasants Kabulis tended to follow the *derha* rates rather than the lower *sawai* rates and would tend to undervalue repayments in kind.[43] For Jhansi district, the Income Tax Officer estimated that Kabuli rates differed from 75 to 300 per cent per annum, with the majority of loans being contracted at a rate of 187.5 per cent per annum – still significantly higher than the 'typical' rate.[44]

In Banaras, Kabuli lenders were mostly lending to artisans, low-value service professions, and domestic helpers. A small number of families engaged in lending in contemporary Banaras are still locally known as Kabulis or Pathans. As to the prevalent interest rates for loans from Kabulis in the city, Thakur Ram Singh, the Assistant Commissioner of Income Tax, agreed with the rate of two *anna*s per rupee (12.5 per cent per month) as the most common rate, though he stressed that Kabuli rates would go up to four *anna*s per rupee per month 'where they think they have to deal with desperadoes and badmashes', adding that Kabulis were capable of recovering their loans through force and intimidation even from these.[45] Lala Babu Lal Vaish, Income Tax Officer at Banaras, went as far in his condemnation of Kabuli practices as to suggest the enactment of a law specifically prohibiting Kabulis from operating as moneylenders though he emphasized Kabuli loans to Banarsi artisans at interest rates of 50 per cent per annum (significantly higher than under the advance systems, but not very different from *qist* rates), and to domestic helpers.

They are disgraceful fellows, because it is the most needy who go to them, and they recover the money by force. It would be difficult for anybody to resist him [*sic!*]. There are many private servants who borrow from them. They know that they won't get money from any other banker or moneylender.[46]

The conception of Kabulis lending primarily to industrial workers is partially related to colonial experience in the Presidency towns and major cantonments like Kanpur, but was again highlighted by the Royal Commission on Labour in India report[47] that sought the enactment of a law against 'besetting' or 'loitering', practices associated specifically with Kabuli lenders (though not uncommon among other moneylenders) in which the lenders would either have agreements with the factory management to enter the compounds on pay day or else set themselves up near the gates of factories or office compounds. The Bengal Banking Enquiry Committee went one step further, and proposed a legal prohibition on 'habitual usury' – in line with British policies designating groups of people as habitual criminals (Singha 1998) – though the context of the recommendation makes it clear that this proposed law was specifically targeting Kabulis.[48] These concerns were taken up by the Indian government that requested recommendations.[49] Eventually, the Indian government declined permission to a bill on prohibiting besetting and loitering due to a lack of consensus, and left legislation on these matters to the provinces.[50] While strictures against loitering became part of money lending legislation in a number of provinces in the 1930s, they were only enacted in Uttar Pradesh in 1976.

The correspondence provides detailed evidence on Kabuli interest rates throughout India that demonstrate that the range of rates in the United Provinces was part of a larger pattern throughout India. Thus, the Inspector of Factories for Delhi, Punjab, Ajmer, and the Northwestern Frontier Province depicted these rates as between 10 and 20 per cent per month,[51] while the Deputy Commissioner for the Santal Parganas argued that Kabuli rates were not different from the *qist* system in which a loan to miners of multiples of 4 rupees at the beginning of a week would be repaid in multiples of 4-4-0 rupees on pay day,[52] though these rates were significantly higher than the *rozahi* rates for Banaras. For industrial workers at Ahmedabad the rates provided fell into the range of 0-0-6 to 0-2-0 rupees per week (roughly 75–300 per cent per annum), with the most typical rates being 9 *pies* per rupee per week (ca. 4.7 per cent) or one *anna* per rupee per month (6.25 per cent).[53] Rates given for other areas show similar fluctuations. Moneylenders who were entering the premises of factories on pay day frequently paid a commission to the factory management in what appeared to be a regularized custom. Monthly commission charges given for Ahmedabad Bania lenders were depicted as 125 rupees.[54] Factories in some parts of India had set up informal arrangements such as in Beawar, Ajmer, in which workers were forced to register debts with moneylenders with the factory management, while the factory would provide the lenders an informal guarantee of repayment, in the process bringing down prevalent interest rates but also enforcing regular payment. The Beawar example is interesting since its inclusion in the correspondence was related to the mill owners' complaints against any attempt to prohibit loitering as it was essential for the smooth functioning of this particular arrangement.[55] As with most other legislative attempts on money lending, official deliberations sought to resolve issues concerning indebtedness through procedural prescriptions rather than policies to improve the economic status of the targeted groups, an issue forcefully raised in this respect by the District Magistrate of Bhagalpur.[56]

Artisanal credit

The last major sub-system of credit markets in late colonial United Provinces that falls within the category of money lending rather than banking is the system of artisanal credit through advances, typically for production purposes. Advance systems to artisans functioned in ways that are entirely different from other credit segments and emphasize the fact that moneylenders – even those classified by the *UPBECR* as 'professionals' – rarely operated solely as lenders. Advances frequently included rates that were significantly lower than any other systems, apart from credit in the bazaar. The primary aim of the advance system, rather than interest accumulation, was the control of labour or of the manufactured product. While this entailed debilitating consequences for the workers' ability to benefit from price rises, it did facilitate access to credit in ways that helped artisanal resilience at subsistence level. The absence of advance systems of lending formed one of the most important reasons for artisanal destitution as noted for instance by A. C. Chatterjee for cotton weavers in Agra or for the blanket industries of Muzaffarnagar.[57] The system of artisanal credit constitutes one of the best researched topics in the history of Indian credit relations, with a considerable number of excellent studies approaching the subject from different angles (Pandey 1981; Roy 1999; Venkatesan 2009; Haynes 2012; for Banaras, Kumar 1988).

As artisanal credit is well researched, it will only briefly be discussed here in order to complement the overview on prevalent lending systems. Sources on artisanal credit in this period are plentiful: apart from a variety of other sources a significant part of the *UPBECR* discusses artisanal credit. The discussion here emphasizes the operation of the advance system in Banaras and artisanal towns in the vicinity. The most important distinction between types of loans (primarily) for production purposes was the differentiation between loans against interest, loans against wages, and loans against the fixed price of the finished product. While the operational modes of these loans differed, and they tended to have diverse effects on the status of the workers involved, there is a clear trend towards uniformity in the rates of profit in lending in the most important artisanal industries that fell within a range from 12.5 per cent to 25 per cent over the relatively short-term periods necessary for the manufacturing process, depicted accordingly for instance for Mirzapur carpet weaving.[58] In a larger town like Banaras, however, a variety of artisanal industries coexisted, and lending systems varied among industries: credit markets reacted rather to the types of goods advanced and the organization process of the industry than to the socio-economic conditions of the target clientele. Within these market segments, lenders had room for adjustments to the borrowers' professional status as well as reputation.

For Banaras, the most important artisanal industry was in silk weaving, with the products marketed especially in south India and Burma, while metropolitan demand for Banarsi silk products was still relatively low.[59] The weavers needed advances not only for silk, but also for chemical bleaches and dyes, and of thread or wire for embroidery, especially the costly *kalabattu* wire, while the knowledge on the design of patterns and its transformation to the looms was kept within a tiny group of families.[60] Both formed conditions under which a system of subordination of artisans through debt could remain remarkably stable. The various entries in the committee's report on silk weaving in Banaras make it clear that the form of subordination was operating irrespective of whether artisans were employed as wage-earners in small-scale workshops (*karkhane*), or earned their incomes by selling the finished products to middlemen or traders. In the latter case, the advance in raw material (and occasionally cash) would be repaid in finished goods, with a commission charged on the advance, and weaving families were generally left with an average daily income of 1 rupee.[61] When working as wage-earners, wages would be paid as advances (*dadan*), carrying no interest but leaving a similar daily income.[62] The financing of the advances, in turn, depended on larger moneylenders, in the case of Banaras increasingly Khatri *sarraf*s who would charge interest to the middlemen and *karkhandar*s at 9–12 per cent per annum.[63] Rates of profit for the *karkhandar*s and middlemen or traders fell into the bracket of 12.5 to 25 per cent before deducting interest on these loans.

Weavers working independently were perforce restricted to the production of cheaper goods that would mostly sell locally as they were unable to afford the costs of buying higher quality raw materials, but would be faced with uniform prices even when offering their goods to different traders, ensuring that independent weavers were worse off than those working under the two advance systems.[64]

The credit system for silk weavers thus did not strive for accumulation through interest or the acquisition of pledged collaterals – advances were contracted on legally valid *chits* that were, however, rarely enforced – but through control of labour that allowed the fixing of prices for the finished goods. From the entrepreneurial perspective, the necessity for the emergence of this system lay in the costs of raw materials. At the same time, reducing workers' incomes allowed entrepreneurs to compete with imported goods despite the relatively poor quality of many Banarsi silk products.[65] Highly skilled labour in the same industries were able to extract greater shares of the profits. The system of labour control employed legally valid contractual instruments but crucially depended on informal labour–capital relations, clearly visible in the dual manners of documenting and operating contractual arrangements in *karkhane*:

> A 'chit' with both debit and credit side in it is also given to the weaver concerned, but it is not certain whether the middleman takes advantage of the weaver's ignorance and illiteracy. When ... the *karkhanadar* sees that almost the full amount of advance is going to be repaid ... he invites him into accepting another advance. The result is obvious. The weaver cannot claim higher wages ... unless and until he repays the money in full....[66]

The adaptation to procedurally defined modernization in this example, signing legally enforceable documents, was voluntary but did not affect the subordination of labour. The *chits* did not need to be enforced legally as the artisans were unable to fully repay their dues before signing up to fresh advances. Similar systems were prevalent in other industries in the United Provinces, such as outlined for Moradabad by the United Provinces Deputy Director of Industries.[67] Here, employers or middlemen would make artisans sign pledges for fictitious sums, carrying interest rates of 24 per cent per annum. While the documents were legally enforceable, they were discarded once the pledges were kept by delivering the finished goods, and interest was not charged. By 'convention', employers would forgo their legal entitlement to interest, unless the workers absconded, substituting for the Workmen's Breach of Contract Act that was repealed in 1925.

For supplementary occupations linked to the silk industries in Banaras, different systems had emerged, some of which did not rely on advances such as in the production of gold and silver wires, though part of the wages here were kept for long periods as a means of labour control,[68] similarly as in low-quality lacquered toys.[69] As a rule, advance systems were in operation in Banaras in industries that were comparatively profitable and paid higher wages, while industries without advance systems tended to show even greater depressions of artisanal incomes, such as in *tikli*s or in iron and steel products.[70] While this might be read as an indication that advance systems facilitated higher wages, it is likely the reverse: where advance systems were absent, artisans did not possess bargaining powers sufficient to claim higher wages, while industries that flourished sufficiently for artisans to make claims on a higher share in profits needed an additional layer of labour control exercised through credit instruments – which, nevertheless, created the need to raise capital from larger lenders, thus being shed whenever markets were sufficiently depressed to ensure workers' compliance.

The invariable conclusion of the committee as well as its witnesses was to seek redress through the cooperative movement – despite the large-scale failure of cooperatives in artisanal industries, especially in Banaras[71] and sufficient evidence for structural incompatibilities that will be discussed subsequently. Artisans were expected to organize in cooperative societies (in proximity with capital), rather than through other forms of association. A strike of artisans engaged in the production of gold and silver thread had taken place in the mid-1920s, but failed to improve wages or work conditions.[72] In silk weaving, several associations had been founded after 1910, but all had failed within a few years, partially due to opposition from middlemen. In 1921, an association for both middlemen and wage-earning weavers had been set up, but failed even sooner.[73] There are numerous examples of *panchayat*s active among Banarsi artisans that enforced minor improvements in work conditions, especially regarding the provision of mid-day meals, but rarely affecting artisanal wages. The system of artisanal credit may have been less directly exploitative than other forms of lending, but by depressing wages under conditions of low competitiveness it facilitated large-scale indebtedness among the urban workforce. Even small calamities led weavers to take up additional loans for consumption purposes, following different systems of lending against interest and pledged securities. The UPBECR notes that '[i]nstances where houses have been mortgaged [were] not rare' among weavers in Banaras.[74]

Recovering interest

The discussion of interest rates in money lending practices shows the variety of credit patterns that continued to affect the population in the United Provinces. There is no clear evidence of major changes in interest rates over time, but one of diversification. *Qist*s to the affluent remained relatively affordable, while the discrepancy regarding interest rates to the poorer target clientele widened, with *rozahi* rates at the higher end coming close to the 'typical' Kabuli rates. The tendency for rates contracted at the *sawai* rather than the *derha* rate continued unabated, showing that credit conditions for peasants with secured tenancy rights continued to ease, though not affecting landless agricultural labour. While the removal from of the 'sanctity of the contract' through the Usurious Loans Act led to a decline in litigation in the higher courts, suits were still brought to the small causes courts, but contractual documents had become merely a supplementary assurance for extra-legal recovery. Essentially, money lending transactions became increasingly unregulated, though not necessarily costlier to debtors.

Rather than looking merely at interest rates, it is necessary to analyse these in relation to credit recovery mechanisms. The vivid depiction of Thakur Ram Singh quoted here illustrates widely held beliefs in the administration that Kabuli lenders were capable of fully recovering loans even from 'desperadoes and badmashes',[75] comprehensively relying on extra-legal means including violence. The violent element in Kabuli recovery methods is highlighted throughout governmental sources, though Kabulis used a range of other methods including public shaming and picketing. Jitendra Nath Roy's deposition makes it clear that signed contracts were treated predominantly as a last option for partial recovery. The Deputy Commissioner of Rae Bareli, S. S. Nehru, argued that Kabulis were the only lenders actually resorting to force[76] – likely exaggerating the absence of violence from other debt transactions, but expressing a tendency – but that extra-legal means of recovery were still prevalent among all classes of lenders.

> Rural bazaar merchants realise 75 per cent. on oral or written demand, and 25 by litigation, which may or may not take its full course.... Kabulis realise by force majeure. Otherwise the ratio is from 70 to 90 per cent. recovery out of court....[77]

Recovery 'on oral or written demand' does not correspond to conflict-free transactions, though threat of force might have been averted through reputational means or the intervention of associational and community bodies.

Shah Muhammad Sulaiman had deplored the unnecessarily long delays in recovery through litigation,[78] a sentiment shared by the majority of witnesses. The Collector of Meerut depicted conditions for loan recovery to be 'poor enough', though his deposition implies that they were worse in court than out of it.[79] Lala Babu Lal Vaish, in turn, stressed that moneylenders did 'not resort to litigation as far as possible' but only when 'compelled to do so', less for recovering arrears but 'for the sake of keeping their prestige'.[80] He estimated bankers' bad debts to be in the vicinity of 10 per cent of their profits. For the *qist* system, he calculated that yearly net profits for the lenders assuming that all capital was lent for every day of the year would come to roughly 25 per cent regardless of the rate of interest charged for different types of *qist*s,[81] indicating a significant loss through defaults and related expenses that rose proportionally with the precariousness of borrowers. The variation of rates shows the relative sophistication of extra-legally operating lenders in factoring in risks and underline the monopoly positions of specific types of lenders. Lending to poorer clientele under these conditions was only possible by evading the law, or through a massive reduction of returns on investment. In the absence of significant policy changes for the improvement of living conditions, policy became based on the presumption that credit for the poor through the regulated systems of lending was to be restricted to clearly productive purposes, exemplified by the argument of W. Gaskell, Commissioner of Income Tax, United Provinces:

> One may be permitted to express the opinion, without being considered cynical, that any extension of credit except for the purposes of trade and agriculture is not expedient.[82]

The core feature of money lending legislation in late colonial India, accordingly, centred on the withdrawal of state guarantees of contractual obligations for debt contracts targeting the poor, anticipating future developments in which only moneylenders capable of enforcing recovery through extra-legal means would flourish. Mitigating policies needed to rely on large-scale capital expenditure by the state through agents like cooperatives, or through similar expenditure through recurring state-funded debt conciliation schemes. These were slow in affecting credit markets, but eventually – in independent India – were capable of providing partial relief to the petty bourgeoisie and landed peasantry, though informal credit practices continued to remain important for these social sections as well.

The failure of cooperative credit

As outlined in the previous chapter, interest in cooperation – especially in credit – was marked by the 1890s. Nicholson's significance as an expert on money lending, for instance, was mostly based on his expertise on cooperative finance. A legal framework was enacted in 1904 with the Co-operative Credit Societies Act. In 1912, the Co-operative Societies Act provided a legal basis for the extension of cooperation into fields unrelated to credit.

In Banaras – both city and district – early cooperative businesses had been started by the 1910s, though these failed rapidly. This failure elicited a (relatively) quick response by the government which set up a commission of enquiry that published its report in 1915. The report described the government's efforts to strengthen the cooperative movement as 'partial and incomplete'.[83] The sustained failure to improve the conditions of cooperation led the United Provinces government to set up another committee in 1925, the Co-operative Committee for the United Provinces of Agra and Oudh, which published its report in the following year. In addition, cooperative measures were dealt with in considerable length by other enquiries, including the Royal Commission on Agriculture (1926) and the various Banking Enquiry Committees. Both played a significant role in augmenting the impression of the government that relief against money lending was to be primarily based on assisting cooperation rather than more direct state intervention. For the United Provinces, the evidence collected by the Royal Commission on Agriculture demonstrated pessimism on the viability of directly intervening through instruments such as *taccavi*, a scheme for loans designed to enable landlords (and tenants with secured tenancy rights) to improve their agricultural land, especially as relief measures. The commission, in its United Provinces section of evidence, highlighted the depositions of H. A. Lane, Revenue and Judicial Secretary to the United Provinces government, that *taccavi* did not provide an alternative to the cooperative movement, or to moneylenders.[84]

Lane's argument crucially hinged on the capabilities of the Revenue Department's administrative staff which would prevent the use of *taccavi* even in the event of sufficient state funding.[85]

In his view, the flexibility of moneylenders could not be emulated by a bureaucracy, unless this bureaucracy comprised a vast layer of local staff which necessitated rigid guidelines to prevent lower-rung corruption. Such rigidity, in turn, would prevent state lending through *taccavi* for all but a small portion of credit purposes. The recent amendment of the Usurious Loans Act to extend its application to mortgages[86] constituted a small, but important step in this regard, though Lane also cautioned that prohibition of moneylenders' businesses would significantly reduce the availability of credit to cultivators.[87] Lane's oral evidence clarifies that *taccavi* was used in the United Provinces predominantly as a tool for providing relief in emergencies, and that the Revenue Department was disinterested in development work. As he also indicated that he had no previous experience with the cooperative movement, his advocation of using cooperation instead of *taccavi* was based rather on pessimism as to the latter's effectiveness than on an informed optimism on cooperation.[88] While the *UPBECR* dealt with *taccavi* loans, especially for encumbered estates, the question of tackling money lending through cooperatives instead of direct state lending for all practical purposes had been settled with the Royal Commission on Agriculture.

While figures cited by the Committee on Co-operation in India show a remarkable growth of the movement already by 1915 also in the United Provinces, both in the number of societies and their capital outlays,[89] their impact remained far below expectations. In the United Provinces, the number of cooperative societies grew from 159 in 1904–05 to 6,000 two decades later, though the membership of primary societies failed to keep up, reaching 145,000 in the mid-1920s after having breached the threshold of 100,000 by 1914 with less than 3,000 societies.[90] The effects of sustained activity on their members' indebtedness to moneylenders, however, were considerable: the *Report of the Co-operative Committee of the United Provinces of Agra and Oudh (CCUP)* calculated that sustained operations had enabled approximately two thirds to become free of moneylenders' loans.[91] This, however, had not facilitated the movement's anticipated take-off, leading the committee to wonder why people did 'did not see sufficiently substantial advantages'[92] in joining it.

> ...[C]o-operation after 20 years is not spreading by its own momentum, as it would if its benefits were felt to be real and substantial. The money-lender is not alarmed, and the interest taken in co-operative societies is so little that very few people consider them to deserve serious attention.[93]

The committee felt that cooperation in the United Provinces had largely developed as credit societies rather than holistically following European examples, and that members failed to adhere to the spirit of cooperation, defined as thrift, avoidance of default and deferred payment, honesty, and mutual responsibility in controlling lending, and the abstention from speculation. This failure to develop a 'true' cooperative spirit was largely held to be responsible for one of the main defects of the system – the 'monopolization of loans by panches and their friends'[94] which also facilitated the transgression of propriety as prescribed in law by the societies' own members in anticipation of future quid pro quos, so that embezzlement was 'not uncommon'.[95] The issue, therefore, remained one of instilling character into the Indian masses which made it even more deplorable that the movement had 'not been more successful in attracting the attention of the educated classes'.[96] In its reduction of developmental concerns to superficial moral arguments, the government's attitudes towards cooperation show remarkable similarity to its other policies on financial markets, reinforcing the impression that the project of defining the 'proper swindle' formed a class-based endeavour of 'civilization' in its colonial mould. The class-basis of propriety, however, was not only visible in the lack of moral education in lending. The committee, for instance, deplored the alleged tendency of borrowers to treat cooperative lending similarly to moneylenders, attempting to default whenever possible. As in the way in which 'indigenous' bankers were occasionally removed from the moral project of defining the 'proper swindle', propriety in financial transactions was not absolute, but a requirement that seemed to be the preserve of the right kind of lender just as much as the right kind of borrower.[97]

Corruption and the inability to follow a cooperative spirit were made out as the primary sources of failure. In contrast to the *UPBECR* which in the context of the failure of artisanal cooperatives related it to resistance by middlemen-lenders arising from greed and an absence of associational spirit, the *CCUP* squarely blamed the members themselves. What is striking in these observations is not so much the common occurrence of corrupt practices, but the inability of the committee's experts to embed these into a debate on the scarcity of 'proper' ways of conducting business that would have provided an avenue for understanding their ubiquity, a feature that is common in debates up to the present.[98] The short passage in the *CCUP* dealing with the cooperative experience in Banaras deserves a full citation, illustrating the employment of a superficial moral argument that abjectly failed to consider the socio-economic contexts of corruption:

The Kashi Bank, Benares, has 59 societies under liquidation and 110 other, of which 30 are not working. The trouble arose from the industrial societies of weavers, basket-makers, fruit-sellers, milkmen, etc., which were formed of unreliable material. The members did not understand the principles or responsibilities of co-operation, and were both poor and dishonest. Some got into arrears beyond their means, and others after disposing of their goods disappeared. Loans were advanced without regard to personal means or security, and in some cases the sarpanch took an unfair share. In such societies constant supervision is even more essential than in agricultural societies, but it was lax and inadequate. Liquidation proceedings are still dragging on.[99]

Particularly striking is the correlation of poverty and dishonesty, considering that cooperation was propagated as an instrument for the poor and by the poor. The state demonstrated not only its exasperation with the failure of cooperation to evolve like the (idealized) blueprint of German or French cooperative movements, but also its unwillingness to link this to contextual parameters rather than ethnic and class-based moral lacunae. Notwithstanding the inability to move beyond superficial moral arguments, the depiction of the failure of cooperation in Banaras is drastic, and serves to explain why the movement failed to increase its membership significantly after the initial spurt, as cooperation relied on initially locking up parts of the meagre capital reserves that artisans and farmers could employ without providing a state-based capital outlay sufficient to overcome the high risks of institutional failure and protracted litigation.

The moral argument on cooperation, however, served an important function partially in attracting volunteers, but also in justifying its inabilities to ensure (the certainly daunting task of) poverty alleviation. Writing already in 1907, S. H. Fremantle, an Indian Civil Service officer, deplored the tendency to imagine cooperation as 'cheap money-lending' and argued that lowering credit costs to agriculturists was not an end in itself, but a means for 'better farming' (Fremantle 1907/1928, 2). The understanding of the difficulties in achieving a breakthrough in agrarian indebtedness through cooperation[100] continued to vie with the more widely held perceptions that cooperation constituted a panacea against money lending, as visible in Wolff's propagation of cooperation as the only way of overcoming the moneylenders' 'ruinous interest rate[s]' that had led India to fall 'a thousand years behind the times' (Wolff 1919, 9; see also Wolff 1902).

The *UPBECR*, while frequently referencing doubts on the viability of the cooperative movement, tended to follow the latter argument, underlining an aversion to engage with a debate on economic rather than juridical-procedural intervention beyond cooperation. The committee failed to make sense of both 'corruption' and the perceived permissibility of default as it failed to take into account the reputational dimensions of debt. For debtors used to reputational dynamics in renegotiating credit obligations, these constituted the key elements of creditor–debtor relationships, and substituting one lender for another did not change the understanding of credit as intrinsically related to reputation.

While a number of witnesses such as (for Banaras) Thakur Ram Singh,[101] or for eastern United Provinces Buddhi Prakash Jain of Allahabad University[102] proposed measures that aimed to bring moneylenders into a regulated legal framework in which registered lenders supplemented cooperative lending for non-productive purposes, these measures were not taken up. The restriction of cooperative credit societies to lend only for productive purposes formed one of the important reasons for continued indebtedness to moneylenders even where cooperatives were functioning well, and for the transgression of cooperative societies' rules. Non-productive purposes for borrowing were widely considered necessary, similar in importance to borrowing for investment purposes – a fact that was highlighted frequently but that could not be addressed without changing the juridical-procedural paradigms of cooperation. A second reason for the continued indebtedness to moneylenders even in the presence of functioning cooperatives, in turn, was the prohibition of cooperative lending for redeeming old debts, highlighted in the Report on Economic Planning in the United Provinces of 1937.[103] This informed another strand of government activity on indebtedness in the 1930s – debt conciliation – that will be discussed later. The report, in turn, implicitly took up the concerns over rigidity in lending that had led Lane to issue warnings on *taccavi*, though this time related to the perceived failure of cooperative credit societies to fully integrate into village society, thereby becoming 'particularly harsh money lending devices'[104] – an indication of the lack of a common intelligibility between juridical-procedural and reputational ways of handling default.

The issue of older debts had been one persistent feature of deliberations on moneylenders, as for instance in the debates in 1895 and 1917 where the primary concern, however, had been imposing limitations on the filing of suits. With the gradual shift towards an increased perception of governmental responsibility, and the failure of cooperation for redress, the debate moved towards the means for debt relief. This relief was not so much envisioned anymore as an emergency measure in the face of public unrest – as after the Deccan Riots – though the urgency of public deliberation was certainly related to the effects of the Great Depression on agricultural livelihoods. Rather, it was informed by a desire to generate a 'clean slate' onto which the policies of financial propriety needed to be based to be effective. The lack of financial resources that the state was willing to employ, however, proved to be a continuing obstacle, so that the outcomes of debt relief and debt conciliation measures tended to be cosmetic.

The dangers of facile credit

Debt relief had been forcefully raised with the Royal Commission on Agriculture by Pundit Govind Ballabh Pant, a leading Congress politician in the United Provinces who became Chief Minister in 1937 and 1950. Pant's deposition demonstrated a strong commitment within the nationalist movement towards debt relief, though he faced hostility in the commission in 1926, based on his political leanings.[105] His subsequent record as chief minister was less straightforward: Visalakshi Menon (Menon 2003, 103–05) argued that there were allegations at the time that the Congress had traded support of moneylenders for the Tenancy Bill in exchange for a delay in bringing legislation related to money lending and debt relief. This delay was consequential as both the United Provinces Moneylenders Bill and the United Provinces Agriculturist and Workmen's Debt Redemption Bill were introduced and passed in mid-1939, but were still awaiting Legislative Council assent when the Congress-led provincial governments resigned, preventing their enactment. The relative caution in bringing in bills against money lending by the Congress government may have also been related to experience in the Punjab. Money lending legislation there had in general been more strident than in the United Provinces. Thus, legislation in the Punjab had already been stipulating registration of moneylenders, but had also led to a communalization of the debate with organizations like the Hindu Mahasabha and other right-wing Hindu groups seizing on perceived anti-Hindu elements in the Punjab Money Lenders Registration Bill to organize protests. The extent to which these groups had been able to mobilize notables and 'respectable' professionals to depict a money lending concern through the prism of communalist slander is apparent from their own collations of newspaper reports on the protests,[106] and the experience may have served as another restraint on the government in the communally charged United Provinces. Within the United Provinces, questions in the legislature sought to showcase a communal bias in money lending legislation and judgments.[107] Yet in 1926, Pant's deposition to the committee was forceful, not only in terms of the general desirability of debt relief but also in its link to the hoped-for successes of cooperation:

> I feel that the agriculturist cannot be saved and set on the road to redemption ... until he is relieved of the village money-lender. No bank can advance money to him on a reasonable rate of interest, nor can the system of co-operative credit be applied successfully so long as his debts are not cleared.... [T]he Government should liquidate the debt and recover it with interest at, say, 8 per cent ... in case of solvent agriculturists.... The cultivator, after he has been once redeemed ... should not be allowed to raise any further loan....[108]

While Pant argued that the government should not have any difficulty in raising a large public loan in Britain for debt redemption in India – which the commission doubted – it is particularly the last sentence quoted here that is instructive in the way debt relief measures were conceived, apart from the concern for the ease of borrowing by *solvent* farmers. As with other commentators, one of the main goals of money lending legislation was not so much to reduce the needs for borrowing, but the opportunities for the mass of the population to do so. The commission took a particular interest in this position in Pant's oral examination, though mostly from an imperial point of view:

> What I am surprised to find ... is this: you want legislation to restrict the credit of the cultivator here.... [Y]ou want the Government to take a bond from him restricting his credit. Belonging to the school of thought to which you do, do you think that ... binding the cultivator hand and foot and hypothecating his crops to Government is either desirable or feasible? ... This ... proposal would not make his position worse, but better?[109]

By the second half of the 1930s some of the hype over cooperation as a means to overcome money lending had worn off. The Reserve Bank of India (RBI) started to publish a bulletin by its Agricultural Credit Department that dealt in detail with its shortcomings. The second of these bulletins introduced the idea of cooperative village banks, seeking to improve cooperative credit markets for the middle farmers rather than the poorer social segments, assuming that it was in the former segment that improvements were viable. It would be simplistic to downplay these intentions as yet another instance of concentrating state assistance at the level of the slightly better-off, however, as rapid poverty alleviation remained unlikely in the absence of significant funding. The RBI made it clear that it supported the general direction of policies, though it was not convinced of their efficacy.

> There is a clamour for the magic wand to produce instantaneous results. Schemes are demanded which will alter the whole situation in the twinkling of an eye.... Such immediate measures of relief as the scaling down of debts, grants of easy instalments, reduction in the rates of interest, curbing the 'rapacity' of the moneylender by regulating his business ... must certainly be adopted. The fact however that these can only be temporary palliatives is in danger of being lost sight of. It cannot be too often repeated that there is no short cut to the solution of the rural problem.[110]

After expressing that moneylenders had benefited from the imposition of the British Indian legal system, but also linking indebtedness to the gradual shift from subsistence farming,[111] the department proceeded to outline the familiar list of cooperative shortcomings, but linked it to reducing credit opportunities for (poorer) farmers as the most important step in addressing indebtedness. It argued that it was not so much 'the dearness of credit'[112] that was to blame for indebtedness, but a more holistic amalgamation of contextual parameters (linked to various social evils including caste and religion). As cooperation had become associated with 'cheap money lending', the village cooperative bank was to be the institution to undertake socio-economic change holistically.[113] The shift from cooperative credit societies to village banks indicated not only a growing emphasis for the concerns of the better-off but, crucially, the alignment of the notion of cooperation with the idea of decreasing credit availability to those not considered creditworthy or, specifically, 'bankable'.

> Hence it is a grave error to suppose that ... indebtedness can be solved by the mere substitution of a new distributing agency; to replace the moneylender by banks is not to replace indebtedness by solvency; on the contrary ... the load of debt may easily be increased by the facility and easy terms of borrowing.... Hence in facile credit lies the danger of an increased mass of burdensome, unproductive indebtedness. It is a mere dream to suppose that the peasant's difficulty will be solved as soon as cheap credit is introduced through banks; it is not removable by mere cheap credit or facile credit, but by the promotion, almost enforcement of thrift, providence and heedfulness in borrowing. There should be alleviation of the terms, but *limitation of the habit of borrowing*.[114]

The emphasized passages demonstrate that the framing of monetary markets had by the late 1930s shifted from the propagation of liberal values in business conduct. Credit market policies were to condense the market. It embodied a change in policy in which credit facilitation and credit market expansion were concentrated on those who were capable of obtaining credit on terms set by the state. While the assumption of a positive impact on agricultural production is plausible, and that a solution to indebtedness among poorer segments needed a different approach than cooperation could still be considered reasonable, it also delineated an enclave for which the extension of credit was considered untenable as long as considerable advances in development were absent. The restriction of formal credit facilities to the better-off hardly formed a step towards changing this. The RBI must have been aware that the restriction of 'facile credit' to the poor would increase their reliance on informal credit agencies, and that the 'enforcement of thrift' remained unviable in the presence of systemic requirements for borrowing. The aims of the RBI, as stated in the bulletin, in promoting 'every one in the village' but 'concentrat[ing] on a few select areas'[115] remained contradictory in Indian village society.

The RBI initiative was rapidly taken up for discussion by the United Provinces government. These deliberations showed that indebtedness of tenants in the United Provinces in 1937 could be estimated at between 30 and 50 *crore* rupees of which roughly equal shares of around 40 per cent were owed to the landlords and moneylenders, another 14 per cent to other tenants, and the remainder to cooperative societies. Approximately 1.75 million tenants were considered heavily in debt.[116] Suggesting legislation on the lines of the Bengal Agricultural Debts Act of 1936 to facilitate rural insolvency as a measure of providing limited one-time relief, the note proceeded to argue for restrictions on credit by preventing agriculturists from 'borrowing in future more than a suitable multiple of the land revenue or rent', 'borrowing from more than one source', and preventing the transfer of land to moneylenders.[117] The setting up of an agricultural credit bank was to be accompanied by credit conciliation boards that should focus on tenants' rather than landlords' debts, implicitly accepting that debt relief measures up to this point had emphasized the latter.[118] Essentially, the government was suggesting to restrict the accessibility of formal credit to tenants in the future, though it was aware that the conditions that forced peasants to borrow from moneylenders remained unchanged. As with many other instances of debt legislation, this contradiction was discursively resolved by the optimistic assumption that these measures would 'virtually eliminate the village bania'.[119] In order to reinforce this assumption, the note suggested severe penalties to borrowers approaching moneylenders after having participated in debt conciliation but suggested extra-legal ways of settling landlords' debts that could not be handled through the Encumbered Estates Act.[120]

As the note proceeded to demonstrate the failures of earlier legislations to even attract significant interest among the tenants, the optimistic assumption on moneylenders appears particularly misplaced, yet it formed a crucial element of most deliberations on debt legislation that shows the futility of colonial debt policies for the less prosperous. With the improbability of an agricultural bank primarily targeting poorer debtors, the discussion of state intervention necessarily returned to measures aiming to restrict business opportunities for moneylenders which – in turn – were likely to restrict available credit to poorer borrowers further, in particular suggesting compulsory registration for moneylenders.[121] With the failure of the United Provinces Moneylenders Bill of 1939, though, these measures received a setback, and were only taken up again several decades later.

Debt relief measures in the United Provinces had received a renewed impetus in 1934 with the enactment of the United Provinces Regulation of Sales Act which standardized the method of calculating the value of land transferred as part of a mortgage in cases of default according to a complicated catalogue of regionally varying multiples of the pledged land's revenue value. Other legislative measures had included the amendment of the Usurious Loans Act to include maximum rates of interest of, respectively, 12 and 24 per cent per annum for secured and unsecured loans, the inclusion of the rule of *damdupat* into the Encumbered Estates Act, and the Agriculturists Relief Act of 1934 that imposed a threshold of 6 per cent per annum interest on moneylenders attempting to recover outstanding loans, after litigation.[122] Especially the latter, as argued by Jwala P. Srivastava, had been proven futile, as creditors evaded it by documenting fictitious principals.[123]

Subsequent debates in the Ministry of Finance showed that debt legislation and notably the Agriculturists Relief Act had been failures – another 'dead letter'.[124] These discussions also provided additional insights into the failure of cooperative societies to affect the position of rural moneylenders in the late 1930s, pointing out that they had considerably scaled down deposits and working capital, concentrating their activities on good debts. They were also showing a relatively strong discrepancy in borrowing and lending rates, accepting deposits at 4 per cent per annum but lending at significantly higher between 12 and 15 per cent. In addition, they continued to fail in loan recovery, attributed to an unwillingness to enforce loans of their own members.[125] The continuity in money lending operations was attributed to borrowers' preferences for moneylenders based on their relatively strong association with lenience.[126] The debate cleared the way for the foundation of an agricultural credit bank to be run 'on strictly commercial lines' and with 'no connexion with the co-operative movement'.[127]

The *taccavi* system of loans, debt conciliation, and the attempts to strengthen the cooperative sector and develop agricultural banking in late colonial India were principally intended to shift the credit markets catering to rural middle classes towards capitalist finance, attempting to cut out the moneylenders similar to Washbrook's argument on the (attempted) elimination of middlemen. In the face of administrative, budgetary, and market realities, however, these efforts never achieved more than cosmetic changes. Their existence allowed the late colonial state the fancy of entering into a dreamy discourse on credit markets, projecting a narrative based on a distant future (in which the ugly realities of credit markets had been overcome) as arguments on the shaping of Indian finance in the present. When directly confronted with the requirements for effecting incremental changes, this narrative quickly collapsed. Lane's warnings on the futility of the system of *taccavi* in even addressing the concerns about money lending need to be read as the resigned statements of a bureaucrat aware that he was merely administering misery. Similarly, Pant's deposition before the Royal Commission on Agriculture – while optimistic – was naïvely based on the willingness of British capital to move into petty agricultural production in India.

This dreamy discourse was not easily shed, even where its shape was pointed out: the RBI policy brief in 1937 may have criticised the desire for a 'magic wand', yet it still maintained that its policy to focus on credit schemes for purposes documentable as productive was commensurate with a strategy of equal treatment within rural society. Where it mattered, however, policy turned towards a contraction of credit markets serving the needs of the mass of the population as the only viable solution within the juridical-procedural parameters of the discourse on containing indebtedness. In the schemes targeting the poor and the petty bourgeoisie, this took the form of restricting the purposes of lending and their contingency on restricting the borrower's future credit to formal sources – an impossible combination considering the limited capital available and the structural needs of borrowing for unprofitable purposes. As involuntarily demonstrated by the RBI, these schemes attempted to contain the *habit* of borrowing rather than the needs for it, and they comprised steps against the 'danger of facile credit' rather than facilitating credit. Money lending legislation in many ways mirrors these attempts. Removing the operation of contractual law provided an incentive to shift business operations towards the extra-legal, creating a case where the state's attempt to impose juridical-procedural formality resulted in its complicity in shaping credit markets operating beyond its own reach, setting aside an economic enclave for continued rampant exploitation. At the same time, these policies tended to make credit significantly more expensive in the long run. Perceiving the threat of cooperative credit societies turning into 'cheap money lending' – certainly not an ideal state but still a significant improvement – the late colonial state set out to curtail the only (partially) viable credit alternative it had designed to target societal needs for credit.

Imperial structures in South Asia have long shaped commerce and finance to their respective needs, and have partially been influenced by them in return. Controversially, this argument was made by Karen Leonard in her work on the 'great firm' in Mughal India, though the controversy was restricted to the role of large businesses in the decline of the Mughal empire (Leonard 1979).[128] Closer in time, Bagchi has shown how colonial rule in mid-nineteenth-century India asserted an influence on the shaping of financial markets, affecting a shift from Indian to 'British Indian' capital within the domain of 'higher money' (Bagchi 1985).[129] Implicit in Bagchi's analysis is the large-scale neglect of petty credit markets, corresponding to the colonial state's attention to the relationship between big capital and government. The governance of petty debt transactions remained at the margins of colonial policy until the results of this negligence appeared to threaten law and order.

While the response to the Deccan Riots formed a significant rupture with regard to government credit policies, the subsequent development of colonial policies soon returned to the pattern depicted by Bagchi. Its main emphasis was on the creation of the conditions for a new equilibrium between big finance and the state. The colonial perception of the Deccan Riots as a rupture prevented a return to the negligence masquerading as *laissez-faire* of the mid-nineteenth century, but the lessons of the Deccan Riots, arguably, were to restrict the visibility of the complicit state, at best by implementing mitigating policies, but primarily by detaching the nexus between big finance and the state from the exploitation through petty finance. Most alleviating measures remained cosmetic in character. The panacea of cooperative credit was capable of addressing some problems, but eventually only shifted the boundaries of exploitation, creating opportunities for somewhat more affluent social strata, but seeking to contain the mass of petty debt rather than creating conditions in which credit to the poor might have worked.

For northern India, the transition from Indian to British Indian capital was far less pronounced than in the cases of Bengal and Bombay that informed Bagchi's analysis. With some notable exceptions, especially the mostly European-origin capital involved in Kanpur that was represented through the Upper India Chamber of Commerce, finance capital in United Provinces firmly remained 'Indian', and rarely relied on the 'British Indian' apex of the credit system.[130] Links between 'indigenous' banking and the Imperial Bank existed, but were far from the norm. Demonstrating the relative decline of Banaras, local 'organized' banks in the mid-twentieth century needed to compete with an influx of (Indian) banks from more important commercial centres of India. The two most prominent 'local' banks eventually failed in this competition, with the Bank of Benares liquidated in 1940, and the State Bank of Banaras (SBB) (by this time an ailing nationalized bank) merging with the Bank of Baroda in the early 2000s (Tiwari 2014). Yet their main competitors well into the post-colonial period remained 'indigenous' bankers and *sarrafs*. The nexus between 'higher money' and the (imperial) state combined with the relative neglect of petty debt remained unchanged, though the direction of the transition in big finance changed in accordance with the changing needs of the Indian state.

The effects of late colonial credit policies dissected financial markets into two spheres, operating on juridical-procedural and reputational parameters. While contact between the two spheres existed, the operational modes of finance and the target clienteles of both spheres sharply diverged. The negative effects of these policies were predominantly born by the poorer social strata who continued to rely on and cope with extra-legal operational modes. The immediate fallout of the project defining the 'proper swindle' in Indian finance, especially in Banaras, was born by an elite segment of society, the 'indigenous' bankers.

The decline of 'indigenous' banking and the struggles of 'organized' finance

The decline of 'indigenous' banking in Banaras was sharper than elsewhere. A number of studies have dealt with the remarkable resilience of banking communities in other parts of India. Rudner's work – discussed in Chapter 5 – has demonstrated the resilience of Nattukottai Chettiar bankers. Timberg and Aiyar (1980) have shown the continued relevance of 'indigenous' bankers even in the late 1970s. At the same time, the data published in the latter work shows a marked tendency of concentration, with Shikarpuri/Multani, Nattukottai Chettiar, and Gujarati bankers significantly more successful in comparison with 'Rastogi' bankers, a category of 'indigenous' bankers in the central north Indian plains. While the categories employed by them do not facilitate clear comparisons in terms of business success – relying on classifications of associational membership or distinctions between 'pure' bankers and other financial entrepreneurs for other communities, without giving these details for Rastogis – the relative decline of the latter is visible in their numbers: discussing the late 1970s, Nattukottai Chettiar bankers number 2,500 (and 40,000 pawnbrokers), Gujarati 'pure' bankers are shown to number 1,500 (plus 3,500 'bankers and commission agents'), while the numbers for Shikarpuri and Multani bankers are given as 550 members of local associations, 650 non-members, and an additional 550 'brokers'. In contrast, the 'Rastogi' segment of 'indigenous' banking is depicted as numbering 500 bankers without further subdivisions. In terms of credit outlays, however, the 'Rastogi' segment with an outlay of 100 crore rupees still managed to remain in a similar bracket as its Shikarpuri counterpart, significantly lower than Gujarati or Nattukottai Chettiar bankers (Timberg and Aiyar 1980, 280). The depiction of credit outlays, however, demonstrates that Timberg and Aiyar, similarly to Rudner, were looking primarily at the segments of financial entrepreneurs depicted in colonial sources as *sarrafs* rather than at the great banking families at the apex of 'indigenous' finance. The distinction between the two groups in colonial sources is often opaque, and the work of Timberg and Aiyar follows the definitions of the *Banking Commission Report* of 1972 that placed its emphasis on the practice of taking deposits, so that these numbers may be partially misleading, given the propensity of banking families to avoid regular deposit taking.

The extent to which the crisis of indigenous banking in Banaras was related to competition from 'organized' banks should not be overestimated. The *UPBECR*, while noting that 'indigenous' bankers were under pressure, makes it clear that this depiction was based rather on an expectation of future developments than on actual data, and that 'indigenous' banking was still flourishing. This is in line with the remembrances of Banarsi bankers and their descendants that depict the 1920s as the last period of 'greatness'. Rather, the decline of 'indigenous' banking in the city needs to be seen in the context of the general decline of Banaras as a commercial centre, related to shifts in trading patterns, the relative eclipse of Calcutta as the economic centre of India (Markovits 2008), and the eclipse of Banaras by other north Indian commercial and industrial cities. The relative unimportance of Banaras as a regional commercial centre in late colonial India can be shown by the membership lists of the respective Chambers of Commerce which are almost exclusively dominated by Kanpur-based businesses.[131] In turn, indigenous banking in the city suffered from a series of economic shocks. The agricultural crisis of the 1930s severely depressed credit markets in general, and 'indigenous' bankers did not manage to avoid its fallout. In post-colonial India, the link between banking and land was exposed by the agricultural reforms that included rural land ceilings, directly affecting the landed 'banking aristocracy' of Banaras, and indirectly affecting the creditworthiness of their clients. The nationalization of Indian banks in 1969 strongly affected the value of capital invested in 'organized' banking, in many ways compromising the original direction of late colonial policies that sought to provide incentives for 'indigenous' bankers in investing their capital in 'proper' banking businesses. Finally, the Urban Land (Ceiling and Registration) Act of 1976 affected investments in urban real estate.

In between these 'shocks' to their businesses lay the main thrust of late colonial and early post-colonial expansion of 'organized' banking. Competition from 'organized' banks had existed since the mid-nineteenth century, though at low levels. Drawing on capital from the major banking families of the city, the first major 'organized' competitor to indigenous banking was founded in 1904 as the Bank of Benares.[132] The bank was occasionally depicted as 'Benares Bank' as well, but was unrelated to an earlier firm of that name (1845–49) which had been depicted George Findlay Shirras as 'another striking example of unsound banking' (Shirras 1920, 353) aiming to invite 'dupes to come in and bring occasionally something in the shape of hard cash with them' (Shirras 1920, 354). By the early twentieth century, the notoriety of banks for scandalous business practices had receded, though the respectability of joint stock banks was far from established (see Chapter 5).

The Bank of Benares opened several branches over the next decades. In his deposition before the UPBEC, its Manager, Mohanlal Bulchand, depicted the bank as one the three large joint stock banks operating in the province.[133] The bank proceeded to grow in its equity and operations until the mid-1930s. In 1936, Bulchand was suddenly replaced as the bank's manager, indicating underlying problems. The bank entered bankruptcy proceedings in 1939, and was liquidated in 1940.

The bank's indirect successor – as a local 'organized' bank operating largely with capital provided by the city's financial elite – was founded in 1946 as the SBB, comprising the *maharaja* of the state of Banaras as director, and figurehead. SBB, in turn, needs to be distinguished from an earlier bank of the same name that operated as the 'central bank' of the princely state of Banaras, a small quasi-dependent state under the residency of Gwalior that had been 'modernized' in the late colonial period by the Resident's agents.[134] As in the case of the Bank of Benares, the SBB expanded significantly, opening several branches across Uttar Pradesh in the 1950s and 1960s, but never became consistently profitable. After banking nationalization, it turned into a sick public sector unit that was eventually merged with the Bank of Baroda in the early 2000s as part of reorganization efforts in the public banking sector (Tiwari 2014).

Both the Bank of Benares and especially the SBB faced competition by 'organized' banks from beyond the United Provinces, markedly limited for the Bank of Benares, as the earliest significant examples of other banking firms opening branches in Banaras are from the early 1930s. While this kind of competition may have hastened the decline of the bank, it is likely that the bank's business practices in themselves were not sufficiently profitable.

Bulchand's depiction of the bank's business practices to the UPBEC clarified that its practices were hardly differing from 'indigenous' banking, apart from the propensity to take deposits, and that it targeted a remarkably similar clientele.[135] His forceful advocacy of distinguishing between the two types of banking almost exclusively based on the frequency of deposit taking made it almost verbatim into the committee's report.

To highlight the frequency of taking deposits as the defining characteristic of 'organized' banking constituted a necessity for the late colonial state, as the differences in practice between 'organized' and 'indigenous' banking were far less pronounced than the use of different nomenclatures suggested. While 'indigenous' bankers and sarrafs were not entirely averse to taking deposits, their legal but also moral constitution remained firmly anchored in the status of full personal liability, making it risky to operate with borrowed money. The main difference between the two strands of banking rested on the juridical form of limited liability, highlighted by Ritu Birla (2009, 39–43) in the definition of the 'proper swindle', and in procedural stipulations that were often followed rather loosely. The crisis of the Bank of Benares, and the difficulties faced by SBB, need to be interpreted along the same lines as the crisis of 'indigenous' banking in the city – as a failure to handle repeated economic crises.

The lack of supportive measures for 'indigenous' banking is striking, especially when compared to 'organized' banks that in practice differed only marginally. In the late 1930s, the RBI half-heartedly attempted to implement one remedy in creating an integrated bill market that would have served the needs of 'indigenous' and 'organized' bankers alike in dealing with hundis.[136] The failure of these efforts was attributed by a large consensus among economists at the time to an assumed unwillingness of 'indigenous' bankers to 'go with the times', or to give up their supposed habits of opacity and secrecy. This consensus was subsequently questioned first by the Shroff Committee Report (see Chapter 7) and more evocatively, by the Study Group on Indigenous Banking in 1971 which argued that it had been the insistence of the RBI on the 'pristine purity of banking concepts [that had] led to the breaking off of the attempts',[137] leading to the discontinuation of all further efforts to provide a supportive structure for 'indigenous' banking.

The characterization of the failure to develop an integrated bill market as an ideological project demonstrates the endeavour to define the 'proper swindle'. RBI policy was informed by hoped-for results of future developments rather than actual practice. The unwillingness to engage with 'indigenous' bankers also facilitated the contraction of credit available beyond the emerging 'formal' credit sector, and thus re-affirmed the containment of debt beyond the reach of the state. While the RBI may have been justified in perceiving other dangers in being involved in the businesses of 'indigenous' banking, a significant part of its decision-making was based on notions of juridical-procedural propriety, informed by an assertion of the superiority of 'modern' banking methods which had not yet fully evolved.

While the Bank of Benares was issuing credit to 'people of rank and status' (see Chapter 5), the provision of credit was not most important business practice. Print media advertisements of the bank consistently highlighted other business aspects, as discussed later. Where the bank was advertising its services, these related invariably to deposits (an indication of its needs for fresh capital), or services on which the bank could finance its operations through commission fees, especially money transfers. A very similar picture emerges when studying the advertising patterns of other banks operating in the city.

The assumed superiority of 'organized' banking lay in the anticipation of reduced rates for credit which – going by these observations – did not constitute the main business of 'organized' banks in Banaras. In any case, 'indigenous' banking rates for 'respectable' customers were highly competitive with the rates offered by banks in late colonial India. More generally, the depiction of favourable lending rates by 'organized' banks compared to rates used by informal lenders was skewed by the different target clienteles and the risks in the recovery of dues. The discursive equation of extra-legal lending with exploitation obscured the elitist character of 'organized' banks. In legislative efforts, this discourse served to facilitate laws that for all practical purposes enforced extra-legality in lending to the less than very affluent. A particularly striking example was the Punjab Debt Relief Act of 1938,[138] which stipulated a link between the legal interest rate by registered moneylenders and the bank rate in which the money lending rates were capped at 2 percentage points above the bank rate, that is, the rate at which banks were able to borrow money from the RBI. Stipulations like these simply disregarded the realities of debt recovery from borrowers less privileged than banks dealing with the RBI.

It does not need remorse for the demise of an elite social stratum like 'indigenous' banking to consider the ramifications of these developments for less affluent borrowers. 'Indigenous' bankers and *sarraf*s had served an important role on financial markets, in facilitating top-down capital flows but also as role models for mercantile behaviour that lenders at the lower ends of the market needed to emulate to gain respectability. In both ways, 'indigenous' bankers in Banaras had served as a governing apex of financial markets, in addition to playing important roles in arbitrating disputes in the 'bazaar'.

The weakening of this governing apex facilitated the demise of the 'traditional' system of Indian finance, though the inability of 'organized' banking to handle the large mass of petty transactions at the base of this system provided the room for the emergence of new extra-legal systems of handling debt, including the entrance of new sets of lenders. The stigma associated with extra-legal lending meant that new lenders were less likely to have been concerned over social status, and more likely attempting to maximize profits even if this compromised their social status. The 'hated' or 'detested' Kabulis and *qistwallah*s – to use the language employed by the Upper India Chamber of Commerce – were less likely to be affected by these developments than lenders to social strata that had been served by less exploitative lenders earlier. Lastly, the withdrawal of the contractual guarantee by the state benefited precisely those lenders who had not relied on the legal apparatus. The decline of 'indigenous' bankers in combination with the entry of new lenders who necessarily were relatively unconcerned with a 'traditional' mercantile ethics undermined the reputational sanctions that had historically been available against breaches of 'respectable' conduct through strong social ties (Granovetter 2011b).

In the 1950s, the All-India Rural Credit Survey (see Chapter 7) stated that 'the private moneylender shows no signs of disappearing'.[139] However, it did not go into the question of whether the composition of moneylenders had changed over time, and chose to present results only in terms of broad categories such as 'moneylenders'. Interest charged by these moneylenders was depicted as unfettered by 'much restraint on themselves'.[140] The Rural Credit Survey provides some information on the changes in the composition of lenders, though based on a sample of responding moneylenders that was considered insufficient.[141] For eastern Uttar Pradesh, the number of moneylenders reporting to have been engaged in this business for less than five years was nil, while five (of a total of eighteen) moneylenders reported to have been in business between five and ten years. For western Uttar Pradesh, out of a total of forty-four respondents, seven had been in business for less than five years, and seventeen for a period of five—ten years, showing a significantly higher fluctuation.[142] It needs to be noted that new moneylenders would have been more difficult to identify, and that the survey is based on the assumedly more stable population of village moneylenders rather than urban moneylenders targeting the poor where significantly greater rates of fluctuation can be assumed. At the same time, the survey report placed an emphasis on the importance of agriculturist moneylenders in lending to small-scale cultivators, especially in the districts of eastern Uttar Pradesh that were covered in the survey (Mirzapur, Ballia, and Jaunpur), with total borrowings by cultivators from this class of lenders in these districts falling in the range of 33 to 49 per cent.[143] Assumedly, the change in the composition of this class of lenders would have taken place in line with the upward mobility of specific sections of rural society since the 1950s and 1960s. In contrast, the *Shroff Committee Report* of 1954 deplored the manner in which the net effects of money lending legislation had been to restrict credit available to the private sector, while also leading to a decline in the numbers and proportions of 'professional' moneylenders.[144] Being primarily concerned with lending for industrial purposes, the statements by the Shroff Committee indicate that the changes in the composition of lenders and the restriction of available credit were more pronounced in urban than in rural India, and led to an increasingly 'amateurish' character of lending. Nevertheless, it is important to note that these changes happened only gradually, and their extent was not yet highly visible in the early decades after independence.

Conclusion

The last decades of colonial rule marked a watershed in the development of financial markets, though one that was characterized by gradual changes rather than clear-cut ruptures as in the case of the juridical-procedural parameters of lending. While the latter created the conditions for the removal of contractual law from the operation of money lending practices, it was in the subsequent decades that the ramifications of this shift developed. Within the realm of extra-legal financial practices, these ramifications extended to the development of interest rates and other transactional obligations, the increasing 'amateurization' of lenders, the demise of the governing apex of 'traditional' finance, and the incipient arrival of new entrants into an economic segment that had been shaped by community relations and mercantile ethics. The most visible change in terms of transactional obligations was the disappearance of legally enforceable penalties which had been one of the main concerns for colonial officials in the early decades of the twentieth century, demonstrating the relevance of the removal of contractual law. Official sources in the middle of the twentieth century rapidly began to show a lack of concern over these, instead shifting their emphasis to the question of interest rates. With the increasing tendency of lenders to rely on extra-legal enforcement, the importance attributed to the acquisition of the collateral through legal means disappeared. In line with the arguments made in the policy debates of the early twentieth century, the shift towards extra-legality demonstrated that colonial policy was highly effective where it mattered most, that is, in removing visible complicity of the colonial state from the governance of an exploitative regime, even if this did not impact the level of exploitation. Indirectly, colonial policy may have facilitated mitigating tendencies concerning a related topic, the incidence of compound interest. Both penalties and compound interest were strongly linked to the value attributed to the collateral. In the rural United Provinces – the main preoccupation of colonial legislation in line with a generally conservative attitude that centred on the prevention of rapid change in the socio-economic fabric of the countryside – compound interest remained a prominent feature of lending, but the rates of compound interest continued to decline slowly, with the *sawai* rate increasingly becoming the norm. To depict the Usurious Loans Act and subsequent money lending legislation as a 'dead letter' is misleading in these circumstances: legislation affected money lending at the higher ends, and in cases where 'modern' financial agents such as cooperatives and banks were competitive as the existence of highly valued securities facilitated the market entry of procedurally 'proper' lenders. In contrast, lending for consumption purposes, and especially towards the poorer end of the spectrum of debtors, eventually became marked by significantly higher rates of (simple) interest, as will be shown in Chapter 8.

Changes in the social composition of lenders were equally gradual. With the gradual demise of its governing apex, the 'traditional' system of finance lost its linkages with other patterns of social organization and hierarchy. The elaborate system of mercantile ethics depicted by Bayly as *sakh* increasingly ceased to be of relevance. The discourse on development emphasized the industrial rather than mercantile employment of capital, creating an added incentive for 'indigenous' bankers and *sarraf*s to seek new business avenues, even though the relatively stagnant industrial economy of a place like Banaras provided little opportunity for this.

The incipient adjustment of reputational dimensions of credit – the shift from *sakh* to *vishvaas*, or from reputational dynamics relying on the enforcement of obligations through elaborate mercantile ethics embedded into strong social ties towards a reliance on the reputational communication of trust – will be discussed in the following chapters. These need to be understood in correlation with the gradual transformation that occurred in the last decades of colonial rule. The large amount of effort involved in extra-legal lending at petty levels prevented more affluent lenders from falling back on these types of business, even if social prejudice against association with the poor would have allowed this shift in behaviour. The increasing domination of lending by 'amateurs' reinforced the removal of 'traditional' regimes of arbitration and social sanction against transgressions of morally acceptable behaviour. While it can be argued that the poorest debtors had benefited little from these in the first place, the gradual disappearance of lending based on the enforcement of obligations through strong social ties weakened the handling of default through reputational means, in turn increasing creditors' risk perceptions. The weakening of strong social ties employed for handling default eventually undermined the only relevant collective dynamic in negotiating the reputational credit contract. Where community structures had played a relatively direct role in 'traditional' finance such as in systems of lending resembling *jajmani* arrangements, these were gradually disappearing.[145] Yet even in the absence of close alignments between community and credit patterns strong social ties had provided some level of protection against further increases in exploitation, and their disruption threatened to remove this element of a debtor's bargaining power, not only their employment by creditors for minimizing default.

While the emerging structure of 'informal' rather than 'traditional' finance underwent incremental but significant changes, the scale of lending remained relatively unaffected. There is little evidence that colonial policies on banking and cooperation led to changes in the needs for credit, and the financial agents preferred by the late colonial state were by and large incapable of supplanting moneylenders. The demise of high-end 'traditional' lending contracted the availability of credit for productive purposes more than for consumption or subsistence. At the lower end of the market, cooperation failed to bring about significant changes in the scale of 'informal' lending, partially due to the fact that it inherently rested on restricting access to credit to certifiably productive purposes. Debt relief measures reinforced this tendency.

In the face of this dilemma, the Indian state began to shift the direction of its 'modernizing' efforts at least after the mid-1930s. It turned to a policy of making indebtedness manageable through its containment, highlighting the dangers of facile credit instead of facilitating credit. The purposes of its policies were increasingly redefined, shifting away from the overly optimistic assessments of the potentials of 'modern' finance that would remove the 'stranglehold' of the moneylender once it had been given an initial push. The promise of credit to the poor – unlocking the 'centuries-old' closet that prevented the unfolding of the entrepreneurial spirits of India's agricultural and artisanal strata through the exploitative moneylender as in the depiction by Wolff – gave way to the dangers of the former's indebtedness. 'Proper' (and relatively cheap) credit needed to be the preserve of those who could demonstrate its 'proper' usage, almost inevitably the affluent. The originally political rather than socio-economic imperative of money lending legislation – of avoiding visible complicity in exploitation rather than seeking to reduce exploitation – reinforced a policy of devising a new financial structure for the better-off, even if this worsened the credit conditions for the remainder of Indian society, an even ghastlier mess for the mass of the Indian population than the one faced by the colonial state at the outset of its legislative efforts.

Notes

1. Lyrics from the song 'A British Bank' in the film *Mary Poppins* (Walt Disney Studios, 1964).
2. It is interesting to contrast this production of impropriety with the differentiation between the legal – indicating what the state considers legitimate – and the licit signifying what people consider legitimate (van Schendel and Abraham 2005). What the Indian state produced by delineating business impropriety was an arena that was considered illegitimate by the state but was nevertheless ignored in its continued operation.
3. The expression 'a tangled jungle of disorderly transactions' is used by *the United Provinces Banking Enquiry Committee Report* (*UPBECR*) to describe the kaleidoscope of financial practices and monetary markets that made up 'indigenous' finance. The *UPBECR* attributes the expression to the earlier Lt Governor, Alfred Comyn Lyall.
4. Royal Commission on Agriculture in India, *Abridged Report* (Bombay: The Government Central Press, 1928), 49.
5. *UPBECR* III, 400–02.
6. Sir Cecil Walsh, 'Peasant and Moneylender in India. A Judge's Experience', *Morning Post* (London), 18 November 1929, in file no. L/PJ/6/1993, India Office Records, British Library.
7. Letter to Dr. Shiels, Colonial Office, by Sir Cecil Walsh, in file no. L/PJ/6/1993, India Office Records, British Library.
8. Memorandum by Sir E. Chamier, 2 December 1929, in file no. L/PJ/6/1993, India Office Records, British Library.
9. *UPBECR* III, 398–99.
10. Ibid. III, 400–05.
11. Ibid. III, 436.
12. Ibid. I, 216.
13. Ibid. I, 209.
14. Ibid. III, 404.
15. Ibid., original emphases; the denominations are given for annual interest except for the expression 'six *pies* per rupee' which designates a monthly interest rate of 3.125 per cent, and 'two annas per rupee', designating a rate of 12.5 per cent per month.

16. Ibid. III, 404–05.

17. Ibid. III, 408.

18. Ibid. III, 410.

19. In order to visualize the differences between interest rates and their prevalent depictions especially concerning compound interest and the frequency of rests, it is instructive to refer to a paper by Ramesh Bellamkonda (Bellamkonda 2007). In one (fictitious) example provided here, a loan of 100 rupees, with the principal repayable in one instalment at the end of one year and an interest rate depicted as 1 per cent compound interest with daily rests equals an annual simple interest rate of 3,678 per cent.

20. *UPBECR* III, 268–70.

21. As a *sarkhat* needed a lower stamp duty if it was registered, this would have been lower than *hundi* rates in many cases. Singh's assertion that the use of *hundi*s was declining needs to be seen in this light, as the *sarkhat*s would fall into the same category of financial instruments than a *hundi*, the main difference being the local character of its circulation and the lower fees in case of registration. Many *hundi*s, however, were not registered either.

22. Government of India, *Benares. A Gazetteer. Being Volume XXVI of the District Gazetteers of the United Provinces of Agra and Oudh*, 1909, 52–53.

23. *UPBECR* I, 75.

24. Ibid. I, 76.

25. Ibid.

26. Ibid. I, 77.

27. Ibid. I, 77–78.

28. Ibid. I, 80.

29. Ibid. II, 189.

30. For an example of a lender's current accounts with borrowers, see ibid. I, 48–49. See also ibid. I, 109–12.

31. Ibid. II, 146.

32. Ibid. II, 164.

33. Ibid. II, 179.

34. Lit.: instalment.

35. Colonial sources frequently depicted these as 'pice', to be distinguished from *pie*s. 1 rupee = 16 *anna*s = 64 *paise/pice* = 192 *pie*s.

36. *UPBECR* III, 400. Nominally, that is, calculated over the entire duration of the loan, this would come to an interest rate of 20 per cent per annum. However, if calculated in a way taking into account the repayment of the principal in instalments, the actual annual interest rate would be close to 45 per cent. For the sake of simplicity given the very different durations of loans quoted here, the approximations for annual or monthly interest rates

given below as representations of the various systems of *qist*s are calculated in the former way.

37. *UPBECR* I, 64.

38. The rates quoted here for Banaras are also consistent with the depositions of other witnesses to the UPBEC from the Banaras area, most notably the 'monograph on the *qist* business in the United Provinces' as part of the deposition by Lala Babu Lal Vaish, Income Tax Officer, Benares, who also added smaller loans of 4 rupees repaid in 6 monthly instalments of 1 rupee each, and of 1 rupee repaid in 72 daily instalments of 3 *pie*s (ibid. III, 297).

39. Ibid. IV, 45.

40. Ibid. III, 404.

41. Ibid. III, 405.

42. Ibid. III, 263.

43. Ibid. III, 298.

44. Ibid. III, 319.

45. Ibid. III, 270.

46. Ibid. III, 319.

47. As the report of the commission noted,

> [t]here are, however, many moneylenders who prey upon workers and depend on the threat of violence rather than the processes of the law. The *lathi* is the only court to which they appeal, and they may be seen waiting outside the factory gate on pay-day ready to pounce on their debtors as they emerge. (*Report of the Royal Commission on Labour in India, 1931*, 235, original emphasis)

For the recommendation on making 'besetting' and 'loitering' criminal and cognizable offences under the law, see ibid., 235–36.

48. *Report of the Bengal Provincial Banking Enquiry Committee, 1929–30*, Vol. I (Calcutta: Bengal Government Press, 1930), 172.

49. 'Correspondence with the local Government on 1: The proposal of the Royal Commission on labour in India that besetting an industrial establishment for the purpose of collecting debts should be made a criminal and cognizable offence, and 2: Mr. N. M. Joshi's Bill further to amend the Indian Penal Code of Criminal Procedure, 1898, introduced in the legislative assembly on 24th Mar. 1933', available online at Digital Repository of Gokhale Institute of Politics and Economics, http://dspace.gipe.ac.in/xmlui/handle/10973/25488 (last accessed 20 May 2020) (henceforth 'Correspondence on Besetting').

50. Ibid., 72.

51. Ibid., 9.

52. Ibid., 14.

53. Ibid., 57.
54. Ibid.
55. Ibid., 10.
56. Ibid., 12.
57. A. C. Chatterjee, *Notes on the Industries of the United Provinces* (Allahabad: Government Press, 1908), 35–36, 56–57.
58. *UPBECR* III, 394–95.
59. Ibid. II, 373.
60. Ibid. II, 372.
61. Ibid. II, 374.
62. Ibid. II, 372.
63. Ibid. II, 373.
64. Ibid. II, 373–74.
65. Ibid. II, 373.
66. Ibid. II, 372, original emphasis. The conflation of middlemen and *karkhandars* in the quotation is due to being part of a larger argument that both systems work in similar fashions.
67. Ibid. III, 377–78.
68. Ibid. II, 375–78.
69. Ibid. II, 379.
70. Ibid. II, 381, 383.
71. Ibid. II, 437.
72. Ibid. II, 376.
73. Ibid. II, 371.
74. Ibid. III, 374.
75. Ibid. III, 270.
76. Ibid. III, 93.
77. Ibid. III, 85.
78. Ibid. III, 398.
79. Ibid. III, 118.
80. Ibid. III, 298.
81. Ibid. III, 299.
82. Ibid. III, 295.
83. *Report of the Committee on Co-operation in India, 1915*, reprinted on behalf of the Government of India by the Reserve Bank of India, Bombay, 1957, 2.
84. Royal Commission on Agriculture in India, *Vol. VII: Evidence Taken in the United Provinces* (Calcutta: Government of India Central Publication Branch, 1927, 208) (henceforth referred to as *RCA* VII).
85. Ibid., 204.
86. Covered by the Usurious Loans (Amendment) Act of 1926.

87. *RCA* VII, 204–05.
88. Ibid., 206–08.
89. *Report of the Committee on Co-operation in India, 1915* (reprinted on behalf of the Government of India by the Reserve Bank of India, Bombay, 1957), 4–5.
90. *Report of the Co-operative Committee of the United Provinces of Agra and Oudh* (Allahabad: United Provinces Government Press, 1926), 3–4 (henceforth referred to as *CCUP*).
91. Ibid., 5.
92. Ibid., 3.
93. Ibid., 5–6.
94. Ibid., 9.
95. Ibid., 11.
96. Ibid., 10.
97. Ibid., 12.
98. See, for instance, Jeffrey (2002).
99. *CCUP*, 14–15.
100. Observing Gorakhpur in the 1930s, Shahid Amin has argued that the colonial state as well as later observers have failed to fully take into account the complexities of peasant life as well as the role of moneylenders in it (Amin 1981). For a consideration of the relationship between co-operation and rural stratification, see Breman (1978).
101. *UPBECR* III, 274.
102. Ibid. IV, 522.
103. *Report on Economic Planning in the United Provinces* (Allahabad: Superintendent, Printing and Stationery, United Provinces, 1937), 63.
104. Ibid., 66.
105. *RCA* VII, 365–66.
106. *A Brief Report on the Criticism on the Punjab Money Lenders Registration Bill and the Resolutions of Protests Passed against It, All over the Country, compiled by L. Salig Ram Bajaj, Honorary General Secretary, Punjab Moneylenders Association, Lahore, 20 April 1925* (Lahore: Arobans Press, 1925).
107. Home Department – Judicial, Question in the Legislative Assembly by Mr. C. N. Muthuranga Mudaliar regarding Kabulis or Pathan money-lenders, National Archives, Delhi, File No. 19/24/34 – Judl.
108. *RCA* VII, 349.
109. Ibid., 366.
110. Reserve Bank of India, Agricultural Credit Department, *Bulletin No. 2: Co-operative Village Banks* (Bombay, 1937), 2 (henceforth referred to as ACD 2).

111. Ibid., 4.
112. Ibid., 19.
113. Ibid., 20.
114. Ibid., 24, emphasis added.
115. Ibid., 29.
116. 'Note for Government on rural indebtedness by the Hon'ble Sir Jwala P. Srivastava, Minister of Finance and Industries, United Provinces', 1, in *Report of the Commission of Enquiry into the Communal Out Break at Cawnpore, 24th March 1931, with Government Resolution Thereon*, document pages 97–108, available online at http://dspace.gipe.ac.in/xmlui/handle/10973/22792 (last accessed 13 August 2021) (the note has been attached to this document, though it formed part of the United Provinces government gazettes of 1937; the note will be referred to henceforth as NRI 1937).
117. Ibid., 2.
118. Ibid.
119. Ibid., 3.
120. Ibid., 4–5.
121. Ibid., 10.
122. For an overview (and the full text) of these acts, see the document 'Bills and Acts on Debt Conciliation, Debt Legislation, and Agricultural Indebtedness', published by the government of the Central Provinces, available online at https://dspace.gipe.ac.in/xmlui/handle/10973/21334 (last accessed 13 August 2021) (the note lacks a title page or other reference details).
123. NRI 1937, 5.
124. 'Note on the discussions on the problem of agricultural indebtedness in the United Provinces held on May 24, 1937, at which the Hon'ble Minister of Finance, Mr. Rangaswamy, Managing Editor 'Indian Finance' and Messrs. Mudie, Kharegat, Waugh, Vishnu Sahai, Teyen, and the Finance Secretary were present', 1, in *Report of the Commission of Enquiry into the Communal Out Break at Cawnpore, 24 March 1931, with Government Resolution Thereon*, document pages 97–108, available online at http://dspace.gipe.ac.in/xmlui/handle/10973/22792 (last accessed 13 August 2021) (the note has been attached to this document, though it formed part of the United Provinces government gazettes of 1937; the note will be referred to henceforth as NPAI 1937).
125. Ibid., 1.
126. Ibid., 2.
127. Ibid., 3.
128. See also Richards (1981).

129. For the involvement of British entrepreneurs in Indian banks, see Leonard (2013).
130. Apart from the Upper India Chamber of Commerce, industry, banking, and commerce were represented from the mid-1930s onwards in the Legislative Assembly by the United Provinces Chamber of Commerce, an exclusively 'Indian' association, founded in 1914.
131. Private & Confidential Memorandum of the United Provinces Chamber of Commerce Submitted to the Chief Secretary to the U.P. Government on the Proposals of the Government for the Delimitation of Constituencies for the United Provinces Legislative Assembly. No. 10296, dated the 25th August 1935, 7–39, British Library, India Office Records IOR/IDC/41. On the opposition of the Merchants Chamber of Commerce to legislative efforts on money lending, see File 11 July 1939, Extract from 'Commerce', dated 10th June 1939, U.P. Money-lending Legislation. Merchants Chamber Opposed. British Library, India Office Records, IOR/LRO/4711.
132. On the history of European banks in India, see, for instance, Sinha (1927).
133. *UPBECR* IV, 100–02.
134. 'Copy of a Confidential Demi-Official Letter No. 101-P dated the 11th May 1940 from Lt. Colonel G. V. B. Gilliam, C. I. E., Resident at Gwalior and for the States of Rampur and Benares to C. G. Herbert, Esq., C. I. E., I. C. S., Secretary to His Excellency the Crown Representative', in *Reports of Political Officers after Their Visits to States within Their Political Charge*, 26 November 1941, P. O. No. 1597 – S/81-41, British Library, India Office Records IOR/L/PS/13/145-2.
135. *UPBECR* IV, 102.
136. For the Reserve Bank's self-depiction on these policies, see Simha (1970).
137. Government of India. Banking Commission, *Report on Indigenous Bankers* (Bombay, 1971), 92 (henceforth referred to as *Report on Indigenous Bankers*).
138. 'Move to Control Money Lending. Punjab Bill', *Times of India*, 23 June 1938.
139. *Report of the Committee of Direction, All India Rural Credit Survey, The Survey Report*, Vol. 1, Part 2 (*Credit Agencies*), 1955, 66 (henceforth referred to as *AIRCS*).
140. Ibid.
141. A detailed discussion of the problems with the sample of moneylenders is provided in *AIRCS*, 455 and 465–67.
142. Ibid., 468.
143. Ibid., 527–29.
144. *Report of the Committee on Finance for the Private Sector* (Bombay: Reserve Bank of India, 1954), 71 (henceforth referred to as *Shroff Committee Report*).
145. *UPBECR* I, 38. On *jajmani* rights, see Wiser (1936) and Fuller (1989).

Part II Debt in Banaras

5

Trust

The notion of 'banker's trust' has a paradoxical quality, like 'burning cold' or 'military intelligence.' Common sense (another paradoxical notion) tells us that bankers have no trust. Perhaps this explains the appeal of Marxist and Weberian assumptions that capitalist economies tend to destroy pre-capitalist social formations based on trust.[1]

The designation of financial markets as M–M' markets implicitly highlights the central role of trust in monetary transactions. Devoid of the commodity element in exchange of goods for money that accordingly expresses valuation differentials rather than assessments of uncertainty, financial markets engage in the transfer of money across time and space, extracting a commission for the necessary infrastructure, but especially for the uncertainty involved. Interest and collaterals, seen in this way, are functions of the level of trust employed. Regardless of its embeddedness in institutionalized or socio-cultural forms, assessment of uncertainty remains an individual process in that the party to a transaction needs to employ a variety of methods selected from the means available. Efforts to institutionalize the assessment of uncertainty as risk have taken a variety of forms, and typically several of these forms coexist, so that a historical analysis cannot describe successions of uncertainty assessing structures but merely point out prominently available methods and the gradual decline into obscurity of others. Yet, at all times, the individual needs to fall back on a variety of registers for handling uncertainty.

A significant part of the literature describing 'modernization' processes and the emergence of capitalist socio-economic orders deviates from this interpretation by describing a supersession of 'traditional' modes of assessing risks by 'scientific' or 'rational' ones, rather than changes in the patterns of coexisting registers. In accordance with the predominant strands of liberal thought at the time, the late colonial Indian state typically fell back on a 'disenchantment' or 'rationalization' trope when thinking in developmental terms, even though the literature on the 'ethnographic' colonial state provides ample evidence that its governing practices were informed by a much more pessimistic understanding of the unknowable qualities (for the British Indian administration) of the subjected population (see, for instance, Cohn 1996). The optimistic evaluation of the potentials of rationalization vied with more pessimistic perceptions of the possibilities of reform: optimism remained preeminent in guiding assumptions on the desirable outcomes, at the same time as the more pessimistic opinions framed responses that eventually marked the boundaries of where 'progress' was at all possible. 'Progress', understood as increasing rationalization through the imposition of procedural 'propriety', became increasingly restricted to financial markets that served the interests of the state as well as the very affluent. For the remainder of the population, the facilitation of credit needed to be replaced by the containment of debt. As the handling of uncertainty continued to lie at the centre of financial transactions, the 'procedural' properties of the definition of the 'proper swindle' as well as their socio-economic ramifications across the diverging financial markets significantly affected the methods of handling uncertainty and, correspondingly, of employing trust.

Trust (and mistrust) needs to be seen as the sub-category of handling uncertainty that identifies the unknowable qualities of interaction between humans. In the terminology employed by Paul Seabright (2010) it forms the practical solution to the existential necessity of living in the 'company of strangers'. According to Georg Simmel (1950, 318), trust constitutes an expectation of future behaviour that is sufficiently certain to provide guidelines for practical conduct.[2] The fallacy of extending the Weberian idea of the disenchantment of the world to the realm of practical conduct that employs notions of trust to deal with the unknowable qualities of strangers' behaviour is that in creating remoteness to what is trusted – the institutional network of 'modernity' anchored in a narrow definition of rational behaviour – the nature of trust itself changes to the extent that Simmel's definition of trust loses the vagueness of its interpretive framework and thereby appears increasingly superior: not anymore being an 'expectation' with 'sufficient certainty' informing practical conduct, but instead emerging as 'knowledge' of a rule-bound system that can be learned and handled 'scientifically'. Its practical fallout is a belief in the inherent superiority – rather than its beneficial applicability in different circumstances – of the particular type of trust described by Niklas Luhmann (Luhmann et al. 1979) as *Systemvertrauen* (system trust).

The fallacy of this understanding of the operation of trust on financial markets can be highlighted by using Seabright's depiction of the rootedness of the recent global financial crisis in one of three 'false lessons' of the Great Depression: that 'if only *confidence* in the financial system could be maintained, the system itself could be *trusted* to survive and prosper' (Seabright 2010, 117, second emphasis added). The seeming tautology of this 'false lesson' can be resolved through the depiction of the experiential basis of trust. But its applicability in complex systems of 'modern' financial markets, through a misunderstanding of this experiential nature needs to be seen as a direct fallout of what Appadurai has described as the 'deep affinity between legal and magical proceduralism' in modern capitalism (Appadurai 2015, 483). In a similar approach, Alberto Corsín Jiménez queries 'how knowledge, responsibility and social relationality have been organized as epistemologically distanced objects in contemporary capitalist regimes of audit and trust-making' (Corsín Jiménez 2011, 178) and discusses the similarities of technocratic, bureaucratic, and occult systems in their needs for the certification of knowledge as robust, in order for it to *be* robust and therefore trustworthy (Corsín Jiménez 2011, 185). Anthropological literature on trust in 'modern' capitalist regimes highlights instances of certification that differ from those of 'occult' systems of divination in the methods employed but not in its underlying inabilities to overcome the shortcomings of trust as the practical employment of human interpretation in dealing with the unknowable characteristics of social interaction. The certification of knowledge as robust, and therefore as an 'expectation' serviceable for providing guidelines for practical conduct in contexts marked by pervasive uncertainty, constitutes an effort in employing trust in situations in which immediate interpersonal knowledge is not readily forthcoming. It provides a short-cut in informing practical business conduct, but it does not alter the necessity of interpretation. It merely shifts the interpretation from the unknowable other transactional party to the similarly unknowable qualities of the certifying agency. Essentially, trust as interpreted in the misapplication of the Weberian discourse on ever-increasing rationalization rests on a semiotic misconception that confuses the remoteness of the certifying agency to the case in which practical conduct requires sufficient certainty with the substitution of interpretation that originally sets the boundaries to knowledge about future social interaction. In its handling of trust (and mistrust), the 'legal and magical proceduralism' of capitalism produces a pretence of sophistication and knowability that continually remains precarious as evidenced by financial 'panics' at times in which confidence in certification is undermined. The effort to overcome these limitations, at the same time, has not been restricted to 'modern' capitalist socio-economic practices but forms a consistent feature of mercantile traditions, even though it differs in the extent to which the replacement of social intimacy as a precondition for robust knowledge is sought by employing the remoteness of certifying agencies.

While 'modern' capitalism tends to emphasize this remoteness, this does not conversely translate into a necessity for alternative regimes of handling trust to be based on proximity. Matthew Carey argues that the 'holy trinity of proximity, familiarity, and trust' that is frequently assumed needs to be questioned as '[p]roximity and familiarity do not necessarily equate to knowability or certainty and cannot be used as a basis for generating expectations and predicting future behavior' (Carey 2017, 8). Instead, in creating a 'temporal collapse' by providing a bridge for expectations of the future into the present, 'trust amounts to confidence in one's expectations, and such expectations cannot arise ab nihilo, but must depend on a certain degree of familiarity with either people, the world, or systemic representations of the real' (Carey 2017, 6). Accordingly, trust and mistrust do not form binary categories but are constitutive of each other as they rest on the management of uncertainties in sequences of exchanges between the individual and its social environment (Carey 2017, 10). Trust, as depicted by Liisberg and Pedersen, instead needs to be distinguished from hope (rather than mistrust) in that its unspecifiable level of certainty bridges uncertainty between people over 'near and probable futures' (Liisberg 2015; Liisberg, Pedersen, and Dalsgard 2015).

Essentially, trust constitutes an element of social interaction that is experiential in its nature and in its handling correspondingly depends on individual life histories so that its precise manner of employment cannot be established a priori. Instead, it is imperative that these manners are perceived as sequences of exchange in which the responses by the object of trust – whether familiar or remote – continue to be interpreted, thus comprising an intricate web of decision-making parameters that continues to evolve. Trust, accordingly, resembles the operation of Mauss' concept of balanced reciprocity in gift-giving. It is the experience of the sequential character of exchanging that serves to establish trust. The seeming tautology in Seabright's depiction – that confidence in the system needed to be maintained for the system to be trusted – thus serves to underline that the magical proceduralism of capitalism depicted by Appadurai (2016) does not affect the basic parameters of the operation of trust in fundamentally different ways than any other regime of handling trust.

The handling of trust on financial markets employs a variety of methods that should be described as registers of trust, depending on the primary patterns in which the experiential sequences that define trust unfold. Turning back to the study of financial practices in northern India, it needs to be stressed that market participants were able to utilize a variety of these registers simultaneously. As stated earlier, it is impossible to delineate clear patterns of transformation defined as shifts in the use of one or several registers of trust. Rather, a history of trust on Indian financial markets needs to outline gradual shifts in prominence in the uses of coexisting registers for specific purposes. For analytical purposes, it is much more promising to rely on a series of concise case studies of these patterns of the employment of registers of trust. Subsequently, I will use this approach in order to discuss two correlated but analytically distinct dimensions in the operation of trust on these markets, with the intention of highlighting broad tendencies that reinforced the dissection of extra-legal and 'formal' finance, while also providing evidence for the obstacles in adjusting to the imposition of the 'proper swindle'. The case studies selected highlight two areas in the employment of various registers of trust over time, first, the practices of debt recovery and their social embeddedness, especially in money lending, and, second, the adaptations of financial entrepreneurs, especially in 'organized' banking, in handling public perceptions of trustworthiness.

Community and alien moneylenders

Trust forms a dimension of transactional practices in which the intersections of markets and moral discourses in society are highly visible, informing individual perceptions of trustworthiness. As discussed in Chapter 2, Hardiman's argument on the impact of the abolition of the usury laws in colonial India depicted the destruction of a 'moral economy' of debt in rural India by the imposition of liberal contractual law onto credit contracts. The rupture portrayed by Hardiman was not based on the emergence of the contractual form but highlights legal enforcement in the recovery of outstanding dues. Hardiman's depiction of the earlier 'moral economy', at the same time, is necessarily vague, given the complexity of debt relations even in a geographical and temporally restricted context like the western Bombay Presidency in the 1870s. Yet the main emphasis of the 'moral economy' argument rests on the assumption that a socially embedded village moneylender – sharing social space and at least partially partaking in the general prosperity (or otherwise) of the villagers – plausibly faced various pressures on the extent to which debtors could be exploited through interest, or particularly the confiscation of pledged collaterals, as the semiotics of landed property created intersections with other moral discourses. In the context of the Punjab, Pervaiz Nazir has deplored that the colonial state dealt with the question of land alienation and growing indebtedness merely through legislation instead of addressing its complexities arising from socio-cultural and politico-economic structures in rural society (Nazir 2000).

Interpreted in this way, the 'moral economy' argument on village lending weaves a rich tapestry of moral discourses enshrining complex patterns of political and economic interdependence that, in turn, inform credit bargaining processes, adding a collective dimension to credit, and therefore may have provided some relief to subaltern debtors. In this context, the increasing reliance on the law for enforcing contractual terms shifted the balance in favour of the lender, as it added an external dimension disturbing the complex web of interdependence. While it remains unclear to what extent the addition of an external politico-legal dimension to debt relationships constituted a significant feature in actual credit practices, many of which remained firmly beyond the reach of Indian courts, the general direction of the argument remains highly plausible. What is more, in terms of the handling of trust the intervention of the colonial state through its courts needs to be interpreted as a more significant external intervention in that they rested on an interpretive framework beyond the experiential foundations in the operation of prominently employed registers of trust: what would have appeared entirely rational and moral to a British Indian small causes judge was not necessarily the expected outcome of litigation by a western Indian villager.[3] Even a cursory glance at late-nineteenth-century judgments in debt cases makes it clear that British Indian judges frequently were exasperated by the claimants' arguments, so that we can infer a considerable level of misunderstanding of the legal tenets by the litigants. The failure to arrive at a consensus of what was considered usurious and exploitative even within the administration of British India – hardly the most complex matter in debt litigations – has been discussed earlier. Equally importantly, British Indian judges frequently expressed their strong mistrust of the intentions of litigants on either side of the transaction so that, conversely, the presumption that the courts would be perceived as neutral and rule-bound arbitrators whose behaviour was sufficiently 'knowable' to be trusted by the litigants in systemic ways is hardly plausible.

A related argument in Hardiman's work discusses the increasing prominence in the western Deccan of outsiders, primarily Marwaris, as moneylenders (Hardiman 1996a). In this, Hardiman takes up the reverse of a long-standing argument on lending that is visible in many cultural contexts – of lending 'to the other, not thy brother'. Similar conceptions informed the Muslim practice of prohibiting usury, especially within the Muslim community that facilitated the predominance of (among others) Armenian and Jewish lenders in Muslim societies, and in India (B. Bhattacharya 51).

In South Asia, similar restrictions on exploiting the needs of fellow community members through usury existed, though typically in uncodified form. In the late colonial period lenders were frequently itinerant. Categories of lenders such as Kabulis or *qistwallah*s benefited from this conception in that their high rates of interest did not evoke severe social sanctions locally. However, the position as outsiders attracted sanctions against the possession of land in the locality, and in turn reinforced the concentration of these lenders' businesses at the lower end of the spectrum of credit markets where loans relied on accumulation through interest alone.

In the case of Marwari (small-town) lenders in the western Deccan described by Hardiman, the infraction of social norms occurred in two analytically separate dimensions.[4] Hardiman's own account stresses concerns over the lack of lenience and solidarity (Hardiman 1996b, 128). In this depiction, the outside lender – being socially disembedded – had little incentive for lenience in times of crisis compared to the embedded village lender. Put more distinctly, the extent to which a village community was able to extract lenience was limited with Marwari lenders, as the collective pressure that could be placed on a lender was significantly lower. At the same time, the affective dimension of lending to highly familiar persons was arguably less pronounced, so that lenders faced less compunctions against recovering dues even in cases of hardship. Colonial sources from the late nineteenth century stress these points as well.

Yet the arguments on this distinction between lenders need to be treated cautiously. First, Marwari lenders, even those not residing within the villages, were still affected by the general ability of debtors to enter into long-standing debt relations. In a highly exploitative business such as money lending, lenience benefited the lender as much as the debtor: a villager unable to pay would remain unable to fulfil contractual obligations regardless of the pressure imposed, and the long-term accumulation of interest depended on the ability of the lender, regardless of social origins, to show lenience wherever necessary. The economic rationale does not preclude lenience out of affect, but it remained an important consideration even in the latter's absence. Lenders also employed affect as a discursive tool in demonstrations of lenience rather than disbursing lenience in contravention of economic rationality. Second, while the collective element in bargaining with village moneylenders offered some restrictions on the level of exploitation, it is implausible to consider this as a unidirectional argument: the village moneylender, frequently belonging to entrenched communities, was also likely to persuade fellow villagers to impose sanctions on a defaulting debtor. Collective forms of punishing transgressions were likely to set boundaries on the behaviour of debtors and creditors alike. While Marwari small-town lenders were less likely to be influenced by these sanctions than village moneylenders, their social standing in instances of collective agency was likely to be limited compared to deeply embedded village moneylenders. Third, literature on the petty merchants and middlemen that made up the bulk of Marwari small-town lenders in the western Deccan suggests that these had developed deep and long-standing ties to their clients, reaching very high levels of familiarity even in the absence of close community ties (for example, Haynes 1999, 2012), and credit flows were more likely to be arranged through these ties of familiarity. Since the dimension of affect in lenience depended on familiarity rather than community membership, it is not clear whether the assumed lack of affect was sufficient to cause considerably different behavioural norms across these categories of lenders.

Rather than reducing the outsider–insider distinction to questions of affect and collective forms of punishing transgressions, it is more fruitful to consider the second dimension in which local embeddedness reinforced distinctions between lenders. Implicitly, this argument can be built upon Hardiman's emphasis on the destruction of the moneylenders' account books which demonstrates the extent to which indebted rioters were aware of contractual law and admissible evidence (Hardiman 1996b, 144). The value of admissible evidence for lenders and debtors alike, however, rose exponentially as soon as mortgages were involved in debt contracts, since small causes courts were more likely to admit other forms of evidence and since the likelihood of protracted litigation that necessitated documentation of evidence increased considerably in mortgage cases. Outsiders as lenders, however, typically faced social sanctions against the acquisition of land from village communities. As Marwari lenders had acquired land pledged as collaterals in the western Deccan for a considerable time, these sanctions had proved to be relatively ineffective, thereby affecting the perceptions of the lenders' trustworthiness. Conversely, Marwari lenders resisting local opposition against land acquisition were less likely to be amenable to show lenience in cases of hardship. Where sanctions against the acquisition of land had been sufficiently efficacious to prevent Marwari lenders from lending against land as security, this would have affected the economic rationale for lenience as a tool facilitating the establishment of long-term debt relationships. In either case, resentment against outsiders as landowners would plausibly have reinforced lifetime experiences that compromised the basis for high levels of trust.

Resentment against outsiders formed a consistent feature of lending in the colonial period. One interesting example of the complex interaction of trust and community was the case of Shikarpuri moneylenders in the Chinese province of Sinkiang (Xinjiang). Depicted locally as 'Hindu moneylenders', these formed a category of 'alien' lenders engaged in extending petty loans to Chinese subjects. Shikarpuri practices of money lending originally seem to have been part of mercantile business but since the late nineteenth century, 'Hindu' moneylenders were increasingly concentrating on lending. British officials posted in the Yangi Hissar district had reacted through 'stern action', by 1919 'refus[ing] to recognise some of the transactions entered into by these Hindus with the local people, and dismiss[ing] many cases which the money-lenders had brought against their clients'.[5] The British consul-general went so far as to describe the 'sharp-witted Hindus' as '[o]ne of the evils of this country'.[6] By the early 1930s, the conduct of Shikarpuri moneylenders had become sufficiently problematic that local magistrates started to see all British subjects in Sinkiang as probable moneylenders. In April 1932, the British consul-general sent a confidential letter to the Government of India, deploring that it had become impossible to settle cases of British against Chinese subjects, inferring that the conduct of 'Hindu' moneylenders affected the influence of colonial officials over judgments by local courts involving 'British' rather than 'British Indian' citizens. The consul-general took steps to repatriate Shikarpuri moneylenders, but asked for assistance from the Indian government by stopping to issue passports.[7] The suggestion caught the Indian administration in a bind, as any such policy 'might be open to criticism … that certain classes of British subjects were being debarred from pursuing what is after all a legitimate occupation and thus subjected to a discrimination....'[8] The ensuing deliberations included proposals to deal with the problem by restricting the entry of 'Hindus' to traders carrying with them high-value goods, or issuing passports 'for trade in goods only'.[9] The government eventually decided against enacting a formal directive, and simply informed the consulate-general in Kashgar that it was willing to cooperate in excluding undesirable British Indian residents from Sinkiang, thus leaving the matter to be solved informally.[10] However 'formalized' or 'rationalized' British policy was, hierarchical patterns within the categorizations of British subjects still could be employed to generate trust or mistrust in financial practices.

In the Punjab, categorizations of moneylenders along communal lines had resulted in impediments for legislative approaches. Communal polarization in a context in which the typical money lending communities were Hindu and most indebted farmers Muslim resulted in a situation in which the question of outsiders did not form an important angle in debates on community identity. When the insider–outsider question eventually came up in debates, the Punjab deliberately refrained from enacting provisions against 'alien' moneylenders. While this was in line with the practice of many provinces, the open communication of the reasoning was not. As reported, the government had come to the conclusion that it was the evil of money lending that needed to be combatted, not the moneylenders' origins.[11]

In the United Provinces, the term 'alien' was primarily used to denote Kabuli (and therefore Muslim) moneylenders, so that concern over 'alien' moneylenders was used as a surrogate for attempts at communal polarization.[12] Itinerant moneylenders from Bihar – usually depicted as Harhias – played an equally important role in money lending to the poor in the eastern parts of the province, targeting the same categories of clients. Though a partial explanation for this lack of concern was to be found in their lesser reputation for violence, the practices of public shaming, besetting, and loitering that were considered the hallmark of their businesses were strongly deplored with Kabulis. Still, the money lending bills introduced in the assembly did not include provisions specifically targeting outsiders. In contrast, the Princely State of Hyderabad in 1946 amended its money lending act exclusively with the intention to restrict the business for 'aliens'.[13] Here, the context was one of increasingly precarious standing of the predominant money lending communities that had supported the rule of the Nizams.

While community did not anymore play a significant role in the governance of interest rates as depicted by C. A. Bayly (1983, 407), the power of *panchayats* to interfere in markets had declined significantly, and instances of *jajmani*-style systems of lending were failing, community identity still impacted considerations of trustworthiness. The ease with which public opinion could be polarized along communal lines over money lending indicates fertile ground for the identification of lenders by community. In some cases, even the terminology used for lenders made use of community features, most ubiquitously in the terms Bania and Kabuli, but extending to other examples such as Harhia.

The distinction between lenders of local and outside origin relates to community in the form of a 'son of the soil' narrative, but there is no indication that this distinction affected lending practices. Where lending was closely linked to the predominant trades followed by communities, their association with money lending remained strong – indicating that lending formed one of the main contact points between mercantile and other social strata – but this did not necessarily inform lending practices. In cases where resentment against 'outsiders' was strong, such as notably in the case of Kabuli lenders, the resulting social ostracism may even have helped the lenders in avoiding other forms of punishing transgressions.

Letters written by concerned readers to the *Times of India* at the time of the deliberations on the Bombay Moneylenders Act of 1946 give an indication of the extent to which urban elite sections tended to employ stereotypical characterizations of community membership. Resentment against Kabuli lenders was pronounced openly, yet factory managements in and near Delhi were still entering into business arrangements with Kabulis, allowing these to enter the premises on pay day, based on an understanding that the settlement of workers' debts on the grounds of the mill was preferable against unsustainable levels of debt.

In May 1938, Presidency Magistrate K.J. Kambata's judgment was reported in the *Times of India*, declaring that 'the court may presume ... that a Pathan money-lender never gives in cash the full amount of the promissory note; and I therefore do not believe the complainant'.[14] In this case, the claimant had not been able (or willing) to produce account books, providing an indication that they would not have corroborated his claims, yet Kambata's reported judgment is significant in the extent to which community membership was used as evidence for the lender's lack of trustworthiness. Another report had highlighted public fears of uncontrolled violence by Pathan moneylenders in Bombay who were depicted as lazy good-for-nothings, having no other profession than intimidating debtors, but had included a variation in the community designation. The report argued that Pathan moneylenders in Bombay were invariably from Baluchistan, and thus unrelated to Pathans from the Northwestern Frontier Province who 'abide[d] by the instruction of their religion prohibiting the taking of interest'.[15] In opposition to the vast majority of opinions, one reader expressed his belief that while Pathan moneylenders were certainly harassing their clients, they were 'at least straight in their business inasmuch as they give a distinct understanding to their debtors ... that they would take such and such interest', unlike – as he claimed – their Marwari counterparts in Pune who tended to cheat.[16] In this depiction, Pathan community membership actually compared favourably in terms of their trustworthiness, though the correlation through lifetime experiences of one set of lenders as intimidating and potentially violent with a higher level of trustworthiness was rare, and intimidation was typically paired in public perception with an equal proclivity for slyness.

The depiction of 'Hindu' moneylenders in Sinkiang and 'Pathan' moneylenders in Bombay shows remarkable similarities. While the employment of culturally derived stereotypes in discussions of trustworthiness was commonplace, the comparison shows that it was public resentment against exploitation in general that formed the basis for their depiction in community-centric ways – in accordance with local prejudices against specific communities – rather than the opposite: references to community formed a way of expressing mistrust but did not plausibly shape the terms of transactions within debt relationships. The prospective debtor approaching a moneylender was still entering a relationship based on a level of trust and mistrust which was shaped primarily by life experiences affecting the perception of the individual case. Attempts at using resentment against money lending for communal polarization remained efforts to benefit politically from public revulsion against money lending in general.

In the late colonial period, the idea that trust deficits between strangers based on the unknowable qualities of the other transactional party could be bridged through community membership and related ascriptive identities – a common understanding in the 'bazaar' economy – was not clearly visible. The experiential background informing an individual's perception of trust in practical conduct involved community, but rather as a belated attempt to categorize patterns of lending than as a sufficiently certain hypothesis to guide practical conduct. As shown for Marwari lenders in the western Deccan, other features of local society affected the organization of credit markets to a greater extent, though their expression still tended to highlight community. Local sociopolitical pressure remained heavily intertwined with community structures and was conflated with the latter discursively, even if it did not impact credit negotiations. That credit practices were subject to these pressures can also be shown in the operation of cooperative credit markets where the preferential treatment of members with higher local standing by the banks' directors attracted heavy criticism as corrupt behaviour. While certainly in contravention of cooperative ideals, these instances marked the embeddedness of cooperative banks in village society including its hierarchical patterns. The concentration of the benefits of cooperation at the top of village hierarchies demonstrates the integration of the idea of cooperation into rural sociopolitical systems rather than their failure, unless the ideal of bank directors operating along the lines of 'proper' procedure was taken literally, unrealistically assuming to overcome prevalent patterns of social organization. A cooperative bank's director, instead, needed to be simultaneously trusted to operate along the lines prescribed by the legal form, and to operate within the confines of village social structure, leading to situations in which the procedural parameters were followed in letter, but not in spirit. The RBI's assessment in the late 1930s that instances of corruption among cooperative credit societies showed that the idea of cooperation had not yet fully been established rather demonstrates its opposite: that cooperation had become well embedded, while the discourse on juridical-procedural propriety remained largely alien, the preserve of managers that needed to straddle the concomitant discursive divide.

Trusting pests and parasites

Where practices of building trust – through juridical-procedural norms, through perceivable experiences of sufficient certainty based on beliefs in 'systemic representations of the real', or through direct interpersonal sequences of exchange – were failing, recovery mechanisms became pervaded by mistrust that produced credit practices characterized by public shaming, intimidation, and even violence. These practices were quintessentially associated with the figure of the Kabuli moneylender, though they were hardly absent elsewhere. In the eastern United Provinces, Harhias – an itinerant category of lenders from Bihar – were depicted as lenders using sophisticated versions of public shaming. According to the *UPBECR*, Harhias specialized in it, including in countering any aggression by defaulting debtors, and in managing livelihood concerns while travelling: the usual method of enforcement centred on visiting the homes of defaulting debtors and sitting in *dharna* – a staged sit-in in protest – in front of their houses, loudly proclaiming the injustices done to them by defaulting. The *dharna* would proceed until at least some demands were satisfied, and the Harhia would demand to be fed by the defaulting debtor's family for the entire time spent in the process.[17] Given the – at surface – non-violent means employed, instances of physical aggression against the lender would have added to the stigma attached to the debtor, so that the recovery strategy of Harhias remained an effective form of extra-legal recovery under conditions of heightened mistrust.

The pervasive level of extra-legality was shared with *qistwallah*s and Kabuli lenders. While there are instances of Kabuli lenders approaching the courts, as discussed earlier, these were rare, and often followed a rationale of last resort for maintaining the lender's reputation. Public perception, however, highlighted the Kabulis' propensity to engage exclusively in extra-legal enforcement practices. Commenting on the case of a particular group of money lending Kabulis from the Ghilzai community in Simla, Sir Horace Williamson argued that 'a Ghilzai money-lender practically never goes to court; he is said to carry his court with him in the shape of a heavy knobkerrie'.[18] Letters to the editor published in the *Times of India* from the 1940s used similar depictions, describing Kabuli lenders as 'burly' and 'stick-wielding'.[19] While the physically intimidating appearance of Kabuli lenders constitutes a ubiquitous element in their depiction, sources on the actual use of violence in the United Provinces are relatively rare, and the added layer of intimidation through demonstrations of martial prowess was likely more beneficial to the lenders than the actual conduct of violence.

The case of Ghilzai moneylenders in Simla (and Delhi) constitutes one of the most detailed descriptions of Kabuli practices for northern India in the mid-twentieth century. Partially, the high level of information was related to the perceptions of these practices as a direct threat by the government, and especially its intelligence community. The debate was started by an intelligence officer, Major Robinson, who raised concerns based on an assessment of the danger of government servants' indebtedness to a foreign community as compromising the secrecy of classified information. Robinson had been engaged in intelligence relating to matters in the Northwestern Frontier Province, and according to one participant in the debate had made this community his 'pet study'.[20] Describing the lenders as 'parasites and pests; misers',[21] Robinson highlighted the incidence of debt to these moneylenders by subordinates, and occasionally even superiors in the offices of the Indian government as well as their servants and menials.

> Nothing could be more objectionable than ... so many clerks – and others – of the G. o. I. ... in the toils of a foreign money-lending community. The bania, with all his drawbacks, is infinitely preferable.[22]

Robinson added that while he had not ascertained the precise contractual obligations involved, his experience from the Bengal Presidency had been that loans to similar target groups there had amounted to 10 lakh rupees, with annual interest reaching 15 lakh rupees. He estimated that the Ghilzai colony comprised around 800 persons, about half of which belonged to its largest sub-group of Sulaiman Khel Ghilzais.[23] Apparently, he argued, the moneylenders speculated that the government would hesitate to interfere in their operations for fear of international entanglements, as 'they kn[e]w where boots pinch'.[24] A subsequent inquiry by the Punjab police corrected Robinson's assessments, declaring that only 46 Pathans in Simla were moneylenders, though these had help from a larger group of assistants. Similarly, there was a group of 112 Pathans in Delhi engaged in lending to government officials and clerks, though only 40–50 of these were 'worth notice'.[25]

The debate gained traction after the intervention by Williamson who related his own experience of a clerk who had borrowed 250 rupees and had not been able to repay within two years.[26] The figures provided for this loan demonstrate an operative monthly interest rate of roughly 9.3 per cent, compounded annually. The use of compound interest by the Ghilzai lenders was untypical for Kabuli rates, but the rate provided here falls within the typical Kabuli rates, demonstrating that office clerks even for the Indian government were as much subject to exploitative rates as farmers or workers. Williamson was dismayed by the extent of indebtedness once starting to investigate the matter:

> I examined the account book of this particular money-lending shark ... and mainly by bluff I effected a settlement of his claim, ... but in ... my examination of his account book, I was astounded at the number of Government servants who appeared to be irretrievably in the hands of these Ghilzais. Scores of ministerial officers in practically every department ... were heavily in debt and there were quite a number of officers of comparatively high rank....[27]

His later depositions qualified that in the military departments, it reached up to the level of the rank of major. Williamson proceeded to investigate, and compiled complaints against intimidation, including 'the worst case' in which a moneylender had physically assaulted an Anglo-Indian woman, though the case was subsequently compounded in court.[28] A more ubiquitous practice was to resort to particularly drastic forms of intimidation and public shaming, including sexual harassment:

> [T]hese money-lenders invade the houses of their debtors and refuse to leave until some instalment is paid; a common practice is for a man to ... sit on the bed of an Anglo-Indian woman.... Why one or two of them have not been shot I am not able to understand. In Agra, ... there were many cases in which Ghilzais insulted and tormented women. This trouble ceased after I had, quite illegally, connived at several Ghilzais being severely thrashed by the police.... I suppose we are now far too civilized even to wink at such procedure.[29]

The subsequent debates demonstrated that civilizational progress was not as high as anticipated, as the discussions remained replete with suggestions of reverting to violence, though the latter tended to be more obliquely worded such as to resort to the administration of a '"warning" by the police, administered in a suitable manner'.[30] Apart from the threat for confidential information flows, concern over the plight of Anglo-Indian women lent urgency to the debates. They highlighted the difficulties in deporting the moneylenders to Afghanistan or even within India, and settled on using the threat of externment, even though it was understood that this threat could not realistically be put into practice. The deportation of Kabuli lenders had already been recommended by the Central Banking Enquiry Committee Report, but was never carried out.[31] Under these circumstances, the most realistic remedy was originally suggested by Williamson:

[T]he only remedy is the one which I applied … to my own office. I issued an
order as follows: 'If any of the staff, ministerial or menial, of this office borrows
a single rupee from these Ghilzai sharks, I will take disciplinary action against
him.' I do not see why such an order should not be passed in every department…
From my examination of one account book I was able to see that the position
is really serious and … dangerous. Most officials in the Government of India
deal with information which has a market value and it is utterly undesirable
that such officials should be hopelessly in debt. Speaking generally, they are
well paid.[32]

Following the issuing of these orders, according to Williamson, would have
solved the problem as the Ghilzais would move elsewhere 'and Simla and
Delhi will be rid of the biggest pest from which they at present suffer'.[33] These
suggestions highlight some general features in the treatment of indebtedness
to moneylenders by the administration: faced with a crisis directly impacting
the government's functioning, the instinctive reaction was to shift the problem
towards the mass of the population, that is, into the *mufassil*. At the same
time, the solution to the crisis lay in disciplinary action against the indebted
clerks, servants, and officers – resembling the containment of debt through
impeding 'facile credit'. As government employees were assumedly 'well paid',
their indebtedness remained their own responsibility, regardless of the reasons
for it.

Notably, the matter of issuing orders against indebtedness remained
controversial. For once, solutions were considered that relied on affirmative
action, with several respondents suggesting to enable government employees
to draw advances from their provident funds to settle extra-legal debts. Yet
such a solution was only possible for high-ranking staff, not to clerks, and
menial employees.[34] It also failed to address the issue of indebtedness to other
lenders, as argued by R. M. Maxwell, who stated that there were 'types of
clerk who are never out of debt and we shall not cure the danger by attacking
Pathan money-lenders in particular'.[35] More importantly, he argued,
any instance of 'welfare work' by superior officers for their subordinates
was considered 'considerably outside the scope' of their work and would
compromise hierarchical relationships, while solutions that relied on setting
up cooperative credit agencies for the employees would encourage further
indebtedness and attract 'only the chronically improvident'.[36] Deliberations
on using the police to guard offices against Pathan moneylenders gained
traction after investigations had shown that a Ghilzai lender had entered the
servants' quarters at the Viceroy's residence in Delhi to collect repayments
from one of the Viceroy's drivers, compromising security arrangements for

high-ranking functionaries.[37] However, these did not lead to any action as special protection to government offices in ways not available elsewhere was inopportune.[38]

The suggestion to invoke disciplinary action against indebted staff was similarly problematic, since the Legislative Department pointed out that the conduct rules for government employees did not include any prohibition against taking loans from moneylenders.[39] Nevertheless, a majority of departments proceeded to issue orders requiring staff members to disclose loans taken from Ghilzai moneylenders, or face disciplinary action. The lack of response – with hardly any cases of indebtedness uncovered – was eventually interpreted as evidence that there had not been a problem of indebtedness after all, very much reminiscent of the treatment of extra-legality in debt relations in general.[40] While the debates led to the inclusion of office orders against indebtedness to Pathan moneylenders into the government servants' conduct rules,[41] the practical solution eventually employed resorted to informal office orders emphasizing 'stern action' against heavily indebted clerks, and threatening these with 'loss of confidence'.[42]

The discussion of the government's responses to the perceived threat of Ghilzai money lending is noteworthy in its resemblance to general patterns of dealing with crises of indebtedness. It also highlights several dimensions that are important for understanding the manner in which recovery practices by extra-legal moneylenders operated in circumstances marked by high levels of mistrust. Kabuli moneylenders certainly were more likely to employ violent means than most others, but the primary intention of their (assumed) martial conduct and appearance remained linked to the facilitation of recovery practices that centred on intimidation and public shaming. While Williamson's statement that he was unable to understand why some of the Ghilzais 'ha[d] not been shot' formed a drastic way of putting it, this appearance primarily prevented counter-violence as well as inhibiting recourse to legal means of resisting being pressurized. Kabuli lenders did not 'carry the courts with them;' rather, they rendered the courts impotent through a show of force, to the extent that even the government of India in a case that was perceived to be threatening its operations reacted timidly. Notwithstanding instances of counter-violence, fear of the Kabulis in combination with the stigma attached to public disclosure of indebtedness had effectively prevented clerks and officers from reporting their dealings with moneylenders. Regarding stigmatization, government policy even had detrimental effects in implicitly threatening sanctions against indebtedness that reinforced the employees' aversion to disclose their debts, so that the only plausible remedy in the eyes of the government lay in placing additional pressures on the debtors, but otherwise turning a blind eye towards a concern originally described as dangerous for the government.

While the Kabulis' practices in Simla were reinforced through intimidation, the crucial dimension in their enforcement practices remained linked to public shaming in ways that differed from those employed for instance by Harhias in the eastern United Provinces in their details, but remained remarkably similar in other respects. Where the Harhia practice of sitting in *dharna* depended on a 'non-violent' performance of the lender as victim of the debtor's vices, Kabuli lenders reached this level of impunity by the appearance of martial prowess, and at least the Ghilzai Kabulis in Simla employed means that went so far as to utilize forms of sexual harassment, attempting to use notions of women's dignity to similar effect. In targeting Anglo-Indians, these instances of public shaming were further compounded by the peculiar social standing of the community that frequently did not possess superior economic means than the bulk of the lower-middle classes, although its distinctive status rested on its ability to publicly showcase 'propriety', especially for Anglo-Indian women as the supposed carriers of family honour (Blunt 2002). At the same time, the fears of the Indian government that indebtedness would compromise the confidentiality of information proved unfounded, as no cases of making use of the information's 'market-value' were uncovered. Ghilzai lenders, it appears, were well aware not only of the political compulsions that prevented their deportation, but also of the threshold at which the government would have felt compelled to act more drastically.

The depiction of the Ghilzai lenders demonstrates the relative pettiness of their businesses, in contrast to the exaggeration of the threat posed by them to the government. In describing the Ghilzais not only as parasites and pests, but also as misers, Robinson was inadvertently pointing out the relative precarity of the lenders. Their profits, he argued, 'sooner or later [went] to Afghanistan to be expended on land acquisition and development, arms and women'.[43] He went on to deplore that the lenders pretended to keep no records of their transactions, and to make 'barely enough profits ... to provide a bare subsistence'.[44] As an intelligence officer working in the Northwestern Frontier Province (and possibly Afghanistan), it is plausible that Robinson had first- or at least second-hand experience of such remittances there, yet the description fits awkwardly with any narrative of exorbitant profits and indicates rather the upwardly mobile lower-class origins of the lenders within Afghan society – sufficiently prosperous to finance small portfolios of starting capital and the original journey, but not affluent enough to acquire landholdings without recourse to a particularly ignoble profession. Robinson had wondered what made 'the Ghilzais ... venture eastwards to exploit ... the mild Hindu',[45] but had apparently failed to fully consider the local socio-economic conditions. Kabulis, similarly to Harhias and *qistwallah*s, engaged in lending in a market niche that was highly profitable in terms of the returns on (relatively small) investment, yet sufficiently risky and disreputable to be eschewed by more affluent lenders, a direct outcome of the precarity involved and the correlated high levels of mistrust.

While the examples discussed earlier deal with a context of relatively low trust, the majority of money lending transactions took place in a context of relatively high trust. Kabuli lending practices were operating at the lowest level of a high-trust lending regime. As mentioned by the assistant commissioner of income tax for Banaras cited in the previous chapter, Kabulis dealt with a particularly mistrusted clientele – referred to as 'desperadoes and badmashes' by Thakur Ram Singh as mentioned earlier. In the light of the discussion of Kabuli lending to government employees it needs to be pointed out that this clientele formed a much larger section of society than anticipated by the respondent, whose derogative depiction demonstrates not only colonial prejudice against lower-class borrowers, but also prevalent perceptions of this clientele by the more affluent lenders Singh would have associated with. Williamson's argument that government clerks were generally well paid was correct to the extent that lower-level government employees tended to get better remuneration than their equivalents outside government employment, even if this obviously did not mean that they were sufficiently creditworthy to approach a more 'respectable' class of lenders.

Even for relatively poor borrowers, extra-legal financial markets generally operated on higher levels of trust than would have been possible for the emerging formal sector. Village moneylenders, for instance, tended to lend solely on the strength of entries in their current account books, and differences between lender and debtor rarely entered the legal system of arbitration unless involving land mortgages. Lending against movable valuables, loans against usufruct rights, and especially unsecured loans in the *qist* system almost exclusively remained outside the scope of the legal system, without comprising similar levels of coercion as shown for Kabuli lenders. This provided avenues for the lenders that could be exploited – colonial sources are replete with examples of borrowers who were repaying much larger amounts than depicted as contractual obligations, and of lenders who manipulated debtors' precarity through an unwillingness to recover dues in time. In many cases, though, these cases reflect uneven levels of information and skills that allowed unscrupulous lenders to take advantage of the high levels of trust employed, rather than being indicative of lower levels of trust in extra-legal finance. The scholarly debate on trust in 'traditional' finance has largely neglected petty debt transactions, instead focusing on trust in 'indigenous' banking.

The 'most perfectly organised' model of extra-legal finance

The embeddedness of trust in social organization and community has been an important area of inquiry in Indian economic historiography concerning trust. This focus partially relates to the visibility of caste-based behavioural codes in archived sources. Merchants who closely followed caste-centric codes of conduct – and were seen as doing so – left identifiable traces to a greater extent than less collectively organized merchants. Summing up the historical experience in early-colonial Banaras, Bayly concluded that caste played an important role especially at higher levels of exchange, that supplemented less visible patterns of organizing trust:

> Caste at the level of geographically extended kin groups had an important role in the organization of trading diasporas.... Nevertheless, it is difficult to see how caste in any sense could have been the prime parameter of mercantile organization in complex cities. Forms of arbitration, market control, brokerage, neighbourhood communities, and above all, conceptions of mercantile honour and credit breached caste boundaries, ... and imposed wider solidarities on merchant people. (Bayly 2011, 117)

'Indigenous' banking certainly made use of caste – more so than petty money lending in urban contexts – yet, as noted by Rudner (1989), caste (and kinship) entered financial markets primarily as a way of minimizing mistrust, one among many methods employed in dealing with the unknowability of strangers. L. C. Jain's depiction of 'indigenous' banking in late colonial India (Jain 1929; see also Jain 1933) forms an excellent source for the variety of means used. Apart from his scholarly work, Jain was a major influence on the direction of policy in the United Provinces as secretary of the the United Provinces Banking Enquiry Committee,[46] though the work primarily discussed here was published beforehand. Noting the manner in which caste played a role especially among the Nattukottai Chettiars in providing preferential terms to fellow caste members, Jain's depiction of their business habits implicitly lists further mistrust-minimizing features. While explicitly referring to Nattukottai Chettiar practices, his analysis consciously illustrated 'indigenous' banking practices in general, using the example of the 'most perfectly organised' group of lenders consisting of 'born bankers' for highlighting common features rather than caste group specificities (Jain 1929, 36).

The Nattukottai Chettiars, according to Jain, trained their children from an early age in financial practices, especially in 'thrift' and 'economy' (Jain 1929, 37). While intended to showcase the equivalence of 'traditional' against 'modern' knowledge, implicitly it depicts a commonality in upbringing that produced a common experiential background that could be made use of in ascertaining behavioural probabilities. The child of a Nattukottai Chettiar banking family could be expected to draw on a similar pool of experiences as his or her caste fellows, and therefore could be trusted more. At the same time, Chettiar practices showed the use of other uncertainty-minimizing techniques. For instance, Jain reported that the usage of unstamped *chits* (on palm leaves) was slowly giving way to stamped *chits* on (more robust and durable) paper (Jain 1929, 38). Central to the high levels of trust, however, was their high level of association, centring on the institution of the temple and the *kovilvasal mariyal* – the association of eminent caste members under the temple's auspices – which among others used the social institution of marriage in imposing sanctions against misconduct. The association was 'remarkable for settling their disputes among themselves without recourse to the law' (Jain 1929, 40).

> The parties at variance reduce their points of difference to the minimum and then lodge their complaints with the manager [of the temple's council], who convenes a meeting of the council, before which both the complainant and the defendant appear, the evidence being recorded by the manager.... The council adjudicates on all matters relating to marriages, monetary transactions, family disputes, etc. The award is given orally and never in writing. As a rule the decision is readily accepted. Those who do not abide by it are not granted the garland of the temple without which no marriage can be celebrated. (Jain 1929, 40–41)

Jain's statement shows the extent to which the Nattukottai Chettiars – and to a lesser extent other communities – were interweaving associational life geared towards the resolution of business disputes with matters pertaining to caste and religious practice. Caste and religion provided the ability to impose sanctions against misconduct that comprised sufficiently strong disadvantages to prevent any serious consideration of breaking with 'tradition' for short term gain. In this way, Jain's statement reflects the importance of caste for credit matters as depicted by Rudner (discussed later). Within Jain's statement, however, lies another matter that is partially obscured by the focus of historians on caste: both parties to a dispute were required – before approaching the council – to 'reduce their points of difference to the minimum'.

In requiring the disputing parties to minimize friction before the settlement process commenced, the council stabilized its powers of arbitration, making the dispute manageable for an intervening agency. This requirement helped to maintain the informality of the resolution process, and preserved the relationship of high trust necessary to maintain an informal business relationship. In order to understand the importance of keeping the settlement of disputes as much as possible away from formal avenues of arbitration for maintaining high-trust relations, it helps to compare this resolution mechanism to the practices of the British Indian legal system: at one level, it resembles the operation of the courts in British India in that it preferred the settlement of strife outside the formal arena. The ubiquitous complaints in colonial sources on the supposedly 'litiginous Indian' illustrate an approach to dispute settlement – related to the low numbers of judicial personnel rather than a high number of legal cases – which depended on and favoured the propensity of disputing parties for extra-legal settlement. At the same time, the practice of the law diverged markedly from the dispute settlement process favoured by the Nattukottai Chettiars. The British Indian legal system (designed for the use in low-trust relationships that require formal certification of procedural propriety) operated on the basis of its own pervasive powers for universal adjudication, while the Nattukottai Chettiar practice (geared towards the maintenance of high-trust relationships) placed emphasis on the interpersonal settlement of disputes before the intervention of an arbitrating agency.

It is imperative here to beware of the fallacy of familiarity, as depicted by Carey. It is not the inter-personality of the settlement process that is crucial here, as an indication of a supposed superiority of personal over system trust. Nattukottai Chettiars were caste fellows, not close kin or friends, with business operations that spanned much of the Bay of Bengal area. Even the high familiarity that can be attributed through joint caste and religious practices was insufficient to overcome the problem of the unknowability of strangers. Rather, high trust is reinforced by informality, and compromised by the recourse to an outside agent with powers of arbitration, embodying a higher level of formality. Informality in business relations, especially in contexts of high uncertainty, requires higher levels of trust than more strongly formalized dispute settlement processes involving powers to impose sanctions against misconduct. The (perceived) need by the disputing parties to approach such an agent in itself signifies the degeneration of high-trust relationships to a level of low trust and, in turn, forms an impediment to the future reconstitution of high trust necessary for the recommencement of informal transactions. In deliberately minimizing its own reach, the practice of Nattukottai Chettiar councils incorporated the idea that high-trust relations were better maintained informally, and provided an arena for the mutual demonstration of reliability and reciprocal goodwill. With regard to Rudner's statement cited at the outset of this chapter, the necessarily high level of formality that characterized the contact with 'capitalist' economy (here the colonial courts) did not necessarily destroy social relations of caste and kinship, but it needed to be shunned, so that it could not compromise future transactional relations characterized by high trust.

The example of the Nattukottai Chettiar council needs to be interpreted as a demonstration of the operational principles of informality and their need for the maintenance of high trust among strangers. This practice resembles the conclusions of anthropological accounts of the organization of the 'bazaar', especially Geertz's depiction of the organization of the bazaar in Morocco (Geertz 1979). Jain's description of 'indigenous' banking practices also makes it clear that other communities active in 'bazaar' lending operated along similar lines, for instance in his depiction of the *gyarah panch* at Indore (Jain 1929, 40). At the same time, Jain's depiction of 'modern associations' of lenders, more in line with the demands of colonial 'modernity' or the 'capitalist economies' mentioned by Rudner, can be interpreted as a gradual process of impoverishment in their ability to reinforce high-trust relationships. According to Jain, these 'modern associations' 'render[ed] a valuable service in bringing the bankers together and binding them to one another in their common interest', though at least the Multani associations were still 'disposing of many disputes among their members who would otherwise have recourse to the law courts' (Jain 1929, 41). Jain's depiction of the Multani associations, however, already shows important discrepancies to the 'most perfectly organised' Nattukottai Chettiars: thus, the disputing parties would record their cases on printed forms before the commencement of a formal investigation, followed by adjudication through a written award. Interestingly, Jain proceeded to point out that it was rare for British Indian courts to reverse the awards if the cases moved to an even higher level of formality as they were 'arrived at after careful scrutiny, as a result of personal knowledge and inquiry' (Jain 1929, 42). Notwithstanding the high propensity of the British Indian judiciary to respect 'traditional' forms of arbitration, this depiction may also indicate an increasing alignment of mercantile considerations of equity with British Indian law.

The emergence of 'modern associations' of 'indigenous' bankers occurred at roughly the same time that the latter increasingly became engaged in deposit-taking. Taking deposits – lending an unknowable stranger's money – introduced an additional layer of complexity to the maintenance of high-trust relations that may have facilitated an incipient shift towards more formalized manners of lending – and therefore low-trust credit relations. As mentioned earlier, the introduction of deposit-taking as the fundamental criterion of distinction between moneylenders and 'indigenous' bankers, and 'organized' banking was mainly an artificial device meant to reinforce the distinction on the lines of alignment with juridical-procedural propriety. When viewed from the perspective of trust in debt relationships, however, this distinction becomes much more plausible – though its proponents hardly intended it in this way: the financial needs of industrial capital could not be served by the 'indigenous' banking sector as the requirements for credit were too large, gestation periods too long, and the risks carried by the creditor too high. The pooling of capital available for investment in industrialization therefore rested on the availability of capital beyond the operational viability of credit systems functioning on the basis of high trust. In terms of its impact on financial markets, the definition of the 'proper swindle' was the condition upon which the British Indian state was able to direct capital flows towards industrialization by setting up a low-trust alternative. The gradual demise of 'indigenous' banking rested on the subordination of large-scale capital flows under an investment regime operating on low-trust conditions that, given the lack of documented collateral certifiable as robust, could not be expanded to cover the credit needs of the masses.

Turning from Jain's discussion of the operation of trust in 'indigenous' banking towards matters of fraud, indicating the operation of mistrust within extra-legal lending, it is striking how much his depiction involuntarily highlights the emergence of a low-trust alternative. The subsequent discussion needs to be qualified in advance: while Jain implicitly argued that it was the availability of low-trust forms of arbitration that reinforced fraud in lending, it is hardly likely that similar forms of fraud did not exist in high-trust credit. Hardiman's 'moral economy' of debt was hardly free of fraud and mistrust (Hardiman 1996b, 124), however much it was embedded in rural social structure.

Jain sought to highlight the respectability of 'indigenous' bankers – with fraud being the preserve of 'a few black sheep' among honourable bankers, especially of lenders dealing with the Indian poor, a familiar discourse:

[I]t must not be supposed that dishonesty, or fraud, and irregularity are the accompanying features of indigenous banking, or money-lending. A dispassionate inquiry will show that almost every banker, and many big money-lenders are ... above reproach. But it is equally true that some money-lenders there certainly are, particularly those with whom the small ignorant borrowers have to deal, who are given to various malpractices. For some malpractices the borrower is also to blame. (Jain 1929, 108)

Jain proceeded to list his complaints on the borrowing habits of poor people which can be summarized as an alleged *habit* of taking on debt without considering the means to repay, thereby compelling creditors to incorporate various safeguards into debt contracts, including illicit ones such as keeping several fake documents for the same transaction for eventual use in case of default. This argument shows the extent to which the conditions of poor debtors that required them to take on loans regardless of their ability to service contractual obligations were disregarded in the debate on the propriety of business practices. It also demonstrates a link between fraudulent or otherwise 'improper' business practices originating from the high-trust system, and the requirements of furnishing admissible evidence in the low-trust system of the law. The transition from high to low trust was one of the chief characteristics in the drive towards the 'modernization' of credit practices in late colonial India.

Jain's argument lists a number of (familiar) 'safeguarding' practices that only make sense within a low-trust system of lending, and the assumption inherent in it that documented evidence was superior to the reputational modes of operation for systems based on relatively high trust: specifically, Jain reported lenders as keeping multiple account books (*bahi*), with one *bahi* reserved for uses in courts; as leaving account books unbound and unstitched, enabling the insertion of additional pages to provide 'proof' for fictitious transactional records; of omitting amount descriptions in words which allowed lenders to add zeros to the figures mentioned in contracts; and of generally making use of fake documents (Jain 1929, 109). As discussed earlier, these 'safeguards' were at times used along the lines of a high-trust system, as in the case of artisanal industries in western United Provinces where such documents were destroyed after full repayment, or used for labour control without being invoked within the legal system. Yet their mode of operation remained inextricably tied to the availability of a low-trust option, a last resort for reinforcing informal transactionalities operating on a high-trust basis as for instance an understanding that signed documents furnishing legally admissible evidence would not be invoked unless there were serious infractions of the informally stipulated behavioural rules. These, in turn, remained necessary since lending to artisans still rested on regimes of petty credit, marked by a widespread absence of contractual relations based on low trust. Adding this layer of complexity – the introduction of low-trust relations into systems working on a high-trust basis, and the continued imperative of maintaining high-trust relations in systems increasingly shifting to low trust – created strains in the relationships between debtors and creditors that could lead to friction, but also provided new avenues for exploitation, or for transgressing behavioural expectations.

Trust, at its root, comprises behavioural expectations that are sufficiently strong to inform decision-making, and both high- and low-trust regimes of lending form operational modes of trust, not trust as such: low-trust regimes of lending compensate the higher original levels of mistrust between transactional parties, in the process establishing trust; high-trust operational modes work on assumptions that minimize the original level of mistrust, and therefore do not need to rely on further reductions of mistrust unless new reasons emerge in the course of the transaction. The increasing complexity of operational modes regarding trust through the multiplication of operational modes available, therefore, corresponded to increases in general mistrust that could be contained only with difficulties, and compromised the precision of handling relations based on trust.

The 'most perfectly organised' caste group of financial entrepreneurs who dominated 'indigenous' finance in major parts of the Bay of Bengal area after approximately the 1870s (Rudner 1994, 44), have been the subject of several studies inquiring into the operational modes of Indian mercantile groups, most prominently by the outstanding work of David Rudner (1989, 1994). The following descriptions are mostly taken from his later work, *Caste and Capitalism*.

Rudner situated his description of Nattukottai Chettiar practices within larger debates on mercantile organization, specifically joining issue with Bayly's depiction, quoted earlier, of caste as an organizing principle for trading diasporas rather than a fundamental organizational aspect of mercantile society. In the process, he provided one of the most nuanced analyses of the principles underlying collective organization among Indian mercantile strata that forms a contradistinction for the argument developed in Chapter 8 on the emergence of a trust-based reputational economy of debt, eschewing the strong social ties that allowed the enforcement of obligations.

Rudner situates the case of the Nattukottai Chettiars within the debates on the uses of caste as symbolic capital (for instance, Cohn 1996, 1987), and specifically David Washbrook's depiction of the 'racialization' of caste in the colonial encounter (Washbrook 1981; see also Virdee 2019), and Karen Leonard's depiction of the potential within localized precolonial castes for supralocal organization (Leonard 1978). Rejecting the emphasis on political organization through caste (Rudner 1994, 21), and taking issue with not only Bayly's treatment of caste but also Sanjay Subrahmanyam's rejection of caste as a major organizing principle of mercantile strata (Subrahmanyam and Bayly 1988), Rudner proceeded to argue for an increased emphasis on *intra*-caste mercantile cooperation (Rudner 1994, 49). The period between the 1870s and the 1930s – after which their business models 'began to unravel in the face of multigovernmental interference' (Rudner 1994, 55) – constitutes the main emphasis of his work. The Nattukottai Chettiar business practices in this period also formed what arguably can be described as one of the most sophisticated Indian variants of a capitalist ethic:

> [C]ontrary to Weber, magic and collectivism are *not* impediments to capitalism. Indeed, they form the basis of a distinctive capitalist ethic in Hindu India.[47]

The 'collectivist spirit of capitalism' (Rudner 1994, 104) manifested by Nattukottai Chettiar business practices provided a link between this-worldly gain and spiritual practice. This 'capitalist spirit' was firmly rooted in a reputational mode of business operation. Echoing Bayly's description of the banking families of Banaras, Rudner remarked that 'a Nakarattar[48] family firm's greatest intangible asset was its reputation' (Rudner 1994, 109). Rudner's depiction of everyday Nattukottai Chettiar lives demonstrates the extent to which religious practice, thrift, and patronage remained central to the community's cultural practices, and economic conduct, yet stops short of describing the almost holistic conception of merchant's credit (*sakh*) that underlies Bayly's work. In highlighting trustworthiness – a concept more contiguous with a track record than Bayly's mercantile ethos – Rudner's idea of reputation centres on an 'impoverished' version of 'credit'. On the possibility of sanctions against misconduct by refusing the grant of the temple's garland, Rudner commented:

> Whether or not such extreme measures were taken, news of his untrustworthiness would spread rapidly.... No Nakarattar would do business with him. A major part of his working capital and an important and reliable source of liquid credit would be denied him. (Rudner 1994, 128)

Rather than reflecting a linear process resembling degeneration, these distinctions need to be interpreted as spatially and temporally bounded reactions by entrepreneurial groups to changing parameters in the handling of trust. Credit markets adjusted to changing conditions and framing processes, and thereby demonstrated different forms of social embeddedness in their precise handling of different registers of trust. While the notions of reputation as *vishvaas* underlying extra-legal credit markets in contemporary Banaras constitute an adjustment of entrepreneurs and markets to 'amateurization', Rudner's depiction of the Nattukottai Chettiars portrays a case of heightened sophistication in the handling of high-trust relationships, yet one that differed from the mercantile worlds depicted by Bayly.

Stating that caste specialization concerning finance should not be essentialized (Rudner 1994, 44), Rudner proceeded to delve into a detailed description of Nattukottai Chettiar business practices and their embeddedness in sociocultural institutions. Apart from processes of arbitration in cases of conflict, his arguments largely depict intense processes of community-centric bonding that augmented the experiential basis for the generation of trust. Caste and finance were interwoven among the Nattukottai Chettiars: Rudner's analysis expressly focused on 'the way a specific caste acted as an institution of banking and trade ... [and] the way a specific financial institution functioned as a caste' (Rudner 1994, 7).

Business and sociocultural life were inseparable. The temple council served as a medium of arbitration through meetings depicted as *panchayats* in accordance with the term's use among other communities, though in practice arbitration was carried out by a single person (Rudner 1994, 127), while the temple's role in the institution of marriage facilitated not only sanctions against misconduct, but intertwined kinship patterns and religious practice. Similarly to the need to maintain high-trust relations by facilitating a high level of interpersonal negotiation before actual arbitration, Rudner also highlights the extent to which '[a]ccess to public information about each other's business ... served to limit situations in which disputes might arise ... due to private misunderstandings' (Rudner 1994, 126), and the fact that arbitration processes were not restricted to any locality, or to centralizing tendencies (Rudner 1994, 127). Moreover, the temple council met regularly to fix the *nadappu* rate of interest in the locality, taking into account the prevalent rates of other lenders (*thavanai*) and local banks, allowing caste members to draw (more cheaply) on the capital held by the collective (Rudner 1994, 91–92). Initials used for the depiction of both firms and persons followed a unified logic demonstrating a lineage of belonging within the caste (Rudner 1994, 109). Similarly, in their dealings with 'organized' banks, Nattukottai Chettiars were able to fall back upon caste fraternity: for risky loans and in cases of default, bank loans were frequently repaid by taking loans from a fellow caste member, at times by taking on credit from another (or even the same) bank (Rudner 1994, 78).

Beyond kinship and the temple, the social embeddedness of business – and the economic embeddedness of sociocultural life – were closely entwined with the institutions of the agency and the *vituti* (rest house). The sharing of social space produced community life (Rudner 1994, 118).

The rest house provided space for commingling and the infrastructure for business transactions (Rudner 1994, 124–26), but also the first place of call for newly arriving caste members, facilitating their introduction among the local community, similarly to the welcome rituals by the temple (Rudner 1994, 124). Both informed a common experiential background for caste members as the community placed a strong emphasis on a prolonged system of apprenticeship during adolescence, sending young Nattukottai Chettiar men to 'family firms with agency houses located to far-flung business stations' as a 'tour of duty' (Rudner 1994, 4). Apprenticeship did not only help young entrepreneurs to familiarize themselves with the family's local branches, but served as an underpinning of communal cohesion, similarly to the early training of (male) children in the fundamentals of business life.

While Rudner's work consciously highlights the aspect of caste in its relationship with the development of capitalism in India, much of his work actually emphasizes the mechanisms by which high-trust relations within extra-legal finance were maintained. In accordance with his own argument that caste as an organizational unit of finance need not be essentialized – and given Bayly's doubts on the role of caste in mercantile organization as well as Jain's classification of the Nattukottai Chettiars as the 'most perfectly organised' group of bankers which implies its coexistence with less perfect but still viable models – caste as a unit of social organization needs to be taken seriously. Yet it primarily needs to be taken seriously as a vehicle of mercantile organization related to either the handling of high-trust relations or the mechanisms for enforcing obligations. Jain's depiction of arbitration and the possibility of punishing transgressions through the office of the temple and the institution of marriage provides just one, and probably not the most important dimension of this process. While the social institutions of the temple and marriage were inextricably linked to caste practices, the minute details of everyday life revolving around the office space and the *vituti* as well as the emphasis on belonging played a similar role in maintaining the preconditions for high-trust relationships. In turn, all these preconditions could be reproduced, if only imperfectly, in socio-culturally more diverse settings, facilitating the operation of high-trust relationships beyond community.

Trust and the 'future of Indian banking'

The development of low-trust alternatives affected 'indigenous' banking significantly, despite the resilience of some groups. It affected the operational modes of petty money lending to the poor and money lending in the 'bazaar' but it was also of central concern for the 'organized' banking sector, the joint stock banks that comprised the 'future of Indian banking' in the words of Mohanlal Bulchand. The juridical-procedural underpinnings of 'modernization' in finance are similarly visible beyond India. 'Modernization', with its core assumptions of rationalization and technological progress, did not form a panacea for the shortcomings of individual assessment by bank managers, centring on evaluations of trustworthiness. The magicality of capitalist 'modernization' in finance lay rather in obscuring the visibility of (and therefore the doubts over) individual handling of trust registers available for judging contextual parameters. Pal Vik's study of the impact of computerization on the roles of local bank managers in Britain since the 1960s is particularly insightful in this regard, depicting the 'considerable discretion over service provision [by branch managers] up until recently' (Vik 2017, 232) and the gradual loss of bank managers' autonomy in decision-making in the wake of computerization. 'Autonomy' here refers to more than just the handling of risk (and therefore trust), yet trust constitutes a major component in it. In looking at the loss of autonomy, Vik also shows how recent the realization of Weber's theorem of rationalization in finance actually is.

In the context of Banaras between the 1930s and the late 1960s, the loss of discretionary powers of decision-making of bank managers to the algorithms of computerized banking systems would have been considered far-fetched, but the idioms of 'scientific banking' and 'rationalization' in finance were well established, more so, in fact, than the actual practices of 'organized' banking at the level of the local bank branch. The Bank of Benares was the most prominent 'organized' bank in the city in the 1930s. The bank's manager, Mohanlal Bulchand, was one of the most important informants from Banaras for the *UPBECR*.

His testimony championed the 'formalization' of banking. Bulchand steadfastly asserted that the future of Indian banking lay in joint stock banks. Conversely, he also emphasized that all other forms of banking did not need any further assistance.[49] In contrast, the Imperial Bank was needed to 'assist [the joint stock banks] by the simplification of the procedure for realization of debts from defaulters'. There also needed to be an 'imposition of restrictions on … the Imperial Bank of India and the exchange banks to prevent them from competing with joint-stock banks and the starting of a State organization which should render financial assistance to [the joint stock banks] in times of stringency'.[50] While the future may have belonged to joint stock banks, they clearly were insufficiently competitive to become this future without state assistance. They struggled in the face of competition from other banks, but also from moneylenders and 'indigenous' bankers who were 'undesirable' or, respectively, did 'not require any assistance'.[51] The preferential treatment he asked for rested on the promise of the juridical-procedural 'propriety'. In practice, however, the Bank of Benares differed remarkably little from 'indigenous' banking: the bank gave loans exclusively to 'people who h[ad] good credit' – notably landlords, 'indigenous' bankers, large-scale silk traders, and middlemen. The use of the term *credit* here needs to be interpreted as denominating *sakh*, though probably a less elaborate version of it. The bank lent either on personal security for an approved list of customers or by demanding vouching by a reputable person. It undertook inquiries in the neighbourhoods and bazaars about the standing of customers and rarely gave loans to unknown debtors against collaterals. It dealt in *hundi*s but not with 'modern' financial instruments.[52]

The extent to which the bank remained embedded in local reputational structures can also be seen from its chairman's letter to its shareholders and investors which highlights the bank's creditors' honour and social standing and humbly addresses their support. Even under the conditions the bank found itself in – with a composition scheme approved by the Allahabad High Court – the statement's language reflects a careful choice of phrasing to honour the goodwill of the investors, attempting to save face for the bank and its director, in fact merging these identities. Noting that the settlement had been reached and vowing that letters by the bank's 'friends and investors' would be individually responded to, the statement emphasized the director's personal humility, though between the lines investors were also informed of continuing difficulties:

> On this occasion I want to announce my heartfelt gratitude to all these friends who placed so much unyielding faith [*vishvaas*] in me and [who] behaved so admirably and with such patience. If all the help and assistance by our investors and friends had not been forthcoming with such readiness, then in the last year

with the burden of work and anxiety that fell on my head, I could not have born all this. I now have just this prayer in good faith and suitable admiration, that the bank will remain, and that the generosity of this scheme of the investors, granted by the High Court may serve to settle its outstanding dues. All my prayer is that with the continued help, sympathy, and assistance of all our merciful friends and helpers, my work may be completed. This is a question of the financial credit [*sakh*] of the nation. To make this lasting for the nation's prosperity is the ultimate necessity. Together we must return the reproachless investors their exhausting efforts. For all of us is this duty – whether [the investors'] manifest unity for the sake of the bank may remain or not – that this goodness may eventually be for the benefit of those the bank management is responsible for.[53]

While the statement constitutes an exercise in humility, its text underscores important points when looking at 'organized' banking from the perspective of the handling of registers of trust, especially when juxtaposed to Bulchand's testimony to the United Provinces Banking Enquiry Committee. Bulchand's deposition had highlighted juridical-procedural forms of handling trust – even while showing that the bank did not actually follow these. Yet the attempt to operate a banking business in Banaras along the lines of a low-trust regime eventually failed. The reasons for this failure have to be interpreted in the context of the larger crisis of finance in the city. However, once entering the crisis, the bank was compelled to simultaneously employ two opposing registers of trust: the legal process mandated bankruptcy proceedings; before entering bankruptcy, however, the bank needed to reach out to its investors – the city's financial elite and landed aristocracy.

Having compromised the trust originally set in the bank – despite the juridical-procedural safeguards – the bank needed to fall back upon the essential characteristics of reputational registers of trust, goodwill and 'faith' (lit.: *vishvaas*). The director's statement even mentioned a notion of 'credit' (*sakh*), and the specific usage makes it clear that it refers to 'credit' as a higher reputational register of trust than 'faith'. In a peculiarly 'modern' use of the concept, the notion of *sakh* was linked to Indian nationhood, contrasting it with the law as a 'British Indian' institution. The imperative to rely on 'faith', the reputational markers of a high-trust register of trust, and 'indigenous' tradition, suddenly needed to be upheld as the 'nation's credit'. Yet the notion of *sakh* could not anymore be used in ways reminiscent of Bayly's depiction, as the bank had already compromised the high-trust registers that made 'informal' lending possible. Not only had the bank had difficulties in reconciling different registers of trust as required by law and actual banking practice, but in entering bankruptcy, 'traditional' notions of liability had been breached irrevocably. Not having fulfilled its obligations under *sakh*, or even the less elaborate ethic of *vishvaas*, the bank fell back on a propagation of 'traditional' ethics applied to the 'modern' concept of the nation rather than directly to itself as a firm. Eventually, its belated attempts to demonstrate its embeddedness in 'traditional' discourses failed, as it was liquidated half a year later, under rules based on conceptions of low trust and limited liability. The director's prayer that – henceforth – the bank would work 'for the benefit' of its investors showcased future adherence to a high-trust register, though it would also have signalled to the bank's debtors that a full settlement of their dues was improbable. Limited liability constituted one of the most important forms of 'organization' for financial businesses, marking what made a bank an 'organized' bank, more so than taking deposits. Yet once the crisis in its fortunes had become apparent, the bank was not anymore able to employ low-trust registers – not without losing all trust by its investors in its reputational standing.

This dilemma of handling contrasting registers of trust simultaneously is visible beyond the bank's bankruptcy proceedings. The following study of advertising patterns in mid-twentieth-century Banaras is based on an archive of newspaper clippings covering all media content related to finance between 1930 and 2011 from the respective leading papers in Banaras (defined by circulation) – until the early 1970s the newspaper *Aaj*, subsequently *Dainik Jagran*.

Local banking advertising spiked in the 1930s and 1940s, then declined in the 1950s and 1960s. After bank nationalization, it reached a new peak in the mid-1970s that lasted until the 1980s, before declining again in the 1990s. Significantly, while the decline of advertising since the 1990s can be related to a shift towards visual media, the earlier spikes reflect changes in the procedural grammar of banking operations. These changes necessitated efforts to reach out to the public to generate trust. This, in turn, is reinforced by a shift in type of banking advertising that centred upon the generation of trust in the banking companies until the mid-1970s, shifting to product-based advertising reflecting consumer aspirations afterwards.

Banking advertising attempted to fulfil several objectives simultaneously, including creating awareness of the bank's brand and its specific products or special offers. Yet concerning the key element of generating trust in early advertisements, juridical-procedural and reputational registers of trust are identifiable. Reputational registers of trust differ from personal trust, yet crucially depend on the ability at need to identify interpersonal experiences producing trust. Bereft of a remote certification process by an assumedly superior agency, they rely on a more knowable certifier whose identifiable personal reputation vouches for unknowable qualities. In juridical-procedural registers of trust this need is replaced by a demonstration of adherence to codified procedural norms that create the illusion of control by the remote and unknowable certifier. Under this definition, various elements discernible in the local banking advertisements fall either in one of these two categories or into a miscellaneous category that may tend towards one category without evidently being part of it. Many banking advertisements in mid-twentieth-century Banaras demonstrate a combination of reputational and juridical-procedural registers of trust, though the predominance of juridical-procedural registers presupposed by their legal form becomes entrenched only after the nationalization of banks in the late 1960s.

Figure 5.1 depicts an example of reputational registers of trust. It announces the reduction of commission fees for money transfers to Calcutta and Bombay for customers frequently transferring money there. However, it is not a reference

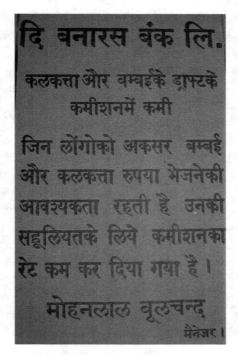

Figure 5.1 Bank of Benares, announcement of reduced commission fees

Source: *Aaj*, 3 June 1936. Archive of the Nagari Pracharini Sabha, Varanasi.

to the bank's product range: the advertisement does not give details on the reduction, or the definition of the term 'frequent'. The bank commissioned half a dozen identical advertisements in paid-for advertising space in *Aaj* between 1933 and 1939, yet decided to leave out detailed information. It could conceivably constitute an example of bad advertising. But it is more plausible that the bank omitted this information deliberately since frequent customers would already have known the rates and target group beforehand, or were considered capable of obtaining the missing information directly from the bank, being in regular contact with it. The sequential character of the advertisements reinforces this interpretation: it remains unclear whether they related to a succession of decreases or intermittent reductions, yet frequent customers would have known.

Then why was the scheme advertised in the first place? At the time of its first appearance in 1933, the Bank of Benares did not have many 'organized' competitors locally. Its competition was from 'indigenous' bankers. The advertisement is hardly visually appealing, undermining an argument that it was intended to showcase the bank's self-professed 'modernity'. The lack of visual appeal, in turn, hardly demonstrated thriftiness as potential customers inclined towards thrift may plausibly have questioned the need to spend money on a visually non-appealing *and* uninformative advertisement. The lack of visual appeal is also uncommon in newspaper advertisements of the time. Douglas E. Haynes (Haynes 2015) has profusely demonstrated the levels of visual sophistication of advertisements in this period, and non-banking advertisements throughout the 1930s were far more sophisticated than those of the Bank of Benares and other banks. The only important detail provided, in fact, was the manager's name, standing in for the bank's reputation, and vouching for the policy's validity in his personal capacity. Its manager was reinforcing the bank's standing with his own reputation.

The practice of using the bank managers' names in advertising, and therefore of managers lending their reputations to the banks, was a recurring feature of banking advertising well into the 1970s, though its frequency declined after the 1940s. As corporate identities gained prominence, the naming of managerial staff diminished to personal touches added to other content. Logos started to be used occasionally by many banks in the mid-1940s, including by the State Bank of Banaras. Logos constituted one of the most easily recognizable juridical-procedural registers of trust in highlighting corporate identity. The frequency of their use was correlated to the gradual disappearance of the names of managerial staff. In the 1930s, bankers lent their name to ensure the bank's reputation, by the 1970s most advertisements were featuring logos and omitted bankers' names. State Bank of India advertisements from the 1960s onwards are particularly instructive as many of these positioned the logo in the bottom right corner, earlier reserved for the bank manager's name. The State Bank of Banaras formed an exception in this regard. It frequently used its logo (typically in the top left corner), but continued to use the names of managerial staff at the bottom right corner well into the 1980s.

The most visually appealing banking advertisement in Banaras in the 1930s reinforces the centrality accorded to managerial staff. By late 1936, Mohanlal Bulchand had been replaced as the bank's manager. An identical advertisement was published four times between August and November 1936 by *Aaj*. An otherwise identical advertisement in black instead of red print was placed in *Aaj* an additional four times between January and September 1937. For a period of over one year, the bank advertised only the changes in its management (Figure 5.2).

The advertisement includes no content apart from the politely phrased intention of the new management to serve its customers well, and the names of its new chairman, manager, and secretary. Apart from these fourteen advertisements, the bank commissioned another twenty-seven advertisements in *Aaj* between 1930 and 1940 (see Table 5.1). All of these were published in sections of the daily that were reserved for paid advertising space, though some may have fulfilled legal stipulations, as in the announcements of prior notice for withdrawals and withholding dividends.

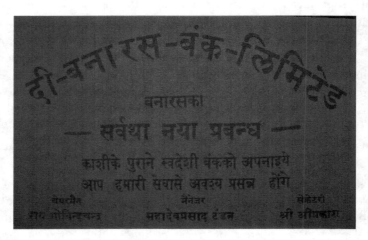

Figure 5.2 Bank of Benares, change of management

Source: *Aaj*, 9 December 1936. Archive of the Nagari Pracharini Sabha, Varanasi.

Table 5.1 Details of Bank of Benares advertising in the 1930s

Content	Number
Hoarding cash at home is not safe. Better deposit in banks. Name of manager.	4
Deposits earn interest. Rates unspecified. Name of manager.	3
Education is expensive. Better use savings account. Rates unspecified. Name of manager.	2
BoB is a swadeshi bank, serving the nation. Name of manager.	2
Listing names of the bank's board and directorate, its branches, and equity.	1
Opening of new branch. Invitation to ceremony. Name of manager.	1
3-month notice required for withdrawing higher amounts. Name of manager.	1
Savings deposits earn interest. Specified rates for different schemes. Name of manager.	2
BoB has paid interest on savings accounts. Specified rates.	3
Details on interest for one-year fixed deposit. Name of manager.	1
Details on equity.	2
Amount of money deposited, details on equity, number/location of branches.	4
Announcement on withholding dividends, regrets for inconvenience. Name of chairman.	1
Reduced commission on money transfers. Unspecified rates. Name of manager.	6
New management.	8
Total	**41**

Source: Collection of digitized newspaper reports on finance from the newspapers *Aaj* and *Dainik Jagran*, obtained from the archive of the Nagari Pracharini Sabha, Varanasi. In possession of the author.

Leaving aside the aforementioned announcements, Table 5.1 shows the key role of reputational registers of trust for advertising. Juridical-procedural registers were mostly absent. The advertisements specifying interest rates for fixed deposits and saving deposits also typically included the manager's name as assurance. Juridical-procedural registers are implicitly visible in the announcements on the bank's equity and deposits, though one of these also featured a comprehensive list of its directorate. The remaining six implicitly juridical-procedural advertisements deviated by not including managerial names. Miscellaneous advertisements served educational purposes – depositing protected against theft, deposits earned interest, and saving schemes served educational expenditure. Even in these, the bank's manager was included as assurance for the claimed benefits of 'organized' banking.

Bank of Benares's advertising can be contrasted to the efforts by other locally operating banks to generate trust. As the only local-origin bank, it benefited from its local embeddedness in employing reputational registers. Banks entering the market from outside partially offset this comparative disadvantage by using both reputational and juridical-procedural registers. One common pattern was to increase the details on their operations, highlighting the bank's size and reliability through enhanced information on equity and deposits, and on interest rates. The Hindustan Commercial Bank even included staff bonuses.[54] These advertisements indicate an incipient shift towards highlighting specific services. Banks from beyond Banaras, in addition, did not advertise with an 'educational' intention, with one exception: in one of the first of these ads in *Aaj*, the Industrial Bank incorporated the slogan (translated from Hindi): 'This is not a lottery. Many people have invested in lotteries, but few have benefited from them.'[55] The perceived need for banks – invariably targeting the well-off and assumedly educated – to elucidate fundamental aspects of 'modern' banking illustrates the extent to which Bulchand's confidence in the future of joint stock banking was based on an awareness of a state-led 'modernization' project rather than customer preferences, or customers' trust in its juridical-procedural parameters.

The competitors of the Bank of Benares frequently included the names of its managerial staff, though local customers would have had little reputational knowledge about them. One prominent way to substitute for individual reputation was to emphasize the number of branches across India and the location of headquarters in the metropolises. Bank headquarters in Calcutta or Bombay indicated business size and embeddedness in the 'modern' economy. In the 1940s, several banks highlighted agencies in New York and London and, in the case of the Kumilla Banking Corporation, in Australia,[56] thus combining the advertising of specific services with an image of 'global modernity'. Demonstrating the decline of Banaras as a financial centre, several banks from the United Provinces since the mid-1940s highlighted their locations in Kanpur and Allahabad. Conversely, the Bihar Bank Ltd. in the 1930s and 1940s closely followed the pattern of the Bank of Benares, reflecting the close regional links.

Another noticeable feature of banks from outside Banaras were their target clienteles. The Bank of Benares typically addressed 'frequent customers', or specified its clientele as 'persons of rank and status' (*shreni*). Several other banks, conversely, advertised their willingness to serve *all* classes of customers, and in the late 1930s the Bank of Benares for the first time omitted the class specification.

Even banks from outside the city regularly employed combinations of registers that emphasized the reputational. A particularly interesting case was the Tripura Modern Bank Ltd. in 1946 (see Figure 5.3). The advertisement was one of the first that specifically highlighted its legal status as a scheduled and clearing bank. At the same time, it proceeded to list the names of its board, starting with the Maharaja of Tripura as guarantor and the Prime Minister of Tripura State as chairman. Though most of the content was used for a detailed description of the business – listing its equity, capital stock, cash and other reserves, deposits, and its banking fund, then proceeding to list its large number of branches mostly in eastern India – the *maharaja*'s involvement was repeated in bold letters as the signee, certifying the bank's reputation through the reputation of his title instead of his name. The State Bank of Banaras – set up by the city's most important banking families – included the *maharaja* of Banaras as director, despite his publicly known indebtedness to these bankers.

Figure 5.3 Tripura Modern Bank advertisement

Source: *Aaj*, 9 January 1946. Archive of the Nagari Pracharini Sabha, Varanasi.

Other banks competed for reputation by announcing that opening ceremonies for branch offices would be attended by widely known Congress politicians, for instance, Dr. Sampurnanand.[57]

Starting in the 1940s but reaching predominance only by the early 1970s, advertisements began to presuppose customer confidence in the juridical-procedural parameters of banking. The Economic Bank went so far as to encapsulate its legal form in the image of a rising sun (Figure 5.4).[58] Yet the advertisement still employed reputational registers through an invitation to the opening ceremony of its Jaunpur branch office that emphasized the personal reputation of bank managers and attending notables. Images of modernity emerged as a hallmark of banking advertising in the 1950s and 1960s, though these remained embedded into the usage of reputational registers of trust. The character of visual contents changed subsequently – after the nationalization

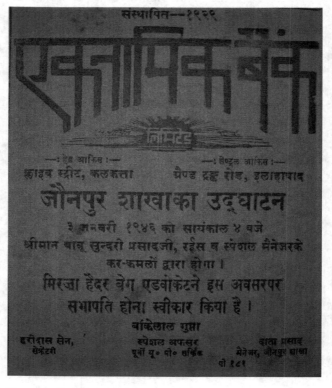

Figure 5.4 Economic Bank advertisement

Source: Aaj, 2 January 1946. Archive of the Nagari Pracharini Sabha, Varanasi.

of Indian banks – with the state utilizing banks as agents of development. In turn, these features tended to be replaced by the 1980s with contents depicting consumerist aspirations.

Conclusion

Trust constitutes an ingenious device for the handling of economic relations in the way it manages uncertainty – not by actually lowering the level of uncertainty faced, but by convincing oneself that it remains manageable. In turn, through its experiential character, information on trust and trustworthiness becomes exchanged, and thereby allows exchange under conditions of high uncertainty. The 'rationalization' and 'formalization' exercises which characterized the project of creating a 'modern' financial sector have tended to obscure the operation of trust on credit markets, creating the illusion of scientifically managing uncertainty as risk, and shifting the object of trust towards distanced agents and institutions. In the process, they reinforced a tendency to place greater value on handling risk, instead of handling trust – an often-overlooked element of the distinction between 'formal' and 'informal' economic relations. This tendency can be illustrated by drawing on James Scott's distinction between types of knowledge (Scott 1998, on markets see in particular pp. 334–35, 351), differentiating between the handling of risk (as a form of *episteme*) and the handling of trust that is firmly anchored in the realm of *metis*. Yet it is notable that the *episteme* of credit merely created the illusion of an absence of trust, though – as with trust itself – the illusion itself produces tangible ramifications for its reproduction, thus creating the conditions for its reliability, as information that can be trusted.

On credit markets in the north Indian *mufassil* the process of distinguishing between the *metis* and the *episteme* of credit relations first needed to be produced itself, before it could become a defining element for credit markets. The distinction between 'modern' and 'indigenous' credit markets remained inextricably tied to the extent of taking deposits in the 1930s in the absence of sufficiently pronounced differences in the practice of credit relations between the favoured juridical-procedural parameters of lending and their reputational counterparts. Birla's distinction between *kaccha* and *pakka* forms of business (Birla 2015, 402–04) – drawing on their respective 'solidity' – needs to be interpreted in this way too. In order to be able to distinguish between solid and unsolid practices, the Indian state first needed to create the conditions under which the former became viable. Lending the money of strangers needed to be facilitated by creating the grounds for the illusion of overcoming uncertainty to become a viable assumption or, ironically, an expectation of the future that was sufficiently certain to serve as a guideline for practical conduct. 'Modernizing' credit did not so much eviscerate the imperative to rely on trust, but it sought to create the conditions – for the favoured segment of creditors and debtors – to operate low-trust regimes in which the reputational dynamics of credit could be minimized and therefore obscured. The reputational handling of high-trust relations, hence, became associated with extra-legal market practices, in turn reinforcing the visibility of market segmentation. This divergence undermined the experience of sufficient certainty in the handling of high-trust relations at the apex of the market that was based on the employment of strong social ties and mercantile ethics for the enforcement of debt obligations. With the incipient demise of this apex, the reputational economy underlying extra-legal finance lost its main collective elements. High-trust market relations based on reputation-as-obligation rooted in collective organizational forms diminished in their importance for the reputational handling of credit.

Notes

1. Rudner (1989, 417).
2. See Möllering (2001) and Simmel (2004).
3. More broadly, and in the context of the Punjab, the complexities of the construction of 'village society' by British Indian administrators has been discussed in detail by Neeladhri Bhattacharya (2018).
4. On Marwari business, see Timberg (2014).
5. Extract from Diary of British Consulate-General, Kashgar, for October 1919, File no. IOR L/PJ/6/1753, India Office Records, British Library, London.
6. Extract from Diary of British Consulate-General, Kashgar, for December 1919, File no. IOR L/PJ/6/1753, India Office Records, British Library, London.
7. Copy of a confidential letter no. 84 – C, dated Kashgar, 14th April 1931, from His Majesty's Officiating Consul-General, Kashgar, to the Foreign Secretary to the Government of India in the Foreign and Political Department, Simla, File no. IOR L/PS/12/2343, India Office Records, British Library, London.
8. Confidential letter from the Deputy Secretary to the Government of India in the Foreign and Political Department to His Majesty's Consul-General, Kashgar, 28 April 1932, File no. IOR L/PS/12/2343, India Office Records, British Library, London.
9. File no. IOR L/PS/12/2343, India Office Records, British Library, London.

10. 'Sinkiang. Proposed exclusion of Hindu moneylenders not engaged in legitimate trade', dated 18 May 1932, File no. IOR L/PS/12/2343, India Office Records, British Library, London.
11. 'Move to Control Money Lending: Punjab Bill', *Times of India*, 23 June 1938.
12. For an example of employing the 'alien' status of Kabulis as a surrogate for communal mobilization against moneylenders, see 'Home Department – Judicial. Question in the Legislative Assembly by Mr. C. N. Muthuranga Mudaliar regarding Kabulis or Pathan money-lenders', National Archives of India, New Delhi, File No. 19/24/34 – Judl.
13. 'Moneylenders' Act Amendment: Hyderabad State Move', *Times of India*, 29 April 1946.
14. 'Note for Rs. 250 for Rs. 23 Cash. Pathan's Charge Fails', *Times of India*, 23 May 1938.
15. 'Bombay's Pathan Money-lenders', *Times of India*, 9 February 1938, ProQuest Historical Newspapers: The Times of India (1838–2003), 12.
16. 'Money-Lenders in Poona', *Times of India*, 25 January 1938, 16.
17. *UPBECR* I, 124.
18. Letter by Sir Horace Williamson, dated 19 June 1935, National Archives of India, New Delhi, Office order regarding the indebtedness to the Pathan moneylenders, F. 288/35-Public (henceforth referred to as Office Order).
19. 'Money-Lending', *Times of India*, 5 November 1935, 8.
20. Note B 12604 by O. K. Caroe, dated 15 June 1935, Office Order.
21. Letter by Major Robinson, dated 30 May 1935, Office Order.
22. Ibid.
23. Ibid.
24. Ibid.
25. Memorandum by J. M. Ewast, Home Department, dated 24 February 1937, Office Order.
26. Letter by Sir Horace Williamson, dated 19 June 1935, Office Order.
27. Ibid.
28. Ibid.
29. Ibid.
30. Memorandum by A. S. Hands, dated 6 August 1936, Office Order.
31. *The Indian Central Banking Enquiry Committee Report*, Volume I, Part I, *The Majority Report* (Calcutta: Government of India Central Publication Branch, 1931), 499.
32. Letter by Sir Horace Williamson, dated 19 June 1935, Office Order.
33. Ibid.

34. Memorandum by J. M. Ewast, Home Department, dated 24 February 1937, Office Order. See also Memorandum by A. S. Hands, dated 6 August 1936, Office Order.
35. Memorandum by R. M. Maxwell, dated 18 May 1937, Office Order.
36. Ibid.
37. Memorandum by J. M. Ewast, Home Department, dated 24 February 1937, Office Order.
38. Memorandum by R. M. Maxwell, dated 18 May 1937, Office Order.
39. Note by the Legislative Department, undated, Office Order.
40. Memorandum by A. S. Hands, dated 6 August 1936, Office Order.
41. Office Memorandum no. 288/35-Public, Government of India, Home Department, dated New Delhi, 18 January 1938, Office Order.
42. Memorandum by R. M. Maxwell, dated 21 May 1937, Office Order.
43. Letter by Major Robinson, dated 30 May 1935, Office Order.
44. Ibid.
45. Ibid.
46. *UPBECR* I, 7.
47. Rudner (1994, 128–29, original emphasis).
48. The term preferentially used by Rudner for the caste group depicted here as Nattukottai Chettiars. Colonial sources tended to use the abbreviated form 'Chetty', instead, though the Chettiar caste comprised a larger variety of sub-castes.
49. *UPBECR* IV, 99.
50. Ibid. IV, 100.
51. Ibid. IV, 99.
52. Ibid. IV, 102.
53. Statement by the director, Bank of Benares, Shri Shriprakash, published in the local daily *Aaj*, 19 December 1939, translation from Hindi by the author. Mohanlal Bulchand had been replaced by a board of directors in 1936.
54. Advertisement, Hindustan Commercial Bank, *Aaj*, 24 January 1947.
55. Advertisement, Industrial Bank, *Aaj*, 23 December 1933.
56. Advertisement, Kumilla Banking Corporation Ltd., *Aaj*, 10 January 1947.
57. Advertisement, Calcutta Commercial Bank, *Aaj*, 25 January 1939.
58. Advertisement, Economic Bank, *Aaj*, 2 January 1946.

6

Obligation

A sahib has got to act like a sahib.... To come all that way, rifle in hand, with two thousand people marching at my heels, and then to trail feebly away, having done nothing – no, that was impossible. The crowd would laugh at me. And my whole life, every white man's life in the East, was one long struggle not to be laughed at.[1]

As discussed extensively in the previous chapters, extra-legal financial markets need to adjust to the heightened levels of uncertainty inherent not only in the credit contract as such but especially in credit contracts that cannot rely on strong mechanisms of enforcing obligations. The guarantee of contractual law for the regulated segment of credit markets by the modern Indian nation-state constituted one of the strongest possible mechanisms, especially from the creditor's point of view, and particularly in favour of the creditor. At the same time, financial markets in India (and beyond) had long experience with producing conditions that facilitated enforceability at need – the various structures of social embeddedness that lay at the heart of the bazaar economy in its South Asian variant. Historically, financial markets in Banaras had been designed to operate in the absence of strong state enforcement of obligation: as a commercial and financial centre that for long periods had been at the margins of imperial structures of authority, and had flourished despite the lack of politico-military control – or possibly precisely because of it – the credit markets of Banaras were well steeped in modes of governance that created possibilities for sanctioning misbehaviour across caste and community membership. Many of these rested on the versatility of reputational flows governing the *hundi* trade. But linked to this trade, the reputation of the local market – a crucial content of information for any trader sufficiently distant or otherwise detached from local conditions to be unable to have reputational knowledge of individual bankers or banking families – rested on the enforcement of obligations by the local bankers and merchants. In the absence of arbitrators specifically employed for these purposes like the *amin* in Geertz's depiction of the bazaar in Morocco (Geertz 1979), it rested on the city's 'indigenous' banking families.

In the absence of politico-military authority, the reputational information networks underlying belonging to the city's financial and commercial 'nobility', provided a loose behavioural code that, in turn, needed to be emulated by lower-order markets to gain respectability and, therefore, reputation. The city's bankers did not need violent means, or the threat of it, as misconduct – once sufficiently pronounced – carried the penalty of losing reputation, and thereby the ability to convert reputation into credit. Vasudha Dalmia, discussing the lavish spending of Bharatendu Harischandra – from the banking families' perspective one of the city's most well-known prodigals – recounts the displeasure of the merchant and banking families with his demeanour, including direct reprimands by the maharaja (Dalmia 1997, 127–29). Harischandra's misconduct may have been a matter of concern for his peers and well-wishers, yet fundamentally it needed the urgent intervention of his betters precisely because it compromised the narrative of reputation woven around the city's banking families as a whole. Breaches of the loose code of conduct for the city's mercantile elite were known to occur, but they needed to be finely calibrated to ensure they remained outside public discourse, lest they damaged the reputation of the local market as a whole.

As importantly, wherever breaches of conduct became known – and the structure of reputational gossip within the market made sure that it was widely communicated – circumspection needed to be seen by lower-order market participants, so that the rationale of emulation for social and economic upward mobility could not be questioned. There was an enormous gap between the city's financial 'aristocracy' and *qistwallah*s or *sahukar*s, yet the common intelligibility of credit and commercial practice, and the reliance of all segments of the market on reputational information flows meant that this emulation of the elite's conduct had significant repercussions for the practices followed even at the lowest segments of the market in terms of value (and reputation). Without the need for emulation, extra-legal credit markets in Banaras lost one of their most fundamental governance structures, and the crisis of 'indigenous' banking in the city – beginning in the 1930s – thus had significantly greater consequences than the mere substitution of elite segments in society. Losing its governing apex meant that the enforcement of obligations within the market even at lower-order segments became weakened significantly, and could remain resilient only in areas marked by stable patterns of socio-economic domination, much more prevalent in rural than in urban Indian society. In the following, these more stable conditions and their impacts on extra-legal credit markets and practices will be depicted subsequently to a discussion of the decline of 'indigenous' banking in Banaras.

Shooting a lion – obligation, mercantile decline, and reputational resilience

One day in the mid-1940s, Shri Radha Raman Prasadji went with a friend to shoot a lion.[2] When I first met him, he felt very proud of it, though he could not say why he went in the first place. Eventually, he said that he had liked rifles as a young man, that he went to the Rifle Club where he met his friend, and that on the spur of the moment they decided to go. They drove to the family of a local retainer, and were led to a place the lion would come to, set up lanterns, readied their photo equipment, hid in a tree, and waited. After shooting the lion, they arranged for an elephant, and triumphantly returned with the dead lion to the adoration of the villagers.

The incident itself is hardly special, a happy remembrance of his youth for a person who was aged ninety-three when I interviewed him. Yet the event needs to be seen in the context of the decline of the banking families of Banaras in the mid-twentieth century, and the changes it affected in the reputational economy of debt, especially the decline of the governing apex of the mercantile ethics described by Bayly (1983) as *sakh*: Shri Radha Raman was the younger descendant of a landlord-cum-banking family. Hunting constituted an aristocratic leisure activity, though his family is from the Agrawal caste. Nevertheless, he inherited a landlord tradition, though his family had lived in urban settings for generations, having shifted from Gaya to Banaras around 1855. They had been moneylenders in western Bihar and became landlords in the late sixteenth century, but maintained their lending activities in Gaya and expanded these in Banaras. Their significant rise in wealth in the late nineteenth and early twentieth centuries was clearly related to lending. Though the family cites the wish of a female family member to undertake *kashivaas*[3] to constitute the reason for their shift, it corresponded to good business strategy since Banaras had reached the heyday of its commercial importance as the 'inland capital of Indian commerce' (Dalmia 1997).

In Radha Raman's time, however, Banaras had declined significantly. The banking families that constituted the city's elite had failed to shift to industrial capital in the way of other business elites.[4] The system of 'indigenous' banking was under pressure to adapt to late colonial 'modernity', while money lending was increasingly associated with moral opprobrium. Hunting lions may be seen as a thrilling pleasure activity, but it needs to be interpreted in the context of an elite trying to hold on to a perceived aristocratic lifestyle and its reputational underpinnings in a context forcing them to become increasingly bourgeois.

The Raman family had been hit hard by this decline. The shooting incidence happened at a time the family had already declined significantly. It had suffered a number of untimely deaths. Radha Raman and his elder sibling Kishori Raman Prasadji were placed under guardianship after the death of their father in 1921. Kishori Raman needed to take over the family business as soon as he reached maturity in 1925. By the time Radha Raman reached maturity, however, he was told to study at Benares Hindu University (BHU) instead of 'wasting away his life in business'. He studied Indian philosophy, stayed on at BHU for his Ph.D., and eventually became a lecturer, partially related to his proximity to Madan Mohan Malviya. Radha Raman started to get involved in business only in the late 1940s, at a time the family slowly moved out of finance. The exact reasons for giving up lending were left unclear by Radha Raman, but families like his felt the need to protect their reputation, and while 'indigenous' bankers were still respected in the city, most of his strand of the family was lending in the 'bazaar', a lower level within the reputational economy of debt much closer to money lending. Public imagination was shifting towards a representation of lenders as greedy and shifty, even sleazy. The figure of the greedy and sly moneylender was prominent in Premchand's novels, written in and on Banaras. Possibly the most notable representation of this image became expressed in the character Sukhilala, played by Kanhaiya Lal in the Bollywood film *Mother India*. *Mother India* was only released in 1957, but the film was based on an earlier film by its director, Mehboob Khan, released under the title *Aurat* in 1940 which figured Kanhaiya Lal in an identical role. *Aurat* may not have had the lasting impact of *Mother India* on Indian cinema,[5] but it was certainly not unpopular, and Mehboob Khan had already made a name for himself by directing several acclaimed films.

As ardent supporters of Gandhi and Malviya, being personally close to both and major donors to the nationalist cause, Radha and Kishori Raman would have keenly felt this condemnation. The policies of the Congress-led government in the United Provinces towards money lending remained ambiguous, but its public discourse was not, and continued to shift to a developmentalist idiom in which the 'anachronism' of money lending was highlighted. Radha Raman, in fact, had briefly flirted with communism in the late 1930s before returning to the Congress. As nationalists, landlords, and bankers, they were also close to the newly emerging political elite, counting several ministers of independent Bihar as well as leading political figures like Jagjivan Ram and Rajendra Prasad as personal friends. Radha Raman became part of several advisory committees on economic policy in independent India. By the time he shot the lion, they were aware of the imminence of the transfer of power from the British, and they knew the outlines of future economic policy sufficiently to be aware of the likelihood of *zamindari* abolition, eventually enacted in 1951.

After *zamindari* abolition, the family needed to turn to new areas: while Kishori Raman was still in charge of the family business, Radha Raman began to diversify their sources of income. On invitation by the maharaja, he became co-founder of the State Bank of Banaras (SBB) in 1946. He was also persuaded by the owners of the Clark's Hotel in Banaras – the most luxurious in town – to become a shareholder. He converted a number of houses the family owned in the Dasasvamedh area, which in his words had paid thousands of rupees in rent into another hotel, the Banaras Lodge. The lodge was initially profitable. The *maharaja* became convinced that he should partner with Radha Raman in setting up his own hotel as part of the Taj Hotel Group of which Radha Raman became a board member and shareholder. He also completed the shift of the family from their old home in the main bazaar area to the Raman Niwas residence in Mahmoorganj, at the time on the outskirts of town. The family had started to live there since the mid-1930s, but had conducted business from Chowk. The shift of business symbolized the transformation from the 'bazaar' to their new businesses, and was depicted accordingly by Radha Raman, who claimed that lending had still needed to operate from Chowk, for prestige as well as for obtaining sufficient information.

The investment in hotels, however, cost a major share of the urban real estate possessed by the family. Radha Raman claimed that he regularly needed to sell houses to maintain the hotel business and pay its staff. He had inherited twenty-two houses in Gaya and twelve in Banaras, and built rural retreats for the family which then were lost in *zamindari* abolition, or had to be sold afterwards. Banaras Lodge is by now a *dharamshala*. It had been unprofitable for most of its time as a hotel. The Taj was highly profitable, but the family incrementally sold its shares. The State Bank of Banaras followed a similar path of evolution. It was founded 1946, then took over first the Bareilli Bank in 1964, and then the Lucknow Bank in 1968; but it failed to become consistently profitable. After its nationalization, the family's shares became practically worthless. According to Radha Raman's grandson Navneet, the family ceremoniously set fire to their shares on their lawn as this was 'the only thing they were still good for'.[6]

Looking back, Radha Raman expressed satisfaction with the course of his life, but also declared himself to be a failure in an entrepreneurial sense. There was a clear sense of entrepreneurial spirit, but eventually most of his business decisions did not turn out as expected. He had accepted this failure – partially as an image of the times he had lived in, partially by pointing out that business had been forced on him. His own idea of his duty to the family was to maintain their status, which required maintaining their lifestyle and their role as patrons more than entrepreneurial success. The funding for their lifestyle and their role as patrons was diminishing, but it ought to have been available, and his entrepreneurial career was mostly determined by the need to find ways to maintain them. In his words, 'Banaras Lodge, Taj hotel, SBB, these were all phases' in this entrepreneurial career, but phases in finding the means for patronage, not ends in themselves. The main difficulty had been *zamindari* abolition.

> This was the real crux of the problem of our family that our zamindari was taken away; we had no resources, and I had to be in politics, but we had no resources, from politics we could not generate resources. That was not possible.[7]

Houses rented out as either homes or shops, according to the family, stopped paying rent, and some were entirely taken over by the people renting them.[8] Most urban real estate was lost in 1976 after the implementation of the Urban Land Ceiling Act. What remained were the family's three major tracts of real estate: the Banaras Lodge complex, the family's residence at Mahmoorganj, and their old, sprawling *haveli* in Chowk, the main bazaar area. Upholding their social status required that the latter two remained in their possession, though much of their land around Raman Niwas, originally a sprawling park, was taken away from the family and developed for real estate. To give up the prime real estate in Chowk would have meant cutting off not only their origins as part of the city's old aristocratic and commercial elite but also much of the family's claim to a status beyond its increasingly bourgeois livelihood, and accordingly was unthinkable. Radha's grandson Navneet remembers that in the 1970s and 1980s major parts of Raman Niwas fell into disuse as the family did not anymore have the means to maintain them. Navneet Raman narrated how the family's income in the mid-1970s was mostly sustained from an automobile repair workshop founded by the family in front of their premises, a depiction that may be exaggerated to some degree but serves to highlight the family's intermittent decline.[9]

Status takes a key role in the family's self-depiction, and the loss of status may be more strongly felt by some of its members than the decline in economic fortunes, especially considering that it is much more prosperous now than in the aftermath of the Urban Land Ceiling Act. The family's self-depiction rests on its history as a landed elite and its role as patrons of the arts and education. Kishori Raman Prasadji was well known in Banaras as a patron of music.

Apart from his role as a patron, musical performances were frequently organized outside the Raman Niwas residence, and both Radha Raman and Navneet Raman stressed that these concerts were still organized until Kishori Raman's demise in the mid-1980s. Attendance was necessarily free as it was unthinkable for an elite family to make money out of patronizing the arts, even if the family had fallen on 'hard times'. While the older generations of the family did not talk about it, Radha Raman's grandson was proud that his family's house was (as he put it) where George Harrison learned to play the *sitar*. Even more costly were contributions to educational institutions: Radha was a lecturer at BHU in the late 1940s but would not accept any salary. The proximity of the family to Malviya meant that they were regular contributors to the university's funds. Another patronized institution, the Sanskrit University, received official university status only in 1958, though Radha Raman claimed that it operated as a full university beforehand, and needed to be funded privately. Yet another institution, the Sanatan Dharma College at Kanpur, was established only in 1970, at a time the family's fortunes had already declined, though they were only one of many contributors. The family had stopped giving patronage in most of the areas of their earlier *zamindari* but still contributed to the upkeep of a number of temples in western Bihar and in Banaras in addition to religious welfare institutions like the Pilgrims' Fund and the *anathalaya* (orphanage). Probably the most lavish instance of patronage consumed most of the family's hoard of jewellery: as moneylenders lending against collaterals the family had acquired large amounts of silver ornaments. In the late 1930s, Radha Raman had learned how to assess the quality of silver and gold from jewellers in the main bazaar, a necessity for lending against movable collateral. However, lending soon became a minor source of income. Instead, much of it was used to change the interior of a temple near their old *haveli* from wood and alloys to silver.

Radha Raman had built several family retreats in western Bihar and the adjoining districts in the United Provinces that were lost as part of the land reforms. He recounted one story that demonstrates the difficulties of living up to their elite status: the commissioner of a district near Gaya had informed them of the incipient land reforms and asked what they intended to do with one of their *haveli*s. Being both a personal and a political friend, Radha decided to donate the building to the district administration and it became the commissioner's headquarters. He did not believe that he had had any chance of selling the *haveli*, yet he was still proud that the commissioner's headquarters was located in one of his family's residences. The one retreat that was kept by the family was in Mussoorie where the family kept on going for holidays well into the 1980s. The house there had a special importance for Radha Raman, yet eventually it, too, was lost to the family.

Marriages and marriage alliances created another problem once the family's decline had set in. Marriage functions were becoming difficult to fund: Radha Raman recounted that a marriage among their status group in the late 1930s used to run up bills of about 2 lakh rupees around Gaya, and 3 lakh rupees in Kanpur. A cousin of his had arrived in Calcutta after partition, having lost most of his possessions. Wanting his cousin to marry as one step in starting his new life, but not having access to sufficient money to arrange the marriage, he needed to fall back on the help of friends. At this time, Radha Raman was staying with a close friend of the family, Sir Vijay Prasad Singh Roy, Governor of Bengal, who eventually offered to take over the expenses for the wedding in return for a promise not to ask for dowry. Radha's son, Shanti Raman, married a descendent of one of the most prominent bankers of Banaras, Raja Sir Motichand Gupta. However, the patronage demands on the Gupta family were even more elaborate. To finance a lavish wedding ceremony, Radha Raman needed to receive the help of two other 'old' banking families from Banaras.

The family faced pressures on the income side as well. Lending was not anymore considered to be a respectable profession and, if at all, it needed to be done in minor and increasingly clandestine ways. Many newly emerging avenues for entrepreneurship were similarly considered closed to the family for reputational reasons, and their income as landlords had diminished drastically. At one time, the family had become involved in setting up a cotton mill in Banaras. However, the mill never became viable. The only trace of it left is in the name of the neighbourhood it was located in. During the interviews Radha Raman did not recount any details of this venture, since he was still a minor at the time. The mill was set up in 1924.[10] It had dropped out of official registers by 1926.[11] The automobile workshop had been set up despite reputational misgivings, but Radha Raman stressed that it was set up only because both he and his brother liked cars. This, apparently, made it possible to overcome an aversion to being associated with a workshop, though automobiles as luxury items and 'modern' technology could more easily be associated with an elite lifestyle.

The family owned several shops that were rented out, but these were not profitable as tenancy laws could easily be abused by tenants who were depicted as frequently defaulting on rent, and the family considered itself too sophisticated to enforce obligations – and had too much status to lose. As a Gandhian with a background in Hindu philosophy, Radha Raman's engagement in politics incurred high expenses rather than being profitable. He complained about incessant train journeys that he needed to pay on his own as he could not accept money from the party or state, reminiscent of his career in academics that increased his family's commitments but did not provide remuneration. At the same time, parts of their lifestyle remained an imitation of aristocratic behaviour. Their residence remained over-staffed until the late 1970s. Laying off employees was out of the question as long as it could be avoided. While hotels were both acceptable as sources of income and profitable, the remarkably simple Banaras Lodge was heavily over-staffed. The ground floor south Indian restaurant operated on their premises without paying rent, and Radha Raman asserted that this was as it should have been as his guests would have had good-quality food nearby.

It is not that Radha Raman took no concern for his family's business. While still lending money, he drastically increased interest rates, and stopped the practice of giving unsecured loans to people they were familiar with. In order to learn his new business as hotelier, he first went to train at the Clark's hotel in Banaras. Starting the partnership with the *maharaja* for the Taj hotel, he also went to train with the Taj Group in Bombay. However, the profits from the hotels were never close to paying for the family's expenses, and he felt incapable of reducing these, even though he was aware that they were ruinous. By the time his son took over as the head of the family, almost their entire wealth was spent and while the Ramans are still maintaining the pretence of their *zamindar* status based on their family's history, the family has become bourgeois in the sources of their income: male family members after Radha Raman's generation mostly studied law or business administration and were successful as employees. Radha himself was proud that they eventually managed to adapt to the decline in their fortunes, as he and his brother made sure everyone valued higher education.

> We knew that it was important to follow the right way. The other families did not really follow the right way and look where they are now [naming two prominent banking families]. They did not know how to deal with the situation but we managed to get our children educated. [They] did not go anywhere after zamindari abolition, but we understood the importance of education.[12]

Becoming 'old' money
The point of narrating the history of the Raman family in this detail is not to evoke sympathy for a family that in the end declined from being super-rich to merely being affluent, nor is it to highlight the roles of the city's elite

in patronizing religion, arts, and education. While this was extensive, and the decline in the fortunes of the city's elite is visibly reflected in the decline of many of its public institutions, patronage in the economy of Banaras was a reciprocal form of exchange: it was undertaken as a process of 'returning' some value to an amorphous concept of a society on which the elite's profits depended. In analogy to Chris Hann and Keith Hart's question of what makes people return the value of the gift (Hann and Hart 2011, 50), it is largely irrelevant what the motivations for patronage were, and more important to understand the reasons why they felt obliged to return value to their 'donors'.

In contrast, the links between the decline of a reputational order centring on the enforcement of obligation through reputational means can be illustrated by the decline of its governing apex of 'indigenous' banking and landlord families that made up an elite comprising both mercantile and aristocratic elements. In turn, this depiction is significant for the larger argument in that it provides insights into the decay of a reputational economy based primarily on the enforcement of obligations, and therefore depending on much stronger social ties, and the corresponding emergence of a differently reputational economy that almost exclusively relied on trust.

As an entry point to this discussion, it is informative to revisit George Orwell's depiction of the 'reversal of the white man's burden', cited at the outset of this chapter. Orwell's argument, regardless of its employability for exculpating colonial rule, depicts a gradual restriction of choice in a reputational economy, and the situation described by him needs to be interpreted as a reputational economy regardless of its political character. What Orwell described was an instance in his career as an official in colonial Burma in which he was called upon by local residents to shoot an elephant that had wandered into town, and destroyed property. He proceeds to describe his growing doubts over shooting the animal, and his eventual resolve to do so as well as his realization – cited earlier – that he had been compelled to shoot the elephant by his own interpretation of the crowd's perception of his reputation, 'a long struggle not to be laughed at'.

Radha Raman's life history demonstrates this process of restricting choice through his own interpretation of others' perceptions of his reputation, though primarily related to the interpretation of his family's reputational perception by his peers, the other 'important' banking and landlord families. Reputation, here, emerges as a category to be upheld – even when its maintenance undermined the material foundations on which it rested. The 'tragedy' of his life was reflected by this inability to bring the two conflicting demands into accordance – buttressing the material foundations of his family's wealth, while also maintaining the publicly communicated role of his family in social life that he had internalized. Reputation is as much an internalized social category as it depends on the attribution by others, one of the reasons it can be used as such a powerful tool for governing economic relations even in the absence of enforcement mechanisms.

It is instructive to relate the perceived need to maintain reputation to the behaviour of people in times of crisis in general. Susana Narotzky and Niko Besnier argue that in times of crisis, 'people operate with coping strategies that enable them to locate increasingly elusive resources' including 'relations of trust and care, economies of affect, networks of reciprocity encompassing both tangible and intangible resources, and material and emotional transfers that are supported by moral obligations' (Narotzky and Besnier 2014, S6). While concerned primarily with precarious social strata, their depiction of people's economic choices made in times of crisis is very much reminiscent of the choices of the financial elite of Banaras in the mid-twentieth century.

> [P]eople invest in multiple aspects of existence that appear at first glance to have little economic substance but end up having economic consequences. Among the poor, social relations often constitute a much safer 'investment' than petty entrepreneurship, contrary to the assumptions that underlie development policies that prioritize microcredit and the entrepreneurial self. Thus, poor Brazilians in the impoverished Pernambuco region affirm that 'money is good, but a friend is better': while money disappears as soon as it is earned, ties of friendship can be counted on in times of need. (Narotzky and Besnier 2014, S6)

While the response to crisis highlighted above emphasizes social ties as assets that may become useful in the course of the crisis, it is imperative to consider the role of reputation even for interpersonal relations. At a higher level of social ties, this role of reputation is even more pronounced than direct social ties, extending into questions of maintaining group membership and status. Reputation stores information on previous behaviour, whether by individuals or by groups that the individual is associated with by the recipients of this information. Reputation thus can be tapped into by decision-makers to provide a basis for assessing informational robustness. It informs the decision-maker on the crucial question of whether to extend trust, facilitating the first step in a trust-based relationship. As reputation consists of the communicated remembrances by others of the assessed individual's or group's conduct, what is being remembered and communicated as such can only partially and indirectly be affected by one's own actions, or the actions of anyone involved in its communication. The strict ideals of publicly visible mercantile conduct were used by the banking families to ensure that only specific types of information entered the reputational communication process, thereby maintaining rudimentary levels of control over one of their most fundamental assets. It is important to note that the operational logic of reputational discourse did not change across market segments, and that lower-order markets operated by their own versions of this logic in addition to the pressures of emulation necessary for entrance into higher-order markets.

However, in order to work as required, reputational information flows needed a reservoir for its storage, a group of peers to judge informational robustness as well as the status derived from it. Maintaining status, or the external perception of his family's reputation, was uppermost in Radha Raman's mind which explains the emphasis on the shooting of the lion in the narrative, leaving aside the way it marked remembrance of youthful exploits. The combination of 'feudal' and mercantile considerations in the wealth of the family – though not uncommon among the elite in Banaras – reinforced this tendency as it resulted in the coexistence of different demands on family status. It did not only shape an internalized demand to behave as both landlord and banker in terms of patronage, it also magnified behavioural restrictions.

Referencing C. A. Bayly's work on Banaras, Jonathan Parry argued that the ideal types of merchant and king follow similar logics in the moral depiction of their roles, especially when considering the spectrum of exchange, including patronage. While the merchant is supposed to make use of all his powers to accumulate through exchange to provide patronage, the king ought to use his military prowess for the same purpose. On the one hand, according to Parry, this discourse provides an apology for this-worldly behaviour: the condemnations of the evils inherent in this-worldly reciprocal exchange (or military violence) 'lack a real sense of outrage' (Parry 1989, 77), being tantamount to condemning a scorpion for stinging. Merchants following the 'nature' of their caste could not be condemned for doing so. On the other hand, there is a constant tension between the obligation to donate, and the acceptance of the practice of gainful exchange (Parry 1989). While Parry emphasizes the 'moral perils' of exchange as represented in the threefold dimensions of the gift – *daan* (the 'pure' gift, as in the receiver's perception of donations), *dakshin* (the 'deserved' gift, as in remuneration for labour and services), and *len-den* (reciprocal exchange) – my point here is to highlight the inherent tensions between accumulation and obligation. Would Radha Raman have been perceived as a failure?

His own perception was obviously ambiguous. His entrepreneurial undertakings failed, so that he failed in his 'duty' to accumulate. Yet his efforts to follow the 'duty' to maintain his family's role in the obligation structure of the market succeeded as much as could have been expected in the face of the failure to accumulate, creating the chance for his family's fortunes to reverse – once the newly chosen path of 'education' facilitated new forms of accumulation in an intergenerational process. The mercantile ethic closely resembles Bayly's depiction of the concept of *sakh*, preferring the long-term strategy of reputational resilience – a prerequisite for regaining wealth in a prospective future upturn in the family's fortunes – over the short-term imperative of maintaining the means for continued accumulation.

Bayly's earlier work on patronage highlights the balancing act between wealth accumulation and reputational preservation. While the trade in *hundi*s could be highly lucrative, reputational preservation ensured that the bankers of Banaras even in the early twentieth century needed to be simultaneously engaged in lending to the state (including the local aristocracy) where returns on investment were significantly lower and less certain (Bayly 1973, 353). Financial conservatism was combined with significant levels of fluidity in secondary trades, particularly as these allowed to make use of short-term accumulation strategies without affecting the need to maintain reputational standing, including the financing of religious activities and political patronage structures (Bayly 1973, 354–55). While the families' 'credit' was their most important possession, religious patronage was of particular importance as it reinforced the family's standing in terms of marriageability which, in turn, augmented the family's 'credit' (Bayly 1973, 362–63). The long-term consolidation of the prerequisites for short-term success relied on maintaining reputation rather than following short-term opportunities for accumulation to the point that the rapid shift of political allegiance by the Banarsi bankers in the 1930s towards nationalism was rooted in the primacy attributed to religious symbolism that could only be safeguarded by becoming 'dissidents' (Bayly 1973, 368).[13]

It is noteworthy that intermittent downturns in the fortunes of 'indigenous' banking families are ubiquitous in the history of Indian merchant families. Few family firms lasted across several generations, at least in positions of prominence (Bayly 1983; Cohn 1960; Mishra 1975). The tendency in the self-depictions of family histories to span centuries, with the Raman family's example provided below, is well suited to cover up intermittent downturns:

The Raman family of Benaras [*sic*] (Varanasi) are the direct descendents [*sic*] of Raja Deepchand Shah, who was the Treasurer ... of Sher Shah Suri.... According to the Royal Farman ..., Sher Shah Suri instructed Raja Deepchand Shah to build the Grand Trunk Road.... In circa 1540 AD, Raja Deepchand was granted the Zamindari of Chainpur, Sasaram and Shahbabad in Bihar by Sher Shah Suri, ... and later helped build the Mausoleum of Sher Shah.... Raja Deep Chand Shahi's son was Raja Yuvraj Shah and his son was Raja Gopaldas Shah, whose son was Raja Durgadas Prasad ji.[14]

This self-depiction then directly proceeds:

In the times to come, the Zamindari headquarters shifted from Chainpur to Gaya, and ... the family ... was also appointed as the Government Treasurer of the British East India Company in circa 1800s [*sic*], and controlled the Zamindari and the Treasury from the Gaya Kothi Palace ... which was donated to the Karanatka Math in the 1980s. In 1859, Raja Durgadas Prasad also was given the Sword of Honour by the British Government of India. In circa 1850s [*sic*] the estate was further expanded ... to cover over 1550 villages in Bihar and United Provinces, and ... became the second biggest Zamindari after the Dharbanga state....[15]

The family here emphasizes its heritage as landlords, partially related to the character of the website, partially representative of their respective incomes, but also related to the higher prestige attributed to land over mercantile activity. Radha Raman's engagement in politics needs to be seen in this light, too. The reputational grammar, following Parry's argument, did not differ between mercantile and landed elites, and in Banaras the two status groups were intertwined in any case (Mishra 1975). Since the ups and downs of banking families across generations were a familiar feature of the market, maintaining reputation served the role of long-term family resilience. Yet it also stabilized the reputational economy of debt, and mercantile practices – by providing continuity within the fluidity that marked exchange relations – and formed a key element in the longevity of 'bazaar' relations.

The specificity of the downturn in the mid-twentieth century rested on the simultaneity of the decline of all 'indigenous' banking families in Banaras, and their inability to regain the means of accumulation they had possessed before. Since the function of reputation as a store of information depended on the continued existence of a peer group serving as a reservoir for the information flows, the simultaneous decline of the banking families counteracted the long-term strategy of reputational resilience. The interface between reputational and material assets could only be maintained as long as one segment of the group possessing high reputation was also in possession of significant material wealth. 'Credit' meant little if it could not be encashed. The downturn thus corresponded to a memory loss of both 'memory banks' (Hart 2000) shaping mercantile worlds up to the mid-twentieth century – money and reputation. Eventually – and discussed in greater detail in Chapter 8 – the loss of memory facilitated a process of informational dis- and re-embedding of the market, cutting loose the reputational economy of debt from its moorings in strong social ties.

The simultaneous downturn of this mercantile elite was related to a number of factors: the city's economy had already stagnated relative to other centres in northern India in the course of the second half of the nineteenth century. Within Banaras, it is not uncommon to hear explanations for the decline in its importance linked to the shift away from riverine trade, especially with the construction of a bridge over the Ganges river that blocked access of larger ships. At the same time, it needs to be taken into account that Banaras was very well connected to other parts of India by both rail and road networks early on. The relative political stability imposed by colonial rule on the fractious region comprising contemporary eastern Rajasthan and western Madhya Pradesh facilitated the emergence of more direct north–south trade routes between north-western India and the western Deccan, however, which – combined with the decline of river-based trade – reinforced shifts in trade patterns away from Banaras and its main southward trade route that closely followed the contemporary route of National Highway 7. This increased the dependence of Banaras on the economic fortunes of Calcutta which, in turn, lost parts of its centrality in Indian trade with the opening of the Suez Canal that redirected intercontinental trade towards Bombay (see Markovits1999, 2001, 2013). Similarly, the shift in trade patterns from opium and indigo to tea and jute created new trading patterns of the Calcutta economy that largely bypassed the produce of the central Gangetic plains. Finally, the Great Depression created massive upheavals especially in the rural north Indian economy that affected trade, and the inability of the city's mercantile and artisanal economy to reinvent itself by setting up large-scale industrial units eventually reinforced the city's decline.[16] Industrialization bypassed Banaras. The city's short-lived cotton mill was mentioned in official sources by 1924, though it closed down soon after. The city at that time also had one metal stamping factory and one printing press.[17] By 1928, these units had closed down, but an engineering works had been set up instead.[18] In 1935, this factory, in turn, had closed, and the city's industrial units were devoid of any heavy industry, with only one joss factory and one hosiery works.[19] It took until the 1950s for the city to obtain a major industrial unit in the form of the public sector Diesel Locomotive Works (DLW).

The origins of the decline of Banaras and, therefore, the decline of its social and cultural elite can be traced to the relative synchronicity of various macro-scale economic trends. As the preceding chapter has shown, though, this discussion needs to be expanded to include the impacts of its reputational economy as well. Even if finance in Banaras was in relative decline, the capital available to its mercantile elite was still enormous. Though investment opportunities in other parts of India may have been more profitable, the organizational structure of the family firm and the reputational underpinnings of this economy should have facilitated the partial redirection of capital flows towards Banaras. There is no a priori reason why firms like the Bank of Benares or the State Bank of Banaras could not have replicated the success story of, for instance, the Bank of Baroda. The city's artisanal industries were sufficiently protected from global and industrial competition through their emphasis on (predominantly silk-based) luxury goods, and recovered fairly well from the devastation of the Great Depression, especially through their ability to use the city's cultural and religious prestige for marketing the recently established 'brand' of the Banarsi *sari* (Kumar 1988). It is noteworthy that its first viable large-scale industrial unit, the public sector DLW, was never truly integrated into the commercial structure of the city.

The decline of the Raman family was mirrored in the family histories of other 'indigenous' bankers in the city. The failure to shift towards 'organized' finance – visible in the history of local banks – was marked when observed from the perspective of the success stories of Indian banking. Yet it needs to be seen in the light of the combination of local economic stagnation and the ramifications of the interplay of reputational dynamics centring on the ability of these families to maintain the enhanced status required for the apex of north Indian credit markets to facilitate the viability of enforcing debt obligations through social ties and mercantile ethics. The banking families needed simultaneously to cope with diminished incomes in maintaining the reputational status necessary for governing high-trust market relations in a manner conducive to enforce obligations extra-legally, and to shift towards operational modes anchored in low-trust relations, including lending the money of strangers, limiting liability, following juridical-procedural stipulations, allowing regulatory intervention, and disclosing assets and liabilities.

The banking families of Banaras failed in handling the ensuing conundrum. The remnants of its 'old' banking families retain a sense of superiority rooted in an increasingly anachronistic understanding of reputation as a means to govern credit markets by ensuring the enforceability of obligations. This interpretation of reputation places emphasis on mercantile ethics and strong social ties instead of partaking in an economy based on the reputational handling of trust. When interviewing members of these families still involved in extra-legal lending in contemporary Banaras, the visible residues of the elaborate ethics of *sakh* had diminished to the pretence of class prejudice – of 'old' money in the sense of 'erstwhile' as opposed to the 'new' upstarts dominating the reputational economy of debt in its contemporary form. But economic success predominantly relied on following the new operational grammar. In other contexts, 'indigenous' bankers remained resilient for a longer period of time, while the dynamics of extra-legal lending in rural India similarly remained more strongly tied to the enforcement of obligations through persistent patterns of socio-economic dominance as will be discussed subsequently.

'Indigenous' banking played various roles in extra-legal finance in its 'traditional' forms that have been characterized here as a reputational economy with sufficiently strong underpinnings through social ties and mercantile ethics to facilitate the enforcement of obligations. These bankers controlled the top-down flows of credit in the bazaar economy. It was their capital that other creditors at lower-order markets could borrow to overcome shortages in their own working capital. They also shaped the emergence of the *hundi* system and, through emulation as well as in their role as arbitrators, the localized financial instruments that can be categorized as *chitti*s. This, in turn, provided one of the main elements of the reputational handling of the credit contract as well as allowing more directly material forms of managing credit relations, especially in relation to the frequent undersupply of bullion and coin.

Following Bayly's depiction of the operation of *sakh*, the depiction of the demise of 'indigenous' banking emphasizes this governing apex of extra-legal credit relations through its moral dimensions, and the importance of emulation. Strong social ties based on caste and kinship were considered less important by Bayly for relatively cosmopolitan and well-connected markets. This does not, however, mean that they were absent. Especially when considering the enforcement mechanisms for transactional obligations, strong social ties played an important role that is partially obscured in the complex market arrangements found in a city like Banaras. Their operation – barring studies that focused on single communities like Rudner's work – can be analysed more fruitfully in village settings. While the focus of this book is strongly on urban credit relations, the inquiry into the operation of strong social ties for the enforcement of obligations necessitates a closer look at rural contexts.

The resilience of strong social ties beyond hinterland towns

For the purposes of analysing these enforcement mechanisms I will focus on the study of money lending practices in Dhanbad district (at the time part of Bihar, now Jharkhand) in the 1970s by Hans-Dieter Roth (2007).[20] Roth originally published his findings in German, though the key findings were reproduced in an enlarged section of the original that was translated into English language (Roth 2007, ii). The foreword by Dietmar Rothermund highlights the exploitative character of money lending despite the flexibility of effective interest rates (Roth 2007, i).

Roth's study provides an excellent entry point into this discussion since his key findings differ from the main emphasis in this work. Roth highlights the monopoly position of rural moneylenders, the role of strong social ties in stabilizing exploitative credit relations, and the extension of exploitation into what Émile Durkheim had depicted as the non-contractual element of the contract (Durkheim 2013) into the control of debtors' labour or, more generally, into an economy of 'favours' that operated in close relationship with interest accumulation. While I had not expected to find significant traces of debt bondage in the urban setting of Banaras, this extension into non-contractual dimensions, and the coexistence of alternative currencies of obligation in terms of money and 'favours' had been a central original assumption of my ethnographic fieldwork (see Chapter 8), a wrong assumption in this context. While debt bondage is sufficiently well documented in Indian postcolonial history (Roth 2007, 77; see also Prakash 1990; Breman 2007), the significantly less stable reputational economy of debt centring on trust that has emerged in Banaras cannot sustain it, or even the less drastic forms of an economy of 'favours' that might have been expected to develop.

Roth's study, however, depicts a different context of credit relations – a system that had been surprisingly stable over a period of about 150 years. Roth depicted exceedingly high (nominal) interest rates, typically falling within the range of 75 to 100 per cent per annum, but also shows that these had not changed significantly since the early nineteenth century, though his depiction of the historical development cannot conclusively rule out intermittent changes (Roth 2007, 49, 58). Variations in interest rates in the 1970s were high, and different prevalent rates could not 'be attributed to objective factors alone' but were 'determined by a number of objective as well as subjective factors' (Roth 2007, 46). Generally, Roth depicted the prevalence of *derha* rates of interest for loans in kind to an extent that cannot be found in available sources for the United Provinces, though his depiction makes it abundantly clear that interest rates frequently went beyond this (Roth 2007, 42–43). For cash loans, Roth showed the variation of interest rates as ranging from 0 to 300 per cent per annum, although rates of 72 per cent or 100 per cent per annum were 'more frequent' (Roth 2007, 46). Surprisingly, extra-legal mortgages fell within broadly the same range of rates as personal-security cash loans, that is, the availability of desirable collateral had no significant impact on the costs of borrowing (Roth 2007, 81). Roth also shows that moneylenders in one of the villages studied had an enhanced interest in acquiring the collateral through credit relations, and therefore kept the interest rate for mortgages low within this range, as opposed to moneylenders in other villages were the land pledged as collateral provided additional security without affecting the costs of borrowing. In addition, interest rates for all kind of loans changed significantly with the caste membership of the debtor (Roth 2007, 81). Roth explicitly highlights caste solidarity among predominantly upper-caste landowners, though implicitly his argument on the structure of lending hinges on the monopoly position of moneylenders in the district that reinforced the strategic dimension in the selection of rates by lenders.

> [A]lthough the bargaining powers of creditors and debtors belonging to low castes are presumed to be equal, this is not so in reality. The strategy of the moneylender is the decisive element in fixing the credit sum ... and consequently also the interest rate. (Roth 2007, 81)

Roth strongly emphasizes the role of the monopoly position in determining credit conditions. Citing Anthony Bottomley (Bottomley 1964, 432–35), Roth depicts village credit markets in India as 'relatively closed' due to local social ties (Roth 2007, 32–33). Taking issue with Bottomley's depiction of interest rates as determined primarily by administration costs and risk costs – rather than opportunity costs and monopoly profit – Roth strongly supports the counter-view by A. G. Chandavarkar (1965) that interest rates in money lending are primarily the outcome of monopoly profits (Roth 2007, 55–56).[21]

In the specific context of Dhanbad district, Roth demonstrates a particularly strong monopoly position of creditors, predominantly based on the ability of strong social ties to prevent the emergence of competition:

> [T]he likelihood that new competitors will intrude in a village credit market is essentially restricted to so-called amateur moneylenders who cannot be taken seriously as competitors for the real moneylenders because their participation in the village credit market is marginal and limited in time. (Roth 2007, 32)

Depicting the case of a new entrant, Roth described the response of local moneylenders as 'incessant threats and attacks by a group of local villagers', forcing the new entrant to close his business 'as quickly as he opened it' (Roth 2007, 32). While strong social ties (and the corresponding capacity to employ violence and intimidation) played an important role in ensuring the continued social cohesion of moneylenders as a group, they also ensured the feasibility of exploitative credit conditions through their use in enforcing transactional obligations, and in creating the preconditions for the emergence of non-contractual alternatives in repayment, especially debt bondage. Stating the persistence of low 'mobility' in demand for credit, that is, the low probability of debtors seeking to develop debt relations with other creditors, Roth distinguishes between voluntary and involuntary commitments by the debtors. The former were stabilized by 'mutual trust', while the latter referred to repayments of debt obligations met through enforced labour, arising out of 'sequels of debt liabilities' (Roth 2007, 36).

Creditors in Dhanbad district were using patterns of dependence linked to caste structure and land ownership 'as far as possible to preclude the risk of delinquency' (Roth 2007, 30), thus minimizing the possibility of renegotiating contractual obligations by other reputational means. The reputational handling of the enhanced future orientation of the credit contract in a context of high default risks was constrained by the management of these risks through strong social ties. Demonstrating the intricate connections between caste and dominance patterns in the villages studied through the use of cancelling rental contracts for housing by the real estate owners, intimidation, and outright violence depicted as the 'lathi strategy' (Roth 2007, 36), he argues that these patterns were rooted in the 'high social status of the lender [which] provides him with a variety of possibilities to dictate and implement his terms of business', especially in minimizing the risk of default (Roth 2007, 30). The hold of dominance patterns, lastly, extended well beyond the credit relationship. The predominance of caste hierarchies, and the corresponding solidarities among the village elite strongly reinforced the creditors' capacity to enforce credit obligations:

> The fact that a small landowning rural upper class controls the key positions of village administration, money market and village cooperatives quickly leads us to the inference that a personal union exists between the office holders in the village cooperative and the moneylenders. Thus, the grotesque situation arises that one and the same group of people guard over interests which pursue opposite objectives.... (Roth 2007, 26)

Roth's study demonstrates that extra-legal finance even in the second half of the twentieth century was capable of maintaining its hold within the credit system. Citing various government reports, Roth estimated that cooperative credit, after an initial period of expansion had reached a share in the rural credit market of about 35 per cent, interpreted by him as failure (Roth 2007, 1–2). Instead, according to his estimations, approximately 3 per cent of all agricultural surplus in India in the mid-1970s was redistributed towards the top through money lending (Roth 2007, 3). By the 2010s, the share of cooperative credit had declined again. The RBI Technical Group to Review Legislations on Money Lending in 2007 estimated that the share of cooperative credit had declined primarily because parts of its share had been taken over by commercial banking.[22] Money lending in rural India certainly declined in its sway over the market, though this decline was much slower than anticipated by Indian policy, and there are indications that the market presence of moneylenders increased again after the early 1990s as indicated among others by Utsa Patnaik (2007).

Money lending in Dhanbad was capable of maintaining its operational modes over long periods of time, including a surprisingly high level of exploitation that went far beyond what can be shown for most other parts of India. Beyond the exploitative rates of interest, Roth's study clearly demonstrates that the functioning of the market did not change significantly since the nineteenth century. At its heart was what Roth depicted as a monopoly position derived from the stability of strong social ties. The relative failure of land reforms in this part of India, combined with fairly resilient upper-caste dominance, reinforced this stability. But beyond patterns of dominance, the market also escaped the demise of enforcement mechanisms for transactional obligations rooted in the decline of elaborate systems of mercantile ethics and the decreasing significance of caste and community that characterized the case of Banaras. Moneylenders were able to make use of caste solidarity and dominance to enforce exploitative credit conditions, minimize default, and even prevent the emergence of 'amateurish' competitors. While the use of social ties for these aims in rural settings has been shown elsewhere (Guérin 2008, 2014), the extent of their continued operational viability in Dhanbad is remarkable, and does not correspond to the diversification of practices also shown in these studies.

Paradoxically, the stability of exploitative credit conditions and the operational modes of the market in Dhanbad underline the importance of the demise of 'indigenous' banking as the lynchpin of a reputational economy capable of enforcing transactional obligations. It reinforces the interpretation that what was important in this demise were its repercussions on the reputational dimension rather than the 'material' dimension of declining top-down capital flows. This argument is crucial in understanding the long-term development of extra-legal financial markets: if the separation of 'organized' banking and extra-legal finance had choked off the availability of capital for extra-legal credit by undermining its top-down capital flows, long-term adjustments in the market would have – over time – undermined the system of petty money lending as well. As will be shown in Chapter 8, though, the availability of capital for money lending does not pose significant problems for extra-legal entrepreneurs. Roth's study, read in this way, confirms this pattern. With the notable decline of 'indigenous' banking across India by the 1970s (Timberg and Aiyar 1980), the capital flows for extra-legal lenders in rural India should have declined similarly. Instead, extra-legal lenders were making use of strong social ties to control the institutional alternatives that had been created, chiefly cooperative credit. One source of capital available for extra-legal credit replaced another, and cooperative credit constituted hardly the only source of capital available to extra-legal lenders.

In turn, the clear-cut dominance patterns in Dhanbad's villages never existed in a diverse and complex urban setting like Banaras – at least not remotely to this extent. Patterns of economic and social dominance certainly reinforced the reputational economy of debt that had developed, but they would not have been capable of suppressing threats to the functioning of the market, for instance the emergence of competition. The process of 'amateurization', after all, was driven by new entrants and the rise of hitherto marginal lenders. The stability of extra-legal lending in rural Dhanbad rested on the strength of the social ties that allowed it to minimize default and impose interest rates according to the status within these ties. Roth depicts the role of caste status within this economy, exemplified by divergent rates of interest for upper and lower castes (Roth 2007, 75). These mark caste discrimination, but they also need to be seen as indices for collective bargaining power. Roth's argument here is reminiscent of Bayly's depiction of punitive interest rates in eighteenth-century Banaras for lower castes that were considered unruly by the upper-caste strata dominating this town (Bayly 1983, 407), but similar patterns cannot be found even in early-twentieth-century Banaras.

While caste discrimination marks a particularly crude system of determining levels of exploitation, its longevity depended on sophisticated means of population control. 'Amateurization' constituted a process of declining hold over credit markets by the topmost layers of local society, the resultant rise of less 'sophisticated' lending practices, and the opening of the market to new competitors. In the area now comprising Uttar Pradesh, the process of 'amateurization' was sufficiently advanced by the late 1920s to ensure that the *UPBECR* was replete with references to it, and the notion was uncontested. In fact, 'amateurization' significantly preceded the decline of 'indigenous' banking in the United Provinces. Roth's depiction of the successful use of strong social ties in rural Dhanbad to resist this process conversely indicates that 'indigenous' banking had not been able to contain this process in the United Provinces – an assessment that corresponds both to Bayly's stress on mercantile ethics and to Rudner's emphasis on caste as intra-caste organization.

While the primary repercussions of the demise of 'indigenous' banking in Banaras were not material in the sense of affecting the availability of capital at the lower levels of the market, the inability to resist 'amateurization' points to the relative weakness of community as an ordering principle for the market. This weakness is itself unsurprising given the much greater complexity of socio-economic relations in Banaras as compared to a village economy, especially in a district in which patterns of dominance remained relatively uncontested. Yet the rise in levels of exploitation through interest (though not through non-contractual elements of the debt contract such as debt bondage) in Banaras did not occur during the period of 'amateurization'. As shown in Chapter 4, interest rates in mid-twentieth-century Banaras and in the United Provinces remained stable, and may even have marginally declined. As will be shown in Chapter 8, interest rates in the city – particularly drastically for poor debtors – have by now significantly surpassed the rates given for Dhanbad by Roth. This increase is even steeper considering that interest rates in late-colonial United Provinces were much lower than the stable rates depicted by Roth.

In Dhanbad, the resilience of strong social ties arrested developments that occurred in Banaras. The resilience of strong social ties in Dhanbad prevented the loss of monopoly positions of entrenched social groups acting as lenders – in contrast to Banaras. In doing so, they stabilized not only levels of exploitation but also practices of exploitation such as debt bondage that significantly declined elsewhere – though certainly not everywhere. But even though the opening of the market to competitors through 'amateurization' led to the destabilization of the 'extrapolations of statuses' perceived as tradition – to refer to the phrase used by Hart for the kinship-based rural economies – in Banaras, this did not result in increased collective bargaining powers for lower-class debtors. Rather, it undermined collective bargaining power in general, in the process creating a market mostly devoid of collective attributes. The patterns of dominance that fortified the cohesion of debt markets in Dhanbad may certainly be seen as the foundations for a particularly exploitative credit system. Yet the decline of the reputational dimensions of enforcing transactional obligations in Banaras undermined the protection offered by collective bargaining powers in shifting the reputational economy of debt from its uses in the enforcement of obligations to an almost comprehensive reliance on the communication of trust. At the core of this development in Banaras was the adjustment of the system of communicating reputations from its reliance on strong social ties – from the elaborate system of mercantile ethics (*sakh*) to a reputational economy relying on trust, depicted locally as *vishvaas* (lit.: faith, trust), the part of the 'amateurization' process that affected extra-legal lending regimes to a much greater extent than the mere replacement of particular groups of lenders.

Conclusion: from *sakh* to *vishvaas*

The enforceability of obligation relied on either the prevalence of strong social ties or the existence of elaborate systems of mercantile ethics that through emulation provided a tenuous structure of governance even for lower-order credit markets. In Banaras, the latter constituted the prevalent mode through the notion of merchants' credit – *sakh* – while the former two are visible in studies focusing on intra-caste organization or in studies highlighting elements of socio-economic dominance. The ability to enforce obligations through reputational means, by definition, favoured creditors over debtors, in particular wherever credit relations were marked by strong hierarchical difference. They stabilized exploitation at the same time as providing a degree of moderation in exploitation through imposing behavioural norms for creditors. Where these structures of market governance did not apply debtors still needed to comply with the reputational dimensions of extra-legal lending, but they did so under even more unfavourable conditions. Kabuli lenders, for instance, were able to transgress even the lower-order emulations of *sakh* as long as they were able to operate on relatively loose reputational dynamics centring on trust and intimidation. Yet their transgression also compromised their ability to shift to higher-order credit markets, one of the reasons why the most exploitative forms of petty lending in colonial India tended to comprise a large component of itinerant lenders who were only capable of reinvesting accumulated capital far away from the markets in which they operated.

The inability to maintain *sakh* in Banaras rested on the inability of the 'indigenous' banking families to maintain the income needed to fund reputational expenditure in patronage through which these families guarded access to higher-order market segments for new entrants. Without the need of engaging in patronage for upward mobility, the emulation of reputational codes of behaviour enforced by the governing apex received strong disincentives. Losing their access to agricultural rents and losing the opportunity to make material gains from forms of lending that fell within the permissible range of conduct combined to undermine the status requirements for imposing emulation as a business strategy on lower-order markets. Shifting to 'organized' finance, in turn, undermined this reputational standing in different ways since it included the necessity to operate on terms that were detrimental to the maintenance of reputation, while the new juridical-procedural parameters of banking were not yet capable of ensuring sufficient levels of trust to form viable alternatives. In the absence of sufficiently strong social ties to govern financial markets in Banaras, the reliance on mercantile ethics reinforced the rapid demise of the city's banking elite. Once the system of elaborate mercantile ethics had been compromised in providing incentives for emulation, the need for maintaining reputational standing collapsed in turn. Yet, in the absence of viable alternatives, the interpretation by members of the city's declining elite that long-term strategies of preserving reputation even in contexts of diminishing incomes would ensure the family's resilience – in line with strategies that had allowed mercantile communities to sustain their fortunes in highly fluctuating markets over centuries – remained entirely reasonable. At the least, it remained plausible as long as the banking families were incapable of realizing that the simultaneous decline of all 'old' families undercut the storage function of reputation underlying the power to impose emulation on lower-order market segments. This interpretation of the need for reputational resilience sought to tide over intermittent decline in order to safeguard the principles under which accumulation had been possible in better times, though the tenacity and obstinacy with which the financial elite clung to its reputational standing eventually only reinforced the emergence of the old forms of reputational dynamics as a caricature of class prejudice. In the course of the early decades after independence, the governance of extra-legal credit markets in Banaras shifted to a much less sophisticated form of mercantile ethics typically described locally as *vishvaas* (see Rotman 2020; Schwecke 2020), indicating the intersection of trust and reputation instead of reputation and obligation. It shifted to the 'upstarts' derided by the former financial elites and the colonial bureaucracy alike as 'amateurs'.

Notes

1. Orwell (1950).
2. The following discussion of the Raman family history is based on a series of interviews with Shri Radha Raman Prasadji conducted in Banaras, unless marked otherwise.
3. Retirement to Banaras in preparation for spiritual salvation after death. See Parry (1994).
4. See, for instance, Goswami (1989).
5. On the importance of *Mother India* for nation-building discourses in independent India, see Schulze (2002).
6. Interview with Navneet Raman.
7. Interview with Shri Radha Raman Prasadji conducted in Banaras.
8. Interview with Navneet Raman. Radha Raman, in contrast, refused to place any blame on the tenants, remarking several times that they simply followed the spirit of the times, and should not be held accountable for doing so.
9. Interview with Navneet Raman.
10. P. H. Swinchatt, *Annual Report on the Working of the Indian Factories Act in the United Provinces for the Year 1924* (Allahabad: United Provinces Government Press,1925), 1.
11. P. H. Swinchatt, *Annual Report on the Working of the Indian Factories Act in the United Provinces for the Year 1926* (Allahabad: United Provinces Government Press, 1927), 19.
12. Interview with Shri Radha Raman Prasadji.
13. On the religious dimensions of market moralities in India, see also Rudnyckyj and Osella (2017).
14. Excerpt from the Raman family webpage, available online from the website http://noblehouse.biz (last accessed 7 February 2020); the website has been temporarily or permanently removed since the date of last access.
15. Ibid.
16. For a study on the broader shift towards large-scale industries by Indian capitalists, see Tripathi (1997).
17. P. M. Swinchatt, *Annual Report on the Working of the Indian Factories Act in the United Provinces for the Year 1924* (Allahabad: United Provinces Government Press, 1925), 3.
18. W. G. Mackay, *Annual Report on the Working of the Indian Factories Act in the United Provinces for the Year 1928* (Allahabad: United Provinces Government Press, 1929), 2.
19. W. G. Mackay *Annual Report on the Working of the Indian Factories Act in the United Provinces for the Year 1935* (Allahabad: United Provinces Government Press, 1936), 2.

20. See Roth (1979).

21. Across disciplines, interest rates are widely held to be determined strongly by lenders' considerations on (*a*) opportunity costs, that is, the possibility of higher returns on investment through investment beyond credit; (*b*) administration costs, that is, costs associated with managing the credit relationship including ensuring repayment; (*c*) risk costs, that is, costs arising from the likelihood of default; and (*d*) monopoly profit, that is, the position of the creditor to impose higher interest rates due to supply constraints in credit. For Roth's treatment of this debate, see Roth (2007, 51–56). For a more general consideration of the debate, see Bottomley (1963).

22. Reserve Bank of India, *Report of the Technical Group to Review Legislations on Money Lending. Mumbai: 2007*, available online at https://rbidocs.rbi.org.in/rdocs/PublicationReport/Pdfs/78893.pdf (last accessed 4 March 2020).

7

Disappearance

This is the kind of stuff one came across in Munshi Premchand's stories only. However, the holy city of Varanasi is witnessing a grim repeat of the sad tales of exploitation in the 21st century. Only the villain has changed from the dhoti-clad wily 'soodkhor' to a sweet-talking lawyer/businessman/city corporator or panchayat member.[1]

By the early 2010s, when I started my research with an ethnographic study of money lending practices in Banaras, extra-legal finance there was flourishing or, it could be said, it was continuing to flourish. It had lost a major share of its predominance in financing trade and petty industry to 'organized' banking, and in doing so had shed its links to elaborate forms of mercantile ethics. It had lost its position in the lives of the city's elites (as lenders), and of the city's upper-middle classes (as debtors and lenders). It had lost its importance in financing high-level investments – especially real estate and education. It even had lost ground to regulated forms of banking in financing various other consumption purposes. As one debtor I interviewed put it:

> The banks have a special credit scheme for purchasing scooters. It makes getting a loan quick and easy, and the bank cannot say no to you. When I want to get a loan to buy a scooter, I go to the bank. When I want to buy anything else, I go to the moneylender.[2]

Within the spectrum of this 'anything else', extra-legal finance continued to be a ubiquitous occurrence: not everyone went to a moneylender for loans, but everyone beyond the upper-middle class knew people who had experience with moneylenders, and had an idea of who could be approached in the neighbourhood. Everyone knew that money lending was flourishing. Within this spectrum of 'anything else', as it turned out, two things really had changed. First, all forms of extra-legal finance had become significantly more exploitative since the late colonial period. And second, the operational modes of extra-legal finance had changed, in some respects subtly, yet – taken altogether – in quite dramatic ways. For Indian public opinion, though, it seemed as if extra-legal finance had ceased to exist, as if it was visible only in Munshi Premchand's stories.

The moneylenders' vanishing act

Within the United Provinces, the lapsing of the United Provinces Moneylenders Bill, 1939, effectively brought to an end the period of considerable legislative efforts to contain money lending (and credit to the poor) for several decades. In 1940, the government passed the United Provinces Regulation of Credit Act, which marginally affected money lending. Specifically, the act prohibited the entering into books of account of a principal higher than what was actually lent, a provision that had little practical value. Commenting on it, the 1965 district gazetteers for Banaras observed that 'this practice [was] more often observed in the breach' (E. B. Joshi 1965, 163). Until well into the 1970s, the Usurious Loans Act and its various amendments remained the only functioning legal restriction on money lending in the state, though there is little indication that more stringent laws elsewhere had different impacts on extra-legal finance. The eventual enactment of the Uttar Pradesh Regulation of Money Lending Act in 1976 certainly did not have any major impact. In the last years of colonial rule in India, however, concerns over money lending still figured prominently in policy discourses, and were covered by media reportage.

Money lending and extra-legal artisanal and trade credit remained a significant source of loans. At the same time, concerns over it vanished – notwithstanding intermittent surges in attention – from public discourse. Not only can a noticeable decrease in attention be detected in the number of mentions of money lending in reportage, there are equally significant differences in the kind of attention it attracted. Given the continued ubiquity of money lending in everyday experience for vast sections of the population, this vanishing remains peculiar, but indicates the growing reliance of moneylenders on extra-legal means preoccupied with establishing trust rather than relying on stronger social ties or the law, thereby withdrawing financial practices from publicly visible concerns. This interpretation rests on three assumptions, each reinforcing the others: (*a*) that moneylenders relying increasingly on a reputational mode of governing credit relations that does not allow for strong enforcement mechanisms would shy away from public attention to a larger extent than those embedded into kinship and community ties and elaborate systems of mercantile ethics; (*b*) that reputational governance structures on markets relying on trust are less easily intelligible to outside observers; and (*c*) that there existed an ideological underpinning informing significant parts of the state and the public that led to an unwillingness to recognize the continued existence of extra-legal finance.

The moneylenders' 'vanishing act' thus embodied the colloquial usage of the trope – of 'doing a vanishing act' to avoid a task or meet a person. It also corresponds to its narrower use in stage magic where it denotes misdirection of attention establishing disappearance from one location, typically to reappear somewhere else. The ephemeral character of trust constitutes an impediment to a wide range of practices related to obtaining evidence, specifically highlighted in 'modern' societies that rely on documentation, quantification, rationalization, and certification. The need for an assurance on the robustness of information does not preclude 'non-modern' evidentiary forms, but tendentially leads to biases (Corsín Jiménez 2011). These biases, in turn, are mirrored in ideological considerations of how a practice like extra-legal finance is supposed to develop in a 'modern' context, broadly following Weberian ideas on rationalization and bureaucratization as measures to enhance calculability.[3] Similarly, materialistic assumptions on evolutionary trajectories rooted in socio-economic relations tend to overlook those relations that do not seem to conform to broader macro-historical patterns. One of the strengths in Barbara Harriss-White's concept of the prevalence of 'awkward classes' in India (Harriss-White 2018) is precisely in emphasizing these classes' positioning in-between hypotheses on class formation.[4] Faced with the resilience of money lending, it was surprisingly easy for the state and the public to look away from the problem rather than focus on its resolution.

In order to depict the decrease in media reportage on money lending, I studied the coverage of topical issues in the *Times of India* between the 1930s and 1970s.[5] As a caveat, this study cannot claim comprehensiveness as it was based on keyword searches: various keywords denoting terms likely to be used to depict money lending practices as well as Boolean combinations of likely terms were employed to identify the sample, which was then narrowed down by deleting mismatches. There is a significant possibility of error, partially related to the possibility of not having included all relevant keywords, and partially to the identifiability of these terms due to problems in print and digitalization quality. As an example, searches for the term 'lender' invariably included results for the word 'leader'. As print quality and preservation problems plausibly can be assumed to recede with more recent publication, they can be expected to have resulted in an exaggeration of later records, and therefore might reinforce the findings of the study.

To identify a baseline, the period from 1931 to 1940 was selected for the '1930s', with the assumption that the number of inquiries and legislative efforts would have distorted the sample. For this period, the *Times of India* published thirty-seven reports on money lending, including in news reportage, editorials, and commentary, and in the published letters to the editor. This does not correspond to a very large concern, but it is significantly higher than in any decade afterwards, while coverage was also more diverse. The newspaper reported on issues of legislation, policy debates and policy recommendations, political campaigns, and litigation as well as on the scandal of the continued existence of money lending, and on offences against moneylenders. It also published local case studies and background information.

In the 1940s (1941–1950), both the extent and the areas of coverage decreased significantly. The *Times of India* reported on money lending only twenty times, twelve of which fell into the year 1946 in which the Bombay Moneylenders Bill was enacted, reflecting its primary area of circulation, but also demonstrating a significant restriction to issues of legislation, policy debate, and litigation. In the same period, the newspaper published a single article on the Hyderabad Moneylenders (Amendment) Act that was debated in this year,[6] and a single article on a debate in the legislative assembly of Mysore on money lending by high-ranking bureaucrats.[7] The Bombay Moneylenders Bill in 1946 constituted the last major legislation against money lending in colonial India. As in the United Provinces, the enactment of money lending legislation in the Bombay Presidency had failed due to the resignation of its provincial government in 1939.[8] New reportage on the topic had started in June 1946, following debates on the amendment of the Bombay Debt Relief Act.[9] The debates over the Moneylenders' Bill and the government's agenda – in the newspaper's words – to combat the 'parasitic and dangerous character'[10] of 'one of the "most ancient and hated" professions in India'[11] were widely reported between late August 1946 and late September 1946, with the last article appearing on 19 October 1946, outlining 'important changes'[12] made in the bill, the most important of which were exemptions for 'trade credit', though the article highlighted relatively minor prescriptions for accountancy practices. The spurt in reportage and publication of readers' letters to the editor on the topic[13] demonstrate the continued prevalence of relatively strong concerns in the newspaper's readership, but the negligible presence of reporting on it during the rest of this decade indicates a significant waning of attention.

Reportage on money lending in the *Times of India* receded drastically in the 1950s and 1960s, reaching negligible levels both in terms of number and content. At the same time, there was a marked spike in newspaper reportage in the 1970s, starting in 1970 and lasting approximately to the end of the state of emergency (1975–1977). While reportage partially focused on legislative measures in the 1970s, the majority of reports in the 1970s emphasized socio-economic dimensions of exploitation, or highlighted reporting on specific money lending scandals. Out of the twenty-six articles covering the topic found for the 1970s (1970–1979), twelve reports discussed various legislative measures, ten reported scandals, and a further three focused on background information, but employed language used for reporting scandals.

A single article published in 1970 actually addressed an improvement in the credit conditions falling under extra-legal finance, ascribed to the spread of banking. Though the report was based on a negligible sample in the vicinity of Delhi, it is noteworthy not only for the drastic reduction in interest rates reported but also since it constituted the only report throughout the period studied here that actually depicted such a development. It noted that moneylenders had reduced average interest rates from 60 per cent to 20 per cent, assumedly per year.

> A visit to two villages revealed that the rapid distribution of bank loans at a nominal rate of interest had adversely affected the money-lenders' income. The farmers now feel that all these years they were being exploited by these money-lenders who used to charge 40 to 75 per cent. With the changing concept of a farmer's credit-worthiness [*sic*] after bank nationalisation, now loans are easily available to farmers who merely have some land or a pair of bullocks or, as in many cases, only their labour to offer to the bankman as security. Two branches of the Syndicate Bank, ... function at the Chatarpur and Fatehpur Beri villages....[14]

The attribution of the success to banking nationalization needs clarification. As persuasively argued by Amol Agarwal,[15] Syndicate Bank was exemplary in addressing the credit needs of relatively less prosperous social segments, particularly in northern Karnataka. This exemplary character also significantly preceded the nationalization of fourteen Indian banks in 1969. Nationalization may have impacted the decision of Syndicate Bank to move towards Delhi, but its overall impact on the continued existence of extra-legal financial markets in northern India was negligible. The track record of Syndicate Bank in terms of financial inclusion merely demonstrates the potentials of socio-economic improvement – if 'organized' banking in India (nationalized or otherwise) had followed the model set by the bank.

The spike in reporting in the 1970s – after decades of declining attention – may seem surprising, but it needs to be interpreted in the light of greater concerns over poverty and developmental issues within public debate at the time. The crisis of the developmental model established after independence became highly visible in the mid-1960s. The Indian state responded by relatively minor attempts at liberalizing its capital goods sector that were soon aborted (Kochanek 1986). Instead, it focused its attention on the Green Revolution in the late 1960s, thus bringing developmental concerns in rural India into the limelight. By the early 1970s, the government started to highlight issues concerning poverty, and led a range of policy initiatives that can be described as attempts to make the industrial policy models of the Nehruvian period work again by tightening regulatory controls, thus allowing it to enhance capital investment in the capital goods sector. The discursive emphasis on poverty alleviation, combined with a tightening of the levers of state control over the economy, brought into focus impediments to development. Whether it was issues related to law evasion and corruption – a category including extra-legal finance, though media attention focused on embezzlement – or a focus on poverty, the figure of the moneylender, exploitation, and debt bondage received greater attention.[16]

This attention was reinforced by the main strand of opposition to the Congress which at this time either revolved on socio-economic issues or highlighted problems associated with the tightening of state controls, depicted as the license-permit-*raj*. The *Times of India* report cited earlier illustrates that even divergent views on policy facilitated greater emphasis on moneylenders: the decision to nationalize (most of) India's private banks in 1969 constituted an important step in directing greater resources to the capital goods sector, but was highly contentious. It helped to abort a slow process of 'modernization' among 'indigenous' bankers in that their investments into joint-stock banks became practically worthless overnight, without providing alternative avenues for profitable investment in the Indian hinterland. The attribution of success to bank nationalization in the two villages in Mehrauli made very little sense in that the Syndicate Bank had had much larger successes in Karnataka that went unreported, despite falling into the newspaper's main area of circulation. Yet the renewed attention made even the successes in two villages in the Union Territory of Delhi 'national' news, particularly in the absence of other successes.

Looking at reporting in Banaras, there are very similar patterns. As records of local newspapers are not digitalized, it was necessary to comb through archived records of newspapers to identify newspaper coverage of financial markets, a task that was greatly facilitated by the preservation of these records in the archive of the Nagari Pracharini Sabha at Varanasi, and by the outstanding help I received from Chandra Kishore Singh. For the period before 1970, this study focused on the daily *Aaj*, which was subsequently overtaken locally in terms of circulation by *Dainik Jagran*. As the general trends for the early decades of this sample (from the 1930s to the late 1970s) followed the pattern established for *Times of India* reportage – relatively strong and diverse coverage in the 1930s, followed by a clear decline, reaching negligible proportions by the mid-1950s, with a temporary spike in the 1970s – the focus here is on the decades from the 1980s to the 2010s. The spike in reporting in the 1970s was mostly related to legislative issues, especially the enactment of the Uttar Pradesh Regulation of Money Lending Act, 1976, and was significantly less pronounced than in the case of the *Times of India*. As a national, English-language newspaper, the *Times of India*'s news coverage differed from that of the local edition even of a major Hindi-language daily that predominantly covered issues within the locality and the state. Newsworthy changes within the locality were mostly absent, or too gradual to evoke much concern.

This pattern of ignoring money lending despite its ubiquity continued in the subsequent decades. In the early 1980s, the local edition of *Dainik Jagran* reported on issues concerning money lending in only five instances, including two cases of violence, one associated with a *len-den* scheme (a catch-all phrase for illicit transactions), and the other directly attributed to a money lending transaction.[17] It also covered the opening of a Grameen Bank in a village near Banaras, and the report expressed the hope that this would lead to a replacement of the local *sahukars*.[18] The follow-up on the opening ceremony noticeably avoided mentioning money lending, despite summarizing speeches held at the event.[19] The paper also covered a speech by Uttar Pradesh minister Baijnath Kureel that argued that legislation against money lending had to be made more effective.[20] The pattern of reporting persisted for the second half of the decade.

In the 1990s, *Dainik Jagran* locally published five reports on money lending, largely continuing the earlier pattern. The contents of reporting shifted marginally: four reports related to violence, a precursor of the trend in the 2000s. In a brief report in 1990, it reported a man being attacked with knives and sticks for defaulting.[21] In 1995, it reported another knife attack and a case of debt-related suicide.[22] In 1996, a young man was killed in a *len-den* affair and his body hidden.[23] Finally, another man was shot in a *len-den* affair in 1997.[24] The absence of reporting on topics other than violence demonstrates an increasing newsworthiness only when the topic was linked to scandal. In the 2000s, this trend largely continued, but reporting spiked to unprecedented extents. The newspaper published forty-six articles related to money lending, thirty-nine in the period from 2006 to 2007, the remainder having been published in 2004 and 2005.

There are several reasons for this spurt in publications and newsworthiness. The reports in 2004 and 2005 show a continued concern over violence and scandal. In a spate of attacks, several people died in relation with money lending, indicating an increasing incidence of violence. The main body of reporting was related to local and central policy. In 2006, the central government started to implement a debt waiver programme specifically targeting weaver communities in Uttar Pradesh. The locally prevalent narrative on this policy and its impacts on money lending linked the eventual success of such a debt waiver programme to a successful crackdown on moneylenders, since otherwise it would merely have led to a lessening of defaults on extra-legal loans.

This narrative is sufficiently plausible, and is frequently encountered when studying the literature on debt, such as the journalistic work of P. Sainath (see later). Moreover, it was frequently added, this crackdown needed to start considerably before the state elections in 2007, so that the effects of the debt waiver were visible in time. This narrative was also corroborated by several police officers of the Uttar Pradesh cadre, though some of these added another dimension, stating that the 'ferocity' of the crackdown was also the outcome of corruption within the force: according to these (unsubstantiated) arguments, a high-ranking officer had attempted to intimidate some well-known and well-connected extra-legal entrepreneurs into paying bribes. Depending on the informant, either the lenders defaulted on these payments or pressure by higher-level politics became too intense, so that the 'gentlemen's agreement' collapsed. There is no possibility of substantiating these allegations and, accordingly, they are mentioned here merely to complement the history of the crackdown. The contents of the reportage will be discussed later. Media coverage of money lending issues decreased towards the end of 2007, and has become negligible since then.

The analysis of media attention demonstrates one aspect of the vanishing extra-legal finance from public attention, despite its ubiquity in everyday life. Being ubiquitous, its continuity did not evoke media concern unless there were contextual reasons for heightened awareness. It is noteworthy that the first term of the United Progressive Alliance government from 2004 to 2009 was marked by debates on developmental issues similarly to parts of the 1970s. The increasing turn towards a discourse emphasizing corruption – loosely reflecting the debate on the license-permit-*raj* in the 1970s – however, did not lead to increased public attention. Corruption and extra-legal finance are sufficiently different – concerns over breaches of regulations in the formal sector and the administration may help to focus attention on informality, and corruption may increase attention to extra-legality, yet the issues are still perceived from different vantage points.

The absence of media attention is only one part of the disappearance of extra-legal finance from public sight. The early independent Indian state was strongly developmental in character. Public discourse until the end of the 1970s remained overwhelmingly centred on the idea of 'development' and 'modernization', and while the conception of the Indian state as 'socialist' is a misnomer, concern over poverty remained an issue that could have focused attention on exploitative financial markets. Moreover, while the main thrust of development policies remained on industry, this thrust might have increased the political will to act in reducing opposition from the capitalist class. The set-up of the government's development strategy rested on industrialization, planning, and 'scientific' management of policy through surveying and statistics (see Chibber 2003; Tyabji 2015). The dominant political alliances included a significant capitalist component – but one whose detachment from the mercantile and petty industrialist economies of the *mufassil* grew over time, regardless of the origins of some corporate houses in the bazaar economy (Damodaran 2008). This strand of India's capitalist class was interested in the growth of 'organized' banking – the setting up of a finance infrastructure that allowed new large-scale business projects – but had severed its earlier links with petty forms of exploitation.

The emphasis of policy on credit markets was highly conducive to the interests of this strand of the capitalist class. Even the contentious decision to nationalize Indian banks did not hurt this segment, but furthered concentration processes in favour of large-scale industrial capital as long as corporate entrepreneurs were able to stay politically aligned to ruling dispensations. The separation of big finance from petty finance that drove the thrust towards looking away from extra-legal finance was driven by desires to enhance the availability of capital for precisely the purposes of India's big capitalists. The difference to the process theorized by Amiya Kumar Bagchi (1985) as a distinction between controlled and 'uncontrolled' credit was primarily in the indigenization of India's capitalists, not in the differentiation between petty and big capital.

The decision to abort the extension of 'organized' banking to 'unbankable' social segments, and to focus on alleviating measures predominantly as an exercise in evading to be seen as responsible for the continued flourishing of extra-legal finance related to two aspects: the presence of India's 'awkward classes' (Harriss-White 2018) and their importance for local- and state-level politics; and the inability of the state to make alleviative measures work. By the late 1930s, this had resulted in the reorientation of policy from facilitating the availability of credit for the mass of the population to the containment of debt by restricting access to credit. The Indian state – with noteworthy exceptions in the renewed thrust towards cooperative credit and more recent partial successes in microfinance, especially in southern India (Shetty 2012; Guérin 2014; Kar 2018) – continued to follow the blueprint of policies that had been established in late colonial India.

The 'awkward classes' that continue to dominate capital in the 'informal' sector – by far the larger sector in terms of employment and very substantial in terms of value added (Harriss-White 2003, 2017) – remained unable to dominate policy to the extent that its interests could only be met through creating loopholes in the regulatory structure (Dietrich Wielenga 2016). They could not overcome the predominance of penalizing measures against money lending, for instance. The aforementioned debates on the Bombay Moneylenders Act exemplify these tendencies. In the state of Bombay, unregistered money lending was prohibited – and registered money lending made less than viable given the rate of default – but the act created sufficient loopholes to allow moneylenders to shift towards comprehensive extra-legality. The stringency of the Bombay Moneylenders Bill of 1938 had already been watered down in the original bill, but the Select Committee that drafted the final bill further weakened it. Discursively, this was justified by distinctions between the vast majority of 'honourable' moneylenders and the 'few black sheep' that supposedly had given the profession a bad reputation. The Home Minister of Bombay, Morarji Desai, had been at pains to declare that the act only sought to 'regulate', not to 'eliminate', money lending.[25] At the same time, the *Times of India* could still denounce moneylenders in general as 'parasites'.[26] Passing laws, in any case, remained of relatively little significance as long as the government lacked the will both to enforce the law and to provide viable credit alternatives.

The failure to provide viable credit alternatives, in turn, allowed money lending to flourish. Given the prevailing rates of default as an indication of the extent of uncertainty within the credit relationship, the model of state-regulated banking was entirely unviable as long as the state was unwilling to extend enormous funds. The emphasis on large-scale industrialization for developmental needs, and the corresponding creation of a financial infrastructure for these purposes thus created the preconditions for withholding this funding from the 'residues'[27] of the bazaar economy, even if it would have been contemplated. The 'scientific' thrust of Indian 'modernization', in turn, created ideological impediments to policies that would have had to engage with the reputational strategies of managing uncertainty and default on extra-legal credit markets, even though these actually worked – if in highly exploitative ways. The ideology of banking policy presupposed the purity of banking concepts in the way they had developed in the western world, not the adaptive way of handling uncertainty through reputational means that characterized extra-legal finance.

Much of the 'organized' banking sector remained concentrated on the major commercial hubs, but there was definite growth in the establishment of banks in less important commercial centres such as Banaras. The Uttar Pradesh district gazetteers for Varanasi district in 1965 showed moderate growth in cooperative credit societies, and reported that eleven banks had set up branches in the city. Banks were lending on average at 5–9 per cent per annum (E. B. Joshi 1965, 164–65). At the same time, it noted that 70 per cent of credit was provided by either 'agricultural' or 'professional' moneylenders who charged average rates of 25–40 per cent per annum. It also reported that the 'trade credit' segment in town continued to be dominated by 'mahajans' who charged 7.5 to 12 per cent per annum plus a brokerage fee of 0.75 per cent. Cheque discounting rates – the practice of advancing money against the security of post-dated cheques – stood at 18–30 per cent per annum for three-month post-dated cheques (E. B. Joshi 1965, 163). The gazetteers also noted that advances against movable collateral were 'common', but that there were 'no records' on their volume, or the interest charged (E. B. Joshi 1965, 163–64). Taking a long-term perspective, the gazetteers took an optimistic assessment of the situation:

> [Rural] indebtedness has been decreasing slowly … as is evident from the fact that the fields which were formerly mortgaged have been redeemed and that the litigation which caused indebtedness has also declined after the abolition of zamindari in the State. (E. B. Joshi 1965, 161)

While *zamindari* abolition, enacted in Uttar Pradesh in 1951, did not directly affect credit markets, its impacts on rural debt markets were broadly positive, however imperfectly the law was implemented. The consolidation of tenurial rights towards the tiller improved the availability of desirable collateral for tenured farmers, helping to bring down interest rates in extra-legal finance, apart from allowing agricultural and cooperative banks to operate more smoothly through minimizing risk, and reporting risk assessment in line with regulatory practice. At the same time, the reasoning provided for the gazetteers' assessment excludes landless segments of the rural population, and are based on relatively unreliable sources – an unquantified but assumedly observable rise in mortgage redemptions. As the report noted, there had been no recent surveys on indebtedness in the district (E. B. Joshi 1965, 161). For urban indebtedness, the report did not offer a projection of trends – indicating that its information was even less reliable – but nevertheless provided one of the few glimpses in early postcolonial sources on money lending in Banaras.

> Indebtedness in the urban areas is generally confined to the people of the lower income groups such as office workers, factory hands, etc., who are the victims of money-lenders. For loans above fifty rupees pawning of valuables is resorted to and when the need for credit is pressing even very valuable articles are pawned for meagre sums. Generally, an interest of nine naye paise[28] per month is charged on every rupee.... (E. B. Joshi 1965, 162)

This depiction of interest rates is noteworthy in that it shows a drastic increase in comparison with the last decades of colonial rule. While the data collected for the *UPBECR* is too sketchy for pawn-brokering to allow generalization, the target group of lenders depicted in this report – 'lower income groups' – corresponds to those of *qistwallah*s and Kabuli lenders. *Qistwallah*s lent relatively equivalent principals (in value) to the 50-rupee loans depicted here at between 3 and 10 per cent per month, while Kabuli rates were higher, most commonly at 12–15 per cent per month. However, these loans were unsecured. Between the late 1920s and the early 1960s, interest rates for secured loans in pawn-brokering rose to the approximate level of unsecured loans in the late colonial period. In fact, this rise is even more dramatic than it appears: debtors who possessed desirable collateral, especially movable collateral, would not even have approached a Kabuli lender or a *qistwallah* charging 9 per cent monthly interest as they would have had cheaper options. If interest is taken as an expression of the lender's risk assessment, then extra-legal lenders in 1960s Banaras would have considered even well-secured loans to relatively solvent debtors as equivalent to the most-risky target group of lenders in the late colonial period. If interest is taken as an expression of the lender's capability to fix higher prices, this rise demonstrates a consolidation of the market position in the segment of petty loans by extra-legal lenders. The district gazetteers' report argued that urban indebtedness remained relatively restricted – to lower-income groups – and therefore was considered less problematic, even though the data indicated a remarkable deterioration in credit conditions. It is notable that the rates given for cheque discounting are significantly higher than most late colonial discounting rates for *hundi*s, although cheques were legally enforceable. Similarly, the 'trade credit' interest rates cited earlier are also higher than in late colonial Banaras, though still relatively competitive with bank interest rates. It also needs to be noted that the bank rate, the rate at which the RBI was lending to banks, had not yet increased drastically. Having reached 5 per cent in late 1964 from 3.5 per cent in 1951, it was set at 9 per cent in 1974, and reached its highest level (by that time considering the repo rate) of 12 per cent in 1991. For 'trade credit', this rate needs to be taken into account, even if its effects on interest rates in extra-legal finance in the 'bazaar' were indirect at best.

The district gazetteers in 1988 reported another rise in the number of operating banks, by that time twenty-five (Swaroop 1988, 38), but did not address issues of money lending except on the number of registered moneylenders. This number had gone up from 5,864 in 1976–1977 to 6,326 in 1979–1980. Moneylenders were not required to register before 1976. Registered moneylenders were charging interest at 14 per cent per annum for secured and 17 per cent per annum for unsecured loans, but these rates were set by the state government, and give no indication of extra-legal rates.[29] The district census handbook for Banaras district of 1951 lists a total number of 2,199 people employed in banking and finance, out of which 1,683 were considered urban. The data provided does not distinguish between money lending and banking, but between employers, employees, and independent workers. It classified 171 people as employers in this category (104 urban), 1,354 employees (1,175 urban), and 674 independent workers (404 urban).[30] Given its organizational patterns, it is unlikely that 'independent workers' were part of 'organized' banking, but the other two sub-categories remain unclear in their composition.

As registration was not yet compulsory, 'employees' may have been employed by moneylenders. In turn, the numbers given for 'employers' outstrips the number of operating banks. Moreover, misreporting needs to considered. Many 'amateurish' lenders may have preferred to emphasize other trades. Conservatively estimated, considering that Banaras in 1951 had around eleven operating banks, with rarely more than one branch office, the census numbers indicate the existence of about 1,500 people engaged in extra-legal finance, approximately 1,200 of which would have been considered urban.

The gazetteers and the census cannot directly be compared as they followed different surveying techniques. Even taking population growth into account, the rise in the numbers of moneylenders between 1951 and 1988 is remarkable since the gazetteers only provided the numbers for registered moneylenders.

While there is insufficient information to estimate the ratio between registered and unregistered moneylenders, the former category constitutes a minuscule proportion of all moneylenders in the city today.

The district census handbook for 1961 provides entirely different numbers that roughly corroborate the estimate for people employed in 'organized' banking – 495 for the entire district despite the expansion of banks in the area – but not the estimate of extra-legal financial entrepreneurs. Using the category 'money lending (indigenous)', the handbook lists 245 people as engaged in extra-legal finance.[31] If this assessment was to be considered accurate, it would indicate a massive drop between the early 1950s and early 1960s, only to be followed by a significantly steeper rise in these numbers afterwards. One possibility to account for this divergence would be increasing 'amateurization' which may have led to the dismissal of moneylenders' employees. At the same time, it is likely that misreporting would have increased as the 'respectable' segment of lending anchored in 'indigenous' banking declined. The changes in the categories used in the 1961 census may also have obscured the number of 'amateurish' lenders. Given the broad tendencies discernible, I have strong doubts over a decline in the numbers of people engaged in the trade at any time.

What remains to be emphasized is the manner in which the composition of the census categories changed, initially combining the two strands of finance, then clearly distinguishing them, including the use of the phrase 'indigenous' to separate it from 'proper' finance. Under the assumption that the discrepancy in numbers indicates 'amateurization' instead of a drastic, intermittent decline, the highlighting of the category of moneylenders not only indicates the growing division of financial markets, but also demonstrates the increasing difficulty for the state to obtain information about the extra-legal segment: moneylenders would have vanished from the view of the census even while the census was attempting to emphasize their difference from banking.

Pristine purity of banking conceptions

The topic of money lending attracted considerable attention in government reports in the 1950s, and sporadically afterwards, but generally disappeared from official records otherwise. In the 1950s and parts of the 1960s, the RBI continued to publish annual reports on trends and progress in banking. Focusing on the 'formal' segment of the market, these reports were emphasizing the establishment of 'organized' banks. Yet the topic – especially in the 1950s – might have addressed extra-legal finance at least in its general statements.

However, the only time they did so was in a brief comment applauding the RBI for its decision *not* to implement the recommendations of the Shroff Committee on maintaining links with 'indigenous' bankers.[32]

The *Report of the Committee on Finance for the Private Sector*, 1954, widely depicted as the *Shroff Committee Report*, constituted one of the two important endeavours to look into extra-legal finance. The report was rendered ineffectual in one of its main recommendations that had sought to establish greater integration through RBI policies designed to include 'indigenous' lending in integrated bill market schemes, reflecting similarly aborted attempts in the 1930s. The recommendation rested on a pessimistic assessment of the banking sector's capacity to expand credit operations to the level required to reach lower-level industrial finance, that is, even within a segment where 'organized' banks were comparatively competitive. According to its mandate, the committee did not engage in a debate on credit for commercial, agricultural, consumption, and subsistence needs where the dominance of extra-legal finance was even more pronounced.

Stating that statistical information regarding extra-legal advances to industry was unavailable, the committee estimated advances by Multani *sarrafs* as approximately 20 crore rupees 'at any time'.[33] The Bombay Shroffs Association was reported having a turnover of approximately 100 crore rupees. In comparison, the committee estimated the total amount of state aid to industries in 1951–52 at 13 crore rupees, including investment in shares. It estimated the working capital of cooperative lenders in the industrial sector at 8.65 crore rupees.[34] The recommendation to integrate the two segments thus needs to be seen in light of a dire need to expand the capital available for industrial credit purposes drastically.[35]

The recommendations on extra-legal finance by the Shroff Committee were far from wide ranging. Essentially, they focused on two issues. According to their evidence, mostly from the Bombay Shroffs Association and the Shikarpuri Shroffs Association in Bombay, extra-legal lenders faced difficulties in rediscounting *hundi*s in banks since legal stipulations defined a bank as exclusively involved in banking, while many extra-legal lenders combined lending with other business. The report recommended measures to allow the banks to circumvent this problem. It also deplored the practice of banks to rediscount *hundi*s merely where they had branch offices, thereby excluding much of the *mufassil*.[36] The committee deliberately refrained from focusing on money lending in general under the assumption that this would be dealt with by the All India Rural Credit Survey carried out simultaneously. Accordingly, it merely stated that 75 to 90 per cent of all internal trade in India was financed by moneylenders and 'indigenous' bankers, and provided information on the *hundi* discounting rates by the Bombay Shroffs Association (4.5–6 per cent plus commission)[37] and the Shikarpuri lenders in Bombay (9 per cent on average, in turn paying 4.5–5 per cent for rediscounting at banks.)[38] It also noted a significant decline in the operations of 'professional' moneylenders and a corresponding rise in the operations of 'non-professionals' in line with the general trend of 'amateurization'.[39] Finally, it provided an overview on the legal restrictions on interest rates in money lending across states which showed that stipulated maximum rates of interest varied from 6 to 12 per cent per annum simple interest, with most states allowing interest rates up to 8 or 9 per cent and expressly or implicitly prohibiting compound interest.[40]

The relatively minor changes in banking practice recommended by the Shroff Committee would probably not have affected the on-going separation of banking and extra-legal finance very much. The clear rejection of even these minor matters by the RBI is even less comprehensible under these circumstances, but it showed a growing perception that *any* linkage between the market segments was to be avoided. For the purposes here, the committee's argument that the composition of lenders in extra-legal finance and their operational modes were changing considerably is most important. It depicted a growing 'amateurization' that can only be interpreted as a decline in adherence to legal and regulatory dimensions of the market, and the growing shift from reputational dimensions allowing the enforcement of obligations to those centring on trust relationships. An acceptance of the committee's recommendations by the RBI would not have stopped this larger trend, but it would have facilitated some form of reintegration of extra-legal finance, even if only at its highest levels.

The *All India Rural Credit Survey Report*, conducted in 1951–52, was the last major survey that looked into questions of extra-legal finance. Later studies, such as the various reports by the National Sample Survey Organisation (NSSO), the *Report of the Study Group on Indigenous Banking*, or committee reports conducted at infrequent intervals added to the data available, but lacked focus on money lending, and depth. Even though the report has been criticized for misguided approaches – especially its policy-orientation, the unsuitability of its conceptual framework, and inconsistent data quality – notably by Daniel Thorner (1960), it provides one of the most informative sources on rural debt. Unfortunately, the Rural Credit Survey did not select Banaras district as one of its 75 district-wise case studies. In any case, the report did not demonstrate significant changes between the 1930s and 1950s.

The predominance of money lending in rural credit was well established by the report. It showed that 44.8 per cent of rural credit was provided by 'professional moneylenders' (lenders with non-agricultural backgrounds), with another 24.9 per cent by 'agricultural moneylenders'. In addition 5.5 per cent of rural credit was provided by 'traders and commission agents' – that is, occasional moneylenders – and another 1.5 per cent by 'landlords'. 14.2 per cent of credit was given by 'relatives', a category comprising interest-free loans in order to distinguish it from money lending.[41] The fact that a loan would be declared interest-free would not necessarily have meant that there were no costs involved, though the report ignored this difficulty in classification. In operational ways, credit from relatives would have differed little from the reputational parameters of lending. The perspective, instead, highlighted exploitation. For 'formal' sources of credit, the report noted that 3.3 per cent of rural credit was provided by the government, 3.1 per cent by cooperatives, and 0.9 per cent by commercial banks, leaving a miscellaneous category of 'others' that accounted for 1.8 per cent.[42]

Noting that moneylenders were 'responsible for much the larger part of the credit which the cultivator obtains',[43] the report criticized suggestions to involve moneylenders in the policies seeking to facilitate credit, noting that it was 'certainly obvious that the moneylender can be allotted no part in the scheme, important or insignificant, notwithstanding a dominance which today is overwhelming'.[44] The report proceeded to argue that the involvement of moneylenders would amount to 'disaster for the whole scheme here put forward'.[45] The question of including moneylenders in government schemes has been controversially discussed at various times in India.[46] Regardless of the merits and demerits of arguments on inclusion[47] – and I broadly agree with the conclusions of the report – the focus on excluding moneylenders had one important impact, especially in combination with the ideological predisposition to propagate 'proper' forms of banking. It misdirected attention to the figure of the lender and the exploitation involved, instead of directing it towards the reasons why moneylenders were capable of providing for the credit needs of the population, while 'proper' credit agencies were not. It prevented the RBI from taking the reputational dimensions of extra-legal credit contracts seriously, and to find credit alternatives that allowed for higher measures of default than could be tolerated in cooperative credit, 'organized' banking, or – subsequently – microfinance. Accordingly, the only viable alternative was a massive outlay of public funds for alleviating poverty, low productivity, and credit conditions – a policy that the Indian state has always deemed necessary without finding the will or the means to implement.

The size of the moneylender's participation in agricultural finance is undoubted. Nevertheless, it is a mistake to imagine that that size is a measure of the place he must occupy in a realistic solution or, conversely, of the peril at which he may be ignored.... Rather, it is an index to the size of the effort that will be needed ... to rectify a chronic maladjustment....[48]

The Rural Credit Survey thus noted the important position of moneylenders, and even highlighted their competitive advantages especially in terms of flexibility,[49] but failed to inquire into the reasons for and impacts of this flexibility. It attributed the strength of moneylenders to their superior local knowledge. Yet in failing to address the need for a reputational handling of uncertainty arising from the enhanced likelihood of default, the report – as its predecessors and successors – failed to take into account the unsuitability of credit relations that did not rely on reputational means for much of the population. It therefore failed to articulate a policy that would have gone beyond the mere repetition of the strategies attempted in late colonial India – only this time in ways that were expected to be planned better.

It would be wholly incorrect to think of the moneylender as only exploiting those needs; he also adapts himself to them. [I]t is his adaptation which explains his survival in the village, whereas the legislation which has sought to control him survives ... only on paper.... [T]here is little that escapes his eye in the circumstances of his debtors.... What co-operatives merely postulate, he actually possesses, namely, a local knowledge of the 'character and repaying capacity' of those he has to deal with.[50]

The report proceeded to list the various means available to moneylenders to pressurize debtors, including the role of strong social ties including caste and local associations like *panchayat*s 'which, because they happen to be intangible, are not on that account any the less powerful'.[51] It even remarks that 'it does not follow that [moneylenders] will invoke the forces of compulsion the moment payment has become due' but that lenders were 'free to follow as flexible a procedure as [they] like[d] in ... the actual operation of lending'.[52] However, the report merely concluded that the role of moneylenders therefore depended on 'what sort of person the particular moneylender happens to be', moving beyond the inquiry into the reasons for their continued success by wondering 'whether there exists, in the village itself, anything which is likely to frighten the moneylender in his turn' and whether there were 'similar sanctions which [could] be used against him'.[53] In other words, the inquiry into the characteristics of extra-legal finance shifted towards pondering the moral character of individual moneylenders and, again, towards the utility of government action against them instead of whether the reasons for their success could be emulated by other credit agencies for extending credit to those considered 'unbankable'.

The report proceeded by pointing out how moneylenders continued to have some links with 'organized' and 'indigenous' banking, implying that cutting the links would be the measure that could 'frighten' moneylenders. This conclusion, expectedly, fed into a set of recommendations that can only be summarized as 'more of the same': a strong reliance on cooperative credit, and commercial banking, the need to fix maximum interest rates, legislation to provide a 'comprehensive system of control and supervision over the moneylender',[54] and the expansion of regulated storage and warehousing facilities that would undermine the role of extra-legal lenders in 'trade credit'.[55] Each of these measures certainly affected the operations of extra-legal lenders. What the report overlooked was that they would drive moneylenders further into extra-legality, while also restricting the capital available to the majority of people as credit in the only segment that actually was able to meet their credit demands, thus again combatting debt by restricting access to credit.

The unwillingness to inquire into the reputational underpinnings of extra-legal finance in ways that would have allowed a deviation from the insistence on fixing future uncertainty in debt relations in favour of the creditor had long historical antecedents. It can be exemplified by the rejection of ideas to bridge the growing gaps between 'organized' and 'indigenous' banking in the late 1930s. Following closely the RBI's self-depiction, V. R. Cirvante's interpretation of this history blamed the 'indigenous' bankers and their unwillingness to change operational modes, based on the availability of credit to them from the Imperial Bank (Cirvante 1956, 38). Cirvante's argument obviously remains questionable. Most 'indigenous' bankers, and particularly the lower range of this category, were incapable of obtaining credit from the Imperial Bank, as explicitly noted by the Shroff Committee, or implicitly demonstrated by David Rudner's depiction of the elaborate ways in which the Nattukottai Chettiars used community features and the institution of the *adathi* to navigate these difficulties (Rudner 1994, 108). In strong contrast, the *Report of the Study Group on Indigenous Banking* reversed the blame, citing the RBI's insistence to uphold the purity of banking conceptions as the key culprit.

A historical review of the efforts to bring about a link clearly shows that pristine purity of banking concepts led to a breaking off of the attempts.[56]

At one time these arrangements could have been made the basis for the growth of an integrated money market.... [T]he hundi could have provided an appropriate basis for the development of a truly integrated bill market adapted to the needs of the local environment. The hardening of attitudes on both sides, however, rendered any direct link or integration with the organized sector difficult.[57]

The report's recommendations, similarly to the *Shroff Committee Report*'s suggestions, remained ineffectual. In a scathing attack on the guiding principles of policy, the Study Group summarized its effects as the replacement of honest moneylenders by dishonest ones.

The net effect of the legislation has been to drive the honest moneylenders out of business and substituting for them dishonest agencies whom the Act intends to regulate and control'.[58]

While this comment correctly assessed the fact that legislation had not helped but actually worsened conditions for people relying on extra-legal credit, it implicitly fell victim to the same assumptions that had convinced the committee of direction of the Rural Credit Survey to disregard the validity of reputational means of handling uncertainty. The debate centred on involving moneylenders instead of emulating what made them successful. Inevitably, it veered off towards arguments on the alleged character of 'the moneylender' – an unresolvable debate: the proponents of integration were always able to point towards lenience as part of money lending, thereby dissecting it into 'honest' and 'dishonest' lenders, and proposing the integration of the former. The proponents of exclusion, in turn, were always able to highlight the exploitative credit conditions imposed by money lending regardless of lenience. The latest round of this debate occurred in 2007 over the findings of the Technical Group to Review Legislations on Money Lending which went beyond earlier recommendations to advocate the restricted inclusion of moneylenders, even providing a legislative blueprint.[59] As with earlier propositions for integration, the recommendations remained ineffectual.

Rather than highlighting the supposed character traits of extra-legal lenders, it is important to note the underlying developments that had led to the 'substitution' of honest by dishonest lenders. The reputational economy of debt that the state's efforts had been seeking to replace since 1855 had informed distinctions between lenders that combined assertions of relative exploitation rooted in the level of risk assessment with generalized attributions of moral standing. The deposition of the Upper India Chamber of Commerce referred to in Chapter 4 provides the best example of the resulting classifications.

Conflating the relative security offered by lending to the prosperous – where default was less likely, and could be balanced by collateral and the stronger imperative to maintain reputational standing in the absence of dire need – lending to the poor became equated with 'dishonesty'. Rich lenders targeting rich clientele, in turn, were designated to be 'honest'. What statements such as the Study Group's depict, instead, is the on-going decline of the higher levels of extra-legal lending and its rootedness in strong social ties and mercantile ethics – the process of 'amateurization'. The report of the Technical Group does not express these notions anymore. Plausibly, the disappearance of 'indigenous' banking after the mid-1970s precluded the reversion to the argumentative trope used earlier.

The conflation of exploitation and moral character is reflected even in the distinction between 'organized' banking and money lending. In the same year as the publication of the Technical Group's report, the Allahabad High Court expressed its outrage at prevalent banking practices that are reminiscent of money lending:

> [I]f [*sic*] loanee is unable to pay ... the instalments, ... proceedings are initiated by employing private agents (often anti-social elements).... [W]e decry money lending because it is immoral to convert the crisis of another into an opportunity to exploit him. Such exploitation of poor people by our banking sectors ... was never visualized by [*sic*] Constitutional framers.... [I]n case of default ... beyond the control of [*sic*] farmer, the bank shall take [*sic*] accommodative attitude of employing coercive tactics and must explore measures like postponing recovery or re-scheduling recovery rather than preying upon farmers in the modernized version of Shylock's pound of flesh.... [T]he loanee is often compelled to affix signatures or thumb impressions on every page of the printed form, which is subsequently filled in by a [different] person.... [The] agreement ... makes it clear that signatures has [*sic*] been affixed thereon at the bottom of every page. Most of the columns are also left blank and entries have been made by some person other than [*sic*] petitioner ... at a subsequent date.[60]

The general preconception of the High Court – that 'organized' banks would be honest creditors in contrast to moneylenders – rests on the unstated assumption that their moral character is rooted in banking regulations that typically prevent them from lending to the poor, or for the purposes for which extra-legal credit is in demand. In cases in which banks were lending to the clientele typically targeted by moneylenders, their resorting to the practices of moneylenders – including intimidation and the manipulation of contractual documents – created outrage. In contrast, the court would not necessarily have castigated the refusal of banks to lend to the target clientele of moneylenders based on their heightened risk assessment, even though this would have constrained the debtors' credit from sources other than extra-legal finance. What is much more remarkable about the High Court's judgment, however, is its advocation of an 'accommodative attitude' for banks in cases of default. Unreflected in this judgment, accommodation and lenience comprise the other element of extra-legal finance, and it is the combination of accommodation, intimidation, and manipulation that defines the operational modes of the reputational economy of debt.

Reverting briefly to the analysis of the Study Group on Indigenous Banking, one of its findings that did instigate legislation was its deploring of the absence of a moneylenders act in Uttar Pradesh.[61] Comprehensive legislation was eventually enacted with the Uttar Pradesh Regulation of Money Lending Act of 1976 that, however, took up stipulations that significantly weakened it. Transactions above a limit of 5,000 rupees were exempted from the provisions as much as 'trade credit', that is, credit transactions between people registered in any trade or industry.[62] The amendment of the act in 1978 repealed the Usurious Loans Act as amended in its application to Uttar Pradesh.[63]

Statistical data published by the Government of India demonstrates a gradual decline of indebtedness to 'non-institutional credit agencies'. These findings are relatively consistent, even if the data provides significant evidence for the continuity of extra-legal finance. The gradual decline appears to contradict the ethnographic evidence depicted in Chapter 8. One fact to consider in this regard is misreporting: while methodologies were selected in the reports to contain this problem, it is plausible that growing extra-legality would affect the reporting of indebtedness to extra-legal lenders, frequently engaging in illegal acts. Where extra-legal credit agencies are not criminalized, credit and debt are still frequently related to attempts to evade taxation or regulation. Whatever the extent of misreporting, it remains necessary to be aware of its probability.

Another aspect to be considered is reporting on the purpose of borrowing – an area where the likelihood of misreporting is even higher. Statistical data definitely shows a gradual increase of credit for purposes in which 'organized' banking has competitive advantages. The data thus predominantly shows the growth of 'formal' credit markets for specific purposes which indicates a relative decline in extra-legal finance regarding its share in the overall credit market. This, however, does not preclude the flourishing of extra-legal markets in areas where it remains competitive.

The household indebtedness survey by the NSSO for 1992 showed a remarkable decline in the incidence of indebtedness to non-institutional sources since the 1970s, and a reversal of the relative shares between institutional and non-institutional agencies. Highlighting the caveat that its sample was 'quite small',[64] the survey reported an incidence of indebtedness for Scheduled Tribe households of 12.0 per cent to institutional sources, and of 6.6 per cent to non-institutional sources. The incidence of indebtedness for Scheduled Tribes was lower than for other groups, indicating low average creditworthiness and low economic dynamism. Incidence of indebtedness was highest for Scheduled Caste households (17.1 and 11.2 per cent, respectively), while for 'other' social groups it was 15.8 and 9.9 per cent.[65] Within the category of non-institutional lenders, the incidence of indebtedness to moneylenders was significantly higher than to relatives and friends (2.3 per cent). Agricultural moneylenders provided 2.3 per cent of credit, professional moneylenders 3.1 per cent, landlords provided 1.1 per cent, while traders provided another 0.7 per cent, and 'doctors, lawyers, etc'. provided 0.1 per cent. The survey reported a residual category of 'others' with 1.1 per cent of credit within this sub-category.[66] Total outstanding debt was 64.0 per cent to institutional sources, and 32.7 per cent to non-institutional sources, with 3.3 per cent unspecified.[67]

By 2002, the relative growth of institutional credit agencies compared to non-institutional ones had been arrested. The NSSO survey for 2002 reported outstanding debt to institutional agencies in rural India for all social groups of 13.4 per cent, comprising 10.9 per cent for Scheduled Tribes, 11.9 per cent for Scheduled Castes, 13.4 per cent of Other Backward Classes, and 15.7 per cent for others.[68] Outstanding debt to non-institutional agencies were 8.1 per cent for Scheduled Tribes, 17.0 per cent for Scheduled Castes, 18.3 per cent for Other Backward Classes, and 12.6 per cent for others, totalling 15.5 per cent.[69] Even though the reversal is notable, the survey data still compares favourably to earlier periods.

The so-called *Radhakrishna Committee Report* on agricultural indebtedness, published in 2007, provides further information for rural India. The report demonstrates the massive growth of credit flows by institutional agencies after the 1970s. Total credit from institutional agencies to rural India grew from 1,675 crore rupees in 1975–76 to 5,244 crore rupees in 1983–84 and 16,494 crore rupees in 1993–94. It massively expanded in the early 2000s, reaching 62,045 crore rupees in 2001–02, 86,981 crore rupees in 2003–03, and 125,309 crore rupees in 2004–05, before reaching the unprecedented level of 180,486 crore rupees in 2006–07.[70] Even taking into account inflation and currency depreciation, this rise is substantial. As importantly, the share of short-term compared to long-term borrowings declined from 70.3 per cent in the mid-1970s to 58.1 per cent in the mid-2000s.[71] The growth of long-term borrowings indicates the increase of credit needs for productive purposes. It also puts the general growth as compared to extra-legal finance into perspective, as the competitive advantages of 'organized' banking are higher for productive purposes. The share of commercial banking from institutional lenders grew significantly faster than cooperative credit, becoming predominant by the 1980s. While its general share declined afterwards, it remained the most important lending agency.[72] Self-help groups linked to banking schemes also reported grew, though they remained marginal overall, reaching 3,080 crore rupees per year in 2005–06.[73] Total debt of agricultural households in 2003 was estimated at 1.12 lakh crore rupees, of which 65,000 crore was institutional and 48,000 crore non-institutional. The report stated that about one third of the latter category was from moneylenders, though the tendency to subdivide the group of extra-legal lenders needs to be considered with caution as most loans in this category would follow similar operational logics.[74] The share of debt of cultivating households to moneylenders declined significantly since independence, though. Moneylenders, according to this classification, provided 69.7 per cent of these loans in 1951, receding to 49.2 per cent in 1961 and 36.1 per cent in 1971, then dropping as low as 16.1 per cent in 1981 and 17.5 per cent in 1991, before rising again in 2002 to 26.8 per cent. Non-institutional credit agencies in total provided 92.7 per cent of credit to cultivating households in 1951. This dropped to 66.3 per cent in 1971, and to 30.6 per cent in 1991, before rising again to 38.9 per cent in 2002.[75] As the difference between non-institutional agencies and moneylenders in operational terms is marginal, the second set of data is of greater importance in understanding the development of extra-legal markets. The sub-category of moneylenders remains open to substantial differences in interpretation, and in any case the intermittent relative decline in the share of creditors classified as moneylenders vis-à-vis other non-institutional agencies – 16.1 and 36.8 per cent respectively at its lowest level in 1991 before rising again – indicates the progression of the 'amateurization' process rather than a decline in money lending. As importantly, considering that credit flows from institutional agencies increased more than one hundred times in value (disregarding inflation) between the mid-1970s and the mid-2000s, extra-legal finance managed to roughly match this increase, indicating how little legal constraints and the decline of 'indigenous' banking affected access to capital.

Among many other aspects, the numbers discussed earlier show a vast increase in the scale of credit markets in which extra-legal and regulated credit practices both participated. Sohini Kar, studying the practices of marketing credit by the loan officers involved in micro-credit schemes in contemporary Kolkata, has argued that the poor are 'enfolded' into global finance (Kar 2017) – that the marketing of credit creates the desire for credit-based consumption, thereby bringing social strata that are inherently precarious into the reach of credit markets, underlying a commodification of affect, social networks, and trust. The increased willingness to take on debt – unless clearly related to subsistence needs which the private micro-credit firms depicted by Kar would hardly serve – indicates a considerable increase in the willingness to take risks, or else a misunderstanding of the risks involved in being indebted. Do we witness in the massive increases in debt intake by people in India and the correspondingly rising incidence of exposure to credit risks a mirror image of the argument in economic history that the desire for higher levels of consumption drives increases in industriousness?[76]

What is notable here is the relative ease with which extra-legal finance, regardless of intermittent drops or rises in its overall proportion in credit – has been able to follow the substantial increase in 'organized' credit. It needs to be pointed out that the liberal argument for fixing the enhanced uncertainty of credit relations in favour of the creditor was rooted precisely in the incentive this provided for increases in the supply of credit. The juridical-procedural parameters of 'modern' finance were developed for this very purpose. Rather than marvelling at the accuracy in predicting the increases in the scale of credit that constituted one of the outcomes of this policy, it is important to highlight how much reputational credit markets were capable of emulating these successes – in the absence of policy design, and while serving significantly more difficult market segments. While the engine of change in the secular process of change in risk-taking attitudes was likely the regulated segment of Indian finance, its extra-legal counterpart managed to follow at a similar pace. 'Financialization', whatever its extent and character in the Indian context, extends to credit markets that would have been depicted as particularly unsuitable for it by many colonial and postcolonial observers.

Returning to the discourse on credit policies in India, the *Radhakrishna Report* recommended a debt redemption scheme specifically targeting loans given by moneylenders. This scheme, reminiscent of failed schemes in the 1930s, was based on banks providing long-term loans to people indebted to moneylenders with the purpose restriction of using the new bank loans exclusively for redeeming extra-legal loans.[77] While there is no reliable data on the success of the scheme, its main defect – as in the 1930s – was that even long-term bank loans were incapable under juridical-procedural rules of 'organized' banking of substituting for the flexibility of extra-legal credit in adjusting obligations to changing circumstances. The scheme, however, played an important role in the crackdown on moneylenders in Banaras in 2006 and 2007.

Before coming to this topic, though, the postcolonial Indian state's handling of extra-legal finance needs to be summarized. The state's attention to money lending shows two divergent trajectories. First, attention gradually slipped away, reflecting the pattern established for media coverage. Undoubtably, issues concerning 'financial inclusion' remained part of the state's institutional architecture, but institutional efforts lacked guidance from higher levels of Indian politics. Concerns over money lending became relevant at specific flashpoints such as in the early 1950s, early and mid-1970s, and the mid-2000s, receding into obscurity afterwards. Second – and more problematically – extra-legal finance diminished as a concern. To put it bluntly, the Indian state – following in the footsteps of the late colonial state after 1918 – remained ideologically predisposed to fail to take money lending seriously, that is, as something that was not just a scandal and exploitation but actually worked in providing credit to social strata not reached by 'organized' finance. The independent Indian state had provided analyses that ran into thousands of pages. Yet the main distinction between arguments was whether late colonial policies should be revamped to include moneylenders in policy schemes or consciously exclude them. While the former was never tried out, the latter became well documented in its failure to effect significant changes. But both positions studiously agreed on ignoring the reasons why money lending worked on the ground, denominated in an increasingly grotesque caricature of the informational advantages held by 'local' moneylenders over (assumedly not so 'local') bank employees. The caricature rested on neglecting the more relevant question of what the supposedly insurmountable informational advantage was being used for – the handling of uncertainty through reputational means, allowing enhanced flexibility in renegotiating credit obligations – and how the 'pristine purity of banking concepts' in their juridical-procedural underpinnings could emulate these means.

In the absence of a change in state policy, extra-legal finance clearly continued to flourish. Policy failed to provide alternatives within the juridical-procedural paradigm of credit. The use of the state's repressive force that informed all approaches on extra-legal finance relying either on their criminalization or on enforced regulation remained impotent – not because the Indian state did not have the capacity to police moneylenders, but because it lacked the capacity to develop policies under which this policing would not have led to even more detrimental outcomes. What the state managed to achieve was to increase the risk premium in interest calculation twofold: by introducing a risk factor into the reputational credit contract by enforcing its operation on the margins of the law; and by undermining the collective elements in how it had worked before, based on the employment of strong social ties and mercantile ethics for the enforcement of transactional obligations. Extra-legal financial entrepreneurs never disappeared. Instead, they vanished intermittently from public sight, all the while adjusting their operational procedures to flourish despite legislation.

Money lending as scandal

Returning to media coverage, in the following I will discuss the emergence of a discourse that can be subdivided into two strands: the scandal of the continued existence of exploitative lending, and the scandal of violence associated with it. In practice, however, both strands were constantly interwoven, though there are distinctive emphases at different times. I will focus on depicting two particularly informative periods of media coverage – the first half of the 1970s, characterized by strong attention towards continued exploitation, and the crackdown on money lending in Banaras in 2006 and 2007. The latter, in turn, provides a bridge into the ethnographic study on the reputational dimensions of extra-legal finance in the subsequent chapter.

Following a decline in its reportage, the *Times of India* initiated a spate in its coverage in early 1970 that lasted approximately until 1976. While its reportage included legislative and policy debates, its core remained firmly centred on the perceived scandal of the continuance of money lending. It also rested on a formidable effort to combine reportage on this scandal with an educational project on the evils of money lending as a representation of greed. Its first article within this period serves as an indication of this trend. Its author, Venkatesh Deshpande, published a parable, involving the fictitious story of a moneylender who out of greed would not donate for religious purposes, and tried to trick a priest into turning over future donations for a meagre one-time payment. Mixing Biblical and Hindu tropes, the story's focus remained on its religious dimension. That the main villain was a moneylender, instead, was primarily used in order to quickly establish his greedy and immoral nature:

> In a small town there lived a business man [*sic*]. His name was Ashamull. He was a moneylender. In a year or two he made a clean sum of Rs. 10,000. He was not satisfied. He raised the rate of interest…. Still he was not happy…. The more he earned, the more his greed for money increased.[78]

While Ashamull proceeds to prevent his wife from donating to the local temple, on the sixth day of the story he starts plotting the transaction that would give him the donations to the temple, ten times the offered upfront payment. On the seventh day, receiving the collected donations, only half his payment has been collected. Enraged, he slaps the face of the god's idol, and his palm gets stuck there, only to be pried free when his wife makes him narrate his devious plan, and offers the equivalent sum of his expected profits as donation.

> From that day, he gave away everything he had as charity. *Moral*: We should not be greedy. We should be satisfied with whatever we get. God's will prevails.[79]

The parable of Ashamull was given significant coverage. It covered a full page, included a major illustration, and the caption was highlighted in both size and font. Addressing a predominantly middle-class readership, the choice of a simplistic educational idiom centring on religious tropes may appear surprising. Yet the choice of moral discourse fit well into the period, a phase of India's developmental project marked by tendencies to exhort middle classes to forego consumerist aspirations in the face of developmental needs, and to disparage notions of profitability in favour of the solidity of salaried employment (Rajagopal 2011). The antipodes of this discourse could be located in the figure of the moneylender, representing the small-town petty bourgeois opposition to the developmentalist thrust. The 'folkloristic' idiom merely reinforced the notion of a (supposed) alignment between urban salaried middle classes and the (alleged) benefiters of their avoidance of consumption that formed the mass of the poorer sections of society, irrespective of the complexity of class interests at the time. In terms of the growing opposition between 'organized' and extra-legal finance, the exhorted behavioural norms for the middle class connected well with the idea of juridical-procedural regulation in public sector banking that was supposed to be extended to the poor masses, while the moneylender stood for its precise opposite, the continuity of immoral and anachronistic ways of ordering credit relations, an impediment to bestowing the benefits of 'modernity' to the poor. The obvious failure of the 'formal' credit system in this expansion merely reinforced the urgency attributed to the educational message.

Deshpande's article constitutes a master narrative for this aspect of the scandal of money lending. The expansion of 'organized' finance was mainly driven by the state's desire to aggregate capital flows for a developmental policy centring on large-scale industrialization that had little to do with the livelihoods of both the petty bourgeoisie and the poorer strata depending on it in the *mufassil*, despite its anticipated trickle-down effects. Propagating the hoped-for long-term benefits of policy in opposition to the lived experience of credit demands and needs, the deprivation of the present was morally legitimized in terms appealing to the urban salaried middle classes, the actual beneficiaries.

This theme of reporting money lending as scandal centring on greed continued over the following years. In April 1973, three men 'connected with a money-lending firm' were held by the police, allegedly having defrauded the Indian Overseas Bank.[80] In December 1973, police arrested a moneylender who had entered an arrangement with a sorter in the foreign post office. The latter allegedly stole remittances, while the moneylender handled their conversion.[81] In August 1975, the Income Tax Department raided another postal sorter who had become a successful moneylender, detailing the riches he had accumulated.[82] In a different raid, it recovered money from a smuggling racket. Here, the fact that the merchant running the racket was a moneylender was merely added – demonstrating additional vice in allegations unrelated to lending.[83] The newspaper reported the suspension of a vendor to the Bombay Port Trust canteen for money lending, again highlighting his riches, obtained from fellow workers.[84] In October 1975, it reported the Maharashtra government's intentions to enact legislation that imposed prison sentences for 'money-lending on the sly'.[85] In May 1976, it reported yet another successful raid, this time against a 'millionaire moneylender' who lived in a village near Delhi and was 'in league with a leading film star of Bombay'.[86] The article emphasized the lender's concealed wealth, partially in his 'dilapidated' home, comprising 'secret chambers from where [the IT department] recovered silver coins of the Mughal period', the unearthing of expensive electrical consumer items and concealment of 'black promissory notes'.[87] The lender was reported charging 24–39 per cent interest per annum – a relatively low range.

As opposed to the theme of greed, the newspaper published three articles that emphasized the socio-economic dimensions of exploitation through extra-legal finance, though employing scandalizing idioms. In June 1973, it published a long article on the plight of Adivasi cultivators exploited by moneylenders in Thane district that highlighted socio-economic conditions of the debtors, patterns of dominance and their use in enforcing credit obligations, and the capacity of moneylenders to offer loans at very short notice. The article also dwelt on the failures of government action.[88]

In contrast, moneylenders were also reported in less disparaging ways, though rarely. In November 1971, the *Times of India* reported the case of

J. P. G. Agarwal, a moneylender who had helped identifying a murderer. The article highlighted the informant's profession as moneylender, detailing how the murderer had pawned various items with him, and how this was used by the police. The tone of the article differed strongly from other reports.

> [T]he court room was packed to capacity. The moneylender, who sported a scarlet bush-shirt and a pair of tapered black trousers, was the object of attention, his reply to a defence question drew laughter from those present.[89]

The defence counsel attempted to use Agarwal's profession to question his moral standing:

> Agarwal ... was asked by defence counsel as to what would happen if a customer turned dishonest. Witness replied that he had had no such dealings, for his business was carried on the basis of trust, and confidence. 'As a licensed moneylender,' defence counsel reminded him, 'you have to pass a signed receipt to your clients giving the description of the articles pawned to you, the amount raised and other such details.' ... Defence counsel: I put it to you that you are a stooge of the police doing business without observing the rules, for this book of entries is a bogus one.[90]

In September of the same year, an article highlighted the failure of government policy by pointing to the practice of debtors from Bombay's working class to pawn their ration cards with moneylenders.[91] Finally, in late 1975 the *Times of India* published a full-page article on two reports on socio-economic conditions conducted by its journalists near Patna and Lucknow, including a large illustration that showed a fat moneylender with his head resting on a strongbox filled with jewellery taking paltry sums from an underweight villager. Despite the scandalizing image, the article provided considerable background information, engaging with bonded labour, intergenerational bequeathing of debts, legislation against money lending, the failure of land reforms, and declining agricultural productivity in the area.[92]

Articles such as these demonstrate that reporting on extra-legal finance could address the issue meaningfully. At the same time, the newsworthiness of such articles was apparently considered low. The idiom of money lending as scandal centred on single instances that supposedly captured public attention, involving crime and greed. The image of extra-legal finance was propagated in ways that implicitly removed it from socio-economic and political considerations. The figure of the moneylender emerged as a sly and greedy criminal, instead of an exploitative entrepreneur who had succeeded in tapping into a market resilient because of the failure of 'organized' banking. The operational modes of extra-legal finance that were routinely handled by millions of people receded into obscurity, overlaid by a caricature of greed, violence, and crime. This caricature, in turn, implicitly absolved the state of its responsibilities to provide viable alternatives as it located the problem of extra-legal finance in human vice.

Media reportage on rural debt increased significantly in the 1990s, especially due to the work of P. Sainath that managed to shift the debate towards socio-economic issues. Sainath's work has been of immense value in publicizing concerns over farmers' suicides.[93] The extent of farmers' suicides in India has been estimated at least at 300,000 instances between 1995 and 2012 (Nagaraj et al. 2014), despite misreporting and misclassification, such as the definition of farmers through land titles, leaving out a considerable section of the agricultural workforce (Nagaraj et al. 2014, 55–57). What is outstanding in this regard is not so much the number of suicides among farmers or their share of overall suicides. Nagaraj et al. estimate these as 23.2 per cent on average between 1997 and 2012 for the worst affected state of Maharashtra, which does not translate into high suicide rates compared to other groups (Nagaraj et al. 2014, 78). Instead, what is outstanding is the extent to which the literature on the subject has been able to link these suicides to agrarian distress.

Farmers' suicides have frequently been linked to debt, including to extra-legal finance, though its causes are manifold, and vary across time and region. A large body of academic literature has been published on this topic which is only tangentially related to this study.[94] Given the multi-causality of agrarian distress and suicides, the debate has been characterized by diverging views. The debate touches this study on the question of the expansion or reduction of 'organized' finance, and on the impacts of 'organized' and extra-legal debt on farmers' suicides. The latter question cannot easily be resolved. Debt to 'organized' finance, including cooperative credit and microfinance, comprises significantly greater rigidity in repayment obligations and enforcement, while extra-legal finance includes increased levels of exploitation. In practice, many debtors in rural India resort to portfolio strategies in acquiring credit – particularly vulnerable debtors as outlined by Guérin (2014) – so that the multiplicity of causes for agrarian distress and suicides is supplemented by a multiplicity of sources of debt, and enforcement strategies. There seems to be very little point in generalizing the role of debt in farmers' suicides beyond stating that it is significant, and complex even at the level of individual instances.

On the expansion or reduction of 'organized' finance in rural India, there are indications in recent decades that 'organized' financial services have declined relative to 'non-institutional' agencies, even while the value of credit from 'organized' finance has increased. Nagaraj et al. depict this as a reduction of 'formal' credit flows, an assessment I am in agreement with when viewed from the perception of individual debtors, the only perspective that justifiably can be used in discussing debt-related suicides.

The space vacated by the state was taken up by private agents ... These agents ... were mostly from the urban centres in the region and, with next to no regulation of their operations, essentially [predatory] (Nagaraj et al. 2014, 81)

What is important here is the characterization of 'private agents' as predatory – going beyond mere exploitation in the context of high socio-spatial distance to the debtors. The implication in the use of the term is that private agents – both 'formal' and 'informal' lenders – do not generally conform to the characterization of extra-legal finance based on a reputational economy centring on trust that is highly exploitative at the same time as being flexible in terms of the re-negotiability of obligations. This, in turn, would indicate a 'formalization' process among the extra-legal entrepreneurs within this category, since the socio-spatial distance is likely to decrease the employability of strong social ties or reputational means centring on trust. As there is no possibility of providing a robust break-up for the impacts of 'formal' and extra-legal finance, this discussion, however, necessarily remains speculative.

Reporting on farmers' suicides formed one of the reasons for the Indian government's decision to set up the Radhakrishna Committee. Indirectly, it therefore had an impact on the crackdown on money lending in Banaras in 2006–2007. Yet the renewed public attention in the wake of this debate also affected the direction of media reportage that shifted from centring on greed to emphasizing socio-economic conditions and the role of violence in extra-legal finance. Socio-economic conditions – while present – became drowned by the latter. In turn, this reinforced the predominance of the second strand of reporting money lending as scandal, violent crime.

The crackdown on money lending in Banaras in 2006–2007 was connected to the Radhakrishna Commission. It was also related to an effort by the Indian National Congress to regain political influence in India's most populous state, and through unverifiable allegations to corruption within the city's police force. However, it also followed a spate in violent crime related to money lending that had started to be reported locally beforehand. As mentioned earlier, these themes had sporadically been reported in the local edition of *Dainik Jagran* from 1970 onwards. However, in 2004 reporting of these crimes significantly increased. The question whether this was due to increased public awareness, increased newsworthiness, or an increase in crime related to money lending itself cannot be answered. If the latter was at least partially correct, it would indicate a considerable intermittent decline in the viability of stabilizing of extra-legal finance through trust and reputation.

In January 2004, the local daily reported a relatively minor case of violence over a debtor's default.[95] This is notable as it preceded more pronounced cases of violence leading to fatalities, but was still considered newsworthy. A relatively similar case was also reported in June 2004,[96] after bigger crimes had been reported: a master tailor was reported killed in a money lending dispute, with the newspaper even publishing a photo of the grieving family, while the daily also reported a knife attack on a weaver, with an image of the wounded man.[97] The fact that *Dainik Jagran* published images shows the increase in newsworthiness. In May 2004, it published a report on the involvement of BHU office workers in money lending practices, briefly reverting to reporting the greed trope.[98] In September 2004, it published an article on a defaulter in a *bisi* circle (see Chapter 8) being gheraoed[99] in his house.[100] Finally, in October 2004 a report was published on the killing of a twenty-five-year-old man, this time with a photo of the body and the man's shuttered shop.[101]

There was a slight decline in reporting in 2005. But, generally, media attention remained on the topic as evidenced by the low profile of one instance of violence reported: seven people were held by the police after a scuffle broke out in a *len–den* affair, and the newspaper followed up on this story by reporting the registration of a first information report.[102] This had been preceded by a report on the suicide of a man indebted to moneylenders, and the killing of a municipal corporation worker, both including images.[103]

Following this trend, *Dainik Jagran* reported a scuffle between a defaulting debtor and a moneylender[104] and the suicide of a *paan* seller related to threats by moneylenders in early 2006, including photos.[105] However, in late April the newspaper significantly enhanced its reporting on money lending. It published an article on the prevalence of usurious credit practices in both the city and its surrounding countryside that called for action against moneylenders who were acting as 'new *zamindars*' and included a cartoon drawing that depicted a vulture (with the caption *suudkhor*, lit.: usurer) salivating while staring at a dove's eggs captioned (in Hindi) accumulated money.[106] In early May, it reported on school teachers dependent on loans from moneylenders.[107] On 23 June 2006, it published a long report on the money lending 'network' of the lawyer Sanjeev Rai, allegedly its mastermind, stating that upwards of 700 families were in his 'blood-soaked claws'.[108] After a lull, the newspaper then provided detailed coverage of the main scandal that had become public since late August 2006.

On 26 August 2006, it announced an intensive police campaign against moneylenders in the city for the next month, as part of a background article on the 'story of suicides hidden in usury'.[109] On the same day, it depicted the arrest of a moneylender by the police, calling for the city's police to bust the 'networks' of moneylenders.[110] It followed up two days later with a report depicting police efforts, and looking at the caste structure underlying an upper-caste-dominated money lending 'network'. Encapsulated was a report on the victims of Sanjeev Rai, who had now emerged as the central figure in the crackdown.[111] The following day, it reported that a debtor had committed suicide after a moneylender allegedly connected to the 'network' had attempted to enforce repayments by all his debtors fearing a police crackdown. The moneylender was reported as absconding.[112] On 31 August 2006, *Dainik Jagran* carried a story about two more first information reports being filed by a rural family that had walked to the city's main police station from their village. The family's original debt was stated to have escalated from 2,000 rupees to 80,000 rupees over five years.[113] On 1 September 2006, the police were reported to have opened a 'mobile' police substation to deal with complaints against money lending.[114] On the following day, moneylenders had been spotted loitering near bank branches on payday. The report called on people's assistance, opening with the statement that everyone was used to 'seeing usurers, but to get rid of them [was] difficult'.[115] By early September 2006, the newspaper had shifted to calling Sanjeev Rai's 'network' a mafia organization. It celebrated the arrest of several lenders associated with this 'mafia' under the headline 'even big fishes are detained now'.[116] One of the suits filed against these lenders, though, was almost immediately given up,[117] but the following day the police filed a first information report against Sanjeev Rai himself.[118]

By November 2006, the crackdown had reached the attention of national English-language media. The *Economic Times* reported on links between the local lenders and Kolkata-based entrepreneurs who had invested in the illegal business run by Rai and others. The opening passage of this article has been cited at the outset of this chapter, but the article proceeded to state that 40 cases had been filed and over 500 complaints received. The operational modes of the lenders were allegedly based on investments by Kolkata-based entrepreneurs to target white-collar employees in Banaras, especially in BHU, the municipal corporation, and the Diesel Locomotive Works. In these three units, the article claimed, between 40 and 50 per cent of the employees had been indebted to the 'racket'.[119]

However, it is the opening passages quoted earlier that are interesting in demonstrating the detachment from the realities of extra-legal finance of a national business newspaper. Premchand's work had certainly emphasized 'wily' money lenders. Yet the depiction in the *Economic Times* – by using terms like 'a grim repeat' and stating that extra-legal finance could 'only' be encountered in fictional literature of the 1930s – either wilfully ignored or simply was unaware of the persistence of extra-legal finance, showing the extent to which its readership had internalized the moneylenders' vanishing act. The local edition of *Dainik Jagran* returned mostly to reporting money lending as scandal in 2007, and largely neglected the topic since 2008. In February 2007, it reported a suicide related to intimidation by moneylenders.[120] In May, it reported a man having burned down his house before committing suicide because of an extra-legal mortgage.[121] In October 2007, a man was killed in a money lending dispute.[122] Finally, in December 2007, it published a colourful account of an instance of intimidation in which the moneylender was alleged to have loitered in front of a debtor's home with a tractor, implying that the vehicle was supposed to be used for violence.[123] The case against Sanjeev Rai figured prominently when in April 2007 a witness turned hostile.[124]

The crackdown was short-lived. When starting my field research in 2011, it was still visible in the way moneylenders needed to be assured that my work was not related to the Indian state. On the ground, however, nothing had changed much for the vast majority of lenders who had not really been affected by it, and did not employ organizational forms similar to the 'racket'. Over the next years, awareness of the crackdown among the moneylenders receded, and by 2017, hardly any person would even bring up the topic.

One aspect that needs to be considered here is the high level of violence visible in the reporting. High levels of violence associated with extra-legal credit, as shown in Chapter 8, were not the norm between 2011 and 2020. Violence – if at all employed – remained mostly confined to low levels. It formed part of the lenders' repertoire in response to evasions of communicating default, and was mostly depicted, including by debtors, as part of strategies to extract a 'price' for lenience in the absence of other employable means. It constituted a form of intimidation that sought to minimize further default in the future. Intimidation tactics cannot be taken lightly. Yet they do not correspond to similarly high levels of violence, of upwards of a dozen homicides between 2004 and 2007, not even counting suicides.

Media reportage is not in itself a good indication of high levels of violence as many instances may have remained unreported, or may not have been linked to extra-legal finance if reported. At the same time, the contrast between the period of 2004–2007 and the time before and afterwards is striking: violent deaths associated with money lending were on average reported less than six times per decade beyond this period, and most of these were reported as suicides. The main difference between this period, and the preceding and following periods is likely the highly organized manner in which one element of the city's extra-legal credit market functioned. It is noteworthy that high-level violence was reported more frequently before the crackdown in mid-2006. The reportage by *Dainik Jagran* makes amply clear that the lending 'racket' allegedly operated by Sanjeev Rai was highly organized compared to the vast majority of transactions in this market. The 'racket' had links to investors outside the city, but it also clearly had a hierarchy of lenders, and employed enforcers. Media reportage tended to club these two categories together, depicting them predominantly as 'associates'.

Enforcers – while not entirely absent – are rare in money lending (see Chapter 8). However, the operation of a hierarchy of lenders constitutes the more surprising element in the operations of the 'racket': it demonstrates an organizational level in which there are clearly defined roles and the regular capital flows needed to sustain these. It shows an organizational level in which extra-legal lending reverted to structures associated with firms, or organized crime.[125] In both these respects, it shows a process of 'formalization' within extra-legal finance that is absent from the market I observed, without reverting to the employment of strong social ties. The reported caste nexus linked local lenders and external investors, and buttressed protection against legal interference, but did not facilitate the enforcement of transactional obligations. In the absence of such as structure of enforcing obligations through social ties, it can be surmised that high levels of organization were only viable in the presence of a high capacity for violence.

Conclusion

Money lending and extra-legal finance did not disappear. Rather, they vanished from public attention, particularly because it was supposed to disappear through the expansion of 'organized' finance, and because this expansion worked sufficiently well for the credit needs of India's industry and elite to enable their detachment from the worlds of extra-legal credit. It would be wrong to state that extra-legal finance flourished because of this lack of attention.

Lenders and creditors alike had merely found ways to operate a credit market that did not rely on sufficiently pronounced links to the higher levels of capital that would have exposed their operations. In the absence of viable alternatives, the state's and the larger public's attention became sporadic. Attention to extra-legal finance increased whenever particular combinations of factors coalesced, and receded once the problem had been determined to be intractable. With 'organized' finance working sufficiently well to provide an alternative for the state's and the elite's needs, attention was followed by apathy in the face of this intractability, reinforced by the reinterpretation of extra-legal entrepreneurs as caricatures centring on tropes of greed, violence, developmental impediments, and the enforcement of the state's regulatory capacity.

The trope of greed related to a much longer history. Colonial sources are replete with references to Shakespeare's *Merchant of Venice*. In public imagination, figures like the character Sukhilala or, for that matter, the moneylender Ashamull served as 'Indianized' equivalents, but even the Allahabad High Court judgment on the practices of nationalized banks referred to the character of Shylock. Similarly, the trope of violence reflected the public imagination of colonial-era Pathan moneylenders regardless of the diversity of their enforcement practices.

The state's attention to extra-legal finance, in turn, centred strongly on the imagination of moneylenders as a developmental problem. This imagination was misplaced in that the real developmental problem was the inability of 'organized' finance as regulated by the state to serve the credit needs of major sections of the population. It was compounded by the unwillingness of the state's decision-makers to contemplate deviations from the juridical-procedural parameters of 'organized' finance – the 'pristine purity of banking concepts' – that might have been employed to substitute for moneylenders. In the absence of a discourse that took seriously the reputational dimensions of extra-legal credit, policy debate shifted between recommendations to integrate moneylenders into the market regulations devised for their replacement, and the reassertion of arguments that policies to replace moneylenders could not rely on their active involvement. Finally, the crackdown on moneylenders in Banaras demonstrates the extent to which the Indian state was and is capable of enforcing its regulatory sway, reminiscent of the example of the Ghilzai lenders given in Chapter 5 – sporadically and intermittently. Once public attention receded from intermittent spurts in proactive policy, extra-legal entrepreneurs still remained the only viable creditors for significant segments of the population, and 'amateurish' moneylenders continued to flourish. What remained was a denial of ground realities and of the ubiquity of extra-legal finance, visible among many other instances in the report on the crackdown by the *Economic Times* cited at the outset of this chapter that characterized money lending as a 'grim repeat' of times only encountered in late colonial India instead of having flourished throughout the intervening period, and that the only thing that had apparently changed was the *dhoti-*clad appearance of the lenders rather than the underlying dynamics of the reputational credit contract.

Notes

1. 'Money-lending Racket Thrives', *Economic Times*, 14 November 2006, available online at https://economictimes.indiatimes.com/money-lending-racket-thrives/articleshow/438438.cms?from=mdr (last accessed 13 March 2020).

2. Interview with a debtor, conducted by the author in Banaras on 18 February 2012, translated from Hindi by the author.

3. For a summary of Weberian ideas on calculability in the context of credit markets, see Vik (2017).

4. For a fascinating study of – among others – class relations in Indian hinterland towns, see the various contributions in Harriss-White (2016).

5. This archive is accessible among others at the University of Göttingen.

6. 'Moneylenders' Act Amendment. Hyderabad State Move', *Times of India*, 30 April 1946, 6.

7. 'Money-lending by Mysore Officials. Criticism in Assembly', *Times of India*, 5 June 1947, 9.

8. 'Control of Money Lending. New Bombay Bill', *Times of India*, 21 August 1946, 7.

9. 'Amendment of Debt Relief Act. Bombay Assembly Agenda', *Times of India*, 6 June 1946, 8.

10. 'Protection from Usurers', *Times of India*, 22 August 1946, 6.

11. 'Money-lending Bill Introduced in Bombay Assembly. "Measure Seeks to Regulate and Not Eliminate Profession"', *Times of India*, 4 September 1946, 5.

12. 'Money-lending Bill', *Times of India*, 19 October 1946, 6; 'Moneylending Bill. Select Committee Makes Important Changes' 'Protection from Usurers', *Times of India*, 28 September 1946, 5.

13. 'Readers Views. Money-lenders' Bill', *Times of India*, 23 August 1946, 6.

14. 'Money-lenders in Villages near Delhi Cut Rates', *Times of India*, 25 August 1970, 4.

15. Amol Agarwal, 'Syndicate Bank: Case of a Forgotten Indian Bank That Pioneered Financial Inclusion', paper presented at the Second Workshop on

South Asian Economic History 'South Asia and the Development Economy', London School of Economics and Political Science, 20–21 May 2019.

16. On bonded labour, and specifically debt bondage in the Indian context, see, for instance, Prakash (1990) and Breman (2007).

17. 'Karj cukaane men shramik ke kuen men girkar mrtyu', *Dainik Jagran* (Varanasi edition), 11 June 1982 (all newspaper report from *Dainik Jagran* cited here are available at the archive of the Nagari Pracharini Sabha, Varanasi; digitalized copies in possession of the author).

18. 'Varanasi men pratham kshetriya gramiin baink ka karyaarambh', *Dainik Jagran* (Varanasi edition), 28 July 1981.

19. 'Gomat, gramiin baink ka udghaatan', *Dainik Jagran* (Varanasi edition), 31 July 1981.

20. 'Sahukari niyaman kanuun ko prabhaavi banaane par jor', *Dainik Jagran* (Varanasi edition), 13 August 1982.

21. 'Bakaaya paise maangne par caakuu maaraa', *Dainik Jagran* (Varanasi edition), 27 March 1990.

22. 'Bakaayaa rupaye maange gaye yuvak ko caakuu maaraa gaya', *Dainik Jagran* (Varanasi edition), 21 March 1995; 'Pati ne karj le gaya thaa, dukhi vivaahitaa ne aatmahatyaa', *Dainik Jagran* (Varanasi edition), 27 September 1995.

23. 'Len-den ke vivaad men galaa dabaakar yuvak kii hatyaa', *Dainik Jagran* (Varanasi edition), 28 December 1996.

24. 'Paise men len-den men yuvak ko golii maaraa', *Dainik Jagran* (Varanasi edition), 13 September 1997.

25. 'Money-lending Bill Introduced in Bombay Assembly. "Measure Seeks to Regulate and Not Eliminate Profession"', *Times of India*, 4 September 1946, 5.

26. 'Protection from Usurers', *Times of India*, 22 August 1946, 6.

27. For a discussion of the use of the 'residue' as opposed to mere remnants, see Kaur (2014). On the historical continuities of the 'bazaar' beyond the mid-twentieth century, see Gupta and Chaliha (2011).

28. India adopted a decimalized system for its currency in 1957 instead of its older system of subdividing the rupee into, respectively, 16 *anna*s, 64 *paise*, and 192 *pie*s. The interest rate given here, accordingly, is 9 per cent per month.

29. Ibid., 43.

30. Census of India 1951, *District Census Handbook: Uttar Pradesh. 27 – Banaras District* (Allahabad, 1955), 44.

31. Census of India 1961, *District Census Handbook: Uttar Pradesh. 53 – Varanasi District* (Lucknow, 1965), 64–65.

32. Reserve Bank of India, *Trend and Progress of Banking in India: Annual Report under Section 36 (2) of the Banking Companies Act, 1949 – During the Year 1954* (Bombay, 1955), 27–28.

33. *Shroff Committee Report*, 34—35.

34. Ibid.

35. Ibid., 36.

36. Ibid., 67–70.

37. Ibid., 67.

38. Ibid., 68.

39. Ibid., 71.

40. Ibid., 158–59.

41. *AIRCS*, 62.

42. *Ibid.*

43. Ibid., 481.

44. Ibid.

45. Ibid., 482.

46. See, for instance, Chavan (2003), Sharma and Chamala (1998, 2003), and Reddy (2007).

47. From the perspective of liberal development policy, see Varghese (2005).

48. *AIRCS*, 149.

49. Ibid., 172.

50. Ibid., 63–64.

51. Ibid., 64.

52. Ibid., 65.

53. Ibid., 66.

54. Ibid., 482.

55. Ibid., 484.

56. *Report on Indigenous Bankers*, 92.

57. Ibid., 98.

58. Ibid., 88.

59. Reserve Bank of India, *Report of the Technical Group to review Legislations on Money Lending* (Mumbai: 2007), available online at https://rbidocs.rbi.org.in/rdocs/PublicationReport/Pdfs/78893.pdf (last accessed 4 March 2020).

60. Allahabad High Court, 2007, *Chander S. O. Buddhu v. State of Uttar Pradesh*.

61. *Report on Indigenous Bankers*, 87.

62. *The Uttar Pradesh Regulation of Money-lending Act, 1976 (U.P. Act 29 of 1976). An Act to Provide, in the Interest of the General Public, for the Regulation of Money-lending Transactions and for the Regulation of Money-lenders, and for Matters Connected therewith, or Incidental Thereto* (Authoritative English Text of the Uttar Pradesh Sahukari Viniyaman Adhiniyam, 1976).

63. *The Uttar Pradesh Regulation of Money-lending (Amendment) Act, 1978 (U.P. Act 1 of 1979). An Act to Amend the Uttar Pradesh Regulation of Money-lending Act, 1976* (Authoritative English Text of the Uttar Pradesh Sahukari Viniyaman [Sanshodhan] Adhiniyam, 1978).

64. Government of India, Ministry of Planning and Programme Implementation. Department of Statistics, National Sample Survey Organisation. *Debt and Investment Survey (NSS 48th Round, January to December 1992): Household Assets and Indebtedness of Social Groups as on 30.6.91* (1998), 33.

65. Ibid., 33–34.

66. Ibid., 34.

67. Ibid., 36.

68. Government of India, Ministry of Statistics and Programme Implementation, National Sample Survey Organisation, *All-India Debt and Investment Survey (NSS 59th Round, January–December 2003): Household Assets Holding, Indebtedness, Current Borrowings and Repayments of Social Groups in India (as on 30.6.2002)* (2006), Statement 13.

69. Ibid., Statement 14.

70. Government of India. Ministry of Finance. Department of Economic Affairs. Banking Division, *Report of the Expert Group on Agricultural Indebtedness* (2007), 47.

71. Ibid., 46.

72. Ibid., 50.

73. Ibid., 65.

74. Ibid., 74.

75. Ibid., 75.

76. I am highly grateful to Tirthankar Roy for pointing out this aspect, as well as the larger question of risk-taking by purpose underlying it. In the absence of much more robust information on the uses for credit – especially considering the incentive and/or need for misreporting credit purposes in postcolonial India – this debate cannot be resolved. But the phenomenal rise in credit after Indian independence – regardless of its sources – points to considerable changes in the perceptions of debt by the Indian population, very much in line with global trends in the same period that are subsumed under the term 'financialization'.

77. Ibid., 5.

78. Venkatesh Deshpande, 'Greed Begets Ruin', *Times of India*, 18 January 1970, 16.

79. Ibid., 16, original emphasis.

80. 'Alleged Fraud on Bank: Three Held', *Times of India*, 14 April 1973, 9.

81. 'Postal Sorter and Moneylender Held', *Times of India*, 6 December 1972, 3.

82. 'Man Who Rose from Rags to Riches in IT Net', *Times of India*, 2 August 1975, 4.

83. 'Rs. 5 Lakh Haul in Poona I-T Raid', *Times of India*, 23 July 1975, 4.

84. 'BPT's "Money-lending" Vendor Suspended', *Times of India*, 14 August 1975, 3.

85. 'Jail Term Soon for Money-lending on the Sly', 'Rs. 1 Cr. Wealth Hidden by Moneylender', *Times of India*, 23 October 1975, 6.

86. 'Rs. 1 Cr. Wealth Hidden by Moneylender.' *Times of India*, 8 May 1976; 13.

87. Ibid.

88. 'Ruthless Exploitation of Thana Adivasis', *Times of India*, 29 June 1973, 9.

89. 'Quadruple Murder Case: Daruwalla Pledged Suit for Loan', *Times of India*, 11 November 1971, 6.

90. Ibid.

91. 'Ration Cards Pawned with Money-lenders', *Times of India*, 15 September 1973, 5.

92. 'Where Lender Is Lord', *Times of India*, 30 November 1975, 8.

93. For an example of Sainath's journalistic work on these issues, see, for instance, P. Sainath, 'Farm Suicides: A 12-Year Saga', *The Hindu*, 25 January 2010, updated 15 December 2016, available online at https://www.thehindu.com/opinion/columns/sainath/Farm-suicides-a-12-year-saga/article16811575.ece (last accessed 11 March 2020). Many of his articles as well as a diverse selection of journalistic and academic work on issues concerning agrarian distress in India can also be found on the highly recommended website of the People's Archive of Rural India (https://ruralindiaonline.org).

94. Some of the debates surrounding the spate of farmers' suicides in India since the 1990s have been discussed, among many other studies, by Vakulabharanam and Motiram (2011), Münster (2012), and Mohanty (2013). For a discussion of the issue of rural credit including farmer suicides, see Shah, Rao, and Shankar (2007). Please note that the list of secondary literature provided here is not even remotely comprehensive or covers all the various arguments brought into the debate by diverse scholars and disciplines.

95. 'Bakaayaa maangne par vyavasaayi ke saath maarpiit', *Dainik Jagran* (Varanasi edition), 30 January 2004.

96. 'Parosii ne dande se piitkar kiyaa ghaayal', *Dainik Jagran* (Varanasi edition), 22 June 2004.

97. 'Lanka men telor maastar ki golii maarkar hatyaa', *Dainik Jagran* (Varanasi edition), 3 February 2004; 'Lenden ke vivaad men bunkar ko maaruu cakuu', *Dainik Jagran* (Varanasi edition), 2 June 2004.

98. 'Bii Ec Yuu men dharaayaa suudkhorii men lipt karamcaarii', *Dainik Jagran* (Varanasi edition), 1 May 2004.

99. A protest form in which a particular person of group is physically prevented from leaving a place by surrounding it with protesters.

100. 'Biisii ke bakaayedaaron ne vyavaasaayii kaa gheraa aavaas', *Dainik Jagran* (Varanasi edition), 17 September 2004.

101. 'Len-den ke vivaad men yuvak ko maarii golii', *Dainik Jagran* (Varanasi edition), 10 October 2004.

102. 'Lenden ke vivaad men kaar svaaron ne uthaayaa, 7 bandi', *Dainik Jagran* (Varanasi edition), 31 July 2005; 'Lenden ke vivaad men maarpit', *Dainik Jagran* (Varanasi edition), 2 August 2005.

103. 'Aarthik tangii ke calte kuen men kuudkar dii jaan', *Dainik Jagran* (Varanasi edition), 15 May 2005; 'Nagar nigam karmii kii golii maarkar hatyaa', *Dainik Jagran* (Varanasi edition), 3 September 2005.

104. 'Bakaayaa maagne par pithaaii', *Dainik Jagran* (Varanasi edition), 29 March 2006.

105. 'Karjdaar paanvaale ne dii jaan', *Dainik Jagran* (Varanasi edition), 10 April 2006.

106. 'Suudkhorii: shahar se ghaon tak "nava zamindaaron" kaa samraajya', *Dainik Jagran* (Varanasi edition), 25 April 2006.

107. 'Suudkhoron ke cakkar men phaanse adhyaapak', *Dainik Jagran* (Varanasi edition), 3 May 2006.

108. 'Suudkhoron ke khuunii panjon men phanse hain saath sau parivaar', *Dainik Jagran* (Varanasi edition), 23 June 2006.

109. 'Suudkhorii men chipii hai aatmahatyaa kii kahaanii', *Dainik Jagran* (Varanasi edition), 26 August 2006.

110. 'Suudkhorii kaa sanjaal', *Dainik Jagran* (Varanasi edition), 26 August 2006.

111. 'Suudkhorii: jaativaar netvarking, vaardvar sarcing', 'Yah hain sanjiiv ke sataaye', *Dainik Jagran* (Varanasi edition), 28 August 2006.

112. 'Suud kaa sanjaal: "Muul" nikalne men jute mahaajaan', *Dainik Jagran* (Varanasi edition), 29 August 2006.

113. 'Tang caacii-bhatiijaa pahunce es. es. pii. Daftar', *Dainik Jagran* (Varanasi edition), 31 August 2006.

114. 'Aparadhiyon ne "maarket" men dhan bhejnaa rokaa', *Dainik Jagran* (Varanasi edition), 1 September 2006.

115. 'Suudkhoron ke calte maut kaa lagaayaa thaa gal', *Dainik Jagran* (Varanasi edition), 2 September 2006.

116. 'Ab karjdaaron se kushalshem puch rahe suudkhor. Karj khatm likhvaane kaa bhii silsilaa shuruu, barii machliyaan ab bhi giraft se baahar', *Dainik Jagran* (Varanasi edition), 4 September 2006.

117. 'Suudkhorii: vaadii mukraa aaropii kaa kliincit', *Dainik Jagran* (Varanasi edition), 6 September 2006.
118. 'Aadhaa darjan ke khilaaf suudkhorii ka maamlaa darj', *Dainik Jagran* (Varanasi edition), 7 September 2006.
119. 'Money-lending Racket Thrives', *Economic Times*, 14 November 2006, available online at https://economictimes.indiatimes.com/money-lending-racket-thrives/articleshow/438438.cms?from=mdr (last accessed 13 March 2020).
120. 'Suudkhoron se pareshaan yuvak ne lagaa lii phaansii', *Dainik Jagran* (Varanasi edition), 14 February 2007.
121. 'Suudkhor ne banaayaa bandhak to aag lagaakar dii jaan', *Dainik Jagran* (Varanasi edition), 24 May 2007.
122. 'Kanuun ke shikanje men suudkhor, mukadma darj', *Dainik Jagran* (Varanasi edition), 6 October 2007.
123. 'Suudkhor khiinc le gayaa traiktar', *Dainik Jagran* (Varanasi edition), 18 December 2007.
124. 'Suudkhorii maamle men gavaah hue pakshadrohii, aaropii sanjiiv barii', *Dainik Jagran* (Varanasi edition), 13 April 2007.
125. On the organization of criminal business practices, and its links to both formal and informal modes of operation, see several contributions in Barbara Harriss-White's and Lucia Michelutti's *The Wild East*, for instance, Bhatia (2019).

8

Reputation

> Least important of all for [the moneylender] is the possibility of having recourse to the law; and almost as unimportant (especially nowadays) is the possibility of acquiring his debtor's property.[1]

Arjan[2] was not the first moneylender I met in Banaras but in some ways the most important. I started contacting him through other people known to both of us as part of a brief feasibility study on ethnographic research in Banaras. He managed to avoid me for several weeks, giving polite excuses that demonstrated how little he wanted to meet me. In the end, he was unlucky. He suffered an accident and became bedridden for sufficient time to run out of excuses. Meeting Arjan was a lucky turn for me, though, since our conversations undermined many of my initial assumptions on money lending. I had expected to find a highly exploitative system of credit depending on debt traps extending into an economy of displacement, an economy of favours (or debt-enforced labour), and significant levels of organization.

What Arjan's self-depiction demonstrated, however, was an almost comprehensively 'amateurish' economy that primarily worked on simple interest aggregation by a highly diverse assortment of lenders following complex operational logics. And it was much more exploitative than anticipated. A particularly frustrating element of Arjan's self-depiction – for me – was the absence of any shred of a Schumpeterian 'entrepreneurial spirit': Arjan had taken over money lending from his father. His clients either had been his father's clients, or their descendants, or they were living in the houses of his father's clients in cases where entire families had moved out. Before passing away, his father had raised the typical interest rate for his loans to 20 per cent per month, and Arjan had not bothered to raise it further, though by 2011 it was a fairly cheap rate for petty loans. He almost never took on new clients and had only ever done this when his existing clients asked him to give loans to friends of theirs. His clients had various social backgrounds, but were only from within the neighbourhood, and the diversity was mostly the outcome of changes in family fortunes over the decades.

By the end of several hours of an increasingly tense conversation I disbelieved almost everything I had heard. Since I knew several people who knew Arjan, I spent a long time afterwards trying to corroborate his story (or rather the reverse). Yet I soon discovered that he had been more honest than I had given him credit for. I asked distant family members about him, talked to some of his friends, and identified and talked to three of his clients. Eventually, I discovered myself questioning the debtors in biased ways.

I decided to delay my archival research. To look first at the present and only then at the archive is – to put it mildly – an unusual approach for a historian. It is eschewed since it tends to reinforce biases on the linearity of historical developments towards the specific state represented by the interpretation of the present. I have very consciously engaged with this possibility throughout my research afterwards but, in the end, an impact cannot comprehensively be ruled out. Yet, if not for having my initial assumptions so brusquely undermined by Arjan, I would have looked for other aspects once I started to engage with the archived materials. I would probably have placed much greater stress on the main emphases in the archived sources, instead of looking for the myriad small details that showed the operation of reputational means of handling uncertainty in debt relations. I think it would have been a poorer study.

Arjan himself was a rentier. He carried on his father's business and had neither the will nor the energy to expand his activities. His lending was sufficiently gainful to avoid any other profession, particularly since his needs were limited. He continued to live in his father's house and was disinterested in expensive consumption. He was interested primarily in what happened in his neighbourhood and the surrounding areas. In fact, he was a gossip, though not in the entrepreneurial sense in which this term will be used subsequently to describe the communication flows of extra-legal finance. While Arjan would typically spend several hours every day hanging around local tea stalls, discussing sundry local affairs and people, he did not need to rely on this for reputational information. His lending business operated on the successfully established principle that he had known his clients all his life, while in turn they knew that he gave preferential terms to debtors who would not transgress common expectations of good conduct. The debtors themselves would try to minimize default and would communicate any difficulties in repayment in advance. Both sides then would agree on what they considered a respectable solution. For Arjan, gossip was a pastime, not an informational tool needed to assess reputations. The neighbourhood was his favourite haunt, not the insurmountable boundary of his entrepreneurial activity related to its informational underpinnings. And money lending was what gave him the opportunity to spend his time gossiping in the neighbourhood, not a means to get rich.

In all this, he was very unlike his father. Arjan's father constantly flitted in and out of his narrative, contrary to most other lenders I talked to. A part of my initial reasoning for conducting a feasibility study had been to assess the possibility of using oral history for bridging the gap between the well-accessible colonial-era documents and their limited availability for the decades after Indian independence.[3] As it turned out, most extra-legal entrepreneurs and debtors had little detailed memory of events more than a few years in the past. But Arjan's depiction of his father's career was highly nuanced. It depicted his father as a successful 'amateurish' new entrant into extra-legal finance in the early decades after independence who then proceeded to adapt his business to his rising fortunes.

Arjan's father had been an elementary-level school teacher primarily for the children of Sindhi refugees. As a school teacher with a local background, he was well placed to take advantage of the local socio-economic disruptions in his early adult life. The Sindhi refugees had not developed sufficiently strong social ties to obtain credit. Yet many refugees needed small loans to tide over the early years of their resettlement. Additionally, Arjan's father – in his role as a school teacher – was a respectable person, especially in the early Nehruvian period with its public emphasis on 'scientific temper'. His role as a teacher brought him in close contact with the resettled Sindhi families and diminished social distance. Having a regular income cushioned him against the risks involved in lending to a newly settled community. More importantly, being the teacher of an indebted family's children provided strong safeguards against default. Lastly, the mid-twentieth century constituted a period of significant change in the petty credit markets of Banaras. The incipient market withdrawal of the big 'indigenous' banking families had started to undermine the established systems of strong social ties and mercantile ethics, creating space for new entrants. The development of 'organized' finance, however, was far from sufficiently successful to allow debtors to turn towards 'institutional' sources of credit.

Arjan's father eventually gave up his teaching position. He had bought a house in one of the better neighbourhoods and shifted from lending to his former clientele to becoming a neighbourhood moneylender. In this new form of extra-legal finance, he was sufficiently successful to attract a steady circle of clients, stabilizing his lending operations. From Arjan's narrative it can be surmised that the first shift occurred in the 1960s, while the stabilization of his business happened one decade later. By this time, Arjan's father was lending at rates of 10 per cent per month. Around the late 1980s and early 1990s, he shifted to 20 per cent per month.

While the information from moneylenders on interest rates for earlier decades is sketchy at best, and other sources are exceedingly rare and even less reliable, most of the older moneylenders I asked agreed that the shift to a rate of 20 per cent occurred between the mid-1980s and the early 1990s. While Arjan maintained this rate even in 2011, the typical rate had further increased to 30 per cent per month. Still, Arjan's father was engaged in expanding his business, though not to other forms of investment. In the way his father was presented, he operated in ways strongly resembling contemporary neighbourhood moneylenders – assessing information on reputational standing through gossip and using this to identify whether or not to enter into relatively stable relationships of credit–debt, but also maintaining a looser form of credit relationship with new clientele.

The production of a monetary outside

Both Arjan and his father constitute facets in a bewildering array of extra-legal financial practices that I have elsewhere described as a 'monetary outside' (Schwecke 2018). The term was chosen to refer loosely to Rosa Luxemburg's concept of the capitalist outside, primarily to highlight the manner in which extra-legal finance (and other market enclaves) constitutes socio-economic segments that diverge from the operational modes prevalent in India's dominant capitalist sector. The Indian economy comprises a large assortment of practices that differ from our understanding of what is capitalist. A number of these practices have attracted recent scholarly attention, including studies that foreground the social embeddedness of 'local' business practices, often related to petty, rural, or non-metropolitan capital[4] as well as studies on particular forms of intermediation.[5] Laura Bear's work is particularly instructive in the way it depicts intermediation and brokerage as functional links between the actual procedures of business and the proceduralism imposed by the regulatory state, thereby defining an arena for the operation of middlemen in catalyst roles in which non-capitalist modes of operation facilitate accumulation. Employing arguments originally depicted by Kalyan Sanyal (2007), Partha Chatterjee (2008) has drawn a distinction between corporate and non-corporate capital, while Birla has used a distinction between *pakka* and *kacca* business practices, distinguishing economic behaviour through its procedural 'solidity' (Birla 2015, 402–04).

This distinction can be used for separating 'organized' and extra-legal finance, in addition to the distinction between 'proper' and 'improper' forms of finance. At the same time, these categorizations lack positive content: like the 'formal–informal' divide, they tend to define categories through a bias in favour of the state-supported, supposedly more modern conception. The same qualification does not arise in an inside–outside distinction since inside and outside define each other. Referring to Luxemburg's concept in a loose fashion without directly employing it emphasizes the relationship with capitalism without needing to describe its operational modes in opposition to capitalism. Luxemburg's concept was articulated vaguely and functions as a catch-all category for everything that is not fully capitalist since its primary intention was to provide a dummy variable proving the need of capitalism to expand continuously (Luxemburg 1913/2003). The capitalist outside therefore encompasses diverse economic regimes. The monetary outside that has been produced in the city of Banaras can thus be seen as one instance of the operation of a capitalist outside without necessarily defining the operations of other such regimes. The main problem in making use of this terminology, accordingly, is to delineate the concept against the loosely employed category created by Luxemburg. On the one hand, this can be done by highlighting the difference in intention: the concept of the monetary outside was not intended to create a link to Marxist conceptions of the contradictoriness of capitalism but to emphasize distinct operational modes that create a need to describe their logics. On the other hand, the delineation of the concepts can be done by referring (briefly) to scholarly engagement within the Marxist debate on the capitalist outside in order to identify possible synergies.

As Chatterjee asserts, many economic practices and relationships in modern India need to be distinguished from capitalist forms of accumulation, thereby making it necessary to re-engage with debates on primitive accumulation. Chatterjee's and Sanyal's arguments, however, clearly relate ongoing primitive accumulation to historically located processes of dispossession in a literal interpretation of the concept – specific groups of farmers losing their means of production through land acquisition alleviated by subsistence-guaranteeing measures, in the process invalidating 'the narrative of transition' inherent in dispossession (Chatterjee 2008, 55). At the same time, many other ongoing forms of non-capitalist accumulation in India cannot be linked to dispossession in this literal interpretation, either because the people involved are already dispossessed of the means of production or because non-capitalist forms of accumulation do not necessarily lead to dispossession. The literal reading limits the processes that can be understood with reference to the concept. Primitive accumulation, in a broader reading, constitutes a range of non-capitalist accumulation processes, the end result of which frames markets that *can be* encroached by capitalism. The original concept postulated that this expansion would happen *eventually* but was disinterested in its teleological thrust in defining *when* and *how*. Instead of the emphasis on dispossession, ongoing forms of primitive accumulation need to be identified through their operational difference from capitalist accumulation.

While Appadurai has underlined the 'deep affinity between legal and magical proceduralism' in capitalism (Appadurai 2015, 483), Birla's distinction between *pakka* and *kacca* forms of business points to a differentiation in which the capitalist form of accumulation is defined as procedure in its assumed rationality as much as the non-capitalist. In Birla's argument, governmentality produces 'proper' (or *pakka*) economic behaviour and therefore an arena in which capitalist procedural rationality can unfold (Birla 2009, 2015). Conversely, procedurally different business practices lack state recognition and affirmation (in part or entirely), even though they remain part of an economy that is (possibly increasingly) capitalist, and often interact with the latter. As 'outside' and 'inside' practices may interact, being parts of a single economy, they cannot always be disentangled. Monetary markets, however, constitute a particularly instructive example: the relative lack of non-procedural elements in the construction of capitalist finance beyond control of labour and its product (see Chapter 2) increases the visibility of the delineation and differentiation processes that led to the production of a monetary outside.

Luxemburg's concept implies the continued presence of primitive accumulation. Without it, the contradictoriness of capitalism would become unsustainable. The capitalist outside accordingly corresponded to an arena of ongoing (necessarily not fully capitalist) dispossession which enables capitalist encroachment in times of crisis, notably crises of over-accumulation. Its role in overcoming capitalist crisis is crucial for Luxemburg, though my loose employment of the concept focuses on the description of an outside, not its functional role. Luxemburg's argument has been taken up – most notably for the purposes of this study – by Harvey's concept of accumulation by dispossession (Harvey 2004) and Patnaik's concept of reserve markets (P. Patnaik 2008).

Harvey's interpretation deviates from Luxemburg's conception by assigning an inventive capacity to neoliberal capitalism, allowing it to delineate arenas and encroach on the outsides so produced. Conversely, the production of the monetary outside played an important role in capitalist expansion within what was delineated as the monetary *inside* by excluding functionally different and competing markets governed by reputational economies of debt in which reputation allowed either the creation of enforcement mechanisms for transactional obligations or the generation of trust in the absence of the former. Patnaik's work argues that the outside in the form of 'reserve markets' need not be subsumed eventually by capitalism, thereby making it possible to locate the major thrust of capitalist expansion in finance within the monetary inside. In essence, Patnaik diminishes the functional role of the outside in times of capitalist crisis to the provision of stimuli for the inside. By linking reserve markets to the capitalist outside, he accepts an implicit functional differentiation between inside and outside. The production of capitalist outsides in the Indian economy does not only highlight the coexistence of these segments within a larger capitalist mode of production. It stipulates an ongoing evolution of the outside in its procedures and operational modes, affecting its functionality in the larger mode of production and thereby the specific location of both inside and outside segments within this mode of production. The monetary outside created in India, and studied here with special emphasis on its operations in Banaras, depended on the interplay of its delineation in law and the responses by market participants to this delineation.

The production of a monetary outside almost certainly was an unintentional result for many of the proponents of the legislation process that started its delineation and facilitated the responses by market participants that over time changed its operational modes. Yet to interpret it in this way misses an important dimension: the intended regulation of the outside was linked to the process of creating a monetary inside. The intent of the late colonial state was not only to help poorer debtors against exploitation by moneylenders but also to construct 'proper' capitalist finance. To many involved officials, relegating the poor to a monetary outside produced in the process was justifiable as a temporary problem in a modernization process. The contradiction, therefore, is not only between the intent of the legislative process and its outcomes but also a misjudgement of the resilience of non-capitalist financial practices, in addition to a misjudgement of the capabilities of capitalist finance in expanding its credit operations – a misplaced hope concerning the assumed superiority of juridical-procedural parameters of finance over reputational ones.

The monetary outside in Banaras

Giving an estimate of the scale of extra-legal finance is difficult. However, it appears to be clear that official data such as the figures provided in the NSSO household indebtedness surveys are underestimating the size of the market, possibly drastically. Moneylenders in the main bazaar area were dismissive of official estimates when I confronted them with the data. In several instances, reactions were replete with incredulity, asking whether I was sure that I was referring to outstanding debts in Uttar Pradesh instead of the city itself. It can safely be assumed that these depictions exaggerated the size of the market. Banaras has a population of about 2 million, and its bazaar remains one of the largest retail and wholesale markets in northern India, yet the population of Uttar Pradesh was above 200 million. Even taking these questions as exaggerations, or possibly boasting, they show a strong mismatch in perceptions. More conservative estimates by extra-legal lenders still presented the scope of trade credit in the bazaar as many times the NSSO estimates.

Rather than asking about the size of the market, it is more fruitful to observe the specific types of markets in which extra-legal finance continues to be competitive. The ethnographic study on which this chapter is based was carried out primarily in the city of Banaras and, to a significantly lesser extent, in the peri-urban areas of the city, where the proximity to the city distinguishes these markets considerably from rural areas. As such, the study cannot shed light on the scope of extra-legal finance in the latter.

Within the urban areas studied here, extra-legal finance refers primarily to credit but extends into speculation. To gauge the extent of extra-legality in finance, the focus will remain on credit markets. Bank credit was sufficiently developed by the 1960s to emerge as a viable alternative to 'indigenous' banking and has since expanded drastically. It does not reach the entirety of the city's population, though. A major segment of the city's population still lacks 'bankability'. While financial inclusion measures have increased the reach of banking services to the poor, most of these are related to the opening of bank accounts and therefore the ability to engage in money transfers. For the lowest strata, bank credit remains entirely inaccessible, while for the larger part of the urban lower classes bank credit constitutes a theoretical possibility but a practical possibility only in specific government-imposed schemes. Typically, bank credit has significant purpose restrictions and depends on fully documented collateral for low-income groups – a major impediment as property titles are often dubious or absent. Where bank credit is available to lower-income groups without purpose restrictions and collateral requirements, many debtors indebted to extra-legal lenders are either unaware of these schemes or have experiential knowledge – frequently second- or even third-hand – of the banks' unwillingness to lend, some of which may not be factually correct. One exception is the Muthoot Finance group, which is frequently perceived as an accessible lender. Yet based on my own observations of footfall in Muthoot Finance branches in the city, its customer base among lower classes is heavily drawing on low-rank white-collar professions. A typical scheme by Muthoot was classified by the company as a consumer goods loan. This category of loans has a principal of up to 3,000 rupees per member, at 25 per cent per annum interest, in addition to a 1 per cent processing fee, repayable in ten months with a two-month moratorium on repayment.[6] While significantly cheaper than any equivalent loan in petty extra-legal moneylending, it is costlier than the prescribed rates for registered moneylenders (24 per cent per annum without commission fees or moratoriums). Moreover, the limit on borrowing and the stringent repayment conditions constitute further barriers. Similar considerations need to be taken into account in Muthoot Finance loans targeting the spectrum served by extra-legal trade credit. A 'Micro-Enterprise Loan' comprises a principal of 15,000 rupees, at an interest rate of 21.05 per cent per annum, with a 1 per cent processing fee, repayable in twelve months with a one-month moratorium. A 'Small and Medium Enterprise Loan' comprises a principal of 75,000 rupees per member, repayable over thirty months, at an interest rate of 23.5 per cent with a 1.5 per cent processing fee.[7] While these loans fell under the category of microfinance in the bank's depiction, other forms of microfinance in the city, especially government-based schemes depending on self-help groups (SHGs), are rare and primarily operate as savings schemes with limitations on withdrawals rather than credit.

The Muthoot Finance loans to 'bankable' clientele detailed here serve as a baseline for what the 'organized' credit market in Banaras is capable of delivering. In turn, registered money lending needs to be interpreted as an in-between category of finance, straddling the categories of regulated and extra-legal credit. My attempts to inquire into the operations of registered moneylenders, unfortunately, were largely fruitless. Registered moneylenders I contacted in the city over several years invariably were unwilling to even meet me. Debtors who had taken loans from registered moneylenders tended to attribute this circumspection to a predilection for including transactional terms that fell outside of the state-imposed regulations, including charging higher interest rates or taking a 'cut' on the principal. I have no way of corroborating this interpretation as the respective debtors also invariably clarified that 'their' moneylender did not engage in these practices and that their assessments were based on the experiences of others. Where these sources of hearsay could be identified, the respective debtors also confirmed that malpractices were common but not in their own dealings.

Just as importantly, in my own assessment the registration process was mostly defunct. My endeavours to even locate the registrars within the municipality proved fruitless, and the cooperation by the local administration in this effort was bordering on hostility. On asking extra-legal lenders why they did not register, it was typically pointed out that registration simply was not possible. In particular, extra-legal lenders argued that licences for money lending needed to be renewed annually. While initial registration might be possible, the licence renewal was not. The lenders' perspective on why registered moneylenders refused to meet me highlighted this aspect.

Apart from the alleged futility of registration, most extra-legal lenders opined that registration would not help them in litigation as courts were considered uniformly hostile to moneylenders regardless of their legal status. An analysis of court judgments related to registered money lenders showed numerous instances of courts providing legal protection, but also cases in which legal protection was denied despite registration. In probably the most important judgment in this respect, the Supreme Court in *Fatehchand Himmatlal and Ors. v. State of Maharashtra*, 1977, had argued that the reversal of the burden of proof in legal stipulations on money lending wherein the creditor needed to provide documented proof of the debtor's capacity to fulfil his or her obligations was legitimate. The court had argued that 'the provision ... is reasonable, because ... the money-lender is sure to be far shrewder' – a statement reminiscent of the legal doctrine of 'expectant heirs'.[8] This judgment, though, does not apply to Uttar Pradesh. However, this and similar judgments may have (mis-)informed lenders into believing that legal redress was not given to them even if their businesses were legal, mirroring the experiential ambiguities of lower-class debtors in accessing banking facilities.

Impressions of administrative apathy or judicial hostility may have informed registered moneylenders' circumspection towards me, in contrast to the accessibility of extra-legal lenders who, after all, were more openly operating in extra-legal or illegal manners. Eventually, I obtained more direct information on the practices of registered moneylenders by observing these in Faizabad, a smaller city roughly 200 kilometres north of Banaras, in a brief, supplementary study. The particular registered moneylender I observed – by accompanying him on his collection rounds, and studying his account books, licence, and other documents – followed prescribed procedure to the letter. He was obviously obtaining significant returns on investment without inflating interest beyond the permissible rate – according to this own testimony, but also considering his obvious prosperity and reinvestment in real estate.

Observing this registered moneylender provided some important details for establishing the baseline for competitiveness of extra-legal finance. They relate to the ambiguity of registered money lending in straddling the juridical-procedural and reputational economies of debt, the rate of default and means of enforcement, and the clientele served, keeping in mind the aforementioned caveats about ethnographic detail. The rate of default in registered money lending, as observed by me in Faizabad, is lower than in extra-legal lending to the poor but very much in line with the lower-end extra-legal trade credit spectrum, partially reflecting the clientele involved. Figure 8.1 provides a visualization of this rate, based on a snapshot from the moneylender's account books, roughly showing an average default rate. Defaults are indicated by dots, while a line in the rows indicates either the repayment of the loan or the lender's abandoning of attempts to obtain further payments. The latter case, according to the lender's testimony, can indicate lenience based either on the acceptance of a loss or on the consideration that repayments were commensurate with expected returns on investment. In the example given in Figure 8.1, the first line depicts full repayment, while the second indicates commensurate repayment as it is preceded by substantial payments not adding up to the outstanding dues.

The ambiguity of registered money lending here is stark. Constituting a fully legal practice, the lender ought to have been able to seek legal redress. The juridical-procedural parameters of credit, after all, are intended to provide the legal system with sufficient information to facilitate this redress. The lender, at the same time, unequivocally stated that he never filed suits in court over contractual breaches, partially since he did not believe judicial redress would be available to him and partially since he believed the

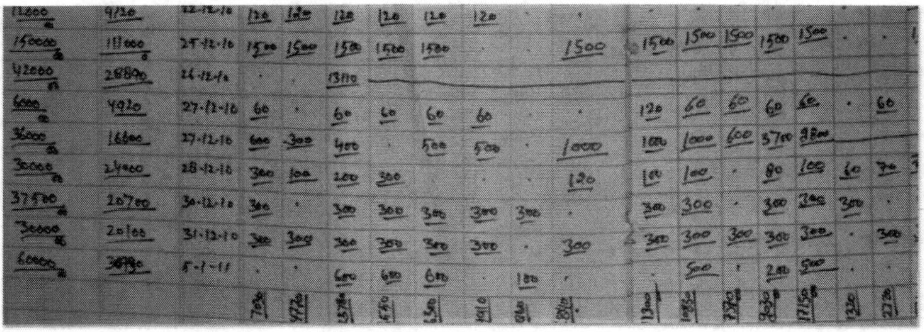

Figure 8.1 Default in registered moneylending in Faizabad

Source: Author.

defaulting debtors to be able to conceal their repayment capacities, rendering the exercise futile.

Roughly estimated, intermittent defaults occurred in about one-fourth of all cases. Most of these cases, according to my analysis of these account books, fell within the category of deferred payments, avoiding absolute losses. Deferments in repayment, though, considerably reduced returns on investment over time through raising opportunity costs and were not compensated by interest for the period of deferment. Accompanying the lender on his collection rounds did not provide any direct information on his enforcement methods as his behaviour in the few cases of default that I observed might be unrepresentative, especially considering my presence. None of these cases involved intimidation. Remarkably, a number of defaults took place openly, without any practices of evasion that are widespread in petty extra-legal money lending, but also without the elaborate forms of advance communication in extra-legal trade credit. The defaulting debtors simply informed the lender of their inability to pay, and the lender informed the debtor that the payment would be due the following week. In one case, the lender subsequently told me that the debtor had defaulted three times in row, and that he was considering whether he would have to accept the loss. In cases of deferred payment, he stated that he would not refuse future loans, though he might not be willing to give higher principals. In cases of absolute default, he would not provide future loans unless the initial payments had been substantial. By and large, relations between the creditor and his debtors appeared to be cordial, but professional, without involving elaborate communication forms that are typical of extra-legal finance where these convey reputational information and generate trust.

While not generalizable, these observations on registered money lending help establish the baseline for competitiveness of extra-legal finance in two ways. First, they indicate the ambiguity of registered money lending in relying to a much lesser extent on juridical-procedural enforcement of obligations. Additionally, the Faizabad example indicates an inability to employ social ties for enforcement which is reminiscent of extra-legal finance in Banaras. Conversely, these observations indicate the absence of strong reputational modes of communication, showing that the assessment of the debtors' reputations is relatively unimportant.

This puzzle can partially be resolved by looking at the lender's clientele. The principals involved in lending – based on a study of the lender's account books from 2010 to 2012 – typically ranged from about 25,000 to 75,000 rupees. The clientele I observed consisted mostly of small but well-established shopkeepers. Occasionally, payments were made by shop workers, though according to the lender, these were still loans to the owners of the commercial establishments. The lender's operations were clearly restricted to well-established debtors with a general anticipation of sufficient means to serve loan conditions. Debtors also entered into long-term relationships with the lender, depositing money with him against interest when not in need of a loan, so that the relative stability of the relationship was maintained. As discussed earlier in the context of Arjan's lending business, long-term relations can substitute for the need to develop elaborate reputational modes of operation.

Returning to the baseline for the competitiveness of extra-legal finance, the example from Faizabad outlines a conundrum: since extra-legal credit at this level in Banaras tends to be significantly more costly for the borrower, why would extra-legal lending not be constrained by registered money lending? Why would borrowers not go to greater efforts to obtain credit from registered moneylenders, especially since these loans involved more favourable conditions than equivalent bank loans? From the lenders' perspective, extra-legality allows higher returns on investment by evading regulations. Yet why would debtors fail to seek out registered moneylenders?

The reason is likely related to capital constraints on the supply side. Registration comes with the need to show documented proof of the origins of the invested capital. In the Faizabad case, one of the reasons stated by the lender for not shifting towards extra-legality was that he invested most of his profits in fully documented real estate and land for which he needed to be able to demonstrate his sources of income. Most of the capital available for extra-legal lending is highly fluid, and short-term as well as typically undocumented. There are practically no supply limits for this kind of capital in Banaras, resulting in the establishment of a market that does not have any monopolistic tendencies. Conversely, fully documented sources of capital for registered lending purposes are limited, creating monopolistic tendencies in registered lending that are abetted by administrative apathy in facilitating the market entrance of newcomers. These tendencies prevent registered moneylenders from expanding their clientele at the same time as constricting this type of lending to the relatively few customers who have already established long-term credit relationships. In turn, the supply restrictions on fully documented capital available for lending create a large market for extra-legal lending targeting the same socio-economic segment, at conditions that are significantly more favourable to creditors.

The competitiveness of extra-legal credit is based on the segments of the credit market that are significantly underserved by 'organized' banks and registered money lending. The vast majority of credit needs of the lower classes for emergency and consumption purposes clearly fall within this category, as do credit needs for which required documentation cannot be provided. The latter forms a significant proportion of credit needs in urban India. The availability of land as a desirable and relatively well-documented collateral facilitates access to regulated rural credit markets, though it leaves a considerable share of the rural population out of their purview. For many urban credit needs among the lower classes, however, collateral exists primarily in movable assets – gold and jewellery – which, in turn, are frequently undocumented. Similarly, purpose restrictions depend strongly on the possibility to document investment plans – an impossibility even for many small-scale businesses. Aggravating this problem is the availability of capital for these credit purposes. While the Muthoot Finance microfinance loans cited earlier involve higher costs of borrowing than registered money lending, they would still be much cheaper than most extra-legal loans targeting this clientele. Yet the restrictions on credit sums in these loans provides another competitive edge to extra-legal finance – obtaining relatively cheap credit from Muthoot Finance at principals of 3,000–75,000 rupees per year leaves many credit demands to be served by extra-legal lenders, especially short-term needs.

Extra-legal finance, hence, remains highly competitive in spite of its costs in the following segments of the urban credit market:

- Loans for all social strata that remain 'unbankable'
- Emergency loans for the poor
- Consumption loans for the poor
- Petty loans in general
- Short-term loans in general
- Loans for not fully documented investment purposes
- Loans for risky investment purposes
- Fast loans
- Loans to unregistered and/or under-documented businesses
- Loans for purposes related to grey or black-market activities
- Loans with purposes/intentions other than capital accumulation through interest
- Loans for which the principals are higher than the principals available from 'organized' finance in this segment
- Loans in addition to credit already obtained from 'organized' finance
- Loans for documented purposes for which the documentation carries the risk of revealing undocumented business activities

Extra-legal credit markets in Banaras can be divided into six different segments, each of which serves multiple but not all of these needs. Some of these segments, particularly the segment of petty lending, need to be further subdivided.

- Pawn-broking
- Petty lending
- Peri-urban lending
- Artisanal credit
- Trade credit
- High-end extra-legal finance

In the following discussion, the segment of high-end extra-legal finance will be omitted as I neither obtained nor tried to obtain access to the sealed-off networks that appear to dominate it. In turn, petty lending needs to be subdivided by target clientele and by lending intention. For the target clientele, mobile and immobile debtors need to be differentiated as the lending strategies to these sub-segments differ considerably. Similarly, within the sub-segment of immobile debtors, lending intentions that emphasize accumulation of interest need to be distinguished from intentions of acquiring collateral. The latter – significantly less frequent – creates economies of displacement through debt that differ strongly from other forms of money lending. Displacement constitutes one outcome of peri-urban lending, too, but the dynamics involved differ significantly. In the following, I will briefly introduce the various segments and sub-segments of the market.

Pawn-broking

Pawn-broking constitutes an essential component of the extra-legal credit market despite the fact that it does not necessarily involve credit. Pawning may or may not involve interest, and without interest it is closer to commodity exchange. However, its operational mode is strongly linked to the extra-legal credit economy. Pawn-brokers typically act as the 'lender' of first resort especially for poor (but not destitute) households. As long as collateral is available, prospective debtors often try to make use of their services first. In turn, the brokers have a different skill profile.

Desirable movable collateral almost invariably takes the form of precious metals or jewellery. Gold that has been registered can be pawned in registered outlets, on better terms, but the majority of items used for pawning are unregistered, and are taken on by smaller jewellery shops. Since gold and jewellery are mostly owned by the upper ranges of the lower classes (and above), a large segment of the population will not be able to make use of pawn-brokers even as lenders of first resort. As importantly, the value of gold and jewellery – even when used as collateral – is frequently above the actual credit needs of lower-class households, restricting the utility of the collateral to higher principals and particular purposes. While most of the credit market served by petty moneylenders targets a spectrum of relatively small loans, pawn-brokers provide an equivalent service for larger sums. Conversely, while pawning in the petty bourgeoisie is still not uncommon, it is most frequently made use of by the upper ranges of the lower classes for education, marriage, bribes for obtaining regular jobs, and similar purposes, all of which include a high capital outlay.

Seeing the pawn-broker as a lender of first resort, accordingly, needs to be qualified. While most people would prefer to pawn collateral rather than take on a moneylender's loan, most jewellers acting as pawn-brokers are neither willing nor capable of actually serving all credit needs. In turn, emotional and status-related attachment to movable collateral restricts the utility of pawning. First, pawning gold or jewellery frequently includes conflicting perceptions and interests within the household, with the potential collateral also marking the status of the family's female members – which can result in conflicting outcomes too. When I spoke to families that had pawned jewellery about conflicts over giving their jewellery to a pawn-broker, the anticipated gendering of perceptions was far from common. Yet where it was visible, it took on various forms. Oftentimes, it was the woman who argued in favour of using jewellery for pawning, though at other times it became clear that the woman's disfavour had been overruled by the male 'head' of the family. Both reactions can be related to status, the former indicating the women's contestation of male-centric decision-making in the financial aspects of the household economy, but also awareness that their status was linked to their ability to contribute to the household's debt portfolio (see Guérin 2014). Conversely, male reluctance to pawn jewellery can be linked to an understanding of status in which the women's ability to showcase financial solidity through wearing jewellery in certain contexts stands paramount. In contrast, in the latter case female family members risking their jewellery through pawning needed to consider the possibility of declining status (see Gandhi 2013; Kar 2013). While there are female moneylenders targeting both male and female clients, and specific credit sources through gendered forms of association that are available exclusively to women, the majority of petty extra-legal loans follow the male-creditor-to-male-debtor model, even accounting for the almost insurmountable difficulties faced by a male researcher inquiring into female-to-female credit flows in India.

From the creditor's perspective, the differences between pawn-broking and money lending lie in the transactional intention, and the skill set required to engage in this business. Pawn-broking in Banaras operates predominantly in two different modes. The first involves interest, the second eschews interest. In the first case, pawn-broking operates in the way of a secured loan. The debtor takes on a loan by the pawn-broker consisting of the principal, future interest payment and repayment obligations, and a collateral. Once the transactional obligations are fully met, the collateral is returned. The pawn-broker is provided an additional opportunity to increase his or her profit since the valuation of the collateral is carried out by him or her. Undervaluing the collateral provides additional income once the collateral is forfeited by the debtor's default. In consequence, loans by pawn-brokers are typically depicted as being cheaper than a petty moneylender's loans, even though the costs of borrowing may actually be equal or higher. Pawn-broking interest rates in Banaras (where these are used) are around 10 per cent per month for relatively small loans – a far cry from the prevalent range of rates for petty money lending. At the same time, the risk costs to the creditor involved in these loans are significantly lower than in petty money lending since pawn-broking with interest by definition constitutes secured loans.

In addition, the frequent undervaluing of collateral constitutes a guaranteed profit to the creditor who simultaneously operates as the assessor of the collateral's value. In fact, pawn-broking with interest deviates from other credit transactions in constituting one of the few cases in which the credit contract resembles the commodity contract. The collateral is 'bought' by the creditor-assessor. The subsequent payment of 'interest' does not so much constitute a charge on the use of capital in the form of rent. Instead, it forms a charge for the time-bound non-utilization of alienation rights within the construction of property (see Hann 2007). Property claims or rights over the collateral are transferred with the promissory element in the contract formed by the right to repurchase the property by timely payment. The key element in this transaction, therefore, is the difference in use values between the exchanged items (collateral and principal) to seller and buyer which, in turn, is reinforced by the informational and skill advantage by the buyer. The enhanced future orientation of the credit contract is absent for the pawn-broker in that the 'bought' collateral already stands in for the amount 'lent'. Accordingly, the comparison between interest rates in the credit transaction of petty money lending and the charge for the deferral of the buyer's alienation rights in pawn-broking with interest is faulty from the creditor's perspective. At the same time, the pawn-broker charging 'interest' uses the unawareness of this difference on the debtor's part – strongly related to the fact that in the absence of experiential alternatives it does not directly affect the seller-debtor's transactional position – to extract enhanced benefits from the contract.

The discussion of pawn-broking with interest also clarifies that pawn-broking itself, that is, without interest, does not constitute credit and should not be confused with the latter. While pawn-broking with interest in Banaras takes place frequently, the majority of transactions in pawn-broking do not involve interest payments. Here, the transactional gains to the broker accrue from his or her superior information on the market value of goods, and of market fluctuations, allowing the pawn-broker, first, to undervalue the collateral and, second, to 'buy' the collateral in periods of declining prices in order to sell later.

In pawn-broking without interest, the pawn-broker's transactional gains depend entirely on the difference between his or her buyer's and seller's price, following the model of the commodity contract. In both segments of pawn-broking, at the same time, this gain depends on (a) the skill of the broker in assessing the current value of the collateral, (b) the skill of the broker in assessing the future development of the market, (c) the informational advantage of the broker over the seller-debtor in this assessment of future price levels, and (d) the difference between the broker's and seller-debtor's availability of capital to tide over the period before the anticipated rise in prices – with the latter frequently approximating zero. The differences in skill sets between pawn-brokers and moneylenders, correspondingly, are vast. For pawn-brokers, skill centres on the ability to assess the desirability of the pawned good in the present and future, which in turn also determines the fixation of 'interest' (where applicable) since the temporary loss of alienation rights determines the time until which the acquired good can be sold. Pawn-brokers who include interest obviously need to be aware of currently prevailing interest rates, but this knowledge is ubiquitous. The skill differential between brokers and their clients in Banaras is considerable, especially since the pawned goods are typically unregistered and undocumented as people who possess registered gold or jewellery are much less likely to have the necessity for pawning them, and can avail themselves of the services of regulated enterprises where the possibility for undervaluing is constricted. The required skills, especially for petty moneylenders, centre on their ability to enforce repayment, for which they need to be skilled in assessing reputations.

Petty money lending

Petty money lending consists of lending to mobile and immobile clientele, and lending for displacement. Together with the trade credit segment, the first two segments comprise the core of the reputational economy of debt in Banaras. Barring the case of Sanjeev Rai depicted earlier, these markets are entirely 'amateurish'. Most lenders engage in lending only as part of their professional activities, and usually do not remain engaged in petty lending for longer than a few years. The fluctuation in the composition of lenders is exceedingly high. They tend to be equally 'amateurish' in their operational modes both when viewed from the juridical-procedural vantage point that originally underpinned the notion of 'amateurization', and when perceiving 'sophistication' in reputational terms as in this study.

One reason for the high levels of fluctuation is the public opprobrium faced by moneylenders. Petty lending constitutes one of the fastest and (arguably) easiest routes to accumulate capital, especially for aspiring and upwardly mobile social strata. Yet public reproach limits aspirational success. Being a moneylender is frowned upon, but condemnation is particularly high for lenders targeting the credit needs of poor clientele. The public image of these lenders as exploiting desperate needs does not apply in similar form to the trade credit segment, or even peri-urban lending. In turn, the rate of default is higher in petty lending, leading to the heightened visibility of reputational dynamics that include intimidation and petty violence. This visibility reinforces an understanding of the operational modes in petty lending that detaches intimidation and petty violence from its reputational underpinnings, and equates them with higher levels of violence that have been prominently displayed in media depictions of money lending. In turn, some petty lenders openly indulge the image thus created – partially in response, partially because their own understanding of their role is shaped through this image, and partially in attempts to cultivate 'tough' and 'streetwise' images of themselves in the hope of minimizing default. Successful accumulation through petty lending therefore increases the material basis of socio-economic status, but actively undermines the acquisition of socio-cultural status, frequently leading to its discontinuation after an initial period of accumulation.

There are two additional reasons for the high levels of fluctuation. The first relates to the considerable risk of default, while the second is based on the effort-intensive character of petty lending. Intermittent default is taking place with such frequency that it carries a constant threat to the profitability of the business. Based on his experiences in Ghana, Hart (2018) argued that it is the default rate rather than the interest rate that defines the profitability of money lending, though there are few instances in Banaras in which money lending actually becomes unprofitable. The frequency of default, however, combined with the reputational dynamics of petty lending have a debilitating effect on many petty lending businesses. As there are no ways to enforce obligations in the reputational economy of debt in Banaras anymore – except for the mostly useless option of violence – intermittent default frequently is met by lenience on the lender's part. The lender's act of lenience, subsequently, is communicated in the same way as any other reputational dynamics, leading to increasing demands for lenience from defaulting debtors. Lenders can attempt to stem this vicious (or virtuous) circle by various means, but many of these means damage the lender's own reputation. Damage to a lender's reputation has the long-term fallout of attracting less reliable clients, thereby increasing the default rate. A loss of the ability to balance lenience and tight enforcement typically has cascading effects on the lender's ability to minimize default, thus significantly compromising the profitability of lending – even if it remains profitable in absolute terms. Once returns on investment decline, the attractiveness of the business diminishes, partially due to social opprobrium, but also because of its considerable labour inputs.

The latter, in turn, reinforce fluctuation not just in lowering profitability as measured against the effort invested. Rather, striking a viable balance between lenience and enforcement of repayments – given the exceedingly high interest rates involved – rapidly leads to successful accumulation. While not all lenders manage to strike this fine line for sufficient time to grow prosperous rapidly, those who do frequently move beyond petty lending, either investing beyond extra-legal finance or moving into the trade credit segment that is considered more legitimate. While interest rates in trade credit are lower than in petty lending, principals are considerably higher and transactions less risky. The efforts involved in enforcement in petty lending are precluding the simultaneous handling of large numbers of debtors, while criminalization and 'amateurization' prevent the employment of wage labour for enforcement. Absolute profitability in trade credit becomes higher as soon as the available capital reaches the level at which a lender can shift to this segment. Success in petty lending, accordingly, undermines its viability. In turn, this dynamic of upward mobility hampers the development of more sophisticated forms of petty lending, for instance, in the maintenance of stable clienteles. The examples of Arjan and his father are exceedingly exceptional in this regard. The obstacles to stabilization reinforce the long-term rise of interest rates.

Petty lending – whether to mobile or immobile clientele – is highly exploitative, and the interest rates hardly ever change according to contextual difference. While many debtors I talked to emphasized their ability to 'play the game' and extract favourable rates, the moneylenders themselves hardly ever stated that they were adjusting rates. Transactions I observed invariably fell under the interest rate prevalent between 2011 and 2019. For petty principals, the prevalent rate was either 30 per cent per month or 1 per cent per day. A few lenders were willing to lend at the rate of 20 per cent per month for particularly reputable debtors, but by and large this rate had disappeared. Most lenders depicted it as the standard rate until the mid-1990s.

Interest rates in petty lending invariably consist of simple interest. Compound rates of interest have largely disappeared from Banaras, except for the sub-segment of lending related to displacement. The disappearance of compound interest is linked to the nature of the loans – short-term loans for low principals. Debtors would be unable to pay the prevailing rates for longer periods of time, as the creditors frequently conceded. Most petty moneylenders would forego interest payments once it became clear that further payments had become impossible for the debtor, but not until the debtor's payments became commensurate with the creditors' expectations. Frequently, lenders asserted that they would simply insist on repayment of the principal after this, though many debtors, in turn, contested these claims. The lenders' claims, however, are plausible. Continued interest payments at the prevalent rate would be unaffordable to any lower-class debtor, thus forcing the debtor to take steps to dispose of their debt by other means, including disappearance, rather than evading the creditor temporarily, and approaching the police. Foregoing interest payments after reaching the anticipated level of returns on investment constitutes a highly rational strategy in these circumstances.

Legal complaints against moneylending are noticeable only in their absence. Police officers I spoke to uniformly remarked that there are no complaints at all. In order to corroborate these statements, the city's police force allowed me to study first information reports filed in approximately half the city's *thanas* between 2011 and 2013.[9] While some of these reports were unreadable – even to native speakers I asked to help me – I was eventually able to study about 1,500 of the approximately 2,000 reports, running into approximately 5,000 of about 7,000 pages of handwritten files. While including complaints against moneylenders, not one of the complaints was against their lending activities. Instead, the complaints comprised alleged offences in which the fact that the accused party was a moneylender was added as additional information, undermining their bona fide credentials.

The decision by moneylenders to forego further interest payment does not follow any visible pattern. Each lender tends to decide differently, and takes different decisions from case to case. The presentation by lenders of their decision-making processes highlighted exasperation. It is typical for petty moneylenders in Banaras to attribute moral deficiencies to their clients, particularly when discussing default. This manner of presenting their decision-making remains predominant even in cases in which the lender accepted the high level of exploitation, frequently leading to the simultaneous depiction of two contradictory assessments. Pointing out the debtors' alleged immorality helps petty moneylenders to justify public reproach since it presents the lender's lenience as willingness to eschew their transactional rights even in undeserved circumstances – approximating altruism in spite of the simultaneously held view that lenience was primarily related to the level of exploitation.

Many petty moneylenders confess to problems in dealing with the moral dilemma of exploitation, and therefore tend to exaggerate their lenience. In relatively stable creditor–debtor relations, I have come across a variety of cases in which the lender acted leniently even if the debtor's inability to pay was not entirely clear. The prerequisite, however, was the commensurability of past repayments with anticipated gains from a transaction. I am choosing the term 'commensurability' in this context precisely because it creates a link between the practice of credit and the notion of returning a gift of commensurate value that underlies the concept of balanced reciprocity. Commensurability constitutes a complex and flexible category. In returning a gift of commensurate value, the decision-making of commensurability comprises an anticipation of the expectations of the other transactional party as well as the giver's understanding of the value involved, further complicated by the flexibility in these assessments depending on changing circumstantial factors. Similarly, what constitutes 'sufficient' gain in petty money lending considers both the lender's and the borrower's expectations (and the respective anticipations thereof by the other party) as well as circumstances – including the debtor's ability to pay and the creditor's need for further gains. In turn, this leads to a process of constantly renegotiating the extent of obligation, which is heavily influenced by the transactional parties' reputations and their ability to communicate these. The notion of being able to 'play the game' invoked by debtors does not so much address changes in interest rates but instead implicitly refers to the process of renegotiating obligations. It addresses actual repayments rather than stated interest rates, though debtors frequently avoided declaring this openly as it demonstrates default as a means of renegotiation.

Interest rates at 30 per cent per month thus provide only the stated level of exploitation, while the actual costs of borrowing are lower. Default, however, carries its own risks in reputational terms. Apart from the question of whether debtors can make use of the renegotiation of the costs of borrowing through default as long as they are capable of paying, it needs to be taken into account that doing so tends to lower the debtor's reputation, giving a significant incentive to minimize default.

Even considering the renegotiation of obligations, petty money lending remains highly exploitative, in fact much more exploitative than its late colonial counterparts. The disappearance of compound interest may appear as a welcome development, but this interpretation misses the impact of the operational modes of these credit markets on the nature of interest payments. Essentially, including compound interest in these transactions makes little sense even for the creditor. Compound rates even at nominally lower interest would lead to an escalation of the default rate, and therefore of the need to renegotiate obligations. It would compromise the stability reached through the employment of reputational means for minimizing default. In addition, since loans in this segment of lending are invariably unsecured, there is no incentive to use compound interest as a means of creating debt traps. For the creditor, trapping the borrower in an inescapable debt relationship is tantamount to writing off returns on investment.

What makes the reputational means in this segment conducive to minimizing default is the prevalence of low principals, which, in turn, increases the creditor's effort and thereby limits absolute gains. Principals start at sums of about 1,000 rupees. They rarely exceed 10,000 rupees. While the willingness to give higher principals would superficially seem to reduce effort for the lender, and increase gains, it actually is the opposite. High principals at interest rates of 30 per cent per month to the clientele involved would almost immediately create the conditions for default, thus forcing the creditor to be lenient. The wide communication of a lender's lenience, in turn, may help to improve his or her image but will invariably lead to claims on the lender's lenience by other debtors – the refusal of which compromises reputational standing, while their acceptance undermines the lender's gains. Low principals help the lender to strike a balance between anticipated returns and reputational imperatives, thus stabilizing the business model.

Loans are frequently repaid within very short periods, rarely exceeding three or four months. For most debtors, taking on a loan is only viable if they are able to increase earnings (or reduce spending) drastically for the period of repayment, or if they are able to obtain credit from other sources, for instance family members. For the creditor, this arrangement results in a doubling of the capital invested over short periods based on the debtor's additional work, reduced consumption, or capital transfers from other sources. For the debtors, taking on a loan corresponds to periods of enhanced hardship that nevertheless remain viable in the short term. Most debtors take on loans frequently but not in direct succession. Debtors' 'careers' typically involve alternating sequences of debt repayment periods and debt-free spells, with the latter needed for recuperation. The necessary intermittent slackening of work effort in turn creates conditions of reduced earnings that increase the likelihood of future credit needs. The system of petty lending in Banaras, in consequence, does not follow the logic of seasonal fluctuations that are so prominent in agricultural or artisanal credit. Instead, it appears as constant credit demand from a macro-perspective, though it is composed of individual cycles of debt.

This depiction of petty lending applies to both mobile and immobile clientele. The differences between these two sub-segments are based primarily on two factors. First, mobile clientele comprises a large number of debtors who can with relative ease increase their daily income in debt repayment periods by enhanced work efforts, exemplified by cycle- and auto-rickshaw drivers. Immobile debtors, in turn, frequently have the benefit of regular incomes, exemplified by shop workers. Regular incomes preclude many opportunities for increasing earnings by putting in longer hours of work. Instead, shop workers and junior-level clerks tend to react by minimizing expenditure – made possible by wage levels that (while abysmally low, and frequently lower than what an auto-rickshaw driver earns) are sufficient to allow low levels of discretionary spending at least as long as housing costs are taken care of through the debtor's family. Mobility, in this regard, refers to two different aspects – the presence of the debtor at regular intervals at known places (marking low mobility), or its opposite, and the likelihood of migration backgrounds. The latter facilitates the use of simultaneously existing support systems beyond the reach of petty lenders in temporarily evading debt obligations, while the former anchors debtors strongly within the reputational economy of debt.

The distinct structures faced by lenders create corresponding differences in the type of lenders involved and their primary skills. Petty lending to immobile clientele is a strictly neighbourhood-centric business. Lenders know their clients and frequently have been in contact with them or people known to them for years. They also are aware of their whereabouts, including their homes, work spaces, and recreational spaces. This knowledge provides advantages in making reputation work, especially to prevent evasion. Conversely, it also offers a certain level of protection to the debtor through the communication flows that establish reputation. Default tends to become common knowledge in the neighbourhood, as do the justifications for default and the lender's responses to these. The frequent need to meet repayment obligations by cutting down expenditure adds to public perceptions of injustice committed by a lender who transgresses behavioural expectations, increasing the reputational fallout for a lender's misconduct. The reputational economy of debt, in comparison with mobile clientele, stabilizes creditor–debtor relations.

This increased stability affects the composition of the group of lenders in ways that may seem counter-intuitive, and initially was surprising for me. When I started my research, I frequently entered a shop expecting the moneylender to be the shopkeeper, only to realize that the lender was one of the workers employed by this shopkeeper. Briefly put, petty moneylending to relatively immobile clientele in Banaras cannot be characterized as an exploitation of the poor by the (petty) bourgeoisie. Instead, it primarily consists of an exploitation of the poor by the slightly better-off poor.

This tendency can be exemplified using the case of one of my first encounters with petty moneylenders. A close friend had initiated the contact with two men from the neighbourhood engaged in lending to local shop workers, and after a long period of waiting for their confirmation, I was stopped outside the shop in which one of them worked by a young man. As it turned out, the person who had stopped me was one of the lenders I was supposed to meet, and he prevented me from entering the shop on the grounds that his employer was currently present, and he was unwilling to discuss his lending activities in front of him. It should be added that both lenders knew that their employer was aware of their business. However, being engaged in petty lending was different from openly discussing this engagement in front of their employer who through his profession, age, and hierarchical difference was expected to know of their activities but was also expected not to be aware of it openly. Both lenders used slack time during their working hours to collect dues. When their employer was present, the two took time off when running errands to visit their debtors. When their employer was absent, they called their debtors over. Both preferred to collect dues at these times since they controlled the environment in which the collection of dues (and the renegotiation of obligations) took place. Having access to the space of a shop, and being seen as in charge of the space, lent gravitas to the young men that they were rather in need of.

While both of them had been in the business for sufficient time to build up a network of clients that allowed them to earn more from lending than from their regular work, they were clearly uncomfortable to speak about it. One of them, in fact, mostly restricted his contributions to an often-repeated statement that he agreed with his peer. Over a period of two hours, I spent at least forty-five minutes assuring the two that I was not working for the police, or the Indian state in any capacity, and that I would never disclose their identity to anyone. These reassurances took a somewhat farcical turn in the aftermath. At this time, I was frequently invited for dinner by a friend in the Uttar Pradesh police who ordered constables assigned to him to drop me off at the place I was staying. In the late night after interviewing the two lenders I was thus dropped in the neighbourhood in a police van with flashing lights and sirens – which the constables enjoyed so much that I had not been able to convince them to stop. The drop-off, in turn, was observed by a young adolescent who lived on the streets of this neighbourhood for parts of the year. The incident became duly communicated through gossip, and by the time I got up late the following morning, I received a call that both lenders had gone into hiding. It took me several days to communicate what actually had happened to a sufficient number of people for someone to be able to reach and inform the lenders and convey my apologies. While I had initially feared that the incident would undermine my ability to contact moneylenders at least in this neighbourhood, it had the opposite effect. Afterwards, many local moneylenders had heard of the story, and I rarely needed elaborate introductions anymore, while the demonstrable fact that nothing had happened to the two lenders (as well as the way I had attempted to reach out to them afterwards) seems to have established my reputation of trustworthiness more effectively than any reassurance.

The two lenders' apparent lack of self-confidence when dealing with a person of assumedly higher hierarchical standing does not necessarily translate into similar behavioural traits when dealing with their clients. Both were sufficiently successful to make significant gains from the business, visible in their showcasing of conspicuous consumption, far beyond the means of a typical shop worker. Their self-depiction made it clear that they cultivated an image of tough, street-wise young men capable of making their way in a rough business, forcing debtors to repay larger sums than these would otherwise be willing to. While I do not doubt that these self-depictions were partially correct, the depictions marked them as lenders of low repute. In turn, this would likely have affected long-term success as debtors with higher levels of reputation would shun them, thus increasing the likelihood of default. This increase would tend to force the lenders to rely more heavily on intimidation, setting off an inescapable vicious circle.

With the neighbourhood as the centre of the market – and Banarsi society relatively prone to engaging in communicating reputations through gossip – entrance-level skills for this market segment are low, as are requirements for starting capital. With principals rarely exceeding 10,000 rupees, starting capital for new entrants may be as low as 20,000 rupees. The regularity of income and the embeddedness into family structures that minimize housing expenses for petty lenders allow the latter to start lending on the sidelines with meagre capital stocks. Successful lending, in turn, can easily supplement income to a considerable extent. Shop workers in Banaras typically earn monthly salaries of about 4,500–7,000 rupees, which means that they are likely to be debtors, while some will be able to save small sums sufficient for the starting capital needs of a petty extra-legal entrepreneur. The relatively low likelihood of shopkeepers to be engaged in petty lending can be explained by two factors, apart from the higher absolute returns in trade credit mentioned earlier. First, the reputational fallout for relatively prosperous social segments in lending to the poor is higher than for other lower-class employees as their engagement in this market cannot be justified by aspirations for upward mobility. Second, the effort-intensive nature of petty lending forms an impediment for shopkeepers in lending to the poor. While both shopkeepers and shop workers work long hours (and for low returns even in the case of shopkeepers), the intensity of work for shop workers is typically lower and, crucially, their long working days allow considerable slack time that, instead, can be used for a variety of purposes – including profitable ones such as collecting dues and obtaining reputational information through gossip.

Shopkeepers are far less frequently involved in this type of lending, though some certainly are. Many shopkeepers cannot easily be involved even if they wanted to. Openly discussing money lending transactions in the shop, let alone using techniques of intimidation on lower-class debtors who will typically respond by highlighting their plight, is hardly conducive to the successful running of a commercial establishment, and shops that are locally known to be places where petty lending happens obtain a bad reputation. A bad reputation, in turn, compromises the ability to obtain loans in the trade credit segment – a regular necessity for many shopkeepers – apart from its fallout on social status. As a result, shopkeepers engaged in petty lending are typically much more circumspect about it than shop workers, who can engage in it in the absence of their employers. In a nutshell, this dynamic corresponds to a considerably less elaborate system of emulating rules of conduct among peer groups than those that used to dominate the market in late colonial times.

While commercial establishments constitute the bedrock of the petty bourgeoisie in Banaras (and for lower-class employment), other forms of creditor–debtor relationships between the petty bourgeoisie and the lower classes exist in tandem. Domestic servants, for instance, frequently rely on loans by their employers in addition to the loans they obtain from other petty lenders. In other professions, contractors and employers take on similar roles. The extent and visibility of reputational dynamics is more muted in these cases since the hierarchical relationship between employer-contractor and employee increases the latter's dependence beyond the immediate credit relationship, thus stabilizing it without a strong need for reputational means. At the same time, especially beyond domestic contexts where familiarity creates bonds that reduce the level of exploitation, most other characteristics of the market segment remain unchanged. Interest rates as a mark of the level of exploitation, principals as an indication of credit needs, and repayment modes differ little.

As an example, one labour contractor openly stated that he was lending at the same interest rates to workers dependent on him despite being aware that he faced lower risks of default than other lenders. The lender was engaged primarily in construction work where he leased out labour and machinery. He also had successfully been involved in local politics at a time, indicating that even more prosperous segments of society at times engage in petty lending.

Atal had migrated to Banaras several decades ago, and sourced most of the workers from his area of origin. Doing so gave him a double advantage in petty lending in that he maintained relations with his native area that could be employed to locate debtors and enforce payment, but also in allowing him to subtract interest payments directly from a worker's wages, or withhold these entirely in rare cases. For him, petty lending was clearly a side-business, and he strongly asserted that while he would not forego payments if at all possible, he was not actually interested in lending as the gains were minuscule compared to his main sources of income. He also did not need to rely on lending for controlling labour as he asserted that there was always sufficient demand for the work he supplied. Instead, he argued, his workers tended to approach him for loans at irregular intervals, and he would face problems in maintaining labour discipline if he did not provide these loans as workers would need to find supplementary work to repay debts to other lenders – making them unreliable. In charging 30 per cent monthly interest, he admitted following the prevailing rates regardless of circumstances. The question made him think, though, and a little time later he came up with a different explanation. If he charged less interest, he said, he would only encourage workers to come to him for their loans, and he would need to spend valuable time lending petty sums.

While forming a subsequent rationalization, the argument was not entirely implausible, implicitly highlighting that lending at lower than the prevailing rates would make it even less worth his while. Atal's statement reflects the aforementioned debate on the relative merits of engaging in the lower levels of extra-legal credit markets for the higher social strata. The high level of relative returns on investment, especially in circumstances where the difficulties of minimizing default were less pronounced, were certainly appreciated by the lower- as well as upper-middle class strata involved. But absolute gains from petty lending were insufficient as an incentive to become involved unless it constituted one of the main sources of income, and the lenders involved had sufficient time on their hands to become engaged for several hours a day.

Mobile clientele tends to be less embedded into neighbourhood social structures. While the communication of reputational dimensions of the market still occurs, the emphasis in the handling of reputational means shifts towards the interpersonal, impacting the patterns of renegotiation. The main difference between petty lending to mobile and immobile clientele rests on the greater likelihood of successful intermittent evasion of the creditor by mobile debtors. This probability affects the socio-spatial ordering of the sub-segment. Taking cycle-rickshaw drivers as an example, many drivers are seasonal migrants with links to their home villages. In cases of high debt, these debtors can consider escaping beyond the reach of petty lenders and then fall back on other credit sources, work in the village economy, or minimize expenditure to pay outstanding loans later. Creditors have few opportunities to prevent this, though it compromises the family livelihoods of debtors by reducing the income from migratory work.

The more important socio-spatial outcome linked to intermittent default is related to attempts to avoid meeting the creditor. While immobile clientele may try to follow this route, their success is limited by neighbourhood structures. For cycle-rickshaw drivers, however, their livelihoods are not entirely dependent on appearing regularly at known places. Most drivers depend on support networks that centre around specific places – the office of the contractor renting out rickshaws, specific rickshaw stands known to customers, particular routes traversed by customers, and recreational spots situated in proximity to the rickshaw stands including tea stalls and *paan* or tobacco stores. Yet, in need, rickshaw drivers are capable of plying other routes for a while, circumventing some of their credit dues.

Superficially, the attempt to evade the creditor may appear useless as outstanding dues would only rise. This interpretation, however, ignores the reputational dimensions linked to the debtors' inability to pay high amounts of interest in absolute rather than relative terms. Disappearing from the creditor's sight – for a season when returning to the village, or for a few days when plying different routes – does not typically lead to progressive increases in outstanding dues since the ability to repay is restricted from the outset, and the creditor's insistence on contractual terms in the face of this inability is reputationally damaging.

To give one example, while interviewing a different lender who will be discussed in greater detail later, I observed a renegotiation arising from the evasion of the creditor by an indebted cycle-rickshaw driver, eventually leading to an incidence of violence. Both parties transgressed specific norms of conduct – default and the attempt to evade the creditor on the side of the borrower, and unwarranted pressure building up to low-scale violence by the creditor – yet both parties employed clearly defined moral discourses to make the other relent. The moneylender appealed to contractual terms and the shame of defaulting, resorted to public shaming, and emphasized the attempted evasion. He also highlighted general untrustworthiness, individually and concerning the collective of borrowers, depicting the latter by profession, class, and place of origin. The lender employed intimidation, mostly shouting, but eventually slapping the borrower's face. These intimidations formed part of the negotiation in that they were expected by the borrower, and were calibrated despite their emotional appearance. Both were aware of their limits. The borrower was deferring to the lender, pleading to mediating circumstances beyond his control, showcasing the depth of his need, expressing embarrassment at his attempts at evasion, professing that it was done in fear of the lender's wrath, thereby flattering the lender's sense of importance, condemning the inequity of the contractual terms and, eventually, using the lender's intimidation against him by pointing out the transgression through the act of violence. Both sides appeared, from a distance, to be locked in a theatrical act of performing a negotiation, with clearly known roles related to specific moral arguments. The outcome of this performance was to be the extraction of a price for lenience, thereby providing a temporary solution, with both sides having won concessions. The arguments were brought up repeatedly, so that different combinations of counter-arguments gave the impression of a well-rehearsed routine negotiation.

In the case depicted here, the defaulting borrower's performance was relatively successful: the (non-involved) moneylender I had come to interview subsequently remarked how much the negotiation had gone beyond the lender's control. To him, the mistake in the lender's performance had been his initial aggressiveness which led the lender to insult the borrower early on, bringing in other rickshaw drivers. In consequence, insults rapidly escalated towards the collective of rickshaw drivers and their (supposedly) Bihari origin which, in turn, led to angry responses from the bystanders. The lender decided to reinstate control and reinforce the hierarchical difference by a sudden turn to violence. In the opinion of the non-involved lender this turn to violence had taken place 'too early': the borrower initially reacted sullenly, refusing to respond, and turning his back on the lender, while some of the bystanders started impressing on the lender that he had gone too far. Eventually the borrower used the incidence of violence to argue that he had already paid a part of the 'price', and the lender found it difficult to regain the upper hand.

The transgressions of good conduct in this case are sufficiently routine and ubiquitous to appear as performance. This depiction obviously fails to address the urgency and gravity for the borrower for whom the need to approach the lender probably constituted the only viable hope of escaping economic distress. The appearance of performance stems from both sides' awareness of a routinely employed reputational discourse in which their various transgressions of propriety were weighed against each other, and in which the most striking act of transgression – direct interpersonal violence – was taking place. Eventually, the performance produced a new agreement, a new precarious balance of trust between lender and borrower.

Compared to immobile debtors, petty lending to mobile clientele involves significantly greater effort for the lender to minimize default and collect dues. It also involves somewhat more sophisticated business practices. While many lenders are still following other professions, they tend to spend long hours at a stretch engaged in lending, and typically have a firmer grasp on how to carry out their business. To illustrate the differences in terms of relative sophistication, I will use the case of Babu. Being able to observe Babu was one of the most fortunate developments during my research. For one thing, Babu and I had common friends, and I was able to learn about his lending activities long after he tired of meeting me. More importantly, though, Babu started lending around the time that I started my research, and I was thus able to observe his own learning processes as an emerging petty lender.

Babu entered petty lending reluctantly. As a young man with a middle-class background, he had been well educated up to the level of graduation in a local but prestigious institution. After graduating, he had taken on employment within the local unit of a corporate enterprise, earning sufficient income to make a decent living without needing to rely on his family's support. Before I met him, his friends related that he had a broadly liberal, 'modern', and educated mindset, making it clear that he needed to be considered progressive by the standards of a sizable city in the north Indian hinterland. Among other things, he had always disliked not only money lending as such, but the entire structure of petty (and frequently enough not-so-petty) exchange that dominates the city's economy – the endless gossip and negotiation, the constant exchange of small favours, the haggling over small margins, and all the other attributes that together compose an important element of cultural practice in a city defined to a large extent by the manner in which a myriad of interlocked transactionalities are constantly playing themselves out. What he had aspired for was the widespread longing among India's younger generations for (supposedly) metropolitan lifestyles associated with a neoliberal consumer and work culture (Srivastava 2007; Gooptu 2013). This culture found its expression in the self-depiction of the country's corporate sector, in relatively sterile computerized and air-conditioned offices, the glitz of metropolitan malls (rather than their mostly decrepit local counterparts), and was associated with broad highways instead of the incessant weaving in and out of traffic jams on narrow, potholed roads that characterize Banaras. It was reflected in the widespread fascination with e-wallets rather than lending petty sums to cycle-rickshaw drivers. In all these ways, Babu was an image of the more fortunate segments of his generation, and a very unlikely moneylender.

Babu's father had been a moneylender, though, specifically to cycle-rickshaw drivers, following the typical patterns of the trade. According to his friends, Babu had been embarrassed about this background, though he was aware that it had paid for his education and thereby given him the chance to move towards a differently aspirational life. He was also much too polite and respectful to his parents to ever indicate anything like this to me. When his father passed away, he left behind outstanding dues owed by his clients. Now having to take over his father's role in providing for the family, Babu decided that he should collect these dues, with the firm commitment that afterwards he would give up money lending. By the time I met him, he had managed to collect these dues, but had not stopped lending. He was clearly uncomfortable, though, in being seen to be engaged in extra-legal finance.

His friends narrated their shock of seeing Babu as a lender. According to their depiction, he had been frequently socializing, but soon after his father's demise started to stay away, and even to avoid them. One evening a group of his friends had spotted him at the stall where I first met Babu. Coming over, they discovered what he was doing and started admonishing him as well as imploring him to stop lending, to no avail. His relationship with his friends had deteriorated afterwards in subtle ways that demonstrate the operation of public reproach of extra-legal finance in its actual practice.

Initially, they berated him every single time they met, and those meetings were becoming less frequent. Over a longer period, though, this rebuke had faded, taking on characteristics of friendly banter, though never entirely losing its underlying tension. Babu had also started hanging out again, though less frequently than before, partially due to the necessity to spend long hours in the evenings collecting dues, but also because of the unresolved tensions. While this qualifies as a mild form of ostracization, Babu himself was keenly aware that his standing had deteriorated, and had become defensive.

The first time I saw him, we met at a tea stall adjacent to a rickshaw stand that his father had frequented, and where some of his clients were frequently based. Babu was clearly a misfit. As mentioned earlier, one of the negotiations I observed there escalated into petty violence, and Babu was openly ashamed by the company he was keeping, even though he held himself apart. At several instances during the interview he was lowering his voice and turning his eyes away from me, while stating variations of phrases like 'this is a bad business; this is a bad society'. He did not give up lending, though. As he put it, it was very lucrative, and he was about to get married. Obtaining the repayment dues left behind by his father had been replaced as both the objective and the rationalization of his extra-legal entrepreneurship by the determination to acquire starting capital for establishing his family. For rationalization, he also used a fairly typical trope among moneylenders, stating that his father's debtors were mostly good men, and that they had besieged him to carry on, since otherwise they would be compelled to obtain loans from moneylenders associated with various vices. Having observed both his behaviour and that of some other lenders, this statement does not appear as implausible as it may seem at first glance, though it still constituted a typical element in the repertoire of rationalizations employed by extra-legal lenders.

Babu's initial experience with money lending had been an abject failure. In his words, he had simply turned up at rickshaw stands, identified his father's clients and demanded repayment. When the debtors started making excuses, he had variously tried to insist on prompt repayment, and to offer payment deferments or reductions in return for clearing the dues. Whatever he had tried, though, he did not manage to obtain more than feeble sums. When he started appearing regularly, his father's debtors evaded him, and he never managed to get information on their whereabouts. He was, in his words, about to give up the attempt to collect his father's dues when he was approached by the owner of the tea stall adjacent to the rickshaw stand.

This meeting was a breakthrough for Babu as an extra-legal entrepreneur. They negotiated a deal in which the tea stall owner received an interest-free loan of 7,000 rupees with favourable conditions of repayment in return for helping Babu with his collections. Over time, this relationship evolved into a low-order business partnership. Babu would occasionally give preferential terms to the tea stall owner, who, in turn, continued to assist him in crucial ways. Initially, the tea stall owner informed Babu on the whereabouts of his debtors, thus providing an edge to Babu's efforts. He also conveyed to Babu how he should approach them, and provided information on their current constraints, and their reputational standing. By the time of our first meeting, this partnership had progressed significantly. Observing Babu's collection routine, it had taken on a key role. Babu was aware of his status as a misfit – a young, educated, broad-shouldered but mild-mannered man who was still ashamed of extracting payments from people so much poorer than himself. Picturing him as intimidating his debtors was impossible, and the rickshaw-drivers habituated to dealing with other lenders would have felt it more keenly. Instead, he left most of the renegotiation to the tea stall owner who had known the drivers for long, and knew whom (and when) to trust. The tea stall owner was behaving more in accordance with my experience of moneylenders than Babu ever could have at the time. In turn, Babu stayed back from the nitty-gritty of the negotiation. He clearly marked his presence. Yet, in standing back, he did so in a way that reinforced the tea stall owner's authority, providing the implicit threat of a member of a hierarchically higher-ranked social stratum who could be called upon to interfere at need, and to make final decisions – almost in the way of a neutral arbitrator, except that of course he was the main beneficiary.

Cooperating with the tea stall owner had one more crucial benefit: as a new entrant to the business, Babu initially knew little of how to make it work. He openly admitted that what he thought he knew initially was mostly made up of the public image associated with moneylenders which corresponded to an image of toughness combined with traces of shrewdness. How to gain reliable knowledge about debtors, how to assess the titbits of reputational information that could be gleaned from gossip, how to handle renegotiations, and how to strike the balance between lenience and threat were unknown to him, and his 'partnership' provided an introduction to these questions on which he was able to build. By the time I met him, Babu had extended this partnership to seven other collaborators at different nodal points for rickshaw drivers. While he was spending a lot of time at the particular stand we met, his routine had changed to a pattern in which he was making rounds of the sites frequented by his debtors, typically centring on a small shop or stall where he would receive information from his partners. Since their opportunities for evasion had been curtailed in this fashion, debtors preferred to meet Babu or his partners instead of evading them, pleading for consideration of their circumstances and trying to renegotiate terms, but also providing advance notice on their ability to repay.

Having consolidated his lending activities, Babu found extra-legal finance too lucrative to give up. Not only did he continue to take on new clients, but he also expanded the capital invested. His friends told me that he would at times ask them to invest money through him, or simply asked for money for his investments. There were rumours, too, that he had started taking on bank loans to increase his liquid capital, though these do not appear likely considering the low amounts of capital that a single petty lender could employ profitably within the limits posed by the time and effort involved. While these rumours were likely incorrect, they indicate that for people observing Babu's lending activities an obvious expansion was taking place.

Relatively early on, Babu had changed his operational principles in another respect. He frequently insisted on introductions of new debtors by other debtors and asked them to vouch for their conduct. In his words, shifting to a system of introductions – vouching for good conduct may be too strong a term as it implies shared liability – proved to be of considerable value. He argued that over the last years of his father's lending activities, profitability had gone down, and this shift increased returns on investment. Introductions spread the reputational fallout of default. In insisting on introductions, Babu gained accomplices in pressurizing debtors to pay their dues, or at least in gaining advance information on their ability to pay. In return, his accomplices could expect greater lenience by Babu as long as their efforts in helping him minimize default were noticeable. The case of Babu depicted here provides significant information on several patterns in extra-legal credit, partially even beyond the segment of petty lending to mobile clientele. These address the reputational dynamics of extra-legal finance, its socio-spatial patterns, the stability of creditor–debtor relations, and the rudimentary forms of sophistication that are identifiable even in the almost comprehensively 'amateurized' system of petty lending. I will return to these issues subsequently.

Displacement, and getting rid of a moneylender

The third segment of petty lending differs strongly from the others – in the extent of professionalism, in the aims of lending and the functional role of the collateral, and in the relatively low importance of its reputational dimensions. It also differs in its scope within the market. The role of immovable assets as collateral in extra-legal finance has rarely been a central concern outside rural areas. The discrepancy in attention is at least partially related to discourses originating in colonial India that highlighted the plight of displaced farmers. To some extent, this rural bias is linked to the fact that farmers losing land also lose their means of production while urban workers and employees losing real estate do not, having already lost theirs. There are also emotional underpinnings to this bias in that the image of farmers driven off their land carries potency. Slum evictions that are enforced in violent ways make headlines; the gradual displacement of urban poor from their homes – family by family – typically does not. Lastly, at least at the centre of urban agglomerations, displacement through debt nowadays predominantly takes place through banks and not moneylenders. With the rise in fully urban real estate prices, the involvement of extra-legal entrepreneurs in displacement has typically shifted to the outer perimeters of urban growth, as will be discussed subsequently.

Historically, this shift is recent in cities like Banaras. The relatively stagnant economies in many north Indian hinterland towns in the mid-twentieth century did not lead to drastic rises in real estate prices. At the same time, the penetration of 'organized' finance into these cities remained relatively shallow, thus creating an impediment to the availability of capital for urban displacement by banks. As importantly, significant tracts of real estate were property of local elites. As discussed earlier, a significant element in colonial debates on money lending was informed by fears over elite decline, but especially in rural India where the decline of traditional tenancy patterns generated fears of uncontrollable movements of displaced agriculturists to the cities.

The middle decades of the twentieth century in Banaras constitute an instructive example of the changes in patterns of urban real estate property due to elite decline. The case of the Assi neighbourhood can be taken as exemplary in this regard. Located at this time at the outer perimeter of the city proper, most of the existing buildings in the neighbourhood were built in the early years of the twentieth century, and a considerable part of these were owned by various wings of one landlord family. Family members were willing to discuss the displacement process after the 1930s, though respecting confidentiality I will not provide further details here than stating that many houses between approximately 1940 and the early 1980s were taken over by moneylenders residing in the neighbourhood. Balancing perceived economic and reputational demands on income and expenditure – with the caveat that this distinction was far from clear-cut – resulted in elite indebtedness that frequently led to the permanent loss of immovable assets to moneylenders who controlled significantly lesser means (and status) but possessed liquidity lacked by the elite.

Similar developments will certainly have taken place with poorer neighbourhoods and debtors, though these were less extensively documented and cannot be identified through oral history. As the focus here is on petty lending and displacement, I will exemplify the dynamics of displacement through debt with a recent example of a *basti* near the Durgakund area, illustrating the manner in which policy and microfinance can contribute to a question that has not been foregrounded here so far, of how to get rid of a moneylender – and of the ambiguous results of getting rid of a moneylender for those indebted to the lender.

The respective moneylender lived in a prosperous compound on the perimeter of a Dalit-dominated *basti*. He owned significant tracts of real estate surrounding it, acquired through lending. The inhabitants of the *basti* had originally squatted on this land decades ago, possession of which had subsequently been regularized. A considerable share of the local population used their regularized property as collateral to the moneylender who in the early 2010s had – according to the remaining families – lent money at compound rates of 20 per cent per month for principals ranging from 1,000 to 5,000 rupees. Real estate was transferred once outstanding dues reached the value of the collateral (as estimated by the lender). Once continuous tracts of real estate were consolidated under his possession, the families were evicted, and the area developed for middle-class housing, which by 2011 had significantly diminished the size of the *basti*, giving it a besieged atmosphere.

During the last government in Uttar Pradesh led by the Bahujan Samaj Party – a Dalit-dominated political party – the *basti* was developed. Under a government scheme, the originally *kacca* (unsolid, not built of masonry) houses were replaced by *pakka* (solid, built of masonry) ones, made of bricks and stone, and with proper ventilation and inside bathrooms as well as anterior sheds for livestock. In the process, real estate titles were made non-transferrable, undermining the legality of their use as collateral. Additionally, the state government facilitated the work of a microfinance programme, with SHGs operating a compulsory savings scheme. Female members of participating families decided on fixed amounts of monthly savings, while withdrawals were limited, with larger withdrawals needing approval by the SHG.

The combination of undermining the transferability of property titles and offering a different scheme for financial needs successfully challenged the moneylender's business. Faced with this challenge, he continued his earlier business practice, yet one indebted family refused to acknowledge its debts. When intimidation failed, the lender was alleged to have resorted to evicting the family using forged property titles. It needs to be added that my attempts to speak to the lender or his family were unsuccessful, so that the narrative is based on depictions by (previously) indebted families. Their statements indicate that the lender misconceived the state government's intervention as a temporary measure. The defaulting family notified the district magistrate, who was sympathetic to their interests. The magistrate ordered the police to arrest the lender – not on charges of money lending (which is difficult to prove), but on charges of forgery. According to local testimony, the lender was marched through the locality by the police, with residents gleefully narrating not only his allegedly rough treatment by the police but also the invective he was subjected to by residents. He was sentenced to imprisonment for two years. According to local residents he refused to lend money to the locals after his release.

The case depicted here constitutes the most drastic incident of state-backed action against moneylenders I have come across in almost a decade of field research. As with the earlier crackdown on money lending, it demonstrates the state's capacity to enforce the regulation of money lending. At the same time, it provides information on the dynamics of displacement through debt that need to be considered especially for the evaluation of its ambiguous fallout.

First, the depiction of the operational principles of lending demonstrates that petty lending for displacement within the city proper constitutes the most exploitative sub-segment of extra-legal credit. Principals were tiny. The compound interest charged made these loans significantly more expensive over short periods of time compared to the typical simple interest rates by petty moneylenders. I was not able to obtain robust information on the frequency of rests at which the interest was compounded, but even annual rests would have a drastic effect on the costs of borrowing. The absence of knowledge on the frequency of compounding among the residents itself is revealing in that it indicates a considerable informational advantage of the lender.

The lending practices also need to be differentiated from the prevalent patterns of the reputational economy of debt in petty lending. The reputational dynamics in petty lending arising from the high incidence of default were absent entirely. This absence can be linked to the intention of lending, which centred on the collateral rather than the accumulation of interest. The provision of credit was tightly linked to real estate development. The gains made from developing real estate clearly surpassed gains from petty lending – which were marginal as a share of the lender's income. What is more, the lender had employed a small number of people as enforcers, a practice that is absent from other forms of petty lending. Interest accumulation could not possibly have compensated for the costs of hiring labour. Instead, the lender's strategy centred on exploiting the value differentials in real estate between the time of the *basti*'s settlement and its value in the early 2010s.

The objective of acquiring the collateral overruled the necessity to minimize default. For the creditor, lending corresponded to a highly profitable long-term investment in which frequent recourse to tiny principals eventually accumulated into vast gains. The problem of temporary default, in turn, was countermanded by the logic of compound interest. Some indebted families highlighted that it had been difficult to make payments as they had been frequently abused and made to wait. From the debtors' perspective, this form of credit was not necessarily more exploitative, though the costs of borrowing were higher. The decision by debtors to take on loans at a compound rate of interest of 20 per cent per month instead of a simple rate of interest of 30 per cent per month is crucial in this respect. Much of the literature on financial inclusion would tend to portray it as an irrational decision and, based on this assumption, link it to the informational advantages of the lender, and recommend 'financial literacy' as a solution.

However, assessing decision-making in this manner entirely misses a major element in the debtors' perspective, and anchors this assessment primarily in the perspective of the creditor. From the perspective of debtors who have little possibility of repaying debt obligations, to obtain a form of credit that gives an incentive to default on interest payments for relatively long periods before the collateral is seized can be an entirely rational decision. This point can be illustrated by looking at the operation of microfinance within the *basti*. The SHGs I studied comprised a pronounced profile in that at least one member of any family involved in the scheme was aspirational and upwardly mobile. My main informant exemplified this pattern. A young shop worker who had recently shifted to better employment, and was going to shift to a new employer approximately two years later, he had taken vocational training courses in various subjects. He was highly appreciated by his employer for being hard-working, disciplined, and willing to learn. He had also made use of legal opportunities against a former employer who had not paid legal minimum wages – no informal sector commercial establishment in Banaras does so, and very few would be able to afford it without massively reducing the workforce employed. His employer confided that he had been thinking of sacking him on the grounds that he suspected a similar move against him – depicted as understandable, and impossible to comply with. His family transferred regular amounts to the microfinance scheme, and had withdrawn some of this money to buy a cow.

Asked about the extent of upward mobility within the *basti*, most SHG members agreed that approximately two-thirds of the families could be characterized that way, with the other third being unable to save even tiny sums. Accordingly, these were not admitted, and often had not even applied as joining the scheme made little sense: if a family could not hope to contribute small sums regularly, locking up capital in a scheme that imposed drastic limits on withdrawals was counterproductive. The replacement of the former moneylender intent on evicting the families after acquiring their pledged collateral with a microfinance scheme thus made considerable sense from a developmental perspective as it reinforced upward mobility. Yet it also forced the remaining one-third of the residents into a trajectory of downward mobility. Having lost the ability to obtain tiny loans at frequent intervals without necessarily needing to pay interest for a long time, they were now forced to seek out petty neighbourhood lenders. While the absolute borrowing costs would be lower in the mid-term, these lenders were enforcing interest payments at least to some extent, regulated by the reputational dynamics of debt in petty lending, or else would cut off credit supply.

The eventual loss of their property involved significant hardship, and compromised employment opportunities, but for a family that was already destitute, displacement serves as a resource for credit at a price that is fairly low once it excludes the value of the collateral. The cycle of displacement through debt needs to be understood from this perspective as well, with the regularization of property obtained through squatting constituting a resource of intergenerational value in obtaining credit needed for subsistence. Eviction, for these debtors, was equivalent to restarting the cycle at a different location. For the aspirational families in the *basti*, however, their indebtedness to a moneylender intent on displacement formed an impediment to upward mobility once the housing conditions had been upgraded. It is noteworthy that the depiction of the downwardly mobile by the other families was frequently crude: they were depicted as alcoholics and drug addicts, stupid, violent, or – in the best of these depictions – as irrevocably sick from a variety of maladies. While other people differed, and while some descriptions were partially applicable, the fallout of getting rid of a moneylender changes according to the precise location of a family within the spectrum of the city's credit economy.

On the perimeters of the monetary outside

Peri-urban lending differs from the displacement through debt of slum-dwellers in two crucial respects. First, the availability of land as collateral indicates greater prosperity among debtors. While similar dynamics among marginal farmers are occurring in many parts of India as well as in the vicinity of Banaras, I have not received any information on these during my fieldwork since its focus was on urban forms of extra-legal finance. Second, the existence of a sufficiently competitive market in land facilitates the accrual of benefits to the debtors from land value differentials over time arising from rapid urban growth. These dynamics allow debtors to pledge parts of their land as collateral to lenders interested primarily in obtaining speculative assets for future development, at the same time banking on increases in the price of their remaining land as compensation.

The desirability of land as collateral leads to a drastic reduction in interest rates. Rates drop to approximately the level of the trade credit segment, though those transactions are mostly unsecured, around 2 per cent per month, rarely going beyond 5 per cent simple interest. The prevalence of simple interest rates is surprising since it can be surmised that the intention of lending is linked to the acquisition of the collateral. However, it can at least partially be explained by the absence of acrimony between debtors and creditors.

In my most informative foray into peri-urban extra-legal finance, I ended up at a petrol pump cum rest house a short motorcycle ride along the highway to Allahabad. I had come there to meet one lender, but this lender had brought along a friend indebted to another lender. While I was still introducing myself, this friend suddenly called out to bystanders, and we were joined by two more lenders and another debtor, the latter indebted to one of the lenders who joined us. I asked this debtor whether he was comfortable speaking with his lender present, and he shrugged the question away insisting that I asked the third lender why he would, in his words, only take aubergines as interest. As he made it clear that he would only answer my other questions once I asked, it turned out that the third lender ran a business selling vegetables at the local *mandi*. He accepted other vegetables, too, and also accepted cash but he preferred taking vegetables as he said he would sell those, and therefore could depict his earnings as agricultural income – which is exempt from income tax in India – and even show documentary proof, just in case anybody ever asked. He also could make an additional profit as he only lent money at the lower-range rate of 2 per cent, but charged interest (in kind) by the buying prices in the *mandi*, before selling them at the going market rates.

Having fulfilled my duty, the debtor opened up. He had taken on a substantial loan from the second lender who charged him 2.5 per cent per month, and pledged one parcel of his land. He needed the money to upgrade his house. He had also earmarked another parcel of land for a loan he needed to pay for his children's education. Once the house was upgraded, and his children were finishing their education, he figured that the city would have grown towards the village to a sufficient extent to make his remaining land much more valuable, and planned to sell most of the rest, keeping enough land to do some farming, mostly for relatively high-value vegetables that he could sell directly.

The lenders, in turn, corroborated this information and made it clear that they were lending as a side-business. If they managed to get hold of a parcel of land, it constituted the best outcome, but they took the interest as well. The land was an investment in a future that seemed certain. With the village located right next to the most important highway leading away from Banaras, land prices were bound to increase drastically. If farmers were able to pay, though, they gained in liquidity which could be reinvested in other loans – providing another opportunity to take possession of land. Agriculture was changing, and eventually the village economy would become 'like in the city'.

The lender I had originally come to meet took a slightly longer-term view. He expected the rate of urbanization to increase, and had started buying land further away. The trick was, he confided, to find land that could be used for growing staple crops now, high-value crops that could be sold in the city directly once distance between village and town receded, and was also located close enough to the main axes of growth, so that it eventually could be sold to a developer. Farmers further into the countryside, he argued, could not yet understand the manner in which land prices would escalate, and he could strike bargains there since the sellers did not realize yet what an urban investor was looking for, or what crops would sell in the city's markets. Having already lived near the city, he said, would make him a fortune, and he even had pledged a small part of his land in this village to another lender as collateral for a loan that he used to buy up land elsewhere.

Asked about lending to poorer households in the village, their answer was replete with bewilderment. Poorer households, the first debtor eventually said, were obviously still around. But their members earned their income mostly in the city, and primarily lived in the village because it was cheaper, and maybe because they still maintained a tiny piece of land to grow produce for their own consumption. Their land had been sold years ago, or lost through debt, when prices had initially started to rise. Now the only real landowners remaining were in possession of sufficient land to profit handsomely from 'development'. Whether they were currently debtors or creditors, they all were part of a 'game'. One looked at the family's needs and decided to follow a certain course with one parcel, then maybe the next year one's needs changed, and one tried to obtain a different piece of land. But nobody would ever lose enough land to be unable to reap the profits 'once the city reaches here'. There also was no need for maintaining reputation and trust – they were all 'good people', they said, and they knew each other well – and if one of them played the game better than others, they deserved the increased gains as no one really had lost out. In fact, many of the transactions were decided upon right at this rest house. It had the best tea, there were always other people from the village around, and if someone wanted to pledge land for a loan, it would initiate a round of discussions that would last until some decision was made several days later.

For the purposes of this study, the depiction of peri-urban lending in Banaras primarily aims to demonstrate the various uses of collateral to overcome the uncertainties associated with the credit contract in extra-legal contexts. In the case discussed on displacement of slum-dwellers through petty debt, the collateral in the form of regularized possession of real estate had constituted the basis for the reproduction of displacement as a subsistence-level resource. For the upwardly mobile residents of the *basti*, the underlying logic of displacement through petty debt had changed once houses were upgraded and microfinance started to provide an alternative. For the villagers in peri-urban Banaras – as long as they had held on to land – the appreciation of land value through urbanization in combination with the relative prosperity of agriculture in proximity to urban agglomerations had created a sense of the value of land that rested on future speculation and had taken on characteristics of a game between friends. The literature on gambling and speculative games in India is replete with practices of betting on future outcomes (Hull forthcoming; Puri 2014, 2015), and extra-legal finance in this context needs to be seen in close association with these practices.

Artisanal credit in contemporary Banaras

The artisanal system of extra-legal credit in Banaras in many ways forms a continuation of historically prevalent structures with minor modifications. Most artisanal groups in Banaras do not anymore have elaborate credit systems specific to their trade, partially due to the decline of important industries like metalwork, woodwork and carpentry, and pottery. As discussed in Chapter 4, these industries were already declining in the 1920s, and credit systems declined with them, while the low-value, low-income artisanal groups did not have elaborate credit systems even then. The prevalence of artisanal credit in the 1920s was tightly linked to the surplus that could be obtained by mercantile capital or workshop owners, and therefore did not extend into industries that depended on subsistence-level production.

Artisanal credit remains the most important form of financing production (and subsistence) in the weaving industries. These industries are dominated by silk weaving, though cotton weaving, carpet production, and weaving based on artificial fibres are also present in the city. Silk weaving, in turn, is dominated by the Ansari community. Socio-spatially, communal tensions and violence between the 1890s and the 1930s led to a concentration of the weaving activity in the Madanpura neighbourhood, adjacent to Godowlia and Laksa, which emerged as the most important Muslim ghetto in town, though the Muslim population was still present in nearby neighbourhoods like Reori Talab and Beniya Bagh, and in other, smaller clusters. Situated on the outskirts of the main bazaar, Madanpura was highly suitable as a location due to its proximity to the main wholesale traders. The history of the Ansari weavers has been traced in detail by Nita Kumar (1988), while other studies have focused on more recent developments, particularly linked to gender, education, and communal violence (Raman 2010; P. Williams 2015). The spatial concentration resulted in ever-denser settlement patterns, and the appreciation of housing costs. Combined with the emergence of socio-economic stratification among the community, it created a gentrification process which drove less prosperous weavers from the neighbourhood, and into newer (or re-emerging) weaving clusters, including Jaitpura. Broadly speaking, these developments led to the migration of handloom production (except for high-value artisanship) and other low-value weaving industries.

Artisanal credit has been discussed in detail in a range of studies covering various industries, regions, and historical periods, so that the discussion here will be brief and its focus on recent changes. Among many other studies, it has been prominently analysed by authors as diverse as Tirthankar Roy (1999), Douglas E. Haynes (1999, 2012), and Gyan Pandey (1981). Generalizing some of the insights from these works, artisanal households used credit relations for both subsistence and production. For production needs, many artisanal households depended particularly on *sahukar*s – and tended to obtain loans from these also for everyday needs. The term *sahukar* at times is used generically for moneylenders below the level of prosperity of *sarraf*s. In contemporary Banaras, however, the term *sahukar* almost invariably describes a moneylender-cum-trader, while petty moneylenders are described derogatively as *suudkhor* (roughly: usurer).

The need for artisanal credit is directly related to seasonal fluctuations in the sale of woven textiles, and it forms both an efficient way of sustenance for weavers and a cause for their frequent inability to acquire larger shares of artisanal surplus. Textile sales have historically been linked to a variety of seasonal fluctuations, depending on the goods involved. Prominent factors were the harvest cycle – which created the liquidity in agricultural households needed for expenditure on consumer goods – and the religious and marriage calendars that roughly follow the former. The relative loss of export markets for Indian textiles during the period of European industrialization exacerbated these fluctuations, and created conditions for Indian weavers to become strongly dependent on locally controlled commercial rather than 'global' capital. In some parts of India, cooperative credit and marketing have partially allowed weavers to overcome this reliance on the *sahukar*. Yet the cooperative movement failed to have any large-scale impact in Banaras, a failure that continued unabatedly into the contemporary period. Jolie Wood (2014) has depicted the associational life of weavers compared to boatmen in contemporary Banaras.

Weavers in Banaras were relatively sheltered from the deindustrialization of India by focusing on high-value and luxury goods. Yet the links between the agricultural, and religious and marriage seasons served to sustain the seasonal fluctuations in demand. In fact, these became stronger over the course of the twentieth century since the 'traditional' reliance on the sale of luxury goods like brocades declined with the westernization of male elite Indian dress codes, and the decline of 'traditional' elites. The silk traders of Banaras responded by shifting production towards the manufacture of *sari*s, an important element of female dress which, in turn, was advertised through local-origins branding. The Banarsi *sari* emerged as a prized item, particularly for marriages and other festivities which, conversely, strengthened the dependence on the religious and marriage calendars in shaping seasonal fluctuations in demand.

These fluctuations, in turn, meant that artisanal production over the off-season was not matched by sales, thus creating the need for credit both in terms of subsistence needs and for obtaining raw materials. Commercial capital was able to exploit the slack periods of demand by providing credit to artisans, and in return tied artisanal household production to specific traders. Having curtailed competition, traders were able to fix the prices for artisanal goods in the low season, thus deflating wholesale buying prices. For both subsistence-consumption and production-related credit, this dependence led to a wide variety of credit practices, particularly regarding the payment of interest. Briefly put, the diversity of practices precludes the identification of patterns on charging interests or on the preference towards accumulation through interest or through controlling labour and prices by the vendors. I have come across merchants who charged high rates of interest up to 20 per cent per month on both consumption- and production-related loans, while others charged significantly less or nothing at all (in interest) even for consumption-related loans. Roughly estimated, I expect that less than half of the city's vendors charge interest on production-related credit.

The decision to charge interest is linked to diverse reasons ranging from moral considerations and a preference for documented or undocumented income to the need or choice to cultivate long-term relations with the producer, the latter more prevalent in high-value goods. As many merchants maintain broad ranges of qualities in their goods, even this rationale does not necessarily translate into identifiable patterns since many vendors will follow uniform credit strategies with different artisans, while others differentiate credit strategies across weaving households. The choice of credit strategy, in turn, reflects on the merchant's reputation in the market and in local society: a lender foregoing interest or charging low rates presents a caring image, not only in terms of social responsibilities but also in terms of caring for the quality of produced goods as high levels of exploitation indicate irresponsible behaviour – undermining the sustainability of artisanal households, and thereby compromising artisanal skill. Conversely, failing to exploit opportunities for generating additional income can be seen as irresponsible behaviour for a mercantile family, though the former dynamic is more prominent. In turn, the reputational dynamics prevalent in petty lending and trade credit are less relevant as the imperative to minimize default is less pronounced. Since both consumption- and production-related credit flows from merchants to artisans are ultimately related to the producer–merchant relationship, the artisanal product takes on an equivalent functional role in the credit relationship to collateral. Outstanding dues can be subsumed under the final price paid to the weaver.

The decision not to charge interest does not necessarily mean that returns on investment for the merchant are lower. Profit margins can easily be as high when fixing the price of goods. The reputational dynamic – of avoiding visible exploitation through interest payments – may communicate a caring attitude, but the reality is more complex in that the level of exploitation is decided by the combination of interest payments, the valuation of the raw materials advanced, and the prices for the weavers' products. Still, many merchants are keenly aware of the need to avoid 'taking too much' to sustain skill levels, thus facilitating social stratification within the Ansari community.

Nita Kumar's nuanced description of artisanal history depicts relatively strong uniformity within communities (Kumar 1988), while Abdul Bismillah has written an outstanding fictional depiction of the everyday aspects of weavers' lives in Banaras (Bismillah 1986). Community traditions, socio-spatial cohesion, and practices of discrimination against Muslims combined with a market dominated by Hindu merchants and the specific traits of this market to create socio-economic homogeneity. This uniformity, however, started to unravel by the 1980s. The market for silk textiles produced in Banaras diversified, with exports gaining a more prominent role, including in Muslim countries in Asia. Enhanced expenditure on luxury items in India and abroad created opportunities for value addition through high-skilled labour. Master weavers increasingly were able to escape the subsistence level of production. Capital accumulation processes within the community, in turn, led to the reinvestment of profits in commercial establishments, and in setting up larger production units beyond the artisanal household. These *karkhane* (workshops) benefited from improved technological applications that allowed the majority of production to shift to powerlooms and to include new raw materials like mixtures of silk and synthetic cloth (art silk).

Socio-culturally, these developments were marked by processes of distinction within the community extending to changes in religious practice – from predominantly Barelvi traditions to the increased inclusion of Wahhabi religious practices – female dress code and gender segregation to housing and educational patterns within richer neighbourhoods (Raman 2010; P. Williams 2015). Dipak Malik has depicted how the expansion of Muslim textile businesses in the late 1980s and early 1990s directly created flashpoints of communal tension, subsumed under the massive campaign of communal violence organized by the Hindu nationalist Bharatiya Janata Party in the early 1990s across northern and western India (Malik 1994). After the early 1990s, communal tensions driven by conflicting socio-economic interests between the (Hindu) mercantile elite and the (Muslim) industrial elite subsided, leading to a moderately stable equilibrium.

This social stratification facilitated the emergence of new credit sources, with more prosperous Ansari entrepreneurs becoming lenders in their own right. As with the merchants, the diversity of credit practices concerning interest payment is considerable. The main difference between the two groups of lenders lies mainly in the intention of lending – fixing prices and controlling labour for the merchants, depressing wages and controlling labour for the workshop owners. Reputational dynamics in these intentions are similar in their functional parameters, though their expression differs according to the cultural contexts. While I have come across Muslim lenders charging interest on top of using credit to depress wages – among them some who unabashedly asserted a distinction between religious injunctions against charging interest and their application in business practice – upward mobility frequently goes in tandem with orthodox religious practice. This pattern limits the charging of interest on loans to workshop employees, though it does not necessarily translate into lower exploitation. Religious and community practices may help debtors, but they also provide opportunities for the employer-creditor in restricting labour mobility and negotiating power. By and large, the choice of being indebted to petty industrialists or merchants rests on the needs of artisanal households. As Guérin has stated, poor families tend to make use of debt for purposes going beyond the immediate credit relationship (Guérin 2014). For an artisanal household still operating their own looms, indebtedness to a merchant provides a measure of stability in sales; for artisanal households working in *karkhane*, indebtedness to the *karkhanedar* increases opportunities for employment. The low inclination of Ansari lenders to charge interest, however, creates difficulties for their debtors in accessing petty consumer credit. Many debtors in this segment were unable to combine work process- and consumption-related loans in the way it is obtainable from merchants. Accordingly, consumption-related loans needed to be taken on from petty moneylenders who invariably resorted to standard rates of interest prevailing in petty lending.

Amateurization and sophistication – extra-legal trade credit

The second-largest segment in the number of transactions and the largest one in value is the segment of trade credit that is centred on the main bazaar area – Chowk and the adjoining neighbourhoods – where it reaches the highest level of sophistication, but spreads to all major commercial areas, though typically the neighbourhood remains the principal unit of market organization. Inter-linkages between commercial areas are frequent but less pronounced than within commercial areas. Outside of the bazaar, lending remains significantly more 'amateurish'. Lenders frequently participate on an ad-hoc basis, and there are few organizational patterns that go beyond gossip and interpersonal relations.

Many traders – within the bazaar or outside it – choose to borrow from moneylenders rather than the 'organized' credit sector in order to evade taxation, receive credit without purpose restrictions, much faster and less cumbersome, and to avail themselves of the greater degree of lenience in repayment. While the bazaar forms an enclave of sophistication, most participants remain 'amateurs' even here. Sophistication increases disproportionately wherever transactions are handled by specialists – facilitators and guarantors – who manage the transactions for a share in the profit (typically 1 per cent per month). Facilitators acquire knowledge on the supply and demand for credit among traders, negotiate the conditions of the transaction, and manage the process of repayment. Their services are reliable and exceedingly fast, even for high sums. Credit can also be arranged for areas outside the city, based on telecommunicated *hundi*s.[10] For most transactions within or across the city's commercial areas, documentation is rarely provided or even needed. Where documentation is given, it typically takes the less elaborate form of the *chitti* rather than the *hundi*.

Guarantors operate as an extra-legal insurance scheme. They take over the risks of default, but have (predominantly reputational) means of ensuring eventual repayment. The presence of specialists does not prevent traders from entering into transactions without their involvement, and even traders who make significant amounts of their income from lending do not necessarily involve specialists at all. A transaction involving facilitators and guarantors is both risk-free and effortless for the lenders, while transactions without specialists tend to be governed sufficiently well by reputational means to ensure the minimization of default. Principals start from about 2 lakh rupees and rarely go beyond 2 crore rupees. Loans are almost invariably short term, the segment in which extra-legal finance has the greatest comparative advantage. Rates of interest depend largely on the principals involved: 10 per cent per month for smaller loans and 5 per cent for larger loans. Interest rates are invariably simple. With good reputational standing, rates can fall as low as 1.5 to 2 per cent per month – competitive with 'organized' banking, especially given its additional advantages.

Sophistication extends to speculation and insider trading, especially in the gold market. There, interest rates fluctuate strongly, including loans with interest on an hourly basis. One per cent per hour was related as a typical rate when involving 'speculation'. Similar rates of interest can also be found among lenders targeting semi-organized gambling rackets. While these loans primarily target desperate gamblers attempting to recover losses, in the more speculative transactions agreed upon in the bazaar these loans are linked to local price variations, at times even during the course of a day. Once the availability of significant amounts of gold, for instance, has become known to some entrepreneurs, prices within the locality can drop drastically. Conversely, if bottlenecks in supply become known through the communication of insider knowledge derived from gossip or through techniques of 'divination' – as

Laura Bear depicted the process of obtaining supposedly robust information by street-level bureaucrats in Kolkata (Bear 2015) – prices may rise significantly over short periods. 'Knowledgeable' entrepreneurs may use speculative trade credit flows to stock up large quantities of gold ahead of these price surges to make windfall gains. As the medium of communicating the necessary information – and indeed the information itself – is dependent on imprecise tools and sources, speculating on price surges frequently fails too.

While this depiction of speculative processes is shared among many entrepreneurs, others derogatively described them as hyperbole. Few entrepreneurs outrightly dismissed the idea of rapidly fluctuating interest rates for speculative purposes, but many showed displeasure at what they considered boastful embellishments. Consequently, I am doubtful that interest rates of 1 per cent per hour occur beyond rare circumstances. What I do not doubt, however, is the availability of loans for hourly rates of interest, indicating an elaborate speculative market, with participants who can either reap substantial windfall gains from having assessed imprecise information correctly, or lose significant amounts of money on short notice. As with other speculative practices based on rapidly fluctuating markets, the dividing line between speculation and gambling can be very thin. While significant levels of speculation constitute important elements in trade credit, very mild practices loosely linked to speculation are much more common. One such practice that is commonly carried out by extra-legal entrepreneurs is related to as cheque discounting. Post-dated cheques are encashed at discounts, typically consisting of a one-time commission depending on the due date.

Most of the bazaar, however, specializes on slower-moving goods even in the wholesale segment. The main retail bazaar in Dal Mandi, in turn, offers a wide variety of consumer goods and, while characterized by high rates of footfall, does not rely considerably on – or provide incentives for – speculative practices. Consequently, much of the trade credit spectrum of extra-legal finance relies on considerably more solid capital flows. The need for extra-legal finance is related to difficulties in documenting credit purposes or, conversely, the intention to obscure income from the Indian state. Loans are available rapidly, at practically no effort to the borrower and without limitations in capital availability for the sums typically involved. As with the speculative credit flows, the market for trade credit operates surprisingly smoothly, almost invariably without the need to secure loans through collateral. In rare cases, the debtor's stock is transformed into collateral *after* default as compensation. Many lenders frown upon these practices, however. Taking possession of a debtor's stock reduces the defaulter's capacity to meet transactional obligations in the long term. As importantly, doing so incurs a heavy reputational fallout for the lender, and saddles the latter with goods that cannot easily be sold. As numerous lenders put it, there is a reason why a trader or shopkeeper stocks certain goods, or is incapable of selling them, and this reason frequently does not apply to another trader. Under normal circumstances, it simply makes more sense for the lender to wait until the defaulting debtor has managed to sell the goods, and then proceed to collect outstanding dues.

In the absence of collateral, reputational dynamics account most strongly for the stability of the trade credit system. Socio-spatial clustering and proximity help in communicating reputations, but the main dynamic rests on the maintenance of sufficient reputational standing to generate trust. Specialists such as facilitators and guarantors may become involved in a transaction once the money involved outstrips the utility of reputational means of generating trust, though many lenders and debtors involve specialists for the ease of doing business provided. In the absence of sufficient information on a market participant knowable through gossip or interpersonal relations, facilitators serve an important role in pooling capital, and in taking over the handling of reputational assessments. In less sophisticated transactions, a dearth of reputational information can be compensated by vouching for good conduct by other, known traders, or through introductions. As in the segment of petty lending, vouching and introductions serve to increase available information, but also spread the reputational fallout of misconduct more widely. The third parties involved indirectly in the transaction share in the negative reputational information that becomes available to the larger community through gossip, and have an incentive to make sure that the transactional terms are kept or, in case of their contravention, that these transgressions are handled in ways that remain within the boundaries set by the reputational parameters of the business.

Debtors and lenders alike face the need to maintain their reputation. One reason is that debtors and creditors may frequently change roles. More importantly though, it is not only the debtor's reputation that is observed and communicated, and – much more pronouncedly than in petty lending – it is not only creditors who rely on assessments of reputational standing. The decision whom to approach for a loan rests as much on established reputations as the decision whom to lend to. While default is less frequent in trade credit than in petty lending, it still occurs sufficiently often, especially intermittently, to lie at the heart of the reputational economy. While trade credit is technically legal, it is insufficiently documented and frequently involves elements that are at best operating in legal grey zones, so that legal redress does not constitute an option. Moreover, seeking recourse to the law attracts negative reputational fallouts that provide a considerable disincentive for any market participant.

The resulting ambiguity of the legal character of trade credit is pronounced. Most market participants were unable to summarize the legal stipulations related to trade credit. Almost invariably, they were loosely convinced that it was legal, or at least that it ought to be legal as it did not involve any 'immoral' practices as opposed to petty lending. It is notable that market participants insisting on the latter perception frequently confirmed openly that one of the main reasons for engaging in extra-legal finance at this level was to avoid taxation or regulatory compliance, both of which were not typically considered immoral. In some conversations with lenders, I took the definition of illegal money lending as defined by the charging of interest (to distinguish money lending from loans by friends or relatives) and omitted the exemptions to trade credit. When confronted with it, all lenders I spoke to immediately pointed out that my concocted legal definition must be incorrect, but few were capable of pointing out how.

Both in petty lending and in extra-legal trade credit, reputation is widely communicated throughout the market. But while much of the reputational dynamics in petty lending centre on the interpersonal relationship between creditor and debtor, and the direct renegotiation of transactional obligations after default, trade credit involves a significantly wider group of market participants and their reputations. This involvement commonly creates perceptions of the existence of an unwritten behavioural code that may be contextually specific and highly fluid, but is nevertheless substantial enough to create a sense of security in creditor–debtor relations, and moral opprobrium once it is considered to be breached.

In one instance, I arranged an improvised discussion group of two lenders and two debtors (indebted to other lenders). They discussed a case I had come across, and subsequently corroborated by interviewing the debtor involved: on intermittent but persistent default, a lender had raided the *sari* shop of the debtor and taken away stock claimed to be of equivalent value as the outstanding dues. The debtor accepted the loss of the *saris* in general but complained about the allegedly inflated amount of stock confiscated. He also was infuriated about the lender's rudeness and lack of circumspection as he had raided the shop openly during business hours instead of forewarning the debtor, and arriving in the early morning when the reputational fallout of the confiscation might have been contained. I had originally asked the discussion group to tell me whether the confiscation of stock was legitimate as it could plausibly be related to a creditor cutting losses. The discussion, however, immediately veered off to debate general moral dimensions of the reputational economy of debt, and eventually resulted in a detailed statement of the moral code to be followed in this situation: on having been informed in advance by the debtor of the imminent default, the lender should have offered to delay repayment twice for one month each without charging interest for these two months. After this, he could have charged additional interest as penalty, or confiscated property up to the amount of the outstanding interest, but not the principal. Charging additional interest as a penalty was the preferable option, as confiscating stock – while legitimate – should only be considered as a last resort. The debtor should have informed the lender of his expected future financial solvency, and the two should have proceeded to work out an arrangement that allowed the debtor to meet his obligations without overly endangering his business prospects, while also fulfilling the creditor's legitimate expectations. The confiscation did not need to be conducted with circumspection, though if the matter would have been solved in another way, it should have been done as secretly as possible. In case of confiscation, this need for circumspection was unnecessary as public knowledge of it formed part of the punishment dealt out legitimately. It was entirely up to the discretion of the creditor. In turn, rudeness constituted a major transgression of acceptable behaviour. Whatever the circumstances, both transactional parties needed to be considered as parts of the same market with rules applying to both, so that rudeness had no place under any circumstances. The creditor was very much entitled to show displeasure, though, and the debtor was similarly entitled once the lender's behaviour was breaching the injunction against rudeness.

The precision of the moral code of conduct outlined above was surprising, and it is important to avoid essentializing it. The same discussants might have arrived at a different interpretation on another day, or when discussing even slightly different cases. Other market participants might stress different moral angles. Obviously, the debtor and lender differed from the discussants' assessment. Yet the outlined behavioural code indicates specific dimensions of the reputational economy involved. First, while the creditor–debtor relationship certainly did not comprise a notion of partnership, it did involve an element of commonality. Both were part of the same market in a way that evoked a loose sense of community. Both needed to be aware that they were not merely involved in an interpersonal transaction, but in a transaction that legitimately was judged by other market participants whose assessment would indicate reputational standing in future transactions. Accordingly, both sides to the extra-legal debt contract needed to proceed with care, together constructing a viable solution to the original problem – persistent default.

Second, the debtor's default was entirely legitimate in itself. Intermittent default was part of the expected course of the business. The debtor was not in any way blamed for his default, since it was expected to be due to circumstances beyond his control. Even the persistence of default was not illegitimate. What was strongly admonished was the failure to communicate default in advance, and to offer a viable mechanism of redress that took care of the creditor's expectations of commensurate returns. In fact, the four discussants strongly agreed that advance communication and assisting the creditor in the eventual collection of dues would have resulted in reputational *gains* for the debtor that went beyond the reputational loss due to persistent default. They were, in fact, perplexed by my depiction of the incident in that it did not appear to involve any steps in this direction.

Third, the incidence of default made it imperative for the creditor to accept lower returns on investment, thereby easing the contractually stated obligations. While the creditor's legitimate claims needed to be taken care of, these could be deferred without additional interest. It is important to note that most extra-legal loans even in trade credit are short-term in character. Foregoing interest for the period of deferment constitutes significant losses through opportunity costs for the creditor who could employ his capital differently during these two months. Calculating at the typical interest rate for the kind of loan represented in the example, the lender was expected not only to agree but to actively offer reducing his returns by 10 per cent. In turn, persisting difficulties in repayment after this period of deferment could be compensated by penalty charges, thus increasing the creditor's gains beyond the stipulated obligations. Essentially, the contractual obligations initially agreed upon constituted a guideline for expected returns and commitments that remained considerably renegotiable.

Finally, circumspection was important, and the creditor had an obligation to consider the debtor's needs to maintain reputational standing. Yet this consideration did not necessarily imply that the creditor had to assist the debtor in maintaining reputation. Instead, the loss of reputation could legitimately be used as sanctions against misconduct. It is also noteworthy that there was no indication that the debtor should have refrained from narrating the alleged creditor's misconduct to me.

With reference to the discussion of the inherently reputational character of extra-legal credit contracts in Chapter 2, it is striking how much the contractual nature outlined in this case differs from both blueprints for credit relationships derivable from European traditions that informed the archetypal credit contract up to the early modern period and, respectively, after. The idea of credit as partnership imposed the obligation on the creditor to partake in the uncertainty inherent in credit, and thereby implicitly fixed the credit contract in favour of the debtor. The reinterpretation of the credit contract through postulating interest as rent, fixed at the time of contractual agreement regardless of future uncertainty, neatly overturned this element in favour of the creditor. In the example of the behavioural code representing the reputational credit contract, in turn, both transactional parties incur different but relatively balanced obligations in maintaining the viability of each other's interests despite the enhanced future orientation of the credit relationship. The relatively balanced nature of these obligations, in turn, reflects the comparatively low hierarchical difference between creditor and debtor in the trade credit segment. Similar dynamics that are visible in petty lending lead to highly different outcomes, with the debtor placed at a significant disadvantage in terms of the level of exploitation expected to be permissible as compensation for the risks involved, despite the element of lenience.

It is tempting to compare the operation of reputation on extra-legal credit markets to a system of parallel currencies or special-purpose monies (Bohannan 1959). A conflation with parallel currencies, however, misses several important aspects of the reputational economy of debt, even though reputation offers a system of value employed in exchange that allows a limited and difficult conversion of reputational into monetary value through credit. One cannot buy or sell reputation, and money converts into reputation with even more difficulties than vice versa, but credit allows for its partial translation into benefits that, in turn, have a monetary value. Rather than falling back on the concept of special-purpose monies, the relationship between the reputational and monetary elements of debt in Banaras can be related to Jane Guyer's interpretation of interfaces, though not 'interface currencies' (Guyer 2004). An interface, according to Guyer, forms a point of meeting where difference is maintained. Where reputation is converted into monetary benefits through the institution of credit, the difference between the two parallel operational principles is maintained – conversion does not directly affect reputation, for instance – but the existence of an interface facilitates the interaction of the parallel principles in ways that make partial conversions possible (though with difficulties) through the intermediation of credit.

Gossip, trust, and reputation

In extra-legal trade credit, the need to maintain reputation attains paramount importance. Losing reputation affects not only the future ability to borrow, but also the ability to lend. Debtors with low reputation are confronted with the situation that lenders will not lend to them, or will lend at higher rates. Those lenders willing to lend to debtors with low reputation are lenders with low reputation themselves, who are less likely to be lenient if the necessity arises, and the debtor's low reputation provides a pretext for refusing lenience. Conversely, these lenders will attract a clientele of low reputation which increases the likelihood of default and, thereby, the likelihood of strong enforcement – further lowering reputation. Losing reputation sets in motion a vicious cycle for both debtors and lenders alike. As debtors and lenders frequently interchange roles, losing reputation on one side of the transactional order almost immediately affects the other side too. The maintenance of high repute, in contrast, sets a virtuous cycle into motion that considerably facilitates the stability of credit relations. The entire system depends on communication flows centring on reputational information.

Reputational communication is primarily 'amateurish'. It rests either on direct interpersonal communication or on gossip. Gossip remains an under-researched topic in anthropology, despite its centrality to ethnography (Besnier 2009, 1). In the Indian context, gossip has been studied primarily in politics and communal violence (see, for instance, Das 1998; Brass 2003), but even in these fields it is frequently treated as a facilitating aspect of the object of inquiry. As discussed earlier, gossip as a means of establishing trust based on reputation provides significant information that cannot anymore be classified as interpersonal, but is not systemic either. It needs to be seen as an amalgamation of a multitude of interpersonal communications in which the original source (or an approximation thereof) – standing in for the robustness of information – remains identifiable with some difficulty. A participant in a communication system based on gossip therefore first and foremost needs to trust his or her own capability to assess the information carried by gossip for its robustness. Most lenders and many debtors highly prized their ability to obtain robust information, frequently expressed in exaggerations about their 'knowledge' and skill in 'playing the game'.

Gossip, however, at all times remains an imprecise tool to assess reputation and, therefore, maintain trust. In most cases related to extra-legal finance, this imprecision does not matter much. It is important here to understand trust as an artifice. Trust generates the pretence of knowledge, and maintaining this pretence stabilizes the transactional order sufficiently for its smooth operation.

Minor miscalculations in reputational assessment do not necessarily undermine trust as the system of lending retains considerable flexibility. High interest rates generate high returns on investment even when the lender is forced to forego some of the stipulated gains. The ubiquity of the understanding that actual returns do not correspond to stipulated obligations allows the lender to reach sufficiently satisfying gains without the detachment between actual and stipulated returns making it necessary to question the reliance on imprecise communication flows. The commensurability of expected returns on investment allows significant room for adjustment in the face of minor disappointments. For the debtor, the expectation of lenience serves to reinforce the understanding of skill in assessing information obtained through gossip regardless of whether lenience took place in precisely the anticipated manner. Generally speaking, the process of trusting reinforces the perceived validity of trust and, correspondingly, the prerequisite of trusting one's own capability of operating on a trust basis – as long as breaches of trust are contained at relatively low levels. The experiential character of trust reinforces the utility of trust and its operational viability. It generates the reasons on which the imprecision of gossip can be ignored, and the disregarding of the imprecision of gossip creates the validity of relying on trust, unless the breach of trust and the level of misinformation through gossip reach an unsustainable level. Relying on trust obtained through gossip becomes rational in its irrationality.

Accordingly, breaches of trust constitute the key aspect of what is communicated through gossip, and their communication is prone to overstatement. Paradoxically, the overstatement of breaches of trust stabilizes a communication order built on reputational information in that market participants take considerable care in avoiding these. The smooth functioning of extra-legal trade credit inherently creates its opposite in the low repute of both petty moneylenders and the clients indebted to them. Petty lending operates relatively smoothly as well, considering that debtors in this segment remain 'unbankable' to the extent that the elaborate juridical-procedural underpinnings of the 'formal' credit sector fail to serve these credit needs. Yet public 'knowledge' about breaches of trust in petty lending is pronounced, and the inherent hyperbole in their communication exaggerates their occurrence. In turn, the comparison between the two systems of lending on reputational terms boosts the anticipation of trustworthiness within the system of trade credit in equally overstated ways.

Frequent exposure to the convoluted logic of credit relations based on trust and reputational gossip increases the likelihood of minor cases of imprecise information, but also of skill involved in assessing information on major breaches. As the system of lending retains the high levels of flexibility necessary to disregard minor faults in calculability, experience in relying on imprecise information creates skill where it is needed. Frequent lenders in the trade credit segment actually become prone to miscalculate often, but only to extents that can still be adjusted. At the same time, they become skilled in identifying major threats to the system's operation. This skill is even more pronounced with specialists – facilitators and guarantors – whose businesses rely on their informational advantages over frequent lenders.

Sophisticated moral hazards

The dynamics of reputational communication intersect with the socio-spatial ordering of the monetary outside. They create boundaries for the operation of the credit systems, but also enclaves of relative sophistication within the market. Before discussing these dimensions, though, it is necessary to observe one more development within the informational underpinnings of extra-legal finance in Banaras in which questions of the communication order and the sophistication in generating robust information are interconnecting: the functional role attained by *bisi* circles in communicating reputations in nuanced ways. The combination of the imprecision of gossip and the difficulties in ascertaining its robustness result in a situation in which gossip may well carry nuanced information. Yet its assessment remains sufficiently doubtful to diminish its perception of robustness. The vast majority of extra-legal credit transactions do not need to rely on highly nuanced information as their inherent flexibility allows for adjustments. Being able to communicate highly nuanced reputational information, however, carries advantages especially in high-stakes transactions. In Banaras, the speculative 'game' of *bisi* has been employed by creditors and debtors alike to offer an alternative system of communicating nuanced trust and reputation, thus constituting a communication system distinct from yet interlinked with gossip.

Bisi constitutes one of the most interesting cases of sophistication in extra-legal finance, though it is not directly related to credit markets, except as a means to avoid borrowing: money circulation schemes such as *chit* funds or *bisi* circles were regarded positively in the drive towards formalizing financial markets in late colonial India. They were considered to constitute 'native' economic practices resembling the underlying tenets of cooperative credit. While the term *chit fund* has emerged as a generic expression for these financial practices, local idioms in Banaras tend to differentiate between the two, with the term *chit fund* describing larger, typically registered financial schemes that have gained notoriety for operating as Ponzi schemes. As opposed to this, *bisi* designates the smaller 'informal' and unregistered versions of the 'game' that is almost ubiquitously 'played' in Banarsi society. According to most 'players' I have interacted with, the 'game' is illegal – as it does not involve registration, or leaves paper trails – though in fact most *bisi* 'circles' fall well below the threshold of legal requirements for registration. *Bisi* forms part of a genre of speculative financial practices that are collectively described as rotating savings and credit associations (ROSCAs), an array of financial practices that are common in much of the contemporary Global South, but have also been known from the North American context (see, for instance, Ardener 1964; Bouman 1995). Jens Zickgraf (2018) has provided an overview on the various kinds of ROSCAs operating in south Indian villages, many of which can be found in contemporary Banaras as well.

Traditionally, a group of twenty players forms one circle, giving the 'game' its name, derived from the Hindi term for twenty. The circle is organized by its head. Rules are agreed upon in advance. The original idea of *bisi* resembles an SHG, though there is an element of gambling in it from the outset which typically is reinforced in the way it is practiced by most groups. Circle members pool money at regular intervals. Each member has a random chance to be allotted the pooled amount once. In this simple (and untypical) set-up, the sequence of winning marks the gambling element at its most basic level. An early slot provides the opportunity for early reinvestment, creating higher returns than if the money had been saved. Typically, though, the gambling element is strengthened. A typical *bisi* played among traders in Banaras works in the following way:

With twenty members contributing 5,000 rupees each per round, the overall pooled amount consists of 1 lakh rupees. However, the first rounds involve an auction. Players who intend to receive the pooled amount early offer to take a reduced amount, up to a pre-designated minimum. This minimum amount, in turn, increases each round. The first player who offers to take the designated minimum receives the slot, otherwise the lowest bid wins. The remainder of the pooled money is redistributed among the players.

Typically, this auction takes place in the first seven rounds, with the exception of the second round, which is reserved for the circle head (see Table 8.1). Auctioning increases the overall profit for the other players, and a skilled player who has acquired sufficient information about other players' intentions can reduce the money paid by making bids. A player who can benefit from early reinvestment can easily recover the initial loss due to the auction. Money lending constitutes one of the most profitable avenues

Table 8.1 A typical *bisi* circle as played by traders in Banaras

Number of players: 20		Pooled amount per round: 100,000 rupees		
Round	Selection by	Minimum Reduction	Maximum Reduction	Minimum Amount Paid
1	Auction	10,000	31,000	69,000
2	Reserved for Circle Head	–	–	100,000
3	Auction	10,000	27,500	72,500
4	Auction	10,000	24,000	76,000
5	Auction	10,000	20,500	79,500
6	Auction	10,000	17,000	83,000
7	Auction	10,000	13,500	86,500
8–20	Lot	–	–	100,000

Source: Ethnographic research by the author.

for reinvestments, but many players also benefit through other investments, exemplified by the owner of a famous low-frills lodge who used the proceeds of *bisi* to construct additional rooms before the start of the tourist season.

Bisi combines the idea of an SHG with practices of gambling, including their communication opportunities. While the 'game' is played among diverse sections of society, many of its players are engaged in extra-legal finance. *Bisi* can be a pastime. While the 'game' is socially disruptive due to the fallout of the incentive to default (see later), its socializing character attracts many people not engaged in extra-legal finance. Many circles are merely intended as an occasion for a friendly get-together. However, the 'game' has specific uses for extra-legal financial entrepreneurs, not only in bringing together a group of people, but particularly by providing a communication platform for nuanced reputational information that crucially supplements the primary mode of communicating reputation through gossip. The importance of the 'game' for the operation of the monetary outside in Banaras can be exemplified by the rags-to-riches story of Murli.

Murli was a shop worker when his employer tasked him with collecting information on prospective players. In return, his employer included Murli in his circles, and protected him from the inherent dangers of the 'game'. In this way, Murli learned how to operate as an extra-legal entrepreneur and, over time, accumulated sufficient capital to start his own extra-legal financial activities. He started lending money to cycle-rickshaw drivers, but also to head circles of shop workers. He continued informing his employer and playing in his circles, with significantly higher amounts involved, yet with lower risks due to his employer's protection.

The combination of petty lending and playing *bisi* was sufficiently profitable for Murli to stop working for wages. He concentrated on his extra-legal activities, and reinvested his profits in buying several small commercial establishments. Using contacts established through his employer's circles, he set up his own circles at higher levels, roughly equivalent to the trade credit segment. Playing *bisi* facilitated his subsequent shift from petty lending to extra-legal trade credit in that it provided the necessary contacts. It also supplemented the reputational information at this level he had already started obtaining as an informer. Eventually, he was sufficiently successful as an extra-legal entrepreneur to start investing in real estate, and he proceeded to initiate the shift to an even higher level of lending (and playing *bisi*), reaching the lower margins of high-end extra-legal finance.

At this point, however, Murli stopped. He feared that the risks he was taking outstripped his needs for further income, not only because the segment of high-end extra-legal finance involved risks he was ill-equipped to deal with as it involved a social space 'where local politics, business, and organized crime met', as he put it, but also because he had earned enough to retire from business, he claimed, and that while being involved in extra-legal entrepreneurship allowed for rapid upward mobility, it also impeded the public acceptance of his social rise. He abruptly terminated his extra-legal activities – in a way reminiscent of renunciation – and sold off most of his shops and real estate to patronize a form of traditional arts, becoming a locally respected public figure.

The example of Murli's extra-legal career illustrates important aspects of *bisi* for extra-legal finance in Banaras. What makes *bisi* risky (and socially disruptive) is its inherent incentive for default. A player who receives an early slot has an incentive to stop contributing to the circle. The lack of juridical-procedural parameters prevents legal redress. Because of this, *bisi* exposes its players to moral hazard, and it is this moral hazard that produces the utility of the 'game' for extra-legal finance as a communication platform for nuanced and robust reputational information. A pastime and mildly speculative practice resembling cooperative finance in late colonial India took on characteristics within the reputational economy of debt in Banaras that allowed market participants to fill an important lacuna in its system of communication.

There are several methods of handling the incentive for default. Defaulting can happen at various stages of the game, often through miscalculations over the ability to contribute. If a member of the circle defaults before receiving the 'slot', the impact is low. Typically, the head of the circle takes over the defaulter's slot. In case of default after receiving one's slot, responsibility for maintaining the circle's cohesion lies with its head. The circle head's reserved slot is primarily intended as an insurance against defaults. Once a second member defaults, other players will start to perceive the circle as instable, augmenting the incentive for default. This can be mitigated in two ways. Circle heads attempt to have a core group of members who are highly trusted. Often, up to five members heading different circles pledge to support each other. The cooperation of these players creates reciprocal expectations of obligation. If even the preselection of players is not sufficient in preventing further defaults, the head of the circle may decide to default as well. This spreads the responsibility for safeguarding the circle's cohesion, increasing the number of players with an interest to act against the defaulters. For a circle head, however, defaulting incurs a loss of reputation that is practically irrecoverable.

The socially disruptive character of the 'game' is evident in attempts by players to pressurize defaulters into continuing their commitments, at times including intimidation and petty violence, but more often simply disrupting relationships. Even when unsuccessful, these practices provide a disincentive for default, resembling the 'price' for lenience by petty lenders. Yet more importantly, *bisi* constitutes an arena for gaining rather than losing reputation. Its utility as an arena for communicating reputations centres on these gains. A sophisticated player of *bisi* may perceive monetary losses from the 'game' as an investment for reputational gains. The utility for gaining reputation is twofold: it facilitates interaction with potential partners, and can even serve as an initiation rite especially when crossing thresholds of lending. As importantly, it allows close scrutiny of the players' behaviour in situations of moral hazard, providing valuable reputational information. The players' behaviour is constantly scrutinized. Defaulting certainly carries significant losses in reputation, yet not all instances of default lead to similar conclusions in reputational information. A player can, for instance, communicate the likelihood of default in advance as long as the default is not wilful, thereby offsetting the loss by demonstrating reliability, resembling the behavioural code in trade credit discussed earlier.

The default of others also provides opportunities for gaining reputation. A player who continues to contribute to the fund after another player's default demonstrates commitment under conditions of considerable risk. There is a variety of manners in which reputational gains can be made – including continued commitment after an early slot or graciously accepting a late slot. The auctioning behaviour, in turn, can indicate means for profitable investment, while preferring the lot may show financial solvency. On entering the auction, the 'betting' behaviour is scrutinized. Negotiating each step of *bisi* carries complex reputational meanings. In turn, the scrutiny for reputational information will be communicated through gossip to a wider audience, though the biggest informational benefits accrue to the players involved.

Bisi allows for sacrifices for reputational gains by offering to take over a defaulter's obligation in part or in total, or in taking part in pressurizing defaulters. The circle heads, in turn, gain reputation by organizing well-functioning circles, and by fulfilling their commitments. Circle heads frequently participate in several circles simultaneously. Losses in one circle can be compensated from gains in other circles. As one player remarked, to have a manageable case of default in one circle while making material and reputational gains in other circles constituted a reasonably good combination, especially if the default in the first circle could be overstated in importance. Where *bisi* is linked to extra-legal finance, it uses the incentive to default as a moral hazard that allows for assessing the robustness of reputational information in ways that cannot be reached by information flows through gossip, even though these assessments in turn are feeding into gossip. *Bisi* accentuates the reputational dynamics of extra-legal finance, forming a parallel information grid to gossip and the socio-spatial ordering of the monetary outside in Banaras.

Socio-spatial dimensions of the reputational economy of debt

There are three different socio-spatial parameters in extra-legal finance in Banaras. Parameters arising from the relative sophistication (and higher capital flows) involved in trade credit have been depicted earlier. The role of collateral in extra-legal finance has ramifications that have been described with respect to urban real estate, displacement, and peri-urban lending. The third pattern reflects the reputational dynamics in petty lending to mobile and immobile clientele, and in trade credit. It is this pattern that I intend to highlight here, observing the linkage between communication flows and its spatial implications.

Regardless of the existence of enclaves of sophistication within the market, contemporary extra-legal finance needs to be interpreted as strongly 'amateurish' by the standards of the late colonial bazaar economy. Lenders targeting the poor in late colonial India were able to cover surprisingly large expanses of space, undermining reputational information flows.

'Amateurization', here, depicts a process of adjustment to the growing prominence of extra-legality in the ordering of the market, and the decline of mechanisms of enforcing obligations through strong social ties. The term reflects the growing importance of a reputational economy of debt centring on the maintenance of trust, and the communication flows underpinning it – especially through gossip so that the neighbourhood has become the principal boundary for most transactions. It is interesting to contrast the relationship between extra-legality and proximity with the example given by Narges Erami and Arang Keshavarzian (2015) on the impact of smuggling on the Iranian bazaar. Erami and Keshavarzian depict the introduction of highly organized forms of extra-legal entrepreneurship as facilitating greater distance between business partners, both in spatial and in social terms, resulting in enhanced short-term orientations – reducing temporal distance – in entrepreneurial behaviour. In turn, these results undermined the regulatory foundations of the bazaar resting on kinship and community, that is, the ability of employing reputational means to enforce contractual obligations. Similarly, Bayly depicted the ties binding 'indigenous' bankers to geographical areas through the local and regional anchoring of patronage networks (Bayly 1973, 355). Proximity, in both cases, facilitated reputational economies based on enforcement mechanisms, while in the Iranian case the introduction of enhanced forms of extra-legality undermined them. In the case of the reputational economy of debt in present-day Banaras, however, the socio-spatial boundaries of exchange were further constricted once the enforcement mechanisms for contractual obligations failed, and the neighbourhood emerged as the key unit of a reputational economy based on short-term transactions centring on trust.

On the lenders' side, the neighbourhood is where information on the reputation of potential clients is available, as most lenders cannot access robust information beyond its boundaries. What is more, there is no need to do so, as demand for credit is always sufficient to allow rapid accumulation. The neighbourhood sets the most important boundary for lending in almost all market segments through their reliance on gossip, but there are additional benefits to this restriction in petty lending such as the existence of nodal points within the neighbourhood that facilitate hierarchical difference and authority.

The most important of these is the shop. It provides an advantage to shop workers as long as their owners are absent, while working in a shop provides leeway in terms of labour discipline that can be exploited to engage in side-businesses. Shopkeepers in Banaras are frequently absent from the shop during the early hours of the day, that is, before most of the business is being conducted. Shop workers not only have privacy in their absence, but are in control of the environment in which the performance of renegotiating obligations is carried out. At the same time, the incentives for using the shop as a nodal point for extra-legal lending add another limitation to the area covered. Lenders become stationary and cannot lend to particularly mobile debtors who can easily evade them.

For the most mobile clientele, the neighbourhood restriction collapses to some extent: here, the nodal points may be strung out across neighbourhoods, as the lenders need to be present at various times of the day at places that assure reliable information flows, ideally in places that debtors cannot afford to avoid. For the debtors, this reinforces the tendency for performance in renegotiations: the defaulting debtor knows in advance that he is likely to meet the lender at certain places, and is therefore prepared to enter the negotiation. While lending to mobile clientele is not strictly bounded within a neighbourhood, the areas covered by these debtors frequently form a contingent area, and the main nodal points where the debtors can be intercepted by lenders – and where information on debtors' reputation (and whereabouts) is accessible – are often centrally located within these neighbourhoods. A third pattern reinforcing the boundedness of petty lending to the neighbourhood is related to residential patterns, as visible in the case of Arjan depicted at the outset of this chapter. Petty neighbourhood lenders like Arjan depend on a stable clientele with strong connections to the neighbourhood in which the lender resides. Often, they live in the same neighbourhood, though they also may be connected to it through friends and relatives, or may have lived there before moving out.

The reputational underpinning of the socio-spatial ordering of extra-legal markets also extends to debtors. Debtors need to avoid the creditors at times, but they also need to be able to locate them, to reach initial agreements, or to renegotiate terms. As importantly, they need to make sure that their reputation is accessible to the lender through gossip, since it is difficult to get a loan from a lender who cannot identify a debtor's reputation. Conversely, there is one spatial dimension that directly counters the importance of the neighbourhood – a geography of shame. Especially with infrequent borrowers, local gossip also carries the certainty of their misfortune becoming publicly known, so that some borrowers try to contact moneylenders in faraway neighbourhoods, accepting low reputational standing to avoid public awareness of their plight elsewhere. As it is difficult to approach a lender who does not know the client's reputation, these debtors frequently rely on introductions by family or friends, which tends to defeat the purpose of secrecy. Yet the geography of shame in petty lending does not revolve around secrecy, but on the handling of reputational information available through gossip. There is a face-saving difference between gossip that is supposed to be secret and gossip that is considered to be openly known. Reputational information that is not supposed to be openly known will also be carried by gossip, but its handling – and thereby its ramifications – are subtly different. Most debtors, however, and especially those who are frequently indebted have little inclination to avoid public awareness. In fact, public knowledge of indebtedness carries reputational significance as it also comprises knowledge about the debtor's behaviour in debt. Being known to be indebted often constitutes the prerequisite for building up the reputational standing necessary to become a market participant.

In trade credit, the role of shame is less pronounced. Typically, debt here has positive meaning in that it shows investment opportunities. At the same time, shops that have fallen on hard times also fall back on extra-legal loans. However, as the handling of debt is central to business, the ability to handle debt at times of distress still allows debtors to transform it into at least partially positive reputation. To illustrate this briefly in one case, a shopkeeper had a strong reputation of being in debt despite his shop's relative profitability. The shopkeeper was known locally as a particularly unskilled gambler who regularly lost money betting on cricket scores without understanding the sport. When I interviewed him formally, he immediately started to turn my awareness of his financial plight into a demonstration of his skills in handling extra-legal lenders. He always got the best rates, he claimed, and eventually he always defaulted, leaving the moneylender with little gain. When I pointed out the accumulation of payments before default in the loans he listed, he shrugged off the comment. Being indebted was part of life, he said, and he was used to it. Having other people know that he was hopelessly in debt was unproblematic, as they also knew how skilled he was in handling it. To some extent, these assertions were correct: while his standing among nearby shopkeepers was not particularly high, he was certainly depicted as shrewd enough to be if not respected then at least accepted in his status. When his debts eventually became unmanageable, he handled his repayment obligations by turning his shop into a part-time petty brothel, attracting public reproach but not in ways that comprehensively undermined his reputation. He finally lost much of his reputation in a different – if related – event, once his wife found out about the prostitution, and took over the shop's management.

Gossip plays similar roles in petty lending and in trade credit, though the extent to which gossip replaces interpersonal communication is more pronounced in the latter. Correspondingly, the neighbourhood pattern is equally visible in trade credit, the main difference lying in the prevalence of commercial over residential patterns. The dependence of the socio-spatial ordering of the market on communication flows is visible in relative sophistication. The central bazaar, located in the Pakka Mahal, subsumes several neighbourhoods into one. The density of communication links for establishing reputation through gossip in this part of the city is considerably greater than beyond it, allowing this merging of commercial areas into a cohesive entity.

Conclusion

Reputation relies on its communication, and the prevalent tool for this communication has severe limits, not just in assessing the robustness of information. Gossip goes well beyond the interpersonal, involving information on people who are *not* fully known. Yet its boundaries lie in the identifiability of the people gossiped upon. One does not need to be intimate with people to be sufficiently interested in engaging in gossip on them, but it is imperative to be able to find out sufficient details for this interest to become sustained. Reputational communication, in the same way as trust, relies on sustaining its experiential character. The supposedly insurmountable 'informational advantage' attributed to the figure of the village moneylender in official reports to demonstrate why 'organized' finance was not replacing these creditors rests on the embeddedness of extra-legal entrepreneurs in the communication structures governing these markets – that, in turn, have been shaped by communication flows on reputational information.

For most of the history of Indian finance, many of its components were shaped by the need to find ways of stabilizing debtor–creditor relations in the absence of state intervention. This long practice of making credit work in the absence of the state as regulator, arbitrator, and guarantor of credit contracts has supplied financial markets in Banaras with diverse repertoires of credit, many of which can be subsumed under the bazaar economy. While Ray postulated the demise of the bazaar, its influence on everyday transactional socialities in Banaras is difficult to overlook. However, extra-legal finance has evolved in ways that underline considerable changes over the portrayal of the bazaar economy across disciplinary divides. It has emerged as a market that at times makes use of what may be described as residues of the bazaar (Schwecke 2021), but in other ways it is closer to the depiction of western African slum economies by Hart (1988). Its repertoires, even when derived from practices associated with the bazaar, have been shaped crucially by the encounter with the political project – driven by both big industrial capital and the Indian state – of 'modernizing' Indian credit markets and with its ramifications. If the absence of the law is what defines the market's extra-legality, its operational principles rely on communication processes that enable market participants to stabilize an exploitative market. This stabilization certainly benefits creditors. Yet it also provides what little protection debtors have at their disposal, without which the level of exploitation would be unsustainable – and without which a vast segment of the Indian population would have no hope of obtaining credit for the purposes they need it for.

Reputation serves diverse ends and cannot be condensed to fulfilling a single functional role. In extra-legal finance as operating in Banaras, however, its most important function – and the reason for its criticality for the market – is to facilitate the generation of high-trust relations in a market that most observers instinctively would construe as non-conducive to the operation of trust. Reputation underpins high-trust relations as the only possible instrument of stability in the face of heightened uncertainty due to the absence of other means to contain default. Rather than the absence of the law, it is the enhanced likelihood of default that creates the need for a reputational economy of debt where the law becomes inoperative. The communication of reputation to secure high-trust relations may appear as a socio-cultural construct – and it takes specific forms due to this construction. Yet ultimately – reminiscent of the way in which the specific form of the credit contract in capitalist economies emerges as a key component in what makes credit capitalist – it takes on material characteristics as the only form allowing the operation of credit flows in the absence of the state and sufficient incentives for acquiring collateral rather than accumulating interest (as argued by the Agricultural Credit Survey cited at the outset of this chapter) and in the face of the decline of the strong social ties and mercantile ethics that defined credit in the bazaar economy.

Observing the economy of Nima, Hart asked what took the place of law in economic relations when the state was absent and extrapolations of statuses defined as tradition had collapsed. In urban north Indian extra-legal finance, this place has been occupied by a conception of trust and reputation that enmeshes these concepts to the extent of becoming indistinguishable. Many market participants used English-language terms whenever they referred to trust and reputation, but they also used these terms interchangeably. If they used a Hindi term, they referred to trust and reputation as *vishvaas*, a term that literally mirrors the Latin roots of *credit* in faith, believing, trusting – but that instead is being used to describe reputation that inherently facilitates high-trust relations on a market otherwise unsuited to it. Bankers have no trust, as David Rudner stated before proceeding to demonstrate the importance of trust among the Nattukottai Chettiars. Moneylenders and their clients in contemporary Banaras *need* to trust.

Notes

1. *AIRCS*, 171.
2. The names of extra-legal entrepreneurs in this book, where given at all, have been changed. Where names are given, they have been added to facilitate a more direct writing style, and were selected to prevent identification, not to further it. Even where extra-legal finance is not illegal, many practices associated with it are. In turn, debt always necessitates respect for privacy. Debtors' names have been omitted entirely. Place names and descriptions for places where the operation of extra-legal financial markets was observed are also deliberately left vague to prevent identification. In general, my ethnographic research was carried out across a large number of neighbourhoods in Banaras, mostly between 2011 and 2017. The neighbourhoods that have been covered the most in this include the main bazaar area (the Pakka Mahal), especially Chowk, Dalmandi, Raja Darwaza, Godowlia, and Golghar, and neighbourhoods in the south and west of the city, particularly Assi, Shivala, Sonarpura, Lanka, BHU, Samneghat, Sigra, Rathyatra, Mahmoorganj, Reori Talab, Madanpura, Laksa, Bhelupur, Sankat Mochan, Kamaccha, Gurubagh, Kashi Vidyapeeth, and Nadesar. In the northern parts of the city (beyond the Pakka Mahal), research was carried out particularly in Lahurabir, Beniya Bagh, Chetganj, and Kotwali.
3. On the problems associated with creating historical evidence from oral sources, see Portelli (1991).
4. See, among others, Haynes (2012) and Harriss-White (2010, 2016).
5. See, among others, Bear (2015) and Levien (2012).
6. See http://www.belstar.in/product.php (last accessed 26 March 2020).
7. Ibid.
8. *Fatehchand Himmatlal and Ors.* v. *State of Maharashtra*, 28 January 1977, 1977 *Latest Caselaw* 39 SC.
9. First information reports filed with the police that do not lead to the initiation of court cases are periodically destroyed instead of being archived, so that earlier reports unfortunately were not accessible any more.
10. Telecommunicated *hundis* use orally transmitted codes. The code sometimes uses the unique identification number of small denomination rupee notes that are cut in half with both sides remaining in possession of the code.

9

Conclusion

The popular image of the village money lender is of a rapacious scoundrel who impoverishes people by lending money at exorbitant rates.... From the [World] Bank's perspective the village money lender is a monopolist who retards the development of free market forces, ... someone to be eliminated in the name of progress. This line has been uncritically adopted by many progressive organizations in India. The actual practice of village money lending is much more complex, however, and we must be wary of oversimplifications.[1]

The production of a monetary outside in Banaras rested on two interlinked developments – the establishment of credit markets suitable for the expansion of capitalism and the responses by market participants in the segments that could not be served by capitalist credit. The former delineated the inside of the larger market by excluding from its outside the crucial principle that allowed for the aggregation of substantial credit flows necessary for mature capitalist accumulation, a conglomeration of regulatory practices establishing the common capitalist intelligibility of the credit contract as an instrument that fixed the enhanced uncertainty of credit relations in favour of the creditor. Faced with its incapacity to extend these regulatory mechanisms to credit practices serving the needs of vast segments of the Indian population – and with its unwillingness to provide the capital that would have sufficiently improved socio-economic conditions for them to participate in it – the Indian state eventually tolerated the prevalence of extra-legality by largely ignoring its existence.

The responses of market participants, in turn, *shaped* what had been delineated as a monetary outside. The delineation process of improper transactions never considered how credit markets were operating beyond the state's reach – apart from caricaturist portrayals of greed, violence, and the supposedly insurmountable informational advantage of 'the moneylender'.[2] Market participants did not need to shape only a market that necessarily operated extra-legally but one that needed to operate in the absence of what had been the predominant forms of making extra-legality work.

The reputational credit contract in India in the nineteenth century rested on the employment of social ties and/or elaborate systems of mercantile ethics rooted in the ability of the market's apex to incentivize emulation. The collapse of these mechanisms was facilitated, even if indirectly, by the project to delineate the monetary inside, although its roots also related to larger socio-economic developments. In consequence, extra-legal finance in contemporary Banaras differs strongly from its colonial predecessors, with its operational viability ensured by the communication flows underlying a reputational economy of debt relying almost exclusively on trust instead of the enforcement of contractual obligations. The emergent system was sufficiently stabilized in the process. It also works relatively smoothly, and at its higher levels even comprises borrowing costs that are competitive with state-regulated banking. For most of the urban poor, it works fairly smoothly in ways that ensure the viability of levels of exploitation through credit that go considerably beyond what was considered outrageous by colonial officials – hardly the most sympathetic judges.

The failure of the 'modernization' project in Indian credit markets since 1855 rested on the ubiquity of default on credit transactions that nevertheless were necessary to sustain livelihoods or fulfil aspirations of upward mobility. The success of extra-legal financial entrepreneurs rested on finding ways in which the pronounced likelihood of default – further enhancing the uncertainty inherent in all credit transactions – could be managed, creating a reputational economy of debt centring on high levels of trust where few observers would expect it. Rather than being the direct outcome of state policy – which only dominated its delineation – extra-legal finance is the consequence of an enhanced likelihood of default, the corollary of socio-economic conditions.

If extra-legal finance is perceived as the result of conditions further enhancing the likelihood of default on credit markets, then the tragedy of its continued prevalence is that policy initiatives that originally sought to regulate or criminalize it have instead merely narrowed down the reputational means available to make credit work, without providing either operational alternatives or improving socio-economic conditions conducive to mature capitalist credit relations. The unwillingness to consider options beyond the 'pristine purity of banking concepts' stipulated as a panacea by the Indian state reinforced the neglect of alternatives, while the empty promises of the benefits of the juridical-procedural parameters of the credit contract enabled it to defer the enactment of viable policies into the distant future. If policies failed, implementing more of the same policies would eventually fulfil the dreamwork of policy planners. Arjun Appadurai's notion of the magical procedurality of capitalism was conceived to describe something that actually worked, but for most lower-class debtors this dreamwork produced a persistent nightmare. There is an eerie resemblance between the planners' belief that following the same strategies that had failed before would lead to different outcomes *this time* and the act of pretence in entering a trust-based relationship – of acting as if one trusted in order to make trust work in spite of its regular breaches. The difference between the two lies in the fact that the artifice of the latter works, if only in the face of minor breaches, while the former continues to be imposed as a grand panacea in spite of its demonstrable failure.

The refusal to contemplate reputational means to handle the enhanced uncertainty of credit relations, finally, needs to be seen in perspective. In Isabelle Guérin's study of microfinance practice in south Indian villages, debtors transgress the juridical-procedural parameters of these schemes – operating under the logic of the capitalist credit contract – by misreporting, while the higher levels of microfinance organizations rely on misreported information to declare the schemes' success. Misreporting, in this case, fulfils two functions in undermining the capitalist conception of credit in order to make it work in a context marked by high levels of default.

Not only is the funding available to debtors through microfinance insufficient to meet needs, despite restrictions on taking on or declaring other loans from 'non-institutional' sources, but alternative credit sources comprise different advantages through the non-contractual element in the credit contract and translate into assets under conditions of chronic indebtedness. Self-help groups collude in misreporting and in employing reputational means to contain the 'misuse' of funds within levels that facilitate the schemes' actual success on the ground as much as their reporting as successes. Credit practice on the ground first needs to transgress the prescribed operational parameters and then use the means available to make credit work in the face of handling the pronounced levels of uncertainty. Both the transgression of juridical-procedural parameters of the credit contract and the employment of reputational means to minimize default permit the schemes to become one of the portfolios of debt available to female villagers, allowing microfinance to serve the actual credit needs of its recipients.

In turn, since the first decade of the twenty-first century, the corporate sector of the Indian economy has been plagued by ballooning debts held primarily by the country's nationalized banking sector. The Indian state's response to this crisis of non-performing assets (NPA) was initially marked by tendencies to change rules regarding the declaration of NPA, thus allowing banks to keep NPA as productive assets in their books, even as repayment became increasingly doubtful. While this policy changed to some extent around the middle of the 2010s, more recent policies introduced by the RBI have followed principles of substantial debt relief in return for the continued commitment to pay reduced debt obligations. With persistent repayment problems, these policies amount to considerable debt forgiveness.

Bailing out corporate firms may be unpopular, and possibly counterproductive, but it is equally true that not bailing out these firms may have disastrous consequences. Regardless of its merits and demerits, what is notable in RBI policy on NPA is that it unintentionally copies the playbook of Banarsi moneylenders. It uses reputational means to extract as much repayment as possible where legal enforcement of debt obligations fails. These policies defer repayments based on assumptions that the standing of the firms and, correspondingly, their ability to communicate default without significant loss of reputation will enforce a part of their debt obligations when they eventually can be met in an undefined future. Essentially, the reputational handling of uncertainty is extended to the one segment of the economy that could be expected to be able to meet the demands placed on the debtor by the notion of the credit contract that fixes uncertainty for the creditor in the present. In turn, the 'sanctity' of the credit contract, 'freely' entered into at the time of agreement by the debtor, and its juridical-procedural underpinnings are compromised in the face of the 'unbankability' of segments of India's corporate sector and the economic fallout of enforcing debt obligations.

The lenience demonstrated by the RBI comes with significant opportunity costs for the Indian state and its nationalized banks even in the best-case scenario of eventual full repayment of credit commitments, but it also relies on the assumption that corporate units *will* eventually repay as much as possible to safeguard their future creditworthiness. Implicitly – in fact very much unstated – the RBI policy on NPA followed a two-step approach, first tinkering with the juridical-procedural parameters of the credit contract by allowing banks to misreport assets, before shifting towards an implicit realization that 'unbankable' credit obligations needed to be served by employing reputational means. In both the cases outlined here, the increased likelihood of default prevents the operational viability of the juridical-procedural parameters underlying the capitalist credit contract, resulting in a lending practice in which creditors and debtors make use of reputational means to make credit work. Extra-legal financial entrepreneurs in Banaras follow the very same logic. Being moneylenders, and having been provided with the opportunity to operate on a credit market that continues to be left to its own devices, the outcome of money lending is exceedingly high levels of exploitation. There is no need to exculpate scorpions for stinging for realistically expecting the likelihood of moneylenders resorting to exploitation. It might be worth considering whether the 'impure' concepts underlying the reputational economy of debt can be applied in less exploitative ways than by Banarsi moneylenders.

Notes

1. Gregory (1988, 52).
2. On the possibility to overcome this supposed advantage by formal credit agents, see, for instance, Kar (2013).

Glossary

anna   a currency unit; until 1957 the rupee was subdivided into 16 *anna*s, 64 *paise*, and 192 *pie*s

arhat   a firm's agency; a managing agency

arhatia/arhatiya   an agent of a firm; a middleman/intermediary, especially in agricultural trade; an intermediary-cum-lender involved in financing this trade and at times in speculation as well

bahi   an account book; the practice of bookkeeping, especially in traditional Indian accountancy

Bania   a member of the *bania* caste group; a moneylender from these castes; sometimes used generically to denote moneylenders

basti   a slum, typically of small or medium size

bepari (*beopari*)   a trader in agricultural produce; a middleman/intermediary in agricultural trade also involved in financing this trade and in speculation; typically a lower-order intermediary than the *arhatia*

bhakti   a diverse group of religious practices across religions in India centring on devotion to God

bisi   derived from the Hindi term for twenty; in Banaras a local variant of money circulations schemes (see *chit fund*) that is invariably unregistered and operates extra-legally, though typically not illegal

chit fund   a money circulation scheme; a rotating savings and credit association; in local usage in Banaras indicating a large and registered scheme that may involve Ponzi schemes

chit   generic term for informally drawn promissory documents typically without legal sanction

chitti   see *chit*

dadan   wages given as advances, especially to artisanal labourers, carrying no interest but typically restricting labour mobility

damdupat   a rule restricting the accumulation of interest, typically interpreted as restricting repayment to twice the principal

darshani hundi   a *hundi* payable to the bearer of the document, often depicted as a sight bill

derha	a set of interest rates; 50 per cent over an agricultural season of up to six months, frequently compounded at twice-yearly rests
dharna	a form of protest typically involving a sit-in
goladari	lit.: storage, warehousing; a system of warehousing that allowed the operation of various credit and speculation practices in the Indian bazaar economy
Harhia	a typically itinerant moneylender to the poor from a community in eastern Uttar Pradesh and Bihar especially known for the employment of public shaming for recovering dues
hundi	a set of financial instruments involving elements of a promissory document and/or bill of exchange; while in circulation, it can be discounted; there are various sub-types of *hundi*s, though the precise meaning is given in the wording for each *hundi*
jajmani	the right/privilege to specific shares of produce, mostly in village economies; this right/privilege can frequently be traded
Kabuli	in the context of credit practices: a typically itinerant moneylender to the poor with a background of migration from Afghanistan or the British Indian border areas with Afghanistan; also depicted as Pathan
Kabuliyat	a term used in nineteenth-century India denoting a promissory document, not necessarily involving Kabuli lenders
kacca	a term depicting a state of being that has not reached its conclusion; typically depicting the aspects of not being ripe or solid (see *pakka*)
kantipat	a (relatively obscure) variant of the rule of *damdupat* that allowed the accumulation of interest to twice the principal
karkhana	pl.: *karkhane*; a small factory or workshop
karkhandar	the owner of a small factory or workshop
len-den	lit.: giving and taking; an expression used to denote exchange; typically depicting exchange relations that are not (entirely) legal or perceived as legitimate
mahajan	a substantial moneylender or banker, frequently involved in trading, especially in wholesale trade, and warehousing; frequently involved in financing trade
muddati hundi	a *hundi* payable at a specified due date, often depicted as a time bill
mufassil	lit.: something that is far away; areas outside the major metropolises, hinterland; in colonial India frequently describing the area outside the Presidency towns

munim	an accountant; typically an accountant for a large family firm, especially among banking families
nazrana	a commission fee for loans against high personal security, typically involving large principals
nidhi	lit.: treasure; a set of collective savings and credit practices, at times involving elements of co-operative credit
paisa	pl.: *paise*; a currency unit; until 1957, the *anna* was subdivided into 4 *paise* (64 *paise* to the rupee); since 1957 the rupee is subdivided into 100 *paise*; in colonial sources occasionally depicted as 'pice'
pakka	a term depicting a state of being that has reached its conclusion; typically depicting the aspects of being ripe or solid (see *kacca*)
Pakka Mahal	description used for the neighbourhoods comprising the old city of Banaras, primarily the main bazaar area of town
panch	lit.: five; here: a member of a *panchayat*
panchayat	a council of 'respectable' community members or local notables; in independent India including a division of the local administrative structure
pie	the lowest currency unit in the subdivision of the rupee until 1957; 3 *pie*s equalled 1 *paisa* (192 *pie*s to the rupee)
qist	lit.: instalment; a system of unsecured loans based on a variety of repayment modes
qistwallah	a petty lender, giving loans according to the *qist* system
rozahi	lit.: daily; a system of payment collection among unsecured loans (see *qist*) with typically daily collections
sahukar	a moneylender; the term is sometimes used generically for moneylenders, but frequently denotes a trader/shopkeeper-cum-lender, both in villages and towns
sakh	lit.: credit; denoting a merchant family's reputational standing
sarkhat	an informally drawn-up promissory document among traders in the bazaar
sarraf (shroff)	a moneylender or banker typically targeting prosperous clientele
sawai	a set of interest rates; 25 per cent over an agricultural season of up to 6 months, frequently compounded at twice-yearly rests
shreni	a honorific for groups of people, loosely describing high social status; people of rank and status
suudkhor	lit.: usurer; a generic term for moneylenders involved in lending to the poor
taccavi	a system of loans by the state or a ruler for the purposes of agricultural development especially of large estates; in colonial

	India mostly used as a measure for alleviating socioeconomic crises
ugahi	lit.: collection; a system of payment collection among unsecured loans (see *qist*) with typically monthly collections
vishvaas	lit.: faith, belief; a term also denoting trust, especially trust in its relationship to reputation; a term frequently used by creditors and debtors in Banaras to describe reputation
zamindar	a landowner; typically a large (and sometimes absent) landowner over land fragmented into a variety of tenancy systems
zamindari	the land owned by a *zamindar*, typically fragmented into a variety of tenancy systems

References

Amin, Shahid. 1981. 'Peasants and Capitalists in Northern India: Kisans in the Cane Commodity Circuit in Gorakhpur in the 1930s'. *Journal of Peasant Studies* 8 (3): 311–34.

Anonymous. 1918. *All About Benares: Containing a Sketch from the Vedic Days to the Modern Times with Many Illustrations, and a Map of Benares and Its Environs.* Madras: K. S. Muthiah & Co. By an Old Resident with a Foreword by P. Seshadri Iyengar.

Appadurai, Arjun. 2015. 'Afterword: The Dreamwork of Capitalism'. *Comparative Studies of South Asia, Africa and the Middle East* 35 (3): 481–85. https://doi.org/10.1215/1089201X-3426325.

———. 2016. *Banking on Words: The Failure of Language in the Age of Derivative Finance.* Chicago: University of Chicago Press.

Ardener, Shirley. 1964. 'The Comparative Study of Rotating Credit Association'. *Journal of the Royal Anthropological Institute of Great Britain and Ireland* 94 (2): 201–29.

Arrighi, Giovanni. 1996. *The Long Twentieth Century: Money, Power, and the Origins of Our Times.* London: Verso.

Bagchi, Amiya Kumar. 1981. 'Merchants and Colonialism'. Occasional Papers. Occasional Paper No. 38. Centre for Studies in Social Sciences Calcutta.

———. 1985. 'Transition from Indian to British Indian Systems of Money and Banking, 1800–1850'. *Modern Asian Studies* 19 (3): 501–19.

———, ed. 2002. *Money and Credit in Indian History: From Early Medieval Times.* New Delhi: Tulika Books.

Banaji, Jairus. 1977. 'Capitalist Domination and the Small Peasantry: Deccan Districts in the Late Nineteenth Century'. *Economic and Political Weekly* 12 (33–34): 1375–404.

———. 2016. 'Merchant Capitalism, Peasant Households and Industrial Accumulation: Integration of a Model'. *Journal of Agrarian Change* 16 (3): 410–31.

Baty, Thomas. 1906. 'Bargains with Money-Lenders'. *Journal of the Society of Comparative Legislation* 7 (2): 392–96.

Bayly, C. A. 1973. 'Patrons and Politics in Northern India'. *Modern Asian Studies* 7 (3): 349–88.

———. 1983. *Rulers, Townsmen, and Bazaars: North Indian Society in the Age of British Expansion, 1770–1870.* 1st ed. Cambridge (Cambridgeshire), New York: Cambridge University Press.

———. 1999. *Empire and Information: Intelligence Gathering and Social Communication in India, 1780–1870.* New Delhi: Cambridge University Press.

———. 2011. 'Merchant Communities: Identities and Solidarities'. In *The Oxford India Anthology of Business History*, edited by Medha M. Kudaisya, 99–121. Oxford: Oxford University Press.

———. 2011. 'The Family Firm: A Microcosm'. In *The Oxford India Anthology of Business History*, edited by Medha M. Kudaisya, 169–83. Oxford: Oxford University Press.

Bear, Laura. 2015. 'Capitalist Divination: Popularist Speculators and Technologies of Imagination on the Hooghly River'. *Comparative Studies of South Asia, Africa and the Middle East* 35 (3): 408–23.

Bellamkonda, Ramesh. 2007. *Real Interest Rates Prevalent in Informal Money Lending in India, and Its Implications for Public Policy Making for Micro Credit in India.* Available online at https://tinyurl.com/esk2xd2h (last accessed 17 May 2020).

Bellot, Hugh H. L. 1906. *The Legal Principles and Practice of Bargains with Money-Lenders in the United Kingdom of Great Britain and Ireland, British India, and the Colonies.* 2nd enlarged ed. London: Stevens and Haynes Law Publishers.

Bentham, Jeremy. 1787/1818. *Defence of Usury: Shewing the Impolicy of the Present Legal Restraints on Pecuniary Bargains in a Series of Letters to a Friend.* London: Payne and Foss.

Bernstein, J. L. 1965. 'Background of a Gray Area in Law: The Checkered Career of Usury'. *American Bar Association Journal* 51 (9): 846–50.

Besnier, Niko. 2009. *Gossip and the Everyday Production of Politics.* Honolulu: University of Hawai'i Press.

Bhatia, Jai. 2019. 'Crime in the Air: Spectrum Markets and the Telecommunications Sector in India'. In *The Wild East? Criminal Political Economies across South Asia*, edited by Barbara Harriss-White and Lucia Michelutti, 140–67. London: UCL Press.

Bhattacharya, B. 2008. 'The "Book of Will" of Petrus Woskan (1680–1751): Some Insights into the Global Commercial Network of the Armenians in the Indian Ocean'. *Journal of the Economic and Social History of the Indian Ocean* 51 (1): 67–98.

Bhattacharya, Neeladhri. 2018. *The Great Agrarian Conquest: The Colonial Reshaping of a Rural World.* Ranikhet: Permanent Black.

Birla, Ritu. 2009. *Stages of Capital: Law, Culture, and Market Governance in Late Colonial India.* Durham, NC, London: Duke University Press.

―――. 2015. 'Speculation Illicit and Complicit: Contract, Uncertainty, and Governmentality'. In 'Speculation', edited by Timothy Mitchell and Anupama Rao. Special issue, *Comparative Studies of South Asia, Africa and the Middle East* 35 (3): 392–407.

Bismillah, Abdul. 1986. *Jhini-Jhini Bini Cadariyan.* New Delhi: Rajkamal Prakashan.

Bissonnette, Jean Francois. 2019. 'The Political Rationalities of Indebtedness: Control, Discipline, Sovereignty'. *Social Science Information* 58 (3): 454–68.

Blunt, Alison. 2002. '"Land of Our Mothers": Home, Identity, and Nationality for Anglo-Indians in British India, 1919–1947'. *History Workshop Journal* 54 (1): 49–72.

Bohannan, Paul. 1959. 'The Impact of Money on an African Subsistence Economy'. *Journal of Economic History* 19 (4): 491–503.

Bottomley, Anthony. 1963. 'The Cost of Administering Private Loans in Underdeveloped Rural Areas'. *Oxford Economic Papers*, New Series 15 (2), July: 154–63. Available online at http://www.jstor.org/stable/2661780 (last accessed 18 July 2014).

―――. 1964. 'Monopoly Profit as a Determinant of Interest Rates in Underdeveloped Rural Areas'. *Oxford Economic Papers*, New Series 16 (3): 431–37.

Bouman, J. C. Fritz. 1995. 'ROSCA: On the Origins of the Species'. *Savings and Development* 19 (2): 117–48.

Brass, Paul R. 2003. *The Production of Hindu–Muslim Violence in Contemporary India.* Seattle: University of Washington Press.

Braudel, Fernand. 1982. *The Wheels of Commerce.* New York: Harper & Row.

Breman, Jan. 1978. 'Seasonal Migration and Co-Operative Capitalism: The Crushing of Cane and of Labour by the Sugar Factories of Bardoli, South Gujarat'. Part 1. *Journal of Peasant Studies* 6 (1): 41–70.

―――. 2007. *Labour Bondage in West India: From Past to Present.* New Delhi: Oxford University Press.

Callewaert, Winand, ed. 2009. *Dictionary of Bhakti: North-Indian Bhakti Texts into Kharī Bolī Hindī and English.* With the assistance of S. Sharma. New Delhi: D. K. Printworld.

Callewaert, Winand, and Swapna Sharma, eds. 2000. *The Millenium Kabir Vani.* New Delhi: Manohar.

Carey, Matthew. 2017. *Mistrust: An Ethnographic Theory* 3. Chicago, IL: Hau Books.

Catanach, I. J. 1970. *Rural Credit in Western India, 1875–1930: Rural Credit and the Co-Operative Movement in the Bombay Presidency*. Berkeley: University of California Press.

Chandavarkar, A. G. 1965. 'The Premium for Risk as a Determinant of Interest Rates in Underdeveloped Rural Areas: Comment'. *Quarterly Journal of Economics* 79 (2): 322–25.

Charlesworth, Neil. 1972. 'The Myth of the Deccan Riots of 1875'. *Modern Asian Studies* 6 (4): 401–21. https://doi.org/10.1017/S0026749X00004285.

Chatterjee, Partha. 2008. 'Democracy and Economic Transformation in India'. *Economic and Political Weekly* (19 April): 53–62.

Chaudhury, Sushil. 2019. 'More on Van Leur's "Pedlar" Thesis'. *Studies in People's History* 6 (2): 202–9.

Chavan, Pallavi. 2003. 'Moneylender's Positive Image: Regression in Development Thought and Policy'. *Economic and Political Weekly* 38 (50): 5301–04.

Chibber, Vivek. 2003. *Locked in Place: State-Building and Late Industrialization in India*. Princeton, Ewing: Princeton University Press.

Cirvante, V. R. 1956. *The Indian Capital Market*. London: Geoffrey Cumberledge, Oxford University Press.

Codr, Dwight. 2016. *Raving at Usurers: Anti-Finance and the Ethics of Uncertainty in England, 1690–1750*. Charlottesville: University of Virginia Press.

Cohn, Bernard S. 1960. 'The Initial British Impact on India: A Case Study of the Benares Region'. *Journal of Asian Studies* 19 (4): 418–31.

———. 1965. 'Anthropological Notes on Disputes and Law in India'. *American Anthropologist (New Series)* 67 (6): 82–122.

———. 1987. *An Anthropologist among the Historians and Other Essays*. Delhi, New York: Oxford University Press.

———. 1996. *Colonialism and Its Forms of Knowledge: The British in India*. Princeton, NJ, Chichester: Princeton University Press.

Corsín Jiménez, Alberto. 2011. 'Trust in Anthropology'. *Anthropological Theory* 11 (2): 177–96. https://doi.org/10.1177/1463499611407392.

Dalmia, Vasudha. 1997. *The Nationalization of Hindu Traditions*. Delhi, New York: Oxford University Press.

Damodaran, Harish. 2008. *India's New Capitalists: Caste, Business, and Industry in a Modern Nation*. Ranikhet: Permanent Black.

Das, Veena. 1998. 'Specificities: Official Narratives, Rumour, and the Social Production of Hate'. *Social Identities* 4 (1): 109–30.

Das Gupta, Ashin. 2001. *The World of the Indian Ocean Merchant 1500–1800*. Oxford: Oxford University Press.

Day, Sophie, E. Papataxiarches, and Michael Stewart, eds. 1999. *Lilies of the Field: Marginal People Who Live for the Moment*. Boulder: Westview Press.

Desai, Madhuri. 2017. *Banaras Reconstructed: Architecture and Sacred Space in a Hindu Holy City*. Seattle: University of Washington Press.

Dietrich Wielenga, Karuna. 2016. 'Repertoires of Resistance: The Handloom Weavers of South India, c.1800–1960'. *International Review of Social History* 61 (3): 423–58. https://doi.org/10.1017/S0020859016000535.

Durkheim, Émile. 2013. *The Division of Labour in Society*. Basingstoke: Palgrave Macmillan.

Elsenhans, Hartmut. 2007. *Geschichte Und Ökonomie Der Europäischen Welteroberung: Vom Zeitalter Der Entdeckungen Zum Ersten Weltkrieg*. Leipzig: Leipziger Universitätsverlag. Herausgegeben mit einem Vorwort von Matthias Middell.

———. 2015. *Saving Capitalism from the Capitalists: World Capitalism and Global History*. Los Angeles: Sage.

Erami, Narges, and Arang Keshavarzian. 2015. 'When Ties Don't Bind: Smuggling Effects, Bazaars and Regulatory Regimes in Postrevolutionary Iran'. *Economy and Society* 44 (1): 110–39. https://doi.org/10.1080/03085147.2014.909986.

Farr, Ian. 2001. 'Farmers' Cooperatives in Bavaria, 1880–1914: "State-Help" and "Self-Help" in Imperial Germany'. *Rural History* 18 (2): 163–82.

Freitag, Sandria B. 1989. *Collective Action and Community: Public Arenas and the Emergence of Communalism in North India*. Berkeley: University of California Press.

———. 1995. 'State and Community: Symbolic Popular Protest in Banaras' Public Arenas'. In *Culture and Power in Banaras: Community, Performance, and Environment, 1800–1980*, edited by Sandria B. Freitag, 203–29. New Delhi: Oxford University Press.

Fremantle, S. H. 1907/1928. *Co-Operative Societies in the United Provinces*. With the assistance of revised by P. M. Kharegat. 6th ed. Allahabad: Government Press, United Provinces.

Fuller, C. J. 1989. 'Misconceiving the Grain Heap: A Critique of the Concept of the Indian Jajmani System'. In *Money and the Morality of Exchange*, edited by. Jonathan Parry and Maurice Bloch, 33–63. Cambridge: Cambridge University Press.

Gambetta, D. 1988. 'Can We Trust Trust?' In *Trust: Making and Breaking Cooperative Relations*, edited by D. Gambetta, 213–37. New York: Blackwell.

Gandhi, Ajay. 2013. 'A Superlative Form: How Gold Mediates Personhood and Property in Mumbai'. *Ethnofoor* 25 (1): 91–110.

Gandhi, Ajay, Barbara Harriss-White, Douglas E. Haynes, and Sebastian Schwecke, eds. 2020. *Rethinking Markets in Modern India: Contested Jurisdiction and Embedded Exchange*. Cambridge: Cambridge University Press.

Geertz, Clifford. 1979. 'Suq: The Bazaar Economy in Sefrou'. In *Meaning and Order in Moroccan Society*, edited by Clifford Geertz, Hildred Geertz, and Lawrece Rosen, 123–244. Cambridge: Cambridge University Press.

———. 1963. *Peddlers and Princes: Social Change and Economic Modernization in Two Indonesian Towns*. Chicago: The University of Chicago Press.

Gooptu, Nandini, ed. 2013. *Enterprise Culture in Neoliberal India: Studies in Youth, Class, Work and Media*. London, New York: Routledge.

Goswami, Omkar. 1989. 'Sahibs, Babus, and Banias: Changes in Industrial Control in Eastern India, 1918-50'. *The Journal of Asian Studies* 48 (2): 289–309.

Graeber, David. 2001. *Toward an Anthropological Theory of Value: The False Coin of Our Own Dreams*. New York: Palgrave.

———. 2011. *Debt: The First 5,000 Years*. New York: Melville House.

Granovetter, Mark. 2011a. 'Economic Action and Social Structure: The Problem of Embeddedness'. In *The Sociology of Economic Life*, edited by Mark Granovetter and Richard Swedberg, 22–45. Boulder: Westview Press.

———. 2011b. 'The Impact of Social Structure on Economic Outcomes'. In *The Sociology of Economic Life*, edited by Mark Granovetter and Richard Swedberg, 46–61. Boulder: Westview Press.

Granovetter, Mark, and Richard Swedberg, eds. 2011. *The Sociology of Economic Life*. Boulder: Westview Press.

Gregory, Christopher A. 1988. 'Village Money Lending, the World Bank and Landlessness in Central India'. *Journal of Contemporary Asia* 18 (1): 47–58.

Guérin, Isabelle. 2008. 'L'argent Des Femmes Pauvres: Entre Survie Quotidienne, Obligations Familiales Et Normes Sociales'. *Revue Francaise de Socio-Économie* 2 (2): 59–78.

———. 2014. 'Juggling with Debt, Social Ties, and Values'. *Current Anthropology* 55 (Supplement 9): 40–50. https://doi.org/10.1086/675929.

Guérin, Isabelle, Bert D'Espalier, and Govindan Venkatasubramanian. 2013. 'Debt in Rural South India: Fragmentation, Social Regulation and Discrimination'. *The Journal of Development Studies* 49 (9): 1155–71.

Guinnane, Timothy W. 2001. 'Cooperatives as Information Machines: German Rural Credit Cooperatives, 1883–1914'. *The Journal of Economic History* 61 (2): 366–89.

Gupta, Bunny, and Jaya Chaliha. 2011. 'Historical Continuity and the Present-Day Bazaar'. In *The Oxford India Anthology of Business History*, edited by Medha Kudaisya, 77–81. Oxford: Oxford University Press.

Guyer, Jane I. 2004. *Marginal Gains: Monetary Transactions in Atlantic Africa*. Chicago, London: University of Chicago Press.

Habib, Irfan. 1964. 'Usury in Medieval India'. *Comparative Studies in Society and History* 6 (4): 393–419.

Hann, Chris. 2007. 'A New Double Movement? Anthropological Perspectives on Property in the Age of Neoliberalism'. *Socio-economic Review* 5 (2): 287–318.

Hann, Chris and Keith Hart. 2011. *Economic Anthropology: History, Ethnography, Critique.* Cambridge: Polity.

Hardiman, David. 1996a. *Feeding the Baniya: Peasants and Usurers in Western India.* Delhi, Oxford: Oxford University Press.

———. 1996b. 'Usury, Dearth and Famine in Western India'. *Past and Present* 152 (1): 113–56.

Harriss-White, Barbara. 2003. *India Working: Essays on Society and Economy.* Cambridge: Cambridge University Press.

———. 2010. 'Local Capitalism and the Foodgrains Economy in Northern Tamil Nadu, 1973–2010'. MIDS Working Paper Series, Chennai.

———. 2016. *Middle India and Urban-Rural Development: Four Decades of Change.* 1st ed. New Delhi: Springer.

———. 2017. 'Rethinking Institutions: Innovation and Institutional Change in India's Informal Economy'. *Modern Asian Studies* 51 (6): 1727–55. https://doi.org/10.1017/S0026749X16000603.

———. 2018. 'Awkward Classes and India's Development'. *Review of Political Economy* 30 (3): 355–76.

Hart, Keith. 1973. 'Informal Income Opportunities and Urban Employment in Ghana'. *Journal of African Studies* 11 (1): 61–89.

———. 1988. 'Kinship, Contract, and Trust: The Economic Organization of Migrants in an African City Slum'. In *Trust. Making and Breaking Cooperative Relations,* edited by Diego Gambetta, 176–93. Oxford: Blackwell.

———. 2000. *The Memory Bank. Money in an Unequal World.* London: Profile Books.

———. 2018. 'A Betting Man's Reflections on Money'. The Memory Bank, 1–17. Available online at https://thememorybank.co.uk/2018/01/09/a-betting-mans-reflections-on-money/ (last accessed 27 August 2021).

Hart, Keith, and Horacio Ortiz. 2014. 'The Anthropology of Money and Finance. Between Ethnography and World History'. *Annual Review of Anhtropology* 43: 465–82.

Harvey, David. 2004. 'The "New" Imperialism: Accumulation by Dispossession'. *Socialist Register* 40: 63–87.

Haynes, Douglas E. 1999. 'Just Like a Family? Recalling the Relations of Production in the Textile Industries of Surat and Bhiwandi, 1940–60'. *Contributions to Indian Sociology* 33 (1–2): 141–69.

———. 2012. *Small Town Capitalism in Western India: Artisans, Merchants and the Making of the Informal Economy, 1870–1960.* Cambridge, New York: Cambridge University Press.

————. 2015. 'Advertising and the History of South Asia, 1880–1950'. *History Compass* 13 (8): 361–74. https://doi.org/10.1111/hic3.12252.

Hull, Matthew. 2020. 'Market Making in Punjab Lotteries: Regulation and Mutual Dependence'. In *Rethinking Markets in Modern India. Contested Jurisdiction and Embedded Exchange*, edited by Gandhi Ajay, Barbara Harriss-White, Douglas E. Haynes, and Sebastian Schwecke, 294–321. Cambridge: Cambridge University Press.

Jafri, S. N. A. 1931. *The History and Status of Landlords and Tenants in the United Provinces (India)*. Allahabad: The Pioneer Press.

Jain, L. C. 1929. *Indigenous Banking in India*. London: Macmillan & Co.

————. 1933. *The Monetary Problems of India*. London: Macmillan.

Jeffrey, Craig. 2002. 'Caste, Class, and Clientelism: A Political Economy of Everyday Corruption in Rural North India'. *Economic Geography* 78 (1): 21–41.

Joshi, Chitra. 2003. *Lost Worlds: Indian Labour and Its Forgotten Histories*. Delhi: Permanent Black.

Joshi, Esha Basanti, ed. *Uttar Pradesh District Gazetteers, Varanasi*. Allahabad: Government of Uttar Pradesh, 1965.

Kar, Sohini. 2013. 'Recovering Debts: Microfinance Loan Officers and the Work of "Proxy-Creditors" in India'. *American Ethnologist* 40 (3): 480–93.

————. 2017. 'Relative Indemnity: Risk, Insurance, and Kinship in Indian Microfinance'. *Journal of the Royal Anthropological Institute* (New Series) 23 (2): 302–19.

————. 2018. *Financializing Poverty: Labor and Risk in Indian Microfinance*. Redwood City: Stanford University Press.

Kaur, Ravinder. 2014. 'Bodies of Partition: Of Widows, Residue, and Other Historical Waste'. In *Histories of Victimhood*, edited by Steffen Jensen and Henrik Rønsbo, 1st ed., 44–63. Philadelphia: University of Pennsylvania Press.

Kochanek, Stanley. 1986. 'Regulation and Liberalization Theology in India'. *Asian Survey* 26 (12): 1284–308.

Kudaisya, Medha M., ed. 2011. *The Oxford India Anthology of Business History*. Oxford: Oxford University Press.

Kulke, Hermann, ed. 1997. *The State in India: 1000–1700*. Delhi: Oxford University Press.

Kumar, Nita. 1988. *The Artisans of Banaras: Popular Culture and Identity, 1880–1986*. Princeton: Princeton University Press.

Labat, Alyssa, and Walter E. Block. 2012. 'Money Does Not Grow on Trees: An Argument for Usury'. *Journal of Business Ethics* 106 (3): 383–87.

Leonard, Karen. 1978. *Social History of an Indian Caste: The Kayasths of Hyderabad*. Berkeley: University of California Press.

————. 1979. 'The "Great Firm" Theory of the Decline of the Mughal Empire'. *Comparative Studies in Society and History* 21 (2): 151–67.

————. 2013. 'Palmer and Company: An Indian Banking Firm in Hyderabad State'. *Modern Asian Studies* 47 (4): 1157–84.

Levien, Michael. 2012. 'The Land Question: Special Economic Zones and the Political Economy of Dispossession in India'. *Journal of Peasant Studies* 39 (3–4): 933–69.

Liisberg, Sune. 2015. 'Trust as the Life Magic of Self-Deception: A Philosophical-Psychological Investigation into Tolerance of Ambiguity'. In *Anthropology and Philosophy: Dialogues on Trust and Hope*, edited by Sune Liisberg, Esther O. Pedersen, and Anne L. Dalsgard, 1st ed., 158–76. New York: Berghahn Books.

Liisberg, Sune, Esther Oluffa Pedersen, and Anne Line Dalsgard, eds. 2015. *Anthropology and Philosophy: Dialogues on Trust and Hope*. 1st ed. New York: Berghahn Books.

Luhmann, Niklas, Howard H. Davis, John Raffan, and Kathryn Rooney. 1979. *Trust and Power: Two Works by Niklas Luhmann*. Chichester: Wiley.

Luxemburg, Rosa. 1913/2003. *The Accumulation of Capital*. London: Routledge.

Malik, Dipak. 1994. 'Three Riots in Varanasi: 1989–90 to 1992'. *South Asia Bulletin* 14 (1): 53–56.

Malinowski, Bronislaw. 2014 [1922]. *Argonauts of the Western Pacific*. Abingdon: Routlegde.

Markovits, Claude. 1999. 'Indian Merchant Networks outside India in the Nineteenth and Twentieth Centuries: A Preliminary Survey'. *Modern Asian Studies* 33 (4): 883–911.

————. 2001. 'Introduction. Circulation and Society under Colonial Rule'. In *Mobile People and Itinerant Cultures in South Asia, 1750–1950*, edited by Claude Markovits, 1–22. London: Anthem Press.

————. 2008. *Merchants, Traders, Entrepreneurs: Indian Business in the Colonial Era*. Ranikhet: Permanent Black.

————. 2013. 'The Colonised as Global Traders: Indian Trading Networks in the World Economy, 1850–1939'. In *the Foundations of Worldwide Economic Integration. Power, Institutions, and Global Markets, 1850–1930*, edited by Christof Dejung and Nils P. Petersson, 158–78. Cambridge: Cambridge University Press.

Martin, Marina. 2009. 'Hundi/Hawala: The Problem of Definition'. *Modern Asian Studies* 43 (4): 909–37. https://doi.org/10.1017/S0026749X07003459.

Marx, Karl. 1967. *Capital: A Critique of Political Economy*. Vol. 1. New York: International Publishers.

Mauss, Marcel. 1970. *The Gift: Forms and Functions of Exchange in Archaic Societies*. London: Cohen & West.

Menon, Visalakshi. 2003. *From Movement to Government: The Congress in the United Provinces, 1937–42*. New Delhi: Sage.

Mews, Constant J., and Ibrahim Abraham. 2007. 'Usury and Just Compensation: Religious and Financial Ethics in Historical Perspective'. *Journal of Business Ethics* 72 (1): 1–15.

Mishra, Kamala Prasad. 1975. *Banaras in Transition: (1738–1795)*. New Delhi: Munshiram Manoharlal Publ.

Mitchell, Timothy and Anupama Rao, ed. 2015. 'Speculation'. Special issue, *Comparative Studies of South Asia, Africa and the Middle East* 35, no. 3.

Mohanty, B. B. 2013. 'Farmer Suicides in India: Durkheim's Types'. *Economic and Political Weekly* 48 (21): 45–54.

Möllering, Guido. 2001. 'The Nature of Trust: From Georg Simmel to a Theory of Expectation, Interpretation and Suspension'. *Sociology* 35 (2): 403–20.

Munn, N. D. 1986. *The Fame of Gawa: A Symbolic Study of Value Transformation in a Massim (Papua New Guinea) Society*. Cambridge: Cambridge University Press.

Münster, Daniel. 2012. 'Farmers' Suicides and the State in India: Conceptual and Ethnographic Notes from Wayanad, Kerala'. *Contributions to Indian Sociology* 46 (1–2): 181–208.

Nagaraj, K., P. Sainath, R. Rukmani, and R. Gopinath. 2014. 'Farmers' Suicides in India: Magnitudes, Trends, and Spatial Patterns, 1997–2012'. *The Journal of the Foundation for Agrarian Studies* 4 (2), July–December: 53–84.

Nazir, Pervaiz. 2000. 'Origins of Debt, Mortgage and Alienation of Land in Early Modern Punjab'. *Journal of Peasant Studies* 27 (3): 55–91.

Oak, Mandar, and Anand Swamy. 2010. 'Only Twice as Much: A Rule for Regulating Lenders'. *Economic Development and Cultural Change* 58 (4): 775–803.

Orwell, George. 1950. *Shooting an Elephant and Other Stories*. Repr. London: Secker and Warburg.

Pandey, Gyan. 1981. 'Economic Dislocation in Nineteenth Century Eastern up: Some Implications of the Decline of Artisanal Industries in Colonial India'. CSSSC Working Papers 37.

Parry, Jonathan. 1989. 'On the Moral Perils of Exchange'. In *Money and the Morality of Exchange*, edited by Jonathan Parry and Maurice Bloch, 64–93. Cambridge: Cambridge University Press.

———. 1994. *Death in Banaras*. Lewis Henry Morgan Lectures. Cambridge: Cambridge University Press.

Parry, Jonathan, and Maurice Bloch, eds. 1989. *Money and the Morality of Exchange*. Cambridge: Cambridge University Press.

Parthasarathi, Prasannan. 2011. *Why Europe Grew Rich and Asia Did Not: Global Economic Divergence, 1600–1850*. Cambridge: Cambridge University Press.

Patnaik, Prabhat. 2008. *The Value of Money*. New Delhi: Tulika Books.

Patnaik, Utsa. 2007. 'New Data on the Arrested Development of Capitalism in Indian Agriculture'. *Social Scientist* 35 (7–8): 4–23.

Peebles, Gustav. 2010. 'The Anthropology of Credit and Debt'. *Annual Review of Anthropology* 39 (1): 225–40. https://doi.org/10.1146/annurev-anthro-090109-133856.

———. 2013. 'Washing Away the Sins of Debt: The Nineteenth-Century Eradication of the Debtors' Prison'. *Comparative Studies in Society and History* 55 (3): 701–24.

Perlin, Frank. 1983. 'Proto-Industrialization and Pre-Colonial South Asia'. *Past and Present* 98 (1): 30–95.

———. 1993. *The Invisible City: Monetary, Administrative and Popular Infrastructures in Asia and Europe 1500–1900.* Aldershot: Variorum.

———. 2020. *City Intelligible: A Philosophical and Historical Anthropology of Global Commoditisation before Industrialisation.* Leiden: Brill.

Persky, Joseph. 2007. 'Retrospectives: From Usury to Interest'. *The Journal of Economic Perspectives* 21 (1): 227–36.

Polanyi, Karl. 2001 [1944]. *The Great Transformation: The Political and Economic Origins of Our Time.* 2nd Beacon Paperback ed. Boston, MA: Beacon Press.

Portelli, Allessandro. 1991. *The Death of Luigi Trastulli and Other Stories: Form and Meaning in Oral History.* Albany: State University of New York Press.

Prakash, Gyan. 1990. *Bonded Histories: Genealogies of Labor Servitude in Colonial India.* Cambridge: Cambridge University Press.

Puri, Stine Simonsen. 2014. 'Speculation in Fixed Futures: An Ethnography of Betting in Between Legal and Illegal Economies at the Delhi Racecourse'. PhD thesis, University of Copenhagen.

———. 2015. 'Betting on Performed Futures: Predictive Procedures at Delhi Racecourse'. In 'Speculation', edited by Timothy Mitchell and Anupama Rao. Special issue, *Comparative Studies of South Asia, Africa and the Middle East* 35 (3): 466–80.

Raheja, Gloria Goodwin. 1988. *The Poison in the Gift: Ritual, Prestation, and the Dominant Caste in a North Indian Village.* Chicago: University of Chicago Press.

Rajagopal, Arvind. 2011. 'The Emergency as Prehistory of the New Indian Middle Class'. *Modern Asian Studies* 45 (5): 1003–49.

Raman, Vasanthi. 2010. *The Warp and the Weft: Community and Gender Identity among Banaras Weavers.* New Delhi: Routledge.

Rao, Parimala V. 2003. 'Peasant in the Nationalist Discourse: Bal Gangadhar Tilak and the Deccan Agriculturists Relief Act 1879'. *Proceedings of the Indian History Congress* 64: 803–21.

————. 2009. 'New Insights into the Debates on Rural Indebtedness in 19th Century Deccan'. *Economic and Political Weekly* 44 (4): 55–61.

Rawal, Tanya. 2015. 'Debt Sentences: The Poetics and Politics of Credit Culture in India, Italy, and the Inland Empire, 1930–Present'. Ph. D. thesis, University of California, Riverside.

Ray, Rajat Kanta. 1988. 'The Bazaar: Changing Structural Characteristics of the Indigenous Section of the Indian Economy before and after the Great Depression'. *The Indian Economic and Social History Review* 25 (3): 263–318.

————. 1995. 'Asian Capital in the Age of European Domination: The Rise of the Bazaar, 1800–1914'. *Modern Asian Studies* 29 (3): 449–554. https://doi.org/10.1017/S0026749X00013986.

Reddy, S. T. Somashekhara. 2007. 'Diary of a Moneylender'. *Economic and Political Weekly* 42 (29): 3037–43.

Richards, J. F. 1981. 'Mughal State Finance and the Premodern World Economy'. *Comparative Studies in Society and History* 23 (2): 285–308.

Robb, Peter. 2013. 'Mr Upjohn's Debts: Money and Friendship in Early Colonial Calcutta'. *Modern Asian Studies* 47 (4): 1185–2017.

Rockoff, Hugh. 2003. 'Prodigals and Projectors: An Economic History of Usury Laws in the United States from Colonial Times to 1900'. NBER Working Paper 9742.

Roth, Hans-Dieter. 1979. 'Moneylenders' Management of Loan Agreements: Report on a Case Study in Dhanbad'. *Economic and Political Weekly* 14 (28): 1166–70.

————. 2007. *Indian Moneylenders at Work: Case Studies of the Traditional Rural Credit Market in Dhanbad District, Bihar.* New Delhi: Manohar. Foreword by Dietmar Rothermund.

Rothermund, Dietmar. 1992. *India in the Great Depression: 1929–1939.* New Delhi: Manohar.

Rotman, Andy. 'Brandism vs. Bazaarism: Mediating Divinity in Banaras'. In *Rethinking Markets in Modern India. Contested Jurisdiction and Embedded Exchange*, edited by Ajay Gandhi, Barbara Harriss-White, Douglas E. Haynes, and Sebastian Schwecke, 234–68. Cambridge: Cambridge University Press.

Roy, Tirthankar. 1999. *Traditional Industry in the Economy of Colonial India.* Cambridge: Cambridge University Press.

————. 2016. 'The Monsoon and the Market for Money in Late-Colonial India'. *Enterprise and Society* 17 (2): 324–57.

Rudner, David. 1989. 'Banker's Trust and the Culture of Banking among the Nattukottai Chettiars of Colonial South India'. *Modern Asian Studies* 23 (3): 417–58. https://doi.org/10.1017/S0026749X00009501.

————. 1994. *Caste and Capitalism in Colonial India: The Nattukottai Chettiars.* Berkeley: University of California Press.

Rudnyckyj, Daromir, and Filippo Osella, eds. 2017. *Religion and the Morality of the Market*. Cambridge: Cambridge University Press.

Sahai, Nandita Prasad. 2006. *Politics of Patronage and Protest: The State, Society, and Artisans in Early Modern Rajasthan*. New Delhi: Oxford University Press.

Sanyal, Kalyan. 2007. *Rethinking Capitalist Development: Primitive Accumulation, Governmentality and Post-Colonial Capitalism*. New Delhi: Routledge.

Saraf, Aditi. 2021. 'Trust amid "Trust Deficit": War, Credit, and Improvidence in Kashmir'. *American Ethnologist* 47 (4): 387–401.

Schulze, Brigitte. 2002. 'The Cinematic "Discovery of India": Mehboob's Re-Invention of the Nation in Mother India'. *Social Scientist* 30 (9–10): 72–87.

Schwecke, Sebastian. 2021. 'Merchants, Moneylenders, Karkhanedars, and the Emergence of the Informal Sector'. In *Routledge Handbook of Colonial South Asia*, edited by Harald Fischer-Tiné and Maria Framke, 145–55. Abingdon: Routledge.

———. 2018. 'A Tangled Jungle of Disorderly Transactions? The Production of a Monetary Outside in a North Indian Town'. *Modern Asian Studies* 52 (4): 1375–419.

———. 2020. 'The Artifice of Trust: Reputational and Procedural Registers of Trust in North Indian Informal Finance'. In *Rethinking Markets in Modern India. Contested Jurisdiction and Embedded Exchange*, edited by Ajay Gandhi, Barbara Harriss-White, Douglas E. Haynes, and Sebastian Schwecke, 147–78. Cambridge: Cambridge University Press.

Scott, James C. 1998. *Seeing Like a State: How Certain Schemes to Improve the Human Condition Have Failed*. New Haven: Yale University Press.

Seabright, Paul. 2010. *The Company of Strangers: A Natural History of Economic Life*. Princeton, NJ: Princeton University Press.

Sen, Sudipta. 1998. *Empire of Free Trade: The East India Company and Making of the Colonial Marketplace*. Philadelphia: University of Pennsylvania Press.

Sewell, William Hamilton. 2005. *Logics of History: Social Theory and Social Transformation*. Chicago: University of Chicago Press.

Shah, Mihir, Rangu Rao, and P. S. Vijay Shankar. 2007. 'Rural Credit in 20th Century India: Overview of History and Perspectives'. *Economic and Political Weekly* 42 (15): 1351–64.

Sharma, Shishir, and S. Chamala. 1998. 'Moneylender and Banker in Rural India'. *Savings and Development* 22 (1): 107–30.

———. 2003. 'Moneylender's Positive Image: Paradigms and Rural Development'. *Economic and Political Weekly* 38 (17): 1713–20.

Shetty, S. L. 2012. *Microfinance in India: Issues, Problems, and Prospects: A Critical Review of Literature*. New Delhi: Academic Foundation.

Shirras, George Findlay. 1920. *Indian Finance and Banking*. London: Macmillan & Co.

Shukla-Bhatt, Neelima. 2014. *Narasinha Mehta of Gujarat: A Legacy of Bhakti in Songs and Stories*. New York: Oxford University Press.

Simha, S. L. N. 1970. *History of the Reserve Bank of India: (1935–51)*. Bombay: Reserve Bank of India.

Simmel, Georg. 1950. *The Sociology of Georg Simmel*. Edited by Kurt H. Wolff. Glencoe: Free Press.

———. 2004. *The Philosophy of Money*. London: Routledge.

Singha, Radhika. 1998. *A Despotism of Law: Crime and Justice in Early Colonial India*. Oxford: Oxford University Press.

Sinha, H. 1927. *Early European Banking in India (with Some Reflections on Present Conditions)*. London: Macmillan & Co.

Srivastava, Sanjay. 2007. *Passionate Modernity: Sexuality, Class and Consumption in India*. Delhi: Routledge.

Stein, Burton. 1985. 'State Formation and Economy Reconsidered'. *Modern Asian Studies* 19 (3): 387–413.

Stokes, Eric. 1969. 'Rural Revolt in the Great Rebellion of 1857 in India: A Study of the Saharanpur and Muzaffarnagar Districts'. *The Historical Journal* 12 (4): 606–27.

Subrahmanyam, Sanjay, and C. A. Bayly. 1988. 'Portfolio Capitalists and the Political Economy of Early Modern India'. *Indian Economic and Social History Review* 25 (4): 401–24.

Subramanian, Lakshmi. 1987. 'Banias and the British: The Role of Indigenous Credit in the Process of Imperial Expansion in Western India in the Second Half of the Eighteenth Century'. *Modern Asian Studies* 21 (3): 473–510.

Suri, K. C. 1987. 'The Agrarian Question in India during the National Movement: 1885–1947'. *Social Scientist* 15 (10): 25–50.

Suter, Mischa. 2017. 'Usury and the Problem of Exchange under Capitalism: A Late-Nineteenth-Century Debate on Economic Rationality'. *Social History* 42 (4): 501–23.

Swamy, Anand, and Latika Chaudhury. 2014. 'Protecting the Borrower: An Experiment in Colonial India'. *SSRN Electronic Journal*. 10.2139/ssrn.2439833.

Swarnalatha, P. 2005. *The World of the Weaver in Northern Coromandel, c. 1750–c. 1850*. Hyderabad: Orient Longman.

Swaroop, Ram, ed. 1988 *Uttar Pradesh District Gazetteers. Varanasi (Supplement)*. Varanasi: Government of Uttar Pradesh.

Taeusch, Carl F. 1942. 'The Concept of "Usury": The History of an Idea'. *Journal of the History of Ideas* 3 (3): 291–318.

Thompson, E. P. 1971. 'The Moral Economy of the English Crowd in the Eighteenth Century'. *Past and Present* 50 (1): 76–136.

Thorner, Daniel. 1960. 'The All India Rural Credit Survey: Viewed as a Scientific Enquiry'. *Economic and Political Weekly* Special Issue (June 1960): 949–63.

Timberg, Thomas. 2014. *The Marwaris: From Jagath Seth to the Birlas.* Delhi: Penguin Books.

Timberg, Thomas, and Chandrasekar V. Aiyar. 1980. 'Informal Credit Markets in India'. *Economic and Political Weekly* 15 (5/7): 279–302.

Tiwari, B. K. 2014. 'Case Study of Benares State Bank Ltd. (BSB) with Bank of Baroda (BOB)'. *Asian Journal of Management Studies and Education* 3 (1): 35–48.

Tripathi, Dwijendra. 1997. *Historical Roots of Industrial Entrepreneurship in India and Japan.* Delhi: Manohar.

Tyabji, Nasir. 2015. *Forging Capitalism in Nehru's India: Neocolonialism and the State, c. 1940–1970.* New Delhi: Oxford University Press.

Upadhyay, Shashi Bhushan. 2011. 'Premchand and the Moral Economy of the Peasantry in Colonial North India'. *Modern Asian Studies* 45 (5): 1227–59.

Vakulabharanam, Vamsi, and Sripad Motiram. 2011. 'Political Economy of Agrarian Distress in India since the 1990s'. In *Understanding India's New Political Economy: A Great Transformation?* edited by Sanjay Ruparelia, Sanjay Reddy, John Harriss, and Stuart Corbridge, 101–26. London: Routledge.

van Leur, J. C. 1955. *Indonesian Trade and Society: Essays in Asian Social and Economic History.* Den Haag: Hoeve.

van Schendel, Willem, and Itty Abraham. 2005. *Illicit Flows and Criminal Things: States, Borders, and the Other Side of Globalization.* Bloomington: Indiana University Press.

Varghese, Adel. 2005. 'Bank-Moneylender Linkage as an Alternative to Bank Competition in Rural Credit Markets'. *Oxford Economic Papers* 57 (2): 315–35.

Venkatesan, Soumhya. 2009. *Craft Matters: Artisans, Development and the Indian Nation.* Hyderabad: Orient Blackswan.

Vicajee, Framjee R. 1900. 'The Rule of Damdupat'. *Journal of the Society of Comparative Legislation* 2 (3): 464–72.

Vik, Pal. 2017. '"the Computer Says No": The Demise of the Traditional Bank Manager and the Depersonalisation of British Banking, 1960–2010'. *Economy and Society* 59 (2): 231–49.

Virdee, Satnam. 2019. 'Racialized Capitalism: An Account of Its Contested Origins and Consolidation'. *The Sociological Review* 67 (1): 3–27. https://doi.org/10.1177/0038026118820293.

Washbrook, David A. 1981. 'Law, State and Agrarian Society in Colonial India'. *Modern Asian Studies* 15 (3): 649–721.

Wertheim, W. F. 1954. 'Early Asian Trade: An Appreciation of J. C. Van Leur'. *The Far Eastern Quarterly* 13 (2): 167–73.

Williams, Philippa. 2015. *Everyday Peace? Politics, Citizenship, and Muslim Lives in India*. Oxford: Wiley Blackwell.

Williams, Tyler. 2019. 'The Ties That Bind: Individual, Family, and Community in Northwestern Bhakti'. In *Bhakti and Power: Debating India's Religion of the Heart*, edited by John S. Hawley, Christian L. Novetzke, and Swapna Sharma, 192–202. Seattle: University of Washington Press.

Wiser, William Henricks. 1936. *The Hindu Jajmani System: A Socio-Economic System Interrelating Members of a Hindu Village Community in Services*. Lucknow: Lucknow Publishing House.

Wolff, Henry W. 1902. *Co-Operative Banking: Its Principles and Practice (with a Chapter on Co-Operative Mortgage-Credit)*. London: P.S. King and Son.

———. 1919. *Co-Operation in India*. London: W. Thacker & Co.

Wood, Jolie. 2014. 'Weavers Unravelled: Comparing Associationalism among Handloom Weavers and Boatmen in Varanasi, India'. *South Asia: Journal of South Asian Studies* 37 (1): 43–59.

Yang, Anand A. 1998. *Bazaar India: Markets, Society, and the Colonial State in Gangetic Bihar*. Berkeley, London: University of California Press.

Zazzaro, Alberto. 2005. 'Should Courts Enforce Credit Contracts Strictly?' *The Economic Journal* 115 (500): 166–84.

Zelizer, Viviana A. 1978. 'Human Values and the Market. The Case of Life Insurance and Death in 19th-Century America'. *American Journal of Sociology* 84 (3): 591–610.

Zickgraf, Jens M. 2018. *Rupien in Der Dollar-Zone: Geld Als Prozess Und Medium Gesellschaftlcher Teilhabe*. Berlin: LIT. Eine Ethnographie.

Index